NANUET PUBLIC LIBRARY

3 2824 00921 9572

JUL 0 2 2001

George Washington Reconsidered

D1227409

George Washington Reconsidered

Edited by
DON HIGGINBOTHAM

NANUET PUBLIC LIBRARY
149 CHURCH STREET
NANUET, NEW YORK 10954

University Press of Virginia
Charlottesville and London

THE UNIVERSITY PRESS OF VIRGINIA
© 2001 by the Rector and Visitors of the University of Virginia
All rights reserved
Printed in the United States of America

First published 2001

⊗The paper used in this publication meets the minimum requirements of
the American National Standard for Information Sciences—Permanence
of Paper for Printed Library Materials, ANSI Z39.48-1984.

Library of Congress Cataloging-in-Publication Data

George Washington reconsidered / edited by Don Higginbotham.
     p.   cm.
    Includes index.
    ISBN 0-8139-2005-1 (cloth : alk. paper)—ISBN 0-8139-2006-X
(pbk. : alk. paper)
    1. Washington, George, 1732–1799.   2. Presidents—United
States—Biography.   3. Generals—United States—Biography.
4. Farmers—Virginia—Biography.   5. Washington, George, 1732–
1799—Influence.   I. Higginbotham, Don.
  E312.G36   2001
  973.4'1'092—dc21   00-043503
  [B]

To
Larry
Christina
David
Hilary
Rob

Contents

Images of the Man

Illustrations

(All illustrations courtesy of the Mount Vernon Ladies' Association)

Acknowledgments

It seemed to me that *George Washington Reconsidered* would be an appropriate addition to the various activities and publications inspired by the bicentennial of Washington's death in 1999. I launched this undertaking during the academic year 1998–99 while I was a visiting professor at the United States Military Academy at West Point. Colonel Robert A. Doughty, head of the Department of History, created an atmosphere there conducive to scholarship as well as teaching. I thank him and all my colleagues there for a most rewarding year. Professor Peter Coclanis, chair of the Department of History at the University of North Carolina at Chapel Hill, has been equally supportive and encouraging. Brian Steele, my research assistant at Chapel Hill, has contributed significantly to my endeavor, always with promptness and good humor. I have profited from the wise counsel of two former graduate students, Stuart Leibiger and Robert McDonald, at various points along the way. Robert F. Jones, Philander D. Chase, William M. S. Rasmussen, and Peter R. Henriques allowed me to profit from their Washington expertise early in the project. I owe a special debt to several fine scholars who wrote essays specifically designed for this volume: Joseph E. Ellis, Dorothy Twohig, and Robert F. Dalzell Jr. and Lee Baldwin Dalzell. Rosalie Radcliffe, my departmental secretary, has saved me from numerous errors thanks to her keen eye and command of the Queen's English. My wife, Katherine J. Higginbotham, continues to read my work and to improve it in ways beyond enumeration. She is always the indispensable one.

Abbreviations

Washington Manuscripts and Printed Sources

MTVL	Mount Vernon Ladies' Association
WPLC	Washington Papers, Library of Congress
GW: Writings	John C. Fitzpatrick, ed., *The Writings of George Washington . . .*, 39 vols. (Washington, D.C., 1931–44)
PGW:	W. W. Abbot et al., eds., *The Papers of George Washington*, in progress (Charlottesville, Va., 1983—), cited by series:
PGW: Col. Ser.	*Colonial Series* (10 vols., completed)
PGW: Rev. Ser.	*Revolutionary Series* (10 of 40 vols. published to date)
PGW: Conf. Ser.	*Confederation Series* (6 vols., completed)
PGW: Pres. Ser.	*Presidential Series* (9 of 20 vols. published to date)
PGW: Ret. Ser.	*Retirement Series* (4 vols., completed)
PGW: Diaries	Donald Jackson and Dorothy Twohig, eds., *The Diaries of George Washington*, 6 vols. (Charlottesville, Va., 1976–79)

Journals and Other Works

PMHB	*Pennsylvania Magazine of History and Biography*
VMHB	*Virginia Magazine of History and Biography*
WMQ	*William and Mary Quarterly*, 3d ser.
Freeman, *Washington*	Douglas Southall Freeman, *George Washington: A Biography*, 7 vols. (New York, 1948–57)
Flexner, *Washington*	James Thomas Flexner, *George Washington*, 4 vols. (New York, 1965–72)
Hening, *Statutes*	W. W. Hening, ed., *The Statutes at Large: Being a Collection of All the Laws of Virginia . . .*, 13 vols. (Richmond and Philadelphia, 1809–23)

George Washington Reconsidered

Introduction

Washington and the Historians

ALTHOUGH THE WASHINGTON literature is voluminous beyond description, there has been only one previous endeavor to present the latest scholarship on the great man in the form of a volume of essays, articles, and book chapters: James Morton Smith's *George Washington: A Profile,* which appeared in the late 1960s. In his introduction Smith surveyed Washington studies from Washington's death to the time of his own endeavor. A major finding was that a subject that had drawn myriad biographers and other historians, lay and professional, seemed to languish for most of the twentieth century. Highly visible Americans had limned Washington in the previous century, including Mason Locke Weems, John Marshall, and Washington Irving. The early days of the seminar-trained historian continued to see talented Americans pursuing Washington, in some cases men who moved from the halls of ivy to the national arena in Washington, D.C., such as Henry Cabot Lodge and Woodrow Wilson. The best-remembered Washington books from the 1920s, by William E. Woodward and Rupert Hughes, came from the pens of writers castigated as debunkers by Washington worshipers. If these authors went too far, in a decade noted for its cynicism and Mencken-like irreverence, they may have been a fairly healthy corrective to the multitude of hagiographers like Weems and Marshall. Small wonder that Nathaniel Hawthorne once exclaimed that Washington must have been born with his clothes on and his hair powdered and that he must have made a low, stately bow on entering the world.[1] The Washington bicentennial of 1932, despite great fanfare, did not generate a spate of new and lasting additions to the Washington library, with one major exception: the best by far edition of Washington's own letters. Edited by John C. Fitzpatrick, a respected Washington scholar, its thirty-nine volumes flowed steadily from the Government Printing Office between 1931 and 1944 under the title *The Writings of George Washington* . . . .[2]

The post–World War II years also initially witnessed no surge of interest in Washington among serious historians. Smith, a Cornell Ph.D. and a professor there at the time of his compilation, seemingly agreed with his own mentor, Curtis Nettels, who in 1946 complained that Washington's continued neglect resulted from the careful investigators' unwillingness to compromise their intellectual integrity by varnishing the Father of Our Country to sell copies.[3] Nettels himself contributed to reviving academic pursuit of Washington, helping to extricate him from the clutches of the popularizers and debunkers. In *George Washington and American Independence* (1951), he thoroughly documented Washington's early commitment to colonial rights and his aggressive actions as commander in chief of the Continental army, behavior that helped move Americans in the direction of declaring independence from Britain.

Smith's *George Washington* showed that Washington's fortunes in American history soon took a turn for the better. Of the twelve essays the editor selected for his volume, all but three reached print after 1947. Two publishing enterprises stand out above all others in terms of what new work was available to Smith and other Washington scholars before the 1970s. First, Douglas Southall Freeman's *George Washington: A Biography* was published in seven volumes between 1948 and 1957. A Richmond newspaper editor, Freeman had impeccable credentials as a military historian derived from his four-volume *R. E. Lee* (1934–35) and his three-volume *Lee's Lieutenants* (1942–44). His Washington also centered on the public man and rested on massive research in primary sources. Every student of Washington is indebted to Freeman for his accuracy and his wonderful fund of information, but it is questionable whether his portrait of Washington casts the Virginian in new shades or hues. One struggles to maintain the focus on the man among the 3,500 pages, which makes us mindful of Abigail Adams's similar concern about Marshall's five-volume Washington. Smith was also able to extract a valuable segment of James Thomas Flexner's *George Washington,* although in 1969 Flexner had completed only two of what became a four-volume opus with its concluding installment in 1972. For his carefully crafted undertaking, Flexner, a prolific author who also eschewed the professoriate, relied on printed sources and drew heavily on Freeman's biography. Readers today probably will prefer Flexner's thoughtful and cadenced prose over Freeman's densely packed narrative, unless they seek more detail or bibliographical information. Flexner was unable to draw upon one of the great documentary publishing projects of the twentieth century, a new edition of the *Papers of George Washington,* just then getting under way at the University of Virginia. It is now well along and in time will come close to ninety volumes.[4]

Just as Smith felt positive about the recent studies available for inclusion in his profile of Washington, I too am encouraged by the scholarship in the decades following the publication of his *George Washington.* Because the essays Smith chose, mostly devoted to the public man, are still well worth reading, I decided to take a different turn, which also mirrors a new trend away from mainline political and institutional history: an examination of the man: his family, his home, his agricultural pursuits, his slaves, his hopes for the West, and his attitudes toward death and afterlife. The last topic seemed as relevant as any in 1999, the year this tome took shape and the bicentennial of Washington's own death. At the same time, balance as well as new accounts necessitated some treatment of the French and Indian War frontier commander, the Revolutionary War commander in chief, and the first president of the United States. A few of these offerings deal with both the public and the private man. A third category of writings here addresses images of the man himself. Those images were his creation, the portraits of his contemporaries, and the configurations of historians.

In fact, it is arguable that the best Washington scholarship of the last fifteen years or so has dealt with the intellectual dimensions of Washington's public image, including his part in creating it. It began earlier, with Marcus Cunliffe's brief but thoughtful biography, *George Washington: Man and Monument* (1958), which ties Americans perceptions to classical influences and acknowledges Washington's remote persona as a factor in the image-sculpting process.[5] Three books appearing in the 1980s dealt directly with this subject. Garry Wills's *Cincinnatus: George Washington and the Enlightenment* (1984) analyzes the symbolism in three of Washington's most famous acts—his resignation as commander in chief of the army in 1783, his crucial support for the Constitution in 1787–88, and his Farewell Address on leaving the presidency. Wills charts his location in Enlightenment painting with seventy-nine black-and-white and six color illustrations. A "virtuoso" at resignations, Washington played on the Cincinnatus theme, perfecting the skill of gaining power by relinquishing power. True to his portraiture, he was a man of reason and brought to reality the classical ideal of a republic. If the Enlightenment needed its heroes, declares Wills, American hero-needs were uniquely republican and met in a single man, Washington.

The temper of the age and the achievements of the man united to forge Washington symbolism, a judgment that Wills shares with Barry Schwartz.

However, in *George Washington: The Making of an American Symbol* (1987), Schwartz pushes the process back in time. It began before the events Wills describes, and it survived a series of Washington's military reversals. Schwartz convincingly maintains that the responsibilities Washington assumed in 1775 led to a psychological need in the Revolutionary mind to advance one leader to a preeminent position. But it is also true that Washington's background as a highly visible French and Indian War hero and well-traveled aristocrat from an influential colony made it easier for his countrymen to elevate him to an exalted state from the beginning of his Revolutionary career. Schwartz, contrary to Wills, discovers Americans inclined to praise Washington in monarchical language, a carryover from the veneration of British kings, until the people crowned themselves in the Constitution, placing sovereignty in their own hands. Paul Longmore, in *The Invention of George Washington* (1988), agrees with Schwartz that Americans resorted to the vocabulary of British monarchy in depicting their number-one hero, but this rhetoric had a peculiar twist: Washington was compared with the ideal of a patriot king popularized by Henry St. John, Viscount Bolingbroke, of a ruler above party or faction and motivated only to serve his people. Thus in the early Revolutionary years, monarchial and republican images of virtue, disinterestedness, and dedication intermingled in the American mind. There is, additionally, evidence that American Protestantism may have exercised a potent part in shaping Washington's image for the middling and lower sort who had minimal awareness of the Enlightenment. The Moses theme—of a savior leading his people out of another form of Egyptian bondage—barely receives more than passing mention by Wills and Schwartz, and none at all by Longmore.[6] It needs more attention in the context of an eighteenth-century American society that still owed much to Puritan values. If we see concurrently in Revolutionary America descriptions of Washington in monarchial, republican, and biblical terms, then his countrymen may not have been as ideological as a generation of "republican" scholars has led us to believe. Or could it be that the patriots carried different ideologies in their heads at the same time?

Several articles evaluate in more detail these and other Washington studies that date from Smith's *George Washington* to 1990, and for that reason no effort is made here to duplicate those historiographical efforts.[7] It might be worthwhile, however, to state that three one-volume biographies of Washington, by John R. Alden, Robert F. Jones, and John E. Ferling, all appearing in the 1980s, remain the best of that particular genre.[8]

Some noteworthy contributions since then require more than passing reference. Washington's drive for both wealth and public recognition began on the frontier before the Revolution in his activities as a surveyor, land speculator, soldier, and legislator. These subjects received expert examination in Warren R. Hofstra, ed., *George Washington and the Virginia Backcountry* (1998). Despite such involvements, Washington never sought a permanent home in the West, like his first employer, Thomas, Lord Fairfax, nor did he appreciate the lifestyles or guerrilla fighting methods of frontier people. He used his wealth and reputation gained in the backcountry to boost his political influence and social and economic standing in the tidewater.[9] The centerpiece of his life among the gentry was Mount Vernon, a Virginia great house of his creation. The story of what it meant to Washington and his own underappreciated originality as an architect are encompassed in Robert F. Dalzell Jr. and Lee Baldwin Dalzell's *George Washington's Mount Vernon: At Home in Revolutionary America* (1998).[10] With no national capitol and no presidential mansion, Mount Vernon took on a symbolic and physical presence unique in American history, a mansion that every American felt he or she was entitled to visit and be entertained by the nation's number-one host and first chief executive.

Washington's generalship in the Revolution has lately generated minimal interest, even among military historians, hardly the appeal it had for historians of Freeman's generation, although one occasionally encounters a lively debate over whether Washington ranks as a fighting general or a Fabian, who, like the Roman commander of antiquity, made holding his army together and wearing down his pursuing adversaries his principal strategy.[11] In any case, he recognized, as general and as president, that national power led to success at home and abroad. In that respect, as Edmund S. Morgan has written cogently in *The Genius of George Washington* (1980), the Virginian had a greater appreciation of the ingredients of national strength than any other member of his generation. The failure of Congress in the Revolutionary War to obtain the authority to raise a substantial, long-term army meant that Washington had to resort to flexible responses throughout the conflict. For all of Washington's complaints about the state militias, Mark V. Kwasny in *Washington's Partisan War, 1775–1783* (1996) discloses a commander in chief who learned how to maximize the effectiveness of irregulars, who came and went and rarely stood in open combat against British regulars. He came to see how a militia under federal control might be made effective and minimize the need for a large standing army, an anathema to Americans, especially in peacetime. He encapsulated that knowledge in his first and only detailed proposals for constitutional reform, which came toward the end of the war in his "Sentiments on a Peace Establishment" (1783).

Yet Washington made substantial contributions to American consti-tutionalism as a critic of legislature-dominated state governments and the weak Articles of Confederation and as a spokesman for constitutional re-form in the 1780s and an enormously influential advocate for the Consti-tution of 1787—all the while retaining his commitment to civil control of the military (a profound contribution in itself) and to republican princi-ples. Glenn Phelps in *George Washington and American Constitutional-ism* (1993) treats in depth this story, long in need of monographic scrutiny. His book also contains the most insightful treatment of how Washington put flesh on the Constitution's Article II, which covers the presidency. A major point, all but ignored in prior accounts of the chief executive's evo-lution, is that Washington initiated the practice of the president, rather than any other federal agency or tribunal, speaking to (and for) the people in the areas of domestic and foreign affairs.[12] Phelps's book, read in con-junction with Matthew Spalding and Patrick J. Garrity's *A Sacred Union of Citizens: George Washington's Farewell Address and the American Char-acter* (1996), provides our best understanding of Washington's thinking about the American Union—how it came about and how to preserve it. Spalding and Garrity prove that the Farewell Address is much more than an attack on parties and entangling alliances (a phrase Washington never used). It contains a prescription for a strong union, national character, and good citizenship, all themes they prefer to stress instead of plowing old ground on Washington's valedictory. Though there remains more new pres-idential terrain to cover, we now have a solid, readable book on his pres-idential tenure: Richard Norton Smith's *Patriarch: George Washington and the New Nation* (1993). One completes a review of recent literature with the feeling that General and President Washington, all hagiography aside, was the linchpin that—to the extent one man could do so—held together a fragile Revolution and afterward a federal Union torn by domestic and foreign controversies in the 1790s.

Washington shared with the other great men of the age the major credit for nation making, and yet we have just now received our first book on Washington's collaborative efforts with any of the other Founders: Stuart Leibiger's *Founding Friendship: George Washington, James Madison, and the Creation of the American Republic* (1999). For a period of nearly ten years, from late in the War of Independence through Washington's first term as president, Washington and Madison grew close both personally and politically as they worked to bolster the military effort, develop the Potomac as an artery for linking the West to the East, invigorate the Con-federation, and organize a Virginia agenda for the Constitutional Convention, which in outline if not more became the core of the national parchment that emerged from the Philadelphia gathering in 1787. They came to sign their letters "affectionately." The ties remained tight in the first presidential term; Leibiger convinces us that Washington was often influenced more by Madison than by Hamilton.

The eventual rupture between the two men over the Jay Treaty and other issues transpired about the same time that Washington and Jefferson ceased all correspondence after Jefferson's letter to Philip Mazzei in 1796 critical of the president's foreign policy fell into the eager hands of Federalist journalists, who gleefully reproduced it for the world to see. Madison profoundly regretted his own break with Washington and continued to speak fondly of him. Jefferson, after the first president's death, visited Mount Vernon to extend his sympathies to Martha Washington, who resented his presence there.[13] Even before his presidency, Washington had terminated a thirty-year friendship with George Mason, who opposed ratification of the Constitution at the 1788 Virginia Convention.[14] As one can see from Leibiger's book, Washington had a tendency not to forgive and forget. Keenly sensitive to criticism and possessed of a fiery temper that only rarely erupted, he dealt severely with three of his generals who displeased him, all, interestingly enough, from the Shenandoah Valley: Horatio Gates, Charles Lee, and Adam Stephen. Madison, Jefferson, and Mason, as well as these generals, were Virginians, and so was Edmund Randolph, the secretary of state after Jefferson and worshipful admirer of President Washington. The president fired and humiliated Randolph on the basis of questionable evidence that he had shared state secrets with the French minister.[15] Washington, however, displayed sound reasoning when he removed another Virginian from his diplomatic post, James Monroe, who as minister to France made known in Paris his distaste for the Jay Treaty. Washington expected more from men he knew well, especially if they were Virginians, and it pained him in the mid-1790s to see his own state leading the way in opposing administration policies.[16]

Just as all the above-mentioned authors provide realistic portrayals of Washington, so too do the contributors of the thirteen essays here seek to offer what Abigail Adams called the "simple truth" about the First of the Fathers. Accordingly, some of the essayists have delineated mistakes and personal failings of the man that Weems and Marshall found to be without faults or frailties. All of the contributors who focus directly on Washington, however, admire him and emphasize his gifts and accomplishments. Can we find some theme, albeit tenuous, that connects the thirteen? I think we can. In some measure or another, each essay implicitly at least deals with a challenge that Washington faced and overcame. Indeed, I am struck by the fact that everything Washington touched in a major way he shaped—in varying degrees of course, but he did so nevertheless. Throughout his life he remained focused; he knew what he wanted. Though hardly brilliant or scintillating, Washington comes through as a highly creative human being.

The first five essays spotlight "The Virginia Localist." As a young man, Washington sought to carry the family name and accomplishments to higher levels than the previous three generations of male Washingtons in his direct line of descent had achieved. He succeeded, building on a tradition of ambition described in Martin H. Quitt's "The English Cleric and the Virginia Adventurer," which traces the family beginnings with the arrival of Washington's great-grandfather John in the 1650s. Seizing the opportunity to advance through the officer ranks of the Virginia militia, Washington became the colonel of the Virginia Regiment that had the responsibility for defending the colony's 350-mile frontier in the French and Indian War. My essay on "Washington and the Colonial Military Tradition" shows that he not only succeeded in his mission but turned his regiment into a remarkably fine unit, one that drew praise from British officers as well as from colonial authorities.

Washington was confronted with still other challenges after the final imperial war when he inherited Mount Vernon. Bruce A. Ragsdale describes how Washington worked to free himself from his indebtedness to Robert Cary & Company by cutting back on luxuries and buying on credit at the same time that he switched from tobacco to more remunerative wheat crops on his Mount Vernon farms. Washington addressed two other challenges at his estate, although he did not solve either immediately. First, as Robert and Lee Dalzell indicate, Washington in the late 1750s began the process of turning his deceased brother's story-and-a-half farmhouse into a mansion befitting a Virginia gentleman and his wealthy bride, the widow Martha Custis, and her two small children. His renovations continued almost without interruption until his death, with the result that Mount Vernon became a reflection of the man and his conception of American republicanism. Slavery too drew his serious attention, as Dorothy Twohig points out. If he failed to find a way to convert to white tenant labor and free his bondsmen during his lifetime, he manumitted his Africans in his will, making a personal statement about the peculiar institution that was not replicated by Jefferson and Madison or most other Virginia grandees of his generation.

"The American Nationalist" constitutes chapters six to ten, which examine Washington's public role from the beginning of the Revolution to his death, two years after giving up the presidency. My "George Washington and Revolutionary Asceticism" looks at a safe man to lead a revolution, one whose family background and personal life were hardly dysfunctional, one not given to inordinate ambition or narcissism. My view of Washington squares with Glenn A. Phelps's interpretation of the commander in chief as a "Republican General," committed to civil control of the military and to republican rather than monarchical goals for the new nation. He shaped his army to be both professionally sound and republican in character. Washington's vision of America included a West securely anchored to the original thirteen states of the East. Both before and during his presidency he did much to bring that vision to fruition through advocacy of internal improvements, interior settlement, and law and order for the region. Covering aspects of this topic, W. W. Abbot, in "Washington, the West, and the Union," says that the West stretched Washington's mind, causing him to dream expansive dreams of a republican empire.

Washington's reveries never ceased to include a grander, more muscular, united America. He never rested on his laurels after helping to secure the writing and ratifying of the Constitution or after serving two terms as president. Joseph J. Ellis reveals how the Farewell Address served both as a means of reflecting on his presidency, with its lasting precedents for the executive branch, and as a way of pointing Americans toward the future, well aware that he was stretching their imaginations just as the Revolution, the West, the Constitution, and the presidency had extended his; that some of his recommendations, with luck, would only be adopted in time. Indeed, Peter R. Henriques sketches a dying Washington, on December 14, 1799, thinking about how he still might, in some limited way, shape what would come after. He reviewed the final copy of his will, with its provisions for freeing his slaves, and he requested that his secretary see to the final ordering and securing of his thousands of letters and other papers. He even controlled his death, instructing his doctors to cease their heroic labors and to let him go quietly and with dignity.

The third and concluding section examines "Images of the Man." As W. W. Abbot writes, the preservation of his treasure-house of manuscripts covering close to half a century was vitally important to Washington. They would define his place for posterity and would, beyond that, provide a mine of information about what Washington saw as a remarkable snapshot of modern history. To Federalist party leaders of the 1790s, Washington's towering reputation was already frozen in history. Or so they wanted to believe.

On most important issues as chief executive, Washington still prevailed as he had earlier in the War of Independence and in the battle over the Constitution. As Edmund S. Morgan depicts this "aloof American," Washington employed his natural dignity and reserve to increase the respect he needed to engage in nation building. He could never have succeeded of course without great energy and dedication, but in an age of deference his imposing physical appearance and body language were weapons in his political arsenal. What, in the final analysis, accounts for Washington's greatness, the question raised by Gordon S. Wood in the final essay? Wood assuredly finds some of the same qualities and virtues that Ellis, Abbot, Morgan, and other essayists advance in this volume. But he notes that we will have trouble appreciating them the way Americans did two hundred years ago because they were all products of a different world, noted for the Enlightenment and the first revolution in the name of both nationhood and liberty in history. Character, however one defines it, seemed to be on everyone's list of what set Washington apart in that now-distant age. It is also on Wood's list, and he explains what character means to him. Those who wish to probe further in their quest to divine Washington's greatness, should turn to a very recent book that raises all the right questions without falling prey to easy answers: Richard Brookhiser's *Founding Father: Discovering George Washington* (1996). The author, among other things, speculates on what it meant to Washington and to his fellow Americans for a man who lost his blood father as a child and who had no offspring of his own to become the Father of His Country.

Notes

1. Quoted in Margaret Brown Klapthor and Howard Alexander Morrison, *G. Washington: A Figure upon the Stage* (Washington, D.C., 1982), 11.

2. John C. Fitzpatrick, *George Washington Himself: A Common Sense Biography Written from His Manuscripts* (Indianapolis, 1933).

3. Curtis P. Nettels, "The Washington Theme in American History," Massachusetts Historical Society, *Proceedings* 68 (1952): 171–98.

4. The Washington Papers undertaking is treated at length by W. W. Abbot, a former editor-in-chief, in chap. 11 of this book.

5. Marcus Cunliffe, *In Search of America: Transatlantic Essays, 1951–1990* (Westport, Conn., 1991), shows the author's continued interest in Washington themes.

6. Robert P. Hay, "George Washington: American Moses," *American Quarterly* 21 (1969): 780–91.

7. Don Higginbotham, "The Washington Theme in Recent Historical Liter-

ature, *PMHB* 114 (1990): 424–37, from which I have borrowed liberally in writing parts of this Introduction; Albert Furtwangler, "George Washington Fading Away," *American Literary History* 2 (1990): 319–27; Kenneth R. Bowling, "An Extraordinary Man: A Review Essay on George Washington," *Wisconsin Magazine of History* 73 (1990): 287–93.

8. Brief but solid are John R. Alden, *George Washington: A Biography* (Baton Rouge, La., 1984), and Robert F. Jones, *George Washington,* rev. ed. (New York, 1986). Much longer is John E. Ferling, *The First of Men: A Life of George Washington* (Knoxville, Tenn., 1988), which fully acknowledges GW's public accomplishments but sees him as a driven man whose lack of self-esteem even plagued him as an American icon.

9. For GW's concern for his reputation at this stage, see William Guthrie Sayen, "George Washington's 'Unmannerly' Behavior: The Clash between Civility and Honor," *VMHB* 107 (1999): 5–36.

10. The new Mount Vernon bookshelf also lists two splendid items that are largely pictorial: Wendell Garrett, ed., *George Washington's Mount Vernon* (New York, 1998); Mac Griswold, *George Washington's Mount Vernon: Landscape of the Inner Man* (Boston, 1999).

11. For example, Dave R. Palmer, *The Way of the Fox: American Strategy in the War for America* (Westport, Conn., 1975), sees GW as an offensive strategist, as opposed to Russell F. Weigley, "American Strategy: A Call for a Critical Strategic History," in *Reconsiderations on the Revolutionary War,* ed. Don Higginbotham (Westport, Conn., 1978), 32–53, who describes the commander-in-chief as defensive-minded, intent on a concept of erosion and attrition. Two other assessments of GW's generalship, although subtle and nuanced, uncover a general who was bold and daring, not unwilling, like British general William Howe, to contemplate a decisive battle if the odds seemed in his favor (John Ferling, "George Washington and American Victory," in *The World Turned Upside Down: The American Victory in the War of Independence,* ed. John Ferling (Westport, Conn., 1988), 53–70; John Shy, "George Washington Reconsidered," in *The John Biggs Lectures in Leadership and Command,* ed. Henry S. Bausum (Lexington, Va., 1986), 39–52).

12. The pre-presidential years are examined briefly in my "George Washington's Contributions to American Constitutionalism," in *War and Society in Revolutionary America: The Wider Dimensions of Conflict,* ed. Don Higginbotham (Columbia, S.C., 1988), 193–213.

13. John Cotton Smith, *The Correspondence and Miscellanies . . .* (New York, 1847), 224–25; Edwin M. Betts and James A. Bear Jr., eds., *The Family Letters of Thomas Jefferson* (Columbia, Mo., 1966), 190.

14. Peter R. Henriques, "An Uneven Friendship: The Relationship between George Washington and George Mason," *VMHB* 97 (1989): 185–204.

15. Mary K. Bonsteel Tachau, "George Washington and the Reputation of Edmund Randolph," *Journal of American History* 73 (1986): 15–34.

16. GW correctly sensed that Virginia was becoming a bastion of Jefferson-

ian Republicanism. The Old Dominion's House of Delegates voted 100 to 50 for a resolution praising the state's senators for opposing the Jay Treaty. All but one of the state's members of the House of Representatives refused to support appropriations for implementing the treaty (Richard R. Beeman, *The Old Dominion and the New Nation, 1788–1801* [Lexington, Ky., 1972], 146–50). GW, on the evening before his death, still had not moderated his opinion of Madison and Monroe. Tobis Lear, his secretary, reported that GW responded with "some degree of asperity" after Lear read aloud from a Virginia newspaper an account of Madison's nominating Monroe for governor and speaking forcefully for his election (Tobias Lear's Narrative Accounts of the Death of George Washington, Dec. 14, 15, 1799, *PGW: Ret. Ser.* 4:543, 547).

The Virginia Localist

1. The English Cleric and the Virginia Adventurer

The Washingtons, Father and Son

MARTIN H. QUITT

From the following account one can draw intriguing parallels between the lives of the first four generations of Washingtons in Virginia. George, the great-grandson of the immigrant John, knew more of his family history than he cared to admit in response to a question about his lineage from an English writer in 1792, and he proudly displayed the Washington coat of arms. He knew that in the first three generations his forefathers had been successful as planters and held county offices and served as members of the House of Burgesses. But, as he pointed out more than once, his great-grandfather John, his grandfather Lawrence, and his own father Augustine had all died relatively young, seemingly on the verge of entering the first circle of the rising plantation aristocracy. George was only eleven when his father passed away. Even more obviously on the brink of higher standing was George's brother Lawrence, who served as a British army officer in the Cartagena campaign against Spain in the early 1740s, inherited the then still-modest estate he called Mount Vernon, and married into the power-ful Fairfax family at nearby Belvoir. But at age thirty-four Lawrence too succumbed to an early death. George inherited his family's drive and am-bition, but he may also have drawn his obvious insecurity as a young man from his family history and his inability, unlike Lawrence and their male ancestors, to obtain an education in England.

Martin H. Quitt, a specialist on Virginia's colonial period, is a professor of history at the University of Massachusetts, Boston. His essay origi-nally appeared in the Virginia Magazine of History and Biography 97

(1989): 163–84 and is reprinted by permission of the Virginia Historical Society.

JOHN WASHINGTON sailed to Virginia in 1656. He belonged to a wave of immigrants that swept ashore during the middle decades of the century and established families that became synonymous with the gentry of the late colonial period. Like many of his contemporaries, he has survived mainly in the glow cast by the famous governing class of the Revolutionary era. John himself is usually remembered in biographies of his great-grandson. Sometimes he is mistakenly identified as George's grandfather, instead of his great-grandfather, as if the closer affinity would more fully justify mentioning him. Viewed in this retrospective light, the motives of John and his generation of leaders sometimes are misunderstood as reflections of their descendants' values. The traditionalism of the eighteenth-century elite, including its devotion to the Anglican church, its loyalty to the crown, its cultivation of gentility, and its general attachment to things English, has been attributed to the inclinations of the immigrant progenitors, who have been depicted as transplanters of Old World ways, as bearers of their English families' values, and as seekers of the status and life-style of English country gentlemen.[1]

The founding generation of leaders needs to be understood in its own terms, however, and John Washington's story is valuable because it illuminates with a narrower but more intense light than that thrown by collective studies the process of immigration as experienced by these men.[2] Washington did not transfer to Virginia the ways of his father, because both their lives were convulsed by the civil war of the 1640s. That upheaval spun John away from his father's world of religious service, geographic stability, and institutional connections into one of commercial adventure, oceanic crossings, and personal ties.

Although his father died before John emigrated, it is unlikely that he had ever encouraged John's career in overseas commerce. Lawrence Washington was a scholarly, sedentary man who had spent his entire adulthood in two organizations, Oxford University and the Church of England. He probably had planned a comparable future for his eldest son, for in an age that celebrated patriarchalism and practiced primogeniture, firstborn sons were expected to follow in their fathers' footsteps.[3] The English civil war disrupted their lives, however, so that those of father and son could not have turned out more differently.

Lawrence Washington was the fifth son of a lesser gentry family in Northamptonshire that was forced to sell its manor house when he was a child. As a younger son he would have prepared for a career away from the land even had his family's fortunes not been in decline, for primogeniture had become a gentry norm.[4] He was seventeen, the median age of all freshmen, when he entered Brasenose College, Oxford, in 1619.[5] Sons of the well-to-do could be younger and those from poorer families older.[6] He did not matriculate until 1621, a not-uncommon delay.[7] He earned the B.A., as did more than half his classmates in a decade when more degrees were granted by Oxford than at any other time before the nineteenth century.[8] Thus Lawrence rode the crest of an educational revolution that carried an unprecedented proportion of youths into one of the universities or inns of court in the eighty years before the civil war.[9] By the time his son John reached the age of eligibility for matriculation in the late 1640s, the impulse behind that expansion had dissipated because of political upheaval.

Although a university education had become part of the prescribed training for country gentlemen, students who stayed for a degree usually were aiming at a professional career in the church, the state, law, medicine, or teaching.[10] A permanent place at the university was not normally considered, because the academic profession had not yet emerged. This fact is important to bear in mind when assessing Lawrence Washington's life, for the circumstances surrounding his eventual departure from Oxford and the birth of his first son have been obscured by the assumption that he was forced to relinquish his place at the university and become a clergyman.

What we know about Lawrence Washington's career at Oxford reveals a man who was methodical and steady in navigating his way up a hierarchical organization. Days after receiving his B.A. in 1623 Washington was elected a fellow of Brasenose College. Under the statutes of the college, a fellow could not have an income of more than a few pounds a year.[11] Throughout the university wealth was usually a disqualification for election to a fellowship.[12] Typically a fellow would spend ten to fifteen years teaching at his college, during which he would take holy orders. If he assumed a college or university office, this service would enhance his chances of being offered a church living. Before the late nineteenth century a fellowship and teaching duties at Oxford were not a profession for life; rather they were steps on a ladder to a career in the church.[13] Lawrence Washington climbed this ladder one rung after another. In 1626 he received his M.A. and in 1627 was appointed lector of Brasenose, the chief disciplinarian of undergraduates in the college, a position he held until he resigned his fellowship.[14] On 26 August 1631 he became a university proctor, a promotion that was not so routine as it appears in accounts of Washington's life.[15]

A year earlier William Laud had been elected chancellor of the university following the sudden death of the incumbent and had become the king's point-man for the suppression of Puritanism there. On 22 August 1631 Laud brought the principal officers of the university before the king and council for a hearing on a series of Calvinist-sponsored sermons attacking the Arminianism of the hierarchy.[16] Three of the summoned officials were dismissed from the university, and the two proctors were forced to resign and allow their colleges to replace them.[17] Four days later Lawrence Washington was chosen by the Brasenose electors to finish his ousted predecessor's term.[18] Only someone who was wholly satisfactory to the chancellor would have been nominated by the college. Although Brasenose is reputed to have had a number of fellows who were not receptive to Laud's ideas, it is inconceivable that Washington was among them.[19]

During his tenure as proctor Washington met every Monday with the vice-chancellor, the heads of the colleges and halls, and the other proctor as members of the newly created Hebdomadal Council. Laud introduced this structure in 1631 as a means of exercising more centralized control over the university and thereby came to know of the proctor from Brasenose.[20]

In 1632 Washington was offered a rectorship in the parish of Purleigh, Essex. About this time he married Amphillis Twigden and their first son was born, but neither the date of marriage nor John's birthday is known. The statutes of Brasenose restricted fellowships to bachelors.[21] When joined to the assumption that Washington had planned on an academic career, these facts have led various writers to believe that he was forced to leave Oxford and take up an unplanned career in the church. One scholar even inferred that Washington's son might have been born out of wedlock and that Lawrence was obliged to depart under a cloud of scandal.[22] Although the case cannot be established one way or the other, it does seem improbable that the Purleigh rectorship was a consolation prize for someone who had been forced to resign an Oxford fellowship so he could marry. The explosive increase of matriculants at the universities had transformed a Tudor shortage of ministers into an early Stuart surplus.[23] A substantial living such as the one at Purleigh was therefore more likely to be conferred on a don who had served his college and university exceptionally well, had pleased the Caroline hierarchy, and was ready to take up the benefice to which a university career was expected to lead.

The familial setting in which John Washington was reared is important to ferret out because it influenced his character and provided him with significant models that he would emulate or rebel against. The relationship between his father and mother, for example, was founded on personal compatibility and leads us to believe that John too would expect companionship to be a major consideration when he married. Lawrence Washington could have become the rector of Purleigh and remained a bachelor, just as Archbishop Laud had. In the seventeenth century an exceptionally high proportion of both sexes never married.[24] Amphillis, however, was an unusually literate girl whom a well-educated clergyman would find companionable.[25] At a time when nine of every ten women in East Anglia could not sign their own names, she composed letters.[26]

Repressive childrearing seems to have been the rule, especially among Calvinists who were preached to about the dangers of obstinacy and willfulness in their young. Parents were urged to break the will of their children. As a follower of the Arminian establishment, Lawrence Washington may have applied a less severe hand to his son, but we should assume that he too was strict.[27] He was an experienced disciplinarian, for as lector of Brasenose he had spent five years as the official responsible for punishing the misbehavior of undergraduates. Thus he was likely to be hard on his children, and most especially on John, for even today parents tend to be more intensely involved and stricter with their firstborn, who do not have older siblings to mediate between themselves and their mothers and fathers.[28]

John grew up in a household that was somewhat larger than average: he had two brothers and three sisters, although the youngest was born probably after John left home.[29] It was not the detached unit of modern times. The Washingtons maintained a close relationship with Amphillis's mother and stepfather, who lived at Tring, Hertfordshire, approximately fifty miles away. Three of their children are known to have been baptized at Tring (the baptismal records of the others, including John, have not been found).[30] This fact suggests that Amphillis regularly spent her lying-in time at her parents' home, while her husband tended to his parish duties at Purleigh.[31] Before the advent of forceps at the end of the century, childbearing was usually an exclusively female affair.[32] The role of a husband in childbirth was so peripheral that when a woman prepared for delivery she could remove herself from his home. Even after her mother died in 1637, Amphillis continued to have her lying-ins at Tring and bore her third son there in 1641.[33] She may have had a support group of women or an especially trusted midwife there whom she preferred to her neighbors in Essex. Her continuing to go to Tring also indicates how comfortable she felt with her stepfather, Andrew Knowling, who left his property and fortune to her children when he died in 1650.[34]

In 1640 Lawrence drew on his standing with the hierarchy to secure a royal recommendation to "a Schollers place" for John, then seven or eight years old, at what was later called the Charterhouse School in London, founded thirty years earlier to serve the sons of poor gentlemen.[35] Lawrence's influence was strong enough only to reserve his son a place on the waiting list, for John did not gain admission. Where he went is not known, although he could have attended the grammar school a few miles north of Purleigh at Maldon, a port on the Blackwater River, which runs into the North Sea.[36] Wherever he went, he was not so far from home to be unaffected when his father's world was overturned three years later.

At the outset of the civil war the Long Parliament moved haltingly to reform the established church but by 1643 launched a campaign against the parish clergy that resulted in nearly 2,800 being persecuted before the Restoration.[37] Lawrence Washington was the ninth named in a November 1643 account of the first hundred "scandalous, malignant priests" whose benefices were sequestered by order of Parliament.[38] The charges brought against the clergy fell into three broad areas: personal morality, religious practices, and political alignment. A deposition taken by the parliamentary committee for Essex in 1643 described Washington as "a common frequenter of Ale-houses, not only himselfe sitting daily tipling there, but also incouraging others in that beastly vice, and hath been oft drunke."[39] Because more than two-thirds of the original one hundred clergymen were described as drunkards, it may well be that his accuser had been primed by the Puritan committee, which was eager to find some cause for removing establishment incumbents.[40] Besides, many years later an acquaintance remembered Washington as "a very worthy pious man . . . [who] appeared a very modest sober person."[41] The truth may never be known. Douglas Southall Freeman's judicious characterization of him seems fair: "He probably was convivial . . . and not averse to sitting over a pot of ale at an inn table."[42] Unchastity, ribaldry, and sabbath-breaking were the most frequently cited moral offenses after drunkenness. The absence of these in the deposition against Washington can be taken to signify that he was a faithful husband, a civil speaker, and an observer of the sabbath.

His brand of Anglicanism, however, is unclear. Again we have to infer much from what was not said about him. Neglect of duties was a common criticism of the harrassed clergy, but it was not leveled against Washington.[43] One can surmise that he was recognized to be as diligent a rector as he had been a fellow at Oxford, where he had earned important appointments. He was also not charged with the High-Church ceremonialism that was associated with Archbishop Laud and that was cited in other cases from Essex.[44] Nevertheless, he was a Laudian and royalist in loyalty, if not in strict liturgical conformity. He allegedly said "[t]hat the Parliament have more Papists belonging to them in their Armies, then the King had about him, or in his Army, and that the Parliaments Army did more Hurt then the Cavaliers, and that they did none at all; And hath published them to be Traitours, that lend to or assist the Parliament."[45] These remarks were too detailed and singular to have been orchestrated by his persecutors. Whether his statements resulted from a moment of indiscretion or were part of a sustained critique of the parliamentary cause can only be surmised.

After his ejection from Purleigh, Washington was able to obtain another, although poorer, living at Little Braxted, Essex, a few miles north of Maldon. Essex County was a stronghold of reformist sentiment, with more than a third of its clergy persecuted during the civil war.[46] There was no shortage of clergy to fill vacated benefices there, as was the case elsewhere.[47] Washington's willingness to conform to Puritan ways may have been a result of his need to provide for his family as well as of an attachment to the area around Maldon. When juxtaposed with the absence of liturgical charges against him in 1643, however, his stay in the church raises the possibility that his Laudianism had been more a matter of institutional and political loyalty than religious commitment.[48]

Lawrence Washington died intestate at age fifty-one or fifty-two in January 1653 and was buried in the nearby parish churchyard at Maldon. The king and archbishop he had openly defended at great risk were both dead, a revolutionary regime was deeply entrenched, and Little Braxted lacked the income or status of Purleigh. It is difficult to quarrel with the judgment that his last years were spent "in defeat."[49]

Had the civil war and Lawrence's expulsion from his benefice not occurred, John Washington might well have matriculated at Brasenose and gone on to a career as a cleric. An increasing proportion of each year's freshman class at Oxford, before and after 1640–60, were clergymen's sons who followed their fathers into the church.[50] John did not turn seventeen until 1649 or 1650, however, when a parliamentary board of visitors purged the university of cavaliers.[51] The long-time head of Brasenose, under whom Lawrence had served as lector and who had no doubt supported him for proctor, had been forced to resign in 1648.[52] Still, it might have been possible for John to matriculate. The visitors concentrated on officials and fellows, not students. The son of another Essex minister, who had been fourteenth among the first hundred sequestered for affirming "that he would drive away all the Puritans out of his Parish," received his B.A. from Oxford in 1652, when Oliver Cromwell was chancellor.[53] Moreover, although enthusiasm for an Oxford education had ebbed during the turbulent forties, by 1650 students were registering at the prewar level, and the university was once again functioning primarily as a place of learning.[54] That John Washington did not attend was likely to have had more to do with his own inclinations than with his not being able to gain admission. The sufferings of his father probably combined with the Puritan ascendancy at the university to push him in a new direction. Oxford had been his father's route to a benefice, but John eschewed a career in the reformed church and found no other incentive to matriculate and pursue a degree.[55]

John was not at Purleigh when his father died in January 1653 or when his mother was buried two years later.[56] In fact the only English references to John in the 1650s place him in London or in London-based commerce. His entry into this arena needs to be explored.[57]

London offered a remarkable diversity of career choices. The death registers of one London parish during the second half of the century identified male decedents by some 360 different occupations.[58] Even in tranquil times such variety could confront a teenager or youth in his early twenties with the hard problem of selection. The civil war compounded the difficulty.

Mid-century London was the epicenter of what Christopher Hill has described as "the world turned upside down."[59] The metropolis quaked during the civil war with pamphlets, books, ballads, street oratory, tavern and coffee shop debates, and private talk that was stirred, writes another English scholar, by "some of the most radical literature ever published in this country."[60] No established institution, value, or way of doing things was exempt from challenge. When the monarchy, the House of Lords, and the episcopacy could be abolished and the king beheaded, no tradition could be taken for granted, no plans based on what the future held could be fully counted upon.

John Washington moved into overseas commerce, probably through apprenticeship, the route into most London occupations. Thousands of youths from all levels of society became London apprentices annually, forming what Steven Smith has depicted as an adolescent subculture.[61] A few months after their father died, John's youngest brother was apprenticed for seven years to a member of the Drapers' Company of London.[62] Although no record of John's apprenticeship has been found, it may be because he did not serve a company. Instead he became involved in the colonial trade, which had become notorious for its domination by individual "colonial interlopers" rather than chartered companies.[63] His father had suffered for his institutional affiliation and loyalty; understandably John preferred personal associations to organizational attachments.

John's oceanic bent could well have stemmed from his boyhood, when he might have been lured by maritime activities at the North Sea port of Maldon. It would be a mistake, however, to view John's transatlantic mercantile career as evolving smoothly and inevitably from a possible childhood inclination into an adult vocation. Unlike the cases of his father and his own two sons, John's passage into adulthood was not facilitated by a certain knowledge of the position and occupation he would hold in society. His father had proceeded in a seemingly preordained manner, steadily and orderly, on the path to a church benefice, and John's sons would take from their father their identities as Virginia merchant-planters and leaders. Neither his father nor his sons, however, were exposed to situations that could compare with the strains of mid-century London, where we can fix John probably in his late teens and definitely in his early twenties. The metropolis contained all the salient ingredients that have made adolescence a worrisome stage in modern society: cultural dissonance, career options, and peer group membership.[64]

During adolescence a boy stretches to become a man by finding a place among the men around him. His sense of who he is builds on the niche he carves for himself in the adult world by committing himself to a career, a marriage, a locale, or even a set of values. His passage into adulthood, then, involves forming an identity for himself within a particular society.[65] In an early modern small town or agricultural village where occupational choices were narrow, the exchange of ideas was circumscribed, and children were expected to follow their parents' path, the developmental task of determining where one fit was not so difficult or so prolonged as it could become in the metropolis. Young men who left their village or small town households for the experience of London would have needed to be remarkably sheltered or single-minded to remain unaffected by the political and religious conflicts, the multitude of career options, and the subculture of other searching adolescents that created a setting in which the formation of identity was likely to be stressful and delayed.

Perhaps no occupation was better suited than overseas trade to a youth who was still trying to find a satisfactory spot for himself. On the one hand, it was the place to be during the 1650s, for the expansionist mood and policies of Cromwellian England brought a new energy and enthusiasm to oceanic commerce.[66] On the other, the Atlantic was so open-ended that it allowed a youth to discover eventually what he wanted to do and where he might want to do it. Its attraction was that it could lead anywhere. It was the perfect location for anyone who had no clear destination.

John Washington, like several other mid-century immigrants who became leaders in Virginia, did not sail to the colony with the intention of settling there. He went there on a business trip and unexpectedly found a patron and a wife, so he stayed. His pattern was repeated by others. A variation was that some, including his brother, made several trips before deciding to remain in the colony permanently. John found enough to keep him there after his first crossing.

Before he came to Virginia John actively participated in the tobacco reexport trade to Europe. The reexport markets already absorbed more than 40 percent of London tobacco imports and would take up about two-thirds by the end of the century.[67] By 1656 John was evidently experienced in this trade, for a merchant, Edward Prescott, asked him to join his ship at Danzig and assist him on a voyage that would take in several Baltic ports and then go to Virginia. Although the terms of the agreement are unknown, Washington was to be a junior partner for the voyage. He sailed to Danzig at his own expense, shared navigational duties as Prescott's second-in-command, and went ashore at different ports to market their freight. From Copenhagen he even traveled by himself overland to sell tobacco in Elsinore.[68]

Temporary partnerships had become a common way for individuals with limited capital but valuable maritime experience to participate as merchants in colonial commerce. Bringing a closure to these relationships, however, could be problematic.[69] It is clear that their original agreement was for Washington to continue with Prescott on both the voyage to Virginia and the return trip to England or the Continent. At some point after their arrival in the colony, however, Washington decided to stay. Prescott apparently consented to the termination of their partnership but not to the terms of a final accounting. An obstacle to a settlement may have been the ship's partial sinking in February 1677 during a storm on the Potomac. Although he was not on board at the time, Washington subsequently helped rescue the ketch, but not before two boats and most of the tobacco they carried were lost. It was after this misfortune that Washington announced his desire to remain in Virginia.[70]

Washington's decision to stay resulted from his having met Nathaniel Pope, who became his father-in-law, benefactor, and sponsor. It was at Pope's plantation that the two partners tried to settle their differences. Washington maintained he had received "nothing in Account of copartnership" and demanded his share. When Prescott countered that Washington owed him money, Pope volunteered to pay whatever might be due Prescott. Pope's good offices did not resolve the dispute, however, for Washington brought an action against Prescott in the Westmoreland County court, where Pope sat as a justice of the quorum. How the case was concluded is not recorded, but the patronage of Nathaniel Pope was more crucial to Washington's future in Virginia than anything he might have wrested in court from his former partner.[71]

The relationship between Pope and Washington is worth examining, because the older man was so unlike the immigrant's deceased father. Whereas Lawrence Washington had been an Oxford don, Nathaniel Pope could not even write his own name until late in life.[72] In the mid-1630s, as Lawrence was settling into the Anglican rectorship at Purleigh that he had attained after a long, steady climb, Pope sailed to Catholic-dominated Maryland, where he quickly established himself as a major participant in the commerce between London and the Chesapeake. His success as a merchant was reflected in his election to the newly created assembly. When the civil war erupted, the religious differences in Maryland made its inhabitants acutely sensitive to developments in England. Pope was not an innocent bystander to an ultimately unsuccessful Protestant rebellion against the proprietary regime from 1645 to 1647. Several of his friends and his son-in-law were directly implicated. But unlike Lawrence Washington, who had openly defended the king's cause at the cost of his personal welfare, Nathaniel Pope was a trimmer. During the crisis he was sent as the governor's emissary to Kent Island, a center of antiproprietary sentiment, and was alleged to have betrayed this trust by depreciating the governor's promises and urging the islanders to remove themselves to Virginia, where he himself settled two years later.[73] Unlike Lawrence Washington, Pope was a survivor who knew how to protect his private interests in dangerous times. John Washington's attachment to Nathaniel Pope, then, is a measure of how far the young immigrant had traveled from the world of his father.

When John Washington encountered him, probably in early 1657, Pope was one of the most prominent merchant-planters and leaders in the Northern Neck. Moreover, unlike the majority of Chesapeake fathers at the time, who did not live long enough to influence the marital choices of their children, Pope had a nubile daughter.[74] Did John marry Ann Pope for love or for her father's patronage? Was Ann drawn to John on her own, or was she pressed by her father to take the young immigrant? Historians generally assume that parental influence and love have usually existed in an inverse relationship. Where parental power was high, instrumental considerations are supposed to have mattered most; conversely, where parents

NANUET PUBLIC LIBRARY
149 CHURCH STREET
NANUET, NEW YORK 10954

were gone, romance is assumed to have held sway.[75] In this case, we can more easily assess the mutual interests of the father and his prospective son-in-law than the nature of the attraction between the future marriage partners.

To be Nathaniel Pope's son-in-law held much promise for a young mariner who wanted to become a full-fledged overseas merchant. Tobacco was the mainstay of that commerce, and it rested on plantation development. In earlier days some involvement by merchants in the productive side was requisite, if only to ensure a sufficient supply for their commerce.[76] Nathaniel Pope's earliest activities in the Chesapeake during the 1630s fit that pattern. He remained foremost a merchant whose planting business served his marketing needs. By the 1650s there were enough growers in the region to allow transatlantic traders to obtain adequate amounts of tobacco without getting involved in its production. Still, the thought of owning land and providing some of one's own tobacco freight, as well as having a base for ancillary commercial services, continued to appeal to ambitious traders. As a long-time Virginia resident wrote in a pamphlet published in London the year John Washington sailed for the colony, "(such preferment hath this Country rewarded the industrious with) that some from being wool-hoppers and of as mean or meaner imployment in England have there grown *great merchants*, and attained to the most eminent advancements the Country afforded."[77] A strategic marriage into an established merchant's family could facilitate that advancement.

If Washington's interest in having the wealthy Pope as a father-in-law is quite understandable, Pope's recruitment of Washington needs to be more fully explored. After all, Pope's daughter could not have had a shortage of suitors, for every unmarried female in the Chesapeake had a pool of bachelors from which to choose during most of the century.[78] A daughter of Nathaniel Pope would have been most desirable even if sex ratio had been more balanced. Why, then, did Washington win the support of the father and the hand of the daughter?

What distinguished Washington was not his money, his social status, nor his English-based connections, the assets that are most often cited as the levers that successful immigrants used to push ahead in Virginia.[79] He had too little money to impress Pope. Indeed, Pope offered to pay what Washington might have owed his partner, Edward Prescott. Moreover, Pope advanced Washington funds that he eventually bequeathed him. The young man's social status was also unlikely to be an especially helpful asset. Although his father came from a lesser gentry family, Washington was not an heir to a country estate and had no conspicuous association with gentility in England. In fact he is identified in his earliest appearances in Virginia records as a merchant, not a gentleman. He was not called a gentleman until after his marriage to Ann Pope.[80] Nor do we know of a letter of introduction from a London merchant that might have brought Washington to Pope's attention.

Washington did, however, possess assets that made him valuable to Ann Pope's father. He had first-hand knowledge not only of the London market but also of the tobacco trade with northern Europe.[81] The Navigation Act of 1651 did not proscribe colonial products from exportation directly to Europe. That prohibition had been part of early Stuart policy and would be reintroduced after the Restoration.[82] In the late 1650s Washington's experience in the Baltic ports would be helpful to Pope's export activities. Furthermore, the newcomer was educated. Pope's own limited schooling had not prevented him from becoming a successful merchant, litigant, or justice, but he had come to realize the utility of learning in his several activities. In fact, a few years earlier a London merchant, apparently in response to Pope's request, had sent him a young man who could "write a very good hand [and] sifer very well" and who therefore could teach Pope's children and keep his accounts.[83] In short, Washington had the requisite skills and experience to help the aging Pope in various ways as a son-in-law. What we cannot glean are the personal qualities that appealed to Ann Pope, but these may well have been the most important reasons for Washington's acceptability.

When Washington met him, Pope had, in addition to Ann, two sons who were under age and a married daughter. He had known his first son-in-law, William Hardich, since their days in Maryland. Pope was a cautious man. He obviously liked Washington but knew that only time could validate his judgment. Thus, in May 1659, some months after Washington married Ann, Pope conferred a 700-acre tract in Westmoreland upon his daughter, but he appointed Hardich and a fellow justice "feofees in trust" to administer the land for Ann and her heirs forever[84] (at the time Ann was carrying the Washingtons' first child). Five days after this conveyance, Pope drafted his will. Both his sons-in-law were witnesses and both received bequests in personalty. The bulk of his estate, however, went to his two sons, one of whom he named sole executor, although the boy was still a minor.[85]

Pope's actions reflected the priorities of someone whose long experience on the bench had familiarized him with husbands who mismanaged or alienated property that belonged to their wives. Under English common law a married woman could own realty, but her movable property was placed at the disposal of her husband, while her real estate was his to manage and profit from. The only decision she could make about her land was whether her husband could sell or mortgage it. In fact, because of his wife's right to be supported during her widowhood by his estate (her dower right), a married man was required to obtain his wife's permission before alienating any of his realty. The consent of wives was supposed to be freely given. To that end courts were expected to examine married women privately before passing titles.[86] As a judge, however, Pope well knew how difficult it must have been for a woman to admit that her consent to a conveyance had been coerced. She, not the jurist, had to live with her husband and bear the consequences of a denial of a transaction. Accordingly Pope adopted the one strategy that could secure for a wife the benefits of her own realty and also insulate her from possible coercion by her husband: he created a separate estate and placed it under the control of trustees.[87]

Although an illness may have prompted him to set up an estate for Ann and also draft his will, Pope did not die until April 1660. During his last months, Pope, physically weakened, found his new son-in-law indispensable. Records of the Westmoreland court show that Washington acted as his father-in-law's attorney during this time.[88] If Pope had created a separate estate for his daughter because he had not known her husband long enough to trust Ann's future to him unconditionally, in the end Pope's family and colleagues on the Westmoreland court had sufficient confidence in Washington to name him guardian of his brothers-in-law.[89]

Both Pope and Washington benefited from their relationship. The older man gained a son-in-law who proved he could reliably assume familial responsibilities during Pope's last year and after his death. Washington, in turn, gained entry to the network of local leaders and became a successful merchant-planter, a member of the Westmoreland governing elite, and the progenitor of a gentry family.

In several ways the story of John Washington illuminates the path taken in the middle of the seventeenth century by many immigrants who later became leaders in Virginia. First, the contrast between his career and that of his father underscores the intergenerational discontinuity that immigration to the colony often represented. John's venture marked a geographical and cultural break with his father's world. Second, for young men involved in the transatlantic trade Virginia was less likely to be a permanent destination than another place to explore before settling down. Without the inducements offered by a patron, it is highly unlikely that Washington would have stayed. Third, what brought such immigrants to the colony in the first instance was trade. The immediate promise of Virginia was that they could become full-fledged merchants there. Fourth, they did not have to possess much money, gentle status, or connections to attract a local sponsor. Wide experience in overseas trade and some schooling were valuable assets that invited recruitment by established leaders. Finally, because of his father's sufferings, Washington sometimes has been presented as a classic cavalier type who transferred to Virginia a strong conformity to the established church and loyalty to the crown. Instead, his story reveals how the dislocations of the civil war produced immigrants from loyalist families who were detached from the traditions in which they had been reared. Men like John Washington came to the New World not to reaffirm an old identity but rather to find a new one.[90]

Notes

1. For examples, see Daniel J. Boorstin, *The Americans: The Colonial Experience* (New York, 1958), 97–143, and various works by Louis B. Wright, such as *The First Gentlemen of Virginia: Intellectual Qualities of the Early Colonial Ruling Class* (San Marino, Calif., 1940), esp. chap. 1; *The Atlantic Frontier: Colonial American Civilization, 1607–1763* (1947; Ithaca, N.Y., 1959), 70; and *Culture on the Moving Frontier* (1955; New York, 1961), 21.

2. The process has been examined for 205 immigrant leaders in Martin H. Quitt, "Immigrant Origins of the Virginia Gentry: A Study of Cultural Transmission and Innovation," *WMQ* 45 (1988): 629–55.

3. On patriarchalism in English culture, see Gordon J. Schochet, "Patriarchalism, Politics, and Mass Attitudes in Stuart England," *Historical Journal* 12 (1969): 413–41, and his *Patriarchalism in Political Thought: The Authoritarian Family and Political Speculation . . .* (New York, 1975), esp. chap. 4. It is traced as a theme in family life generally by Lawrence Stone in *The Family, Sex, and Marriage in England, 1500–1800* (New York, 1970), 151–218. On patriarchalism and primogeniture among the great landowners, see Lawrence Stone, *An Open Elite? England, 1540–1880* (New York, 1984), esp. 69–86. On occupational continuity between generations as an ideal among artisans, see Robert Blair St. George, "Fathers, Sons, and Identity: Woodworking Artisans in Southeastern New England, 1620–1700," in *The Craftsman in Early America*, ed. Ian M. G. Quimby (New York, 1984), 89–125, esp. 97. See also Paul S. Seaver, *Wallington's World: A Puritan Artisan in Seventeenth-Century London* (Stanford, Calif., 1985), 76.

4. On the circumstances of his father, who died intestate in 1616, see Charles A. Hoppin, *The Washington Ancestry and Records of the McClain, Johnson, and Forty Other Colonial American Families*, 3 vols. (Greenfield, Ohio, 1932), 1:94–109, esp. 101, 104. On primogeniture within the gentry, see J. P. Cooper, "Patterns of Inheritance and Settlement by Great Landowners from the Fifteenth

to the Eighteenth Centuries," in *Family and Inheritance: Rural Society in Western Europe, 1200–1800,* ed. Jack Goody, Joan Thirsk, and E. P. Thompson (Cambridge and New York, 1976), 214, and Joan Thirsk, "The European Debate on Customs of Inheritance," ibid., 186–87, 190.

5. Data regarding his entrance, matriculation, and degrees are taken from C. B. Heberden, *Brasenose College Register, 1509–1909* (Oxford, 1909), 138.

6. Lawrence Stone, "The Size and Composition of the Oxford Student Body, 1580–1910," in *The University in Society,* ed. Lawrence Stone, 2 vols. (Princeton, N.J., 1974), 1:29–30.

7. For reasons that are unclear, more than a third of his entering class put off registering (ibid., 85, graph 17). The practice was university-wide (ibid., 83–87).

8. Ibid., 24, graph 6, 95, table 4, 94, table 3.

9. In 1621 matriculations were the highest in forty years and more than twice the annual average of the previous two decades (ibid., 110; L. F. Salzman, ed., *The Victoria History of the County of Oxford,* 13 vols. [London, 1939–96], 3:23 [hereafter cited as *VCH*]). The term *educational revolution* comes from Lawrence Stone, "The Educational Revolution in England, 1560–1640," *Past and Present* 28 (1964): 41–80.

10. Stone, "Size and Composition of Oxford Student Body," 17–28.

11. *Brasenose College Quartercentenary Monographs* 2:9 (1909): 18.

12. V. H. H. Green, *A History of Oxford University* (London, 1974), 29.

13. Arthur Engel, "Emerging Concepts of the Academic Profession at Oxford, 1800–1854," in Stone, *University in Society,* 308. This career path dated from the Middle Ages (Green, *History of Oxford,* 29).

14. Hoppin, *Washington Ancestry* 1:111. For the duties of the lector, see James McConica, ed., *The Collegiate University* (Oxford, 1986), 14.

15. Hoppin, *Washington Ancestry* 1:111; Freeman, *Washington* 1:528. Until 1628 the two university proctors had been elected annually by the regent masters. The proctors had enjoyed wide powers and have been described as "the most influential figures in the University" (Green, *History of Oxford,* 6). On efforts in 1628 and 1629 to reform the election of proctors, see Charles E. Mallet, *A History of the University of Oxford,* 3 vols. (London and New York, 1924–28), 2:241–42; G. C. Brodrick, *A History of the University of Oxford* (London, 1891), 109–10; Mark H. Curtis, *Oxford and Cambridge in Transition, 1558–1642: An Essay on Changing Relations between the English Universities and English Society* (Oxford, 1959), 44.

16. The role of Caroline Arminianism as a cause of the civil war has recently been debated. See Nicholas Tyacke, "Puritanism, Arminianism, and Counter-Reformation," in *The Origins of the English Civil War,* ed. Conrad Russell (New York, 1973), 119–43; Nicholas Tyacke, *Anti-Calvinists: The Rise of English Arminianism, c. 1590–1640* (Oxford, 1987); Peter White, "The Rise of Arminianism Reconsidered," *Past and Present* 101 (1983): 34–54, esp. 41n for a definition of Arminianism; P. G. Lake, "Calvinism and the English Church, 1570–1635,"

ibid., 114 (1987): 37–76, esp. 74–75, for an analysis of the "positive aspects of Arminianism."

17. For the August 1631 conference, see Tyacke, *Anti-Calvinists,* 82; Curtis, *Oxford and Cambridge in Transition,* 173–74; Mallet, *History of the University of Oxford* 2:305.

18. The term ran until April 1632 (Anthony Wood, *Athenae Oxonienses,* 2 vols. [London, 1691–92], 1:869, 872 [microfilm]).

19. Mallet, *History of the University of Oxford* 2:304.

20. Curtis, *Oxford and Cambridge in Transition,* 44; Mallet, *History of the University of Oxford* 2:333.

21. *Brasenose College Monographs* 2:9 (1909): 18.

22. Charles H. Browning, "The Washington Pedigree: Corrigenda and Addenda," *PMHB* 45 (1921): 320–63, esp. 348–49. The passion that such an inference could engender sixty years ago is evident in Charles A. Hoppin's response, presented as a notarized affidavit in "The Good Name and Fame of the Washingtons," *Tyler's Quarterly Historical and Genealogical Magazine* 4 (1922–23): 315–52. On the basis of recent demographic findings, the likelihood of John Washington's having been born out of wedlock is remote. Even at their peak, illegitimate births hovered only at 4 percent and were virtually nonexistent among gentle folk. See David Levine and Keith Wrightson, "The Social Context of Illegitimacy in Early Modern England," in *Bastardy and Its Comparative History: Studies in the History of Illegitimacy and Marital Nonconformism . . . ,* ed. Peter Laslett, Karla Oosterveen, and Richard M. Smith (Cambridge, 1980), 158–75. In the Essex parish of Terling between 1590 and 1640, they found that only one of fifty fathers of illegitimate children whom they could identify was of gentle status (163). Much more common were prenuptial conceptions. Approximately one-fourth of all births in sixteen English parishes between 1600 and 1650 resulted from premarital intercourse (23, table).

23. Mark H. Curtis, "The Alienated Intellectuals of Early Stuart England," *Past and Present* 23 (1962): 25–43.

24. Between 1620 and 1700 the proportion of persons who never married ranged from approximately 15 to 27 percent (E. A. Wrigley and R. S. Schofield, *The Population History of England, 1541–1871: A Reconstruction* [Cambridge, Mass., 1981], 261, table).

25. Alan Macfarlane, *Marriage and Love in England, 1300–1840* (Oxford, 1986), 154–58, argues that companionship was a continuing expectation of English couples for centuries and that it was a distinguishing feature of the Western concept of marriage.

26. David Cressy, "Literacy in Seventeenth-Century England: More Evidence," *Journal of Interdisciplinary History* 8 (1977): 146 and tables on 148, 150. A letter by Amphillis Washington is reprinted in Hoppin, *Washington Ancestry* 1:127.

27. On the repressiveness of child rearing generally in the sixteenth and sev-

enteenth centuries and of Puritan parents in particular, see Stone, "Family, Sex, and Marriage in England," 161–78; Joseph E. Ilick, "Child-Rearing in Seventeenth-Century England and America," in *The History of Childhood*, ed. Lloyd deMause (New York, 1974), 303–50. On the differences between Calvinist and moderate Protestant child-rearing modes, see Philip Greven, *The Protestant Temperament: Patterns of Child-Rearing, Religious Experience, and the Self in Early America* (New York, 1977), 21–261. Linda Pollock, *Forgotten Children: Parent-Child Relations from 1500 to 1900* (Cambridge, 1983), 199, like Greven, believes that "the method used to discipline a child varied according to the parent and child rather than the time period."

28. Cecile Ernst and Jules Angst, *Birth Order: Its Influence on Personality* (New York, 1983), 87–88; Lucille Forer with Henry Still, *The Birth Order Factor: How Your Personality Is Influenced by Your Place in the Family* (New York, 1976), 8–9, 47, 222.

29. Whether the Washington household had any servants or other inmates is not known. The mean household size in England from the late sixteenth century to 1901 was approximately 4.75 (Peter Laslett, ed., *Household and Family in Past Time: Comparative Studies in the Size and Structure of the Domestic Group* . . . [Cambridge, Eng., 1972], 126).

30. Hoppin, *Washington Ancestry* 1:122.

31. Pregnant women commonly returned to the homes of their parents for delivery through the eighteenth century (Catherine M. Scholten, *Childbearing in American Society, 1650–1850* [New York, 1985], 22).

32. Vivian C. Fox and Martin H. Quitt, *Loving, Parenting, and Dying: The Family Cycle in England and America: Past and Present* (New York, 1980), 36, 215; Scholten, *Childbearing in American Society*, 23–24, 34.

33. Hoppin, *Washington Ancestry* 1:122, 129.

34. Ibid., 140.

35. The letter of recommendation to Sutton's Hospital is printed in ibid., 139.

36. *VCH: Essex* 1: Geological Map. The school is described in ibid., 2:516–17.

37. A. G. Mathews counted 2,425, while I. M. Green raised the total to 2,780 (Mathews, *Walker Revised: Being a Revision of John Walker's Sufferings of the Clergy during the Grand Rebellion, 1642–60* [Oxford, 1948], xv; Green, "The Persecution of 'Scandalous' and 'Malignant' Parish Clergy during the English Civil War," *English Historical Review* 94 [1979]: 508). On Parliament's slow start, see ibid., 515, and Derek Hirst, *Authority and Conflict: England, 1603–1658* (Cambridge, 1986), 195.

38. John White, *The First Century of Scandalous, Malignant Priests, Made and Admitted into Benefices by the Prelates, in Whose Hands the Ordination of Ministers and Government Hath Been* (London, 1643), 4 (microfilm).

39. Ibid.

40. Green, Persecution of Parish Clergy," 510. See also Jim Sharpe, "Scandalous and Malignant Priests in Essex: The Impact of Grassroots Puritanism," in

Politics and People in Revolutionary England, ed. Olin Jones, Malyn Newitt, and Stephen Roberts (New York, 1986), 253–73, esp. 264–65.

41. Hoppin, *Washington Ancestry* 1:125; Matthews, *Walker Revised,* 167.

42. Freeman, *Washington* 1:529.

43. Green, "Persecution of Parish Clergy," 519–20. Sharpe suggests that some sequestered ministers fell victim to the "heightened expectations concerning clerical conduct" that existed at the time ("Scandalous and Malignant Priests in Essex," 267).

44. Green, "Persecution of Parish Clergy," 511. Matthews lists 152 Essex clergy who were sequestered. Examples of those charged with ceremonialism are on nearly every page (*Walker Revised,* 144–71).

45. White, *First Century of Scandalous Priests,* 4 (microfilm).

46. This total was well above the national average of 28 percent (Green, "Persecution of Parish Clergy," 522–24). On reform ferment during the civil war there, see *VCH: Essex* 2:56ff.

47. Green, "Persecution of Parish Clergy," 526.

48. Green finds that 42 percent of the sequestered clergy continued in the church and believes that this high rate would have been unlikely "if the sufferers as a whole had been strong supporters of the policies of Charles I and Laud in the first place" (ibid., 525, 527). Washington's case, however, suggests that some clergy may have strongly supported the establishment for reasons other than doctrine.

49. Freeman, *Washington* 1:529. Freeman mistakenly gives his age at death as fifty-four and the year as 1652. See Hoppin, *Washington Ancestry* 1:110, 126, which is also Freeman's source, and note 5 above.

50. Stone, "Size and Composition of Oxford Student Body," 39. For the use of a less neutral term than "1640–1660," see Barry Coward, "Was There an English Revolution?" in Jones, Newitt, and Roberts, *Politics and People in Revolutionary England,* 10.

51. Charles I marched into Oxford in October 1642, and the university became the headquarters of the royalists until it was captured by parliamentary troops in June 1646 (*VCH: Oxfordshire* 3:25; Mallet, *History of Oxford University* 2:353, 368–69). In May 1647 Parliament charged the visitors to investigate men who had failed to take oaths abjuring the royalist cause, men who had fought against parliamentary forces, and men who contravened parliamentary ordinances, including those dealing with doctrinal matters (Brodrick, *History of the University of Oxford,* 140). For the visitors' four-to-five-year activities at the university, see Mallet, *History of Oxford University* 2:371–79. He characterizes their efforts as moderate (370). The not-so-dispassionate contemporary historian Anthony Wood charged the visitors with effecting "the great rout of Royalists" (*Athenae Oxonienses* 2:744 [microfilm]).

52. Samuel Radcliffe had been head since 1614 (*VCH: Oxfordshire* 3:210, 214).

53. See the case of Edward Thurman and his son Henry, both of whom at-

tended Christ Church (Joseph Foster, *Alumni Oxonienses,* 4 vols. [Oxford, 1891–92], 3:1484; Matthews, *Walker Revised,* 165; and White, *The First Century of Scandalous Priests,* 5–6 [microfilm]). Thurman was the only sequestered Essex minister whose son is identified in Foster. Cromwell was elected chancellor in 1650 (Mallet, *History of Oxford University* 2:390).

54. Stone, "Size and Composition of Oxford Student Body," 110. A low of eight matriculations was reached in 1648.

55. John might have attended for a year or more and dropped out before registering. Such a pattern was an especially common occurrence at midcentury, when the proportion of freshmen who neither matriculated nor received a degree was abnormally high (ibid., 85, 87, 109).

56. Hoppin, *Washington Ancestry* 1:141, 144. Two weeks after his father died, his mother wrote her brother a letter in which she sent regards from her children, except from two who were not home (127).

57. A. Wrigley, "A Simple Model of London's Importance in Changing English Society and Economy, 1650–1750," in *Pre-Industrial England: Geographical Essays,* ed. John Patten (Folkstone, Kent, 1979), 191–217, attributes to London a "modernizing" influence on people who came there from rural villages. On effects of the London experience on the outlook of Virginia immigrant leaders, see Quitt, "Immigrant Origins of the Virginia Gentry," 635–38.

58. Thomas R. Forbes, "Weaver and Cordwainer: Occupations in the Parish of St. Giles without Cripplegates, London, in 1654–1693 and 1729–1743," *Guildhall Studies in London History* 4 (1980): 119–32. I have tallied the individual occupations he itemizes for 1654–93 at 360, excluding only those listed under his general category of "status."

59. Christopher Hill, *The World Turned Upside Down: Radical Ideas during the English Revolution* (New York, 1972).

60. Valerie Pearl, "Change and Stability in Seventeenth-Century London," *London Journal* 5 (1979): 6.

61. Steven Smith, "The London Apprentices as Seventeenth-Century Adolescents," *Past and Present* 61 (1973): 157.

62. Hoppin, *Washington Ancestry* 1:129.

63. Robert Brenner, "The Civil War Politics of London's Merchant Community," *Past and Present* 58 (1973): 68, 76.

64. For a wise analysis of the biological, cultural, and psychological aspects of adolescence and the possibilities for its historical treatment, see John Demos, "The Rise and Fall of Adolescence," in his *Past, Present, and Personal: The Family and the Life Course in American History* (New York, 1987), 92–113. The term *dissonance* is his (104). See also Fox and Quitt, *Loving, Parenting, and Dying,* 331–34.

65. The classic formulation of the formation of adolescent identity comes from the many writings of Erik Erikson; see especially his *Identity: Youth and Crisis* (New York, 1968). His thesis suggests how the execution of Charles I in 1649 may

have affected a youth like John Washington, who was brought up in a royalist household (159).

66. Derek Massarella, "'A World Elsewhere': Aspects of the Overseas Expansionist Mood of the 1650s," in Jones, Newitt, and Roberts, *Politics and People in Revolutionary England,* 141–48.

67. John R. Pagan, "Growth of the Tobacco Trade between London and Virginia, 1614–40," *Guildhall Studies in London History* 3 (1979): 255; Paul G. E. Clemens, *The Atlantic Economy and Colonial Maryland's Eastern Shore* (Ithaca, N.Y., 1980), 37–38; Arthur P. Middleton, *Tobacco Coast: A Maritime History of Chesapeake Bay in the Colonial Era* (1953; Baltimore, 1984), 124.

68. Details of the voyage and partnership are gleaned from interrogatories filed in Westmoreland County court in May 1667 as a result of Washington's suit against Prescott (Westmoreland County Deeds, Wills, and Patents, 1653–59, 77–78 [microfilm]). The interrogatories were partially stained before they were microfilmed in 1947. Fortunately, two of them had been printed earlier in Hoppin, *Washington Ancestry* 1:147–49.

69. On the importance of temporary partnerships in colonial trade, see Brenner, "Civil War Politics of London's Merchant Community," 66.

70. Hoppin wrote that Prescott was prepared to return to Europe without Washington when he was shipwrecked (*Washington Ancestry* 1:147). The interrogatories make it clear, however, that Washington did not decide to stay until after he had helped save the vessel.

71. Edward Prescott did not fare as well as his former junior partner. Although the bulk of his Virginia property was in Westmoreland County, he was commissioned to the Northampton court. In 1660 he was suspended for "several scandalous mutinous and seditious words" directed at the assembly that probably stemmed from his unhappiness with decisions that had gone against him when that body sat as an appellate court in private causes (Hening, *Statutes* 2:15, 1:549; Hoppin, *Washington Ancestry* 1:150n). His will was recorded in March 1662 (Westmoreland County Deeds and Wills 1, 1653–71, 191–92 [microfilm]).

72. Not until 1657 did Pope sign his name on documents. Previously he affixed his mark to deeds (Hoppin, *Washington Ancestry* 1:277).

73. Details of Pope's career in the Chesapeake are gleaned from ibid., 1:248–84.

74. Two-thirds of the married men leaving inventories in Charles County, Maryland, between 1658 and 1705 left children who were all under age eighteen (Lorena Walsh, "'Till Death Us Do Part': Marriage and Family in Seventeenth-Century Maryland," in *The Chesapeake in the Seventeenth Century: Essays on Anglo-American Society,* ed. Thad W. Tate and David L. Ammerman [Chapel Hill, N.C., 1979], 12n). Three-fourths of the children born in Middlesex County, Va., in the seventeenth century lost one parent, and more than one-third lost both before they reached twenty-one or married (Darrett B. Rutman and Anita H. Rutman, *A Place in Time: Explicatus* [New York and London, 1984], 80–81, and Dar-

rett B. Rutman and Anita H. Rutman, *A Place in Time: Middlesex County, Virginia, 1650–1750* [New York and London, 1984], 114).

75. The inverse correlation between parental power and romance in choice of a marriage partner owes much of its force in American scholarship to Daniel Scott Smith's seminal essay, "Parental Power and Marriage Patterns: An Analysis of Historical Trends in Hingham, Massachusetts," *Journal of Marriage and the Family* 35 (1973): 419–28. Although overstated in parts, Macfarlane's *Marriage and Love in England* provides a valuable corrective to the even more extreme proposition that romance in marriage is a modern innovation. Perhaps the baldest and most influential statement of that position is Edward Shorter, *The Making of the Modern Family* (New York, 1975).

76. Brenner, "Civil War Politics of London's Merchant Community," 69.

77. John Hammond, *Leah and Rachel, or, The Two Fruitfull Sisters Virginia and Mary-land* (London, 1656), in *Narratives of Early Maryland, 1633–1684,* ed. Clayton C. Hall (1910; New York, 1967), 299.

78. Martin H. Quitt, "Virginia House of Burgesses, 1660–1706: The Social, Economic, and Educational Bases of Political Power" (Ph.D. diss., Washington University, 1970), 70–71, 348.

79. See, for example, Bernard Bailyn, "Politics and Social Structure in Seventeenth-Century Virginia," in *Seventeenth-Century America: Essays in Colonial History,* ed. James M. Smith (Chapel Hill, N.C., 1959), 90–115.

80. Westmoreland County Deeds, Wills, and Patents, 1653–59, 105–6 (microfilm); Deeds, Wills, and Patents, 1661–62, 23 (microfilm).

81. Their isolation from the European market normally left Chesapeake planters feeling that English merchants, with their "daily Opportunities of looking abroad in the World," could take advantage of them (*An Essay upon the Government of the English Plantations on the Continent of America* [1701], ed. Louis B. Wright [San Marino, Calif., 1945], 43). For the putative authorship of this essay, see Carole Shammas, "Benjamin Harrison III and the Authorship of *An Essay upon the Government of the English Plantations on the Continent of America,*" *VMHB* 84 (1976): 166–73.

82. The act of 1651 is printed in Samuel R. Gardiner, ed., *The Constitutional Documents of the Puritan Revolution, 1625–1660,* 3d ed. (Oxford, 1906), 468–71. See also Thomas C. Barrow, *Trade and Empire: The British Customs Service in Colonial America, 1660–1775* (Cambridge, Mass., 1967), and Charles M. Andrews, *The Colonial Period of American History,* 4 vols. (New Haven, 1934–38), 4:43–44.

83. See the letter of Nicholas Hayward to Nathaniel Pope, Nov. 1652, in the Northumberland County Record Book, 1652–58, 11 (microfilm).

84. Westmoreland County Deeds, Wills, and Patents, 1653–59, 127 (microfilm).

85. Westmoreland County Deeds and Wills, 1, 1653–71, 115 (microfilm).

86. Marylynn Salmon, *Women and the Law of Property in Early America*

(Chapel Hill, N.C., and London, 1986), 14–19. The preamble to a Virginia statute of 1674 that mandated private examinations indicated that these had been "the usual way in the country for many Yeares" for conveying estates that belonged to a wife by right of her inheritance (Hening, *Statutes* 2:317).

87. The evolution of separate estates under the rules of equity is examined by Salmon, *Women and the Law of Property,* 81–119. Pope's action suggests that Salmon may be overstating the protection that private examinations afforded married women in the early Chesapeake (ibid., 18–22).

88. Westmoreland County Wills, Deeds, and Patents, 1653–59, 135 (microfilm).

89. Washington's appointment as guardian is noted at the end of Nathaniel Pope's appraised estate (Westmoreland County Deeds, Wills, and Patents, 1661–62, 8–9 [microfilm]).

90. The story of the Washingtons illustrates Christopher Hill's argument that the civil war resulted in an important transformation of English values: "Economics has replaced religion" (*Some Intellectual Consequences of the English Revolution* [Madison, Wis., 1980], 59). For a fuller exposition of his thesis about the effect of the civil war on the shift to possessive individualism, see Hill's "A Bourgeois Revolution?" in *Three British Revolutions: 1641, 1688, 1776,* ed. J. G. A. Pocock (Princeton, N.J., 1980), 109–39. See also Lawrence Stone, "The Bourgeois Revolution of Seventeenth-Century England Revisited," *Past and Present* 109 (1985): 44–54.

2. Washington and the Colonial Military Tradition

Don Higginbotham

The essay that follows emphasizes that Washington did not think of himself as a militiaman but rather wished to be considered a military professional. As a result of the four imperial wars with France between 1689 and 1763, a growing number of provincials had acquired considerable military experience. In their desire to behave as professionals and, if possible, to acquire British commissions, we see an example of what some historians call the anglicization of American colonial society in the mideighteenth century—a desire to be British in every way: in fashions, in architectural styles, in the education of their children, in the way they practiced law and viewed their legislative bodies, and so on. The colonists created in time of war what might be called semiprofessional forces. That is, these specially raised units, outside the militia structure, enlisted for a year or more, served beyond their respective colonies if necessary, came under stricter military law than that imposed on the militia, and fought under officers who, like Washington, read military treatises and crafted their standards and procedures after those of the British officers with whom they served. Consequently, America's adopting a professional army — "a standing army"—in the Revolution was a logical and predictable extension of evolutionary military practices. Most of the ranking officers in the Continental army in 1775–76 had held commissions in the last imperial conflict.

I have written extensively on Washington and on the American Revolution. This essay originally appeared as chapter 1 of my George Washington and the American Military Tradition (© 1985 by the University of Georgia Press, Athens, Georgia 30602) and is reprinted by permission of the publisher.

IN OUR MIND'S EYE, the picture of Washington the colonial military figure is that of the militia officer. Washington, like other Virginians and indeed like colonials elsewhere, preferred to be addressed by his military title. From his middle twenties to the time of the Revolution, he was usually referred to as Colonel Washington. When he posed for Charles Willson Peale's portrait in 1772—his earliest known countenance on canvas—he elected to do so in his old uniform, with its blue coat and red facing, evidently the same uniform that he donned for sessions of the Second Continental Congress in the spring of 1775. Although it is not surprising to see that Peale depicted Washington wearing a sword and gorget, the standard accoutrements of an eighteenth-century officer, the artist's work includes an item not found in portraits of British officers of the period. There is a gun over the Virginian's shoulder, which Douglas S. Freeman, Washington's distinguished multivolume biographer, believes to be a rifle rather than a musket.[1] Why did Peale add such a weapon? Was it to signify the importance of firearms in this New World society for all men, both officers and the rank and file? If Freeman is right about its being a rifle, there is a real frontier flavor to the portrait. Long rifles (as opposed to shorter central European models) were confined to the American backcountry. Probably first crafted in Pennsylvania, they were the invention of colonial gunsmiths who had responded to the need in hunting and Indian warfare for a weapon superior in range and accuracy to the musket, which was used by professional armies with their practice of delivering short-distance volley fire.

Today, perhaps in keeping with Peale's intent, we may be tempted to see exemplified in that portrait a colonial military tradition distinct from the professional tradition of the mother country. We may be all the more inclined to do so if we think of the specific event of the French and Indian War for which Washington is best remembered: his bravery during the defeat of British General Edward Braddock's army near the Monongahela River on July 9, 1755, an army whose objective had been to seize French Fort Duquesne at the forks of the Ohio, the location of modern Pittsburgh. He seems to personify the virtues of forest-wise Virginia fighters as compared to British regulars clad in crimson coats who were trained to wheel, advance, and give battle in long, exposed lines three rows deep.

To be sure, Washington and the other Virginians fought heroically in the Battle of the Monongahela. "I luckily escapd with[ou]t a wound," he assured his mother, "tho' I had four Bullets through my Coat, and two Horses shot under me." Braddock's regulars, surprised and confused by their foes who assailed them from the protection of wooded areas, were disgraced, many of them fleeing the scene. We never saw more than "five or six" of the enemy at any one time, reported one member of the Braddock expedition, "and they Either on their Bellies or Behind trees or Runing from one tree to another." Washington subsequently recalled that "before it was *too late*" he had offered unsuccessfully to take charge of the provincials and engage "the enemy in their own way." As the afternoon wore on, the army suffered staggering casualties from a blistering cross fire. When Braddock's forces began their retreat, Washington assisted in loading the mortally wounded general into a cart. Then Washington, though still quite weak from a recent illness, traveled throughout the night and part of the next morning to reach the rear guard and supply train, with instructions that provisions, medical supplies, and wagons be hastened forward.[2]

Washington was as proud of the Virginians as he was contemptuous of the redcoats. "The Virginians," he exclaimed, "behavd like Men, and died like Soldier's; . . . I believe that out of 3 Companys that were there that Day, scarce 30 [men] were left alive." The regulars, in contrast, "behavd with more cowardice than it is possible to conceive." It was their "dastardly behaviour" that "exposd" the provincial troops, who "were inclined to do their duty to almost certain death . . . they broke and run as Sheep pursued by dogs; and it was impossible to rally them."[3]

Washington and the other surviving Virginians became heroes in the Old Dominion. "Our Brave Blues" they were hailed, since they wore the customary colonial uniform: blue breeches and blue coats with red facings. According to one story that Virginians doubtless relished in telling and retelling, Braddock, as he lay bleeding on the field, "would cry out my dear Blue's . . . give em tother fire." In the final days before he expired from his wounds, the general "could not bare the sight of a red coat." Upon seeing a regular, "he raved imoderately, but when one of the blues [appeared], he said he hop'd to live to reward em."[4]

A romantic rendition of the French and Indian War deeply embedded in our folklore portrays this battle as proving the superiority of American militia over British redcoats and demonstrating the irrelevance of European military theory and practice in the New World. Actually, the Monongahela disaster only confirmed and reinforced variations on these themes already present in provincial culture. Americans had always believed that militia composed of upstanding citizens were more trustworthy than professional soldiers, who were seen as the dregs of society. Militia were also better fighters because they were motivated by a desire to defend their homes and families rather than by a lust for plunder. The roots of this American militia ethos were imported from England at a time when the Stuart monarchy was turning from a centuries-old militia system to professional soldiers as its first line of defense. Certain seventeenth- and eighteenth-century British writers, who kept alive a radical whig tradition in the parent kingdom and whose works were widely disseminated in America, glorified an English militia that had not effectively existed in modern times and exaggerated the benefits of scarcely trained yeomen in arms because of their dislike and fear of salaried, full-time forces.

Colonial literature abounds with militia themes. In Puritan New England, they often found expression in annual artillery sermons. We discover an example of such thought as early as 1710 in the fledgling colony of South Carolina, where a planter boasted: "If regular troops excell in performing the Postures, . . . militia is much superior in making a true shot. . . . A planter who keeps his body fit for service . . . is doubtless a better soldier . . . than a Company of raw fellows raised in England."[5]

Braddock's devastating defeat brought these sentiments into sharper focus and elevated them as never before to a high level of public approval, if numerous pamphlets and newspaper essays on the subject are reliable indicators. Few were as simplistic in explaining the outcome as the contributor who intoned that redcoats "fight for pay" while Americans take arms "to revenge the Blood of their nearest Friends or Relatives, or to redeem them from a Captive State." Another commentator thought the tragedy lay in the decision not to confine "British Veterans" to garrison assignments, which would have allowed the dispatching of an entire army of colonial "Irregulars" to the Ohio. Perhaps no American penman was more savage in his treatment of Braddock himself than Boston's Charles Chauncy, a Congregational minister, who charged that the general "had no Idea of the *manner of fighting* in use here" and that he had with "great contempt" ignored throughout the campaign the advice of his provincial subordinates.[6] The main thrust of colonial arguments, as Douglas E. Leach summarizes them, was that "Americans, through long experience in fighting both the stealthy Indians and the shrewd French in the wilderness, had developed a special expertise that was neither possessed nor appreciated by the regulars, who supposedly were trained only for open European-style warfare. This idea led slowly but inexorably to another—that under certain favorable conditions a small force of well-armed and woods-wise colonists could rout a much larger, more ponderous formation of professional soldiers. It was an intriguing proposition, not easily forgotten."[7]

With varying degrees of emphasis, according to time and place, the notions that American warfare was unique and hardly required formal training would have a tenacious life. We encounter them just before Lexington and Concord as the colonists praised the advantages of their own militias and deplored the evils of standing armies, particularly the British army currently in their midst. Essayists in the American press reminded Parliament and the king's ministers that a war with her colonies would be for Britain a repeat writ large of Braddock's fiasco in the Pennsylvania wilds. One "Ranger," as he styled himself, explained the Braddock formula in this fashion: the king's regulars would be allowed to land and initially advance without opposition, after which "we can *bush fight* them and cut off their officers very easily, and in this way we can subdue them with very little loss."[8]

Either specifically or by implication parts of the militia ethos found expression during the Revolutionary era in the state constitutions, in the writings of the Antifederalists (and sometimes the Federalists as well), and in the second amendment to the federal Constitution, a part of the Bill of Rights, which states that "a well regulated Militia, being necessary to the security of a free State, the right of the people to keep and bear Arms, shall not be infringed." In the minds of some Americans, the militia ethos was almost as viable in the nineteenth century as in the republic's dawning days. When in 1940 Senator Bob Reynolds of North Carolina warned Hitler not to take lightly American boys who grew up with squirrel rifles in their hands, he implicitly gave testimony to an attitude not wholly dead.

Yet Washington, notwithstanding the Peale portrait and the Braddock campaign, does not lend himself to any personification of the American militiaman. We have explained, of course, why the superficial Washington student might think he should. As we will note later, Washington's duties as commander in chief of the Continental army have prompted still other of his admirers to tie him almost exclusively to a professional military tradition. We will endeavor to demonstrate subsequently that he was not an uncritical apologist for either a militia or a professional ethos.

Truth to tell, Washington never held a high opinion of the militia as an institution, nor did he ever think seriously of himself as a militia officer.

He knew that in colonial America there was an enormous gap between the theory and the reality of the militia. Militia training had always fluctuated between being haphazard and being nonexistent. As an organization the militia could hardly be highly effective when it included almost all free white adult males and when officers owed their appointments to their political and social standing. For example, in Frederick County, a frontier area and the scene of much of Washington's French and Indian War activity, the county lieutenant was Thomas, Lord Fairfax, Virginia's only resident nobleman, and the colonel of the Frederick regiment was His Lordship's relative, George William Fairfax.

Had Washington wished to be totally candid, he might have acknowledged the dubiousness of receiving his first militia commission as a major and as adjutant of the southern militia district of Virginia, which meant that he had the responsibility of overseeing the militia training in a wide region of the colony, one distant from his own home. Training days in Virginia as elsewhere were usually honored in the breach and were social occasions as much as anything else when they did occur. A generation before Washington's own military baptism, Governor Alexander Spotswood exclaimed that Virginia's militia was "the worst in the King's Dominions."[9]

Sustained crises, especially the eighteenth-century wars with France and Spain, required the recruiting of special forces, either under the direct control of a colony such as Virginia or as part of an intercolonial army operating alone or in conjunction with a British military expedition. Four companies of Virginians, including Washington's half brother Lawrence who afterward became adjutant for the entire colony, had been among the several thousand provincials who participated in the unsuccessful British attack on the Spanish Caribbean fortress of Cartagena in 1741. The Virginians with Braddock, the heroic blues, also were not militia but rather two companies of rangers and one of carpenters, present because of their skills in woodland warfare. Contrary to contemporary myth, Braddock appreciated those skills.[10]

Washington himself during the French and Indian War was always something between a militiaman and a professional soldier—from his viewpoint decidedly more the latter. In 1754, after Governor Robert Dinwiddie sent Major Washington on his now-famous but fruitless journey to order the French out of the Ohio Valley, Dinwiddie established what became known as the Virginia Regiment, to be recruited from able men, and he chose Washington as lieutenant colonel and second-ranking officer. On the death of his superior, Colonel Joshua Fry, Washington was promoted to colonel; however, the regiment was disbanded before the year's end, and he resigned rather than suffer the humiliation of accepting a lesser rank. It was as a volunteer and special aid to the general that he had fought with Braddock. Since the general's defeat and the withdrawal of his remaining redcoats to Philadelphia made it clear that Virginia would have to defend herself, the colony's leaders reconstituted the Virginia Regiment. Washington once again agreed to serve, accepting a high-sounding commission as "Colonel of the Virginia Regiment & Commander in Chief of all Forces now raised & to be raised for the Defence of this His Majesty's Colony."[11]

During the next three years (1755–1758), charged with the task of anchoring the colony's frontier defenses, he labored to make his regiment a first-rate military unit. In this capacity, he proved to be a good soldier for at least two reasons. First, he relished a military life. "My inclinations are strongly bent to arms," he asserted on one occasion; and on another he voiced his ambition of "pushing my Fortune in the Military way." Second, he had taken his military education seriously, grasping every opportunity to increase his "knowledge in the Military Art." He obtained that education by the tutorial method, which was also how doctors and lawyers learned their crafts in the colonial period. This tutorial method for soldiers meant discussions with battle-tested veterans, independent reading, observation, and firsthand practice. Washington had listened to his brother Lawrence reminisce about the Cartagena campaign of 1741 with their friend and relative by marriage, Colonel William Fairfax, who himself had once fought in Spain. He had read Caesar's *Commentaries;* a translated version of *A Panegyrick to the Memory of Frederick, Late Duke of Schomberg,* an acknowledged master of the art of European warfare (a book he purchased from a cousin at a cost of two shillings sixpence); and Humphrey Bland's *Treatise of Military Discipline,* the so-called Bible of the British army and affectionately known to generations of officers as "Old Humphrey." On a trip to Barbados with Lawrence he made note of the island's defensive capabilities, including the works of Fort James, a "pretty strongly fortified" post. Part of his firsthand practice in the art of war came before his three-year stint as commander on the Virginia frontier. It began in 1754 when, leading a tiny contingent of men, he tasted the joy of victory over Ensign Jumonville at the Battle of the Meadows and soon afterward felt the pain of defeat when he surrendered Fort Necessity to a superior French party in July of that year. Rarely an indecisive military man, not even at age twenty-two, he had given no thought to retreating before a superior foe. Cool in the face of danger, he never lost his nerve, which his subsequent conduct under Braddock illustrates.[12]

Braddock's campaign not only afforded Washington further experience on the battlefield, but it also gave him the opportunity to witness the day-to-day activities of a professional army. That he was a conscientious observer is indicated by his copying in a small notebook the army's daily general orders for his own edification and future study. Interestingly, Washington eschewed the harsh judgments of Braddock's performance that streamed from his contemporaries and confined his negative comments to the behavior of the enlisted men. He felt that the king's officers had showed courage and disregard for their own safety. (Three decades later he said gently of his old commander that he was "brave even to a fault" and in an orthodox campaign would undoubtedly "have done honor to his profession.") He still in 1755 had enormous respect for the British army. He had thirsted for a royal commission from Braddock. His persistence in that ambition would influence his subsequent actions, large and small—even to the point of mastering the art of fencing, still one of the social graces for an officer but hardly more than that.[13]

Though not yet twenty-four years of age, Washington had considerable experience in arms when he assumed direction of the reconstituted Virginia Regiment, and he strove to impart that knowledge to his unit through his officers. Had he reflected on the matter, he might have stated that a military leader, regardless of rank, should be a teacher, as he himself would again demonstrate on a wider stage in the Revolution. One of the most valuable lessons that a military commander can impart is a sense of fairness to one and all. Washington's first surviving written address to his officers made that point: "you may . . . depend upon having the strictest justice administered to all; . . . I shall make it the most agreeable part of my duty to study merit and reward the brave and deserving. . . . partiality shall never biass my conduct, nor shall prejudice injure any."[14]

Most of Washington's subordinates would have agreed that the colonel was substantially true to his word, which more than anything else explains why he gained their respect. He had it because of his actions, not because he was an officer, nor even because his was a deferential society in which men looked up to their social and economic betters and the term *gentleman* applied to the few rather than the many. Today officers are entitled to respect because they are officers. Even so, there are varying degrees of regard, determined by the manner in which superior officers conduct themselves. In contrast, the view in Washington's America was somewhat the reverse: the man by his character and performance gave dignity to the office; the office was less likely to give luster to the man. This view may have held particularly true in colonial military services, where squabbling and factionalism seemed to run rampant. Washington implicitly acknowledged the conditions for respect when he cautioned his juniors to "remember, that it is the actions, and not the commission, that make the Officer—and that there is more expected from him than the *Title*."[15]

He repeatedly instructed his field officers and company captains to be proper and correct in dealing with their own subordinate officers and men. Enlistees were to be assured that all promises to provide them with pay, provisions, and equipment would be met on schedule as far as possible. He, like perceptive military leaders throughout American history, pointed out that soldiers performed best under officers they knew and respected. Accordingly, he ordered that recruits "be put under the Command of Officers who enlisted them."[16]

Throughout his public life Washington stressed efficient administrative procedures and high ethical standards of behavior, traits which manifested themselves forcefully during his frontier command. Officers were to keep careful records, providing him with periodic reports of numbers present and absent, of monies on hand, and of supplies and equipment available. Both officers and men who deviated from the straight and narrow felt his retribution. Along with desertion, nothing aroused his wrath like abuse of the civilian population, not only for reasons of humanity but also because his forces depended upon the private sector for countless forms of assistance. In a lengthy document entitled "General Instructions to all the Captains of Companies," Washington declared that his officers' foremost objective was to protect and establish cordial relations with the inhabitants. In this one regard he had been openly at odds with Braddock during 1755. To Washington's mind, the general had displayed little tact or patience in dealing with colonials in all walks of life. Moreover, the years after Braddock's defeat brought more serious Anglo-American tensions as Britain hastened thousands of redcoats to North America. Their needs and their close proximity to colonials led to controversies over quartering troops on civilians, confiscating supplies and equipment, and recruiting servants.[17]

As for tactical training, Washington's ideas were not very different from those of British officers who were his contemporaries. Like most provincial officers, he was less than fully aware that some of his British counterparts had considerable familiarity through both military literature and direct European experience with flexible responses, including guerrilla or partisan warfare. (Historical opinion, in fact, now holds that Braddock himself was no theoretical old-school tactician. He had exercised the necessary precautions for moving a European army through a dense wilderness until the very day of his defeat, when in the afternoon before the battle his staff failed to perform alertly after crossing the Monongahela.) Even so, British ranking officers in the colonies such as Henry Bouquet, John Campbell, earl of Loudoun, and John Forbes after 1755 put new emphasis on training their regulars to shoot at targets, advance over rugged terrain, and respond to surprise attacks.[18]

Washington predictably stressed the value of "bush" tactics for the Virginia Regiment. "I expect you will take great pains to make your Soldiers good marks-men, by teaching them to shoot at Targets," he continually reminded his company officers. These admonitions further undermine the fiction that every American owned a gun and knew how to use it. In the aggregate, however, his sermons and exhortations pointed in another direction: toward British army practices. "For this desirable end," he counseled his officers to read extensively in military literature, beginning with Bland's treatise and then other works "which will give us the wished-for information." He specifically ordered instruction in "the New platoon way of Exercising," by which he meant procedures introduced in the king's forces by the duke of Cumberland.[19] Washington must have known that anything associated with "Billy" Cumberland, the captain general of the British army, would receive a positive response. Triumphant over the Pretender at Culloden and a veteran of the War of the Austrian Succession, the duke had persuaded his reluctant father King George II to hurry royal regiments to the defense of Virginia, although the duke could not be blamed for Braddock's rout. Virginians named in honor of Cumberland a fort, a county, a mountain range, a mountain gap, and a river.

Cumberland might be referred to endearingly as Billy by his rank and file, but he hardly advocated running a military organization by democratic methods; nor did Washington, who early in a subsequent war castigated them as New England ways. "Discipline is the soul of an army," he declared, repeating that time-honored maxim. "It makes small numbers formidable; procures success to the weak, and esteem to all." A disciplined army was also a clean, neatly uniformed army, a conviction Washington emphasized in his regimental communications. To insure that specified drill and ceremonial procedures were correctly followed, "even in the most minute punctilio's," Washington ordered every captain of a frontier fort to send a noncommissioned officer and two enlisted men to his headquarters in Winchester to receive exact instruction, which would then be imparted "on their return" to "the rest of your Command." Not if he could help it would his Virginians resemble the British caricature of colonial soldiers, with their unkempt hair, droopy stockings, carelessly slung weapons, and movements out of step and out of line. The Virginians were, in his eyes, neither militia nor even semiprofessionals; they surely were not to be equated with provincials serving in other parts of America. They *were* professionals because arms was "their profession."[20]

Washington was consciously endeavoring to transform his Virginians into a force that would be more equal to a British army regiment than any ever raised in English America. He told Governor Dinwiddie of doing things "more after the British Manner," "of pay[ing] that Deference to her Judgment & Experience." As his second-in-command Lieutenant Colonel Adam Stephen confided to Washington, "I think the more our Form resembles that of the Regiments on the Establishment The better pretensions we will have to be Established." The colonel, who had sought from Braddock a royal commission for himself, pressed to have the entire regiment taken into the British army. He could cite a precedent well known to him and other Virginians for such action. His brother Lawrence had received a regular's commission, since the colonial troops recruited for the Cartagena undertaking were royalized and placed under Virginia's Governor William Gooch—"Gooch's American Foot." Washington remembered that, even though the expedition had been a fiasco, Lawrence personally had received most favorable treatment from the governor; Lawrence had been so impressed with the overall commander Admiral Edward Vernon that he had named his Potomac River plantation Mount Vernon.[21]

Long desirous of changing the colors of his coat, Washington had additional reasons for his quest that related to his command of the Virginia Regiment. Twice British captains heading small bodies of men in his operational theater had refused to obey his orders because he held only a Virginia commission. Conflicts over rank and jurisdiction between professional and local forces were not uncommon in the colonial wars, and they would pose recurring problems for American military leaders in future conflicts. Matters came to a head when Captain John Dagworthy, claiming to hold a valid British regular commission and leading Maryland troops at Fort Cumberland on the Maryland side of the Potomac, persisted in thwarting the activities of Washington and his subordinates at a post that was administered jointly by Virginia and Maryland. The Virginians were so sensitive about the issues involved that in 1756 Washington journeyed all the way to Boston to present before General William Shirley the case for placing his regiment on the royal establishment. He carried with him a petition drawn up by his officers, stating that they should not be treated as inferiors to British officers of lower or similar rank, particularly since the Virginians shared equally with regulars the duties and dangers of wartime assignments.

Whatever precedents might be drawn from previous imperial struggles, Shirley felt he lacked the authority to grant Washington's request, though he managed to iron out the dispute at Fort Cumberland in Washington's favor. Washington transparently impressed Shirley, who remarked in a different context to Governor Horatio Sharpe of Maryland that "I know no Provincial officer upon this Continent" so deserving of a high position if an intercolonial force were dispatched against Fort Duquesne.[22] That was, however, small consolation to Washington, who undertook several such efforts on behalf of his officers and himself. The last one in 1757 was directed to Lord Loudoun, Shirley's successor as British commander in chief in America. Washington once again made a lengthy trip, this time to Philadelphia, to see His Lordship. During his interview, Washington presented a brief memorial from his officers, based on a thicker document originally designed to enlist the support of Governor Dinwiddie. This parchment is worthy of attention because it spells out so clearly the officers' perceptions of themselves and of their accomplishments. Some had served since the formation of the original Virginia Regiment in 1754.

They accurately claimed "that the Virginia Regiment was the first in arms of any Troops" in America during the French and Indian War, having completed "three years hard & bloody Serivce." Unlike other troops (in what was obviously a slap at the remnant of Braddock's regular regiments and at British forces in general), they had had no "agreeable recess in Winter Quarters" since "the Nature of the Service in which we are engagd, and the smallness of our Numbers . . . keep us constantly in Motion." But what if it should be said that "the Troops of Virginia are Irregulars, and cannot expect more notice than other Provincials"? At pains to explain that they were not militia, should any confusion exist on that score, militia being part-time or seasonal soldiers, the Virginians could legitimately state that they needed "nothing but Commissions from His Majesty to make us as regular a Corps as any upon the Continent. . . . We have been regularly Regimented and trained; and have done as regular Duty for upwards of 3 Years as any regiment in His Majesty's Service."[23]

When Loudoun rejected the appeal of Washington and his subordinates, we can only imagine their disappointment and frustration. His Lordship did not give a high priority to the Southern frontier and the capture of Fort Duquesne but rather stressed the immediacy of launching an offensive toward the Great Lakes. It must have seemed to Loudoun, who had only recently set foot in America, that he was bombarded by the colonists with an unending stream of requests. For example, approximately one hundred provincials descended on his headquarters and offered to serve as gentlemen volunteers—as Washington had done to Braddock—in order eventually to obtain a king's rank. These provincials included such prominent Virginians as young William Henry Fairfax and William Byrd III.[24]

Yet for Washington, Loudoun's rejection of his appeal was only one of multiple frustrations associated with his frontier command; the others would have been bearable, might even have withered away, had he possessed the authority and resources accompanying a royal commission to back him up. If Washington was a teacher, he was a student as well. Douglas Freeman has written that "recruitment, discipline, and fort building" were, along with British-colonial military controversies, "hard lessons in the school of experience." "I am wandering in a wilderness of difficulties," Washington complained to the House of Burgesses Speaker John Robinson. Responsible for a line of forts stretching over 350 miles, the longest exposed frontier in America, Washington seemed perpetually thin on necessities— first one, then another, and often several at once (clothing, provisions, equipment, arms and ammunition). Reluctant though he was, it became necessary in emergencies to impress from civilians, though as a consequence, "they threaten[ed] . . . 'to blow out my Brains.'"[25]

Most of all, Washington lacked manpower. Although Dinwiddie had boasted to Loudoun that Washington was unsurpassed as a recruiter, the governor had cautioned London officials not to anticipate Virginians' rushing to the colors. The Old Dominion was a colony of freeholders who treasured their independence and resented regimentation. Recruiting lagged so badly that at its low tides the regiment had under four hundred effectives and never reached the fifteen hundred authorized.[26]

Throughout he had to rely on the militia to help occupy distant posts and respond to French and Indian forays. Even at its best, the militia, which Washington always saw as little more than a necessary evil, functioned chiefly as a form of selective service. Men were drafted from their county companies and then were re-formed into new, temporary units while on duty. When they were summoned, Washington always had several concerns: would they be reasonably well armed, would they turn out in adequate strength, and would they remain long enough to be useful? They were invariably minus weapons. One contingent of two hundred Culpeper County men reported with a total of only eighty firelocks.[27] Instead of arriving promptly, militia trickled in, fewer than requested, or ignored the call completely, expressing indifference or fear for their safety. In October 1756, Washington discovered that when one-third of the militia in Augusta County were ordered out, one-thirteenth showed up. At first the militiamen summoned in some emergencies could not be compelled to stay more than thirty days, including the time it took to reach their stations and return home (a process that could absorb half the month). Generally, militia legislation specified that draftees were accountable for longer tours, but the acts of 1756 and 1757 stipulated that they could not be retained beyond December 1 of the year in which they took the field, nor could they be dispatched outside the colony. While numbering twenty-seven thousand men on paper, the colony's militia failed to meet the manpower requirements of the war and were no more effective than efforts "to raize the Dead," according to Washington.[28]

Militia posed other headaches. Often disorderly and insolent, they suffered scant retribution for their ill behavior since they were not subject to the martial law governing the Virginia Regiment. Patterned after the British Mutiny Act, this law passed by the General Assembly authorized the death penalty for desertion, mutiny, and disobedience. After one surprisingly good militia turn-out, a messenger brought a report of the approach of a sizable Indian war party. Before this intelligence proved to be erroneous, several hundred assembled militiamen at Winchester vanished. The express "might as well have ridden down the street shouting that a thousand war-crazed savages were entering the town," wrote Douglas Freeman. "Men . . . pictured themselves as already scalped. . . . they began to pour out of Winchester on the roads to the gaps of the Blue Ridge. With scarcely a pretense of concealment, they deserted en masse."[29]

These irregulars felt, quite correctly, that the uniformed officers and men of the Virginia Regiment looked down on them. There are habitual tensions when soldiers of dissimilar training and standards are thrown together, as Washington and his Virginians had learned during their prior service with British regulars and as he would be reminded later by friction between Continentals and militia in the Revolution. When a Prince William County militiaman made himself insufferable with his own condescending remarks about "the blues," he was slapped in the guardhouse. His comrades broke in and released him, and then, to show their contempt for superior authority, they "pull'd down the House," said Washington. (It was a typical eighteenth-century gesture of defiance: to take apart piece by piece a structure that symbolized immorality or oppression as the case might be; whorehouses and tax collectors' quarters were ever favorite targets.) The original culprit, feeling his oats after feeling his freedom, now swore that the officers of the Virginia Regiment were a pack of "Scoundrels and that he could drive the whole Corps before him." Washington concluded his account of this episode in tantalizingly brief fashion, although it is obvious that he and his officers looked the other way while an unnamed member of the regiment cured the obstreperous one of his "imprudence."[30]

While most militia did not imitate the violence of the Prince William men, they were scarcely reticent about protecting their interests. Even those that fulfilled their service would rarely stay beyond their calendar date. Nor did they suffer in silence if their basic needs were unmet, if promises could not be kept, if they saw better ways of running an army. "Every *mean* individual has his own crude notion of things, and must undertake to direct," complained Washington. "If his advice is neglected, he thinks himself slighted, abased, and injured; and, to redress his wrongs, will depart for his home."[31]

If these men knew their rights, it was not always because they were the respectable citizen-militia that inspired idealistic prose in both England and America. Sensitive to constituent pressures, the General Assembly more often than not restricted drafts to men "not free-holders or housekeepers qualified to vote at an election of Burgesses." Even when men of modest or better means were so unlucky as to have their names pulled from a hat, they were normally permitted to escape service by hiring a substitute or paying a £10 fee. Consequently, Washington increasingly drew upon the lowest orders of society, whom he once portrayed as "loose, Idle Persons that are quite destitute of House and Home." In time, every form of mankind was recruited, drafted, or impressed, including elements that mostly fell outside the militia structure—the "willfully unemployed," absconding husbands and fathers, indentured servants, vagrants, free blacks, and Indians. It was primarily those persons not a part of the organized militia who were conscripted into the regiment itself for longer service, but as always the results for Washington were depressing. One entreaty to the Cherokee, for instance, netted seven warriors and three squaws. This would not be the last American war in which military commanders would scrape the bottom of the barrel of human resources.[32]

Why did Virginia's colonial government not act more decisively to win the war on her borderlands? Part of the problem was the frontier nature of the war itself. Most Virginians saw themselves as unaffected by the struggle, which appeared to be far away and seemingly constituted no real threat to the Old Dominion. Indeed, as Washington himself admitted to Lord Loudoun, some felt the conflict had been unnecessary, precipitated by the expansionist lustings of Governor Dinwiddie and the Ohio Land Company. Consequently, unwilling to make a less-than-popular war downright divisive, the colony left its productive citizens—the freeholders—largely alone, except for short-term militia service, which could usually be avoided. Instead, it conscripted men for the Virginia Regiment who had no voice in political life, or it turned to recruiting soldiers from outside the Old Dominion, a high percentage of the latter being foreign-born. Since the flotsam and jetsam of that era had so little stake in the outcome, and since their pay and treatment under the military code made them literally second-class citizens in comparison to the militia, it is understandable that enlistments lagged and that desertion rates were high in the Virginia Regiment. The Reverend James Maury reported in June 1756 that "no person of any property, family, or worth" had enlisted in the Virginia Regiment.[33]

Small wonder that Washington was not an eternal optimist, that his idealism about mankind was more tempered than that of many American revolutionists. He was ever mindful of the self-interested dimension in people, which must have owed something to his failure to secure the voluntary enlistment of responsible citizens in defense of their own soil during the French and Indian War. Washington might have concluded his first military career a total cynic except for a dramatic upswing in his fortunes in 1758. The years 1755–1757 had been dismal not only for Washington's small command but also for British-American fortunes everywhere. The loss of Oswego on Lake Ontario and Fort William Henry in New York were coupled with Loudoun's failure to take the French fortress of Louisbourg. But William Pitt, the new head of the London ministry, breathed fresh life into the creaky war machinery and dug liberally into the royal treasure chest in order to reverse the tide. A three-pronged offensive for 1758 targeted Duquesne, Quebec, and Louisbourg, with Brigadier General John Forbes to command the army of regulars and provincials assigned to drive on the forks of the Ohio.

Here was an opportunity for Washington, always an aggressive, offensive-minded officer destined in both his military careers to spend the great preponderance of his days on the defensive. While he had closed the door on all hopes of obtaining a king's commission, he thirsted to accompany Forbes, but in a capacity commensurate with his experience and accomplishments. He urged Brigadier General John Stanwix to "mention" him "in favorable terms" to Forbes as a man far above "the *common run* of provincial officers." Similarly, to Colonel Thomas Gage, a fellow Monongahela veteran, he pleaded for a good word because he had been "much longer in the Service than any provincial officer in America."[34]

Both Forbes and Washington held a generally low opinion of provincial troops, though Washington would have claimed otherwise for the officers and some men of his own regiment, which was designated along with other colonial forces to join the second campaign against Fort

Duquesne. Forbes, who characterized American officers as a "bad Collection of broken Innkeepers, Horse Jockeys, & Indian traders," considered Washington a notable exception. So did Forbes's colonels. At their request, he diagrammed a suitable line of march for a heavy column of four thousand men—the approximate number Forbes might deploy—penetrating densely forested country, together with a scheme for promptly forming "an Order of Battle in the Woods."[35]

It is quite likely that Forbes adopted a modified form of Washington's plan in mid-November. After months of back-breaking road-building, the general undertook a race with winter and the calendar as well, since most of his provincials were to be mustered out on December 1. Washington had recommended that three divisions proceed ahead of the main body, and now Forbes made such a disposition of his army, with orders for the three divisions to hack out the remaining portion of the trail and lead the advance on the French stronghold. Washington, the only provincial to head a forward division, commanded the Virginia, North Carolina, Maryland, and Delaware units. But there was no ambush to repulse or battle to be won. The outnumbered French, seeing their adversaries had overcome both weather and wilderness, burned their fort and departed shortly before Forbes's scouting parties arrived.

A campaign that ended anticlimactically had nonetheless appreciably deepened Washington's military knowledge. Forbes commanded the largest army in which Washington had served, and his crisply fashioned general orders dealing with quick assemblages, protection of weapons in inclement weather, inspection of equipment, and so on must have been absorbed by the Virginian with all the care he had devoted to Braddock's instructions. A sound and energetic officer, Forbes had made his mark as an administrator, talented in putting an army together and then maintaining it. So far Washington too had been chiefly an administrator, holding together a scattered wilderness command by dint of husbanding his pitifully inadequate resources. Had Washington perceived his future, he would have seen that his disappointments over missing out on formalized engagements had been more than compensated by his lessons in the Forbes school of management techniques. In any event, he had played a part in realizing his most pressing goal as colonel of the Virginia Regiment: the seizure of the forks of the Ohio, from which the French had spewed out hostile tribesmen to ravage the borders of the Old Dominion.

Washington's second goal, gaining crimson regimentals for his Virginians, had met with failure. It was a disappointment doubtless rekindled by the presence, with Forbes's army, of part of the Royal American Regiment. It takes no imagination to speculate that Washington would have loved to command the Royal Americans or, better still, to have seen his Virginia Regiment given the same status. The Royal Americans constituted the only British regiment (officially, the 60th Foot) composed largely of provincials, although the colonists were frozen out of the officer ranks, a circumstance that must have rankled Washington and his Virginia officers. Even so, Douglas Freeman may not have exaggerated in claiming that the veteran commander of the Royal Americans, Colonel Henry Bouquet, both "by temperament and training . . . probably was second only to Forbes among all the soldiers from whom Washington could learn."[36]

Washington and Bouquet shared one soldierly quality, the ability to engender a strong esprit de corps in their officers. That sense of oneness among the Virginians was owing to a number of things, including Washington's persistent labors to secure them regular status, his eagerness to defend them from critics in Williamsburg, his striving to meet their material needs, and his fair and impartial treatment of them. Although there is considerable evidence of the officers' esteem for him, that esteem was manifested most poignantly at the close of 1758. With Duquesne taken, with a royal commission apparently forever beyond his grasp, with marriage beckoning, and with a seat in the House of Burgesses awaiting him, Washington resigned his commission in the service of Virginia. We find high regard expressed in the "Humble Address" signed by officers of his regiment as Washington took leave of them. "Judge . . . how sensibly we must be Affected with the loss of such an excellent Commander, such a sincere Friend, and so affable a Companion," they wrote. Though obviously aware that his decision was final, they could not help adding that "your Presence only will cause a steady Firmness and Vigor to actuate in every Breast . . . while led on by the Man we know and Love."[37] To our ear, the prose is stilted and effusive, but the substance is worth our reflection. It is high praise in any language, particularly for a twenty-six-year-old provincial officer. No doubt any officer, then or now, would find it intensely rewarding to be so regarded by those he had led in the field.

Captain Robert Stewart, a Scot who had been with Washington throughout the war (including the Braddock campaign when the two colonials had helped the mortally wounded commander from the field), wrote Washington in after years: "I think without vanity we can assert that there never was and very probably never will be such another Provincial Regiment." Stewart was undoubtedly correct. Washington, the teacher, had succeeded in spite of adversity. His young officers—almost wholly innocent of military lore in the beginning, according to Dinwiddie—had gained the esteem of Forbes and Bouquet. His enlisted men also had performed ably. "The General has complimented me publickly on their good behavior," he boasted to Governor Francis Fauquier, Dinwiddie's successor. Forbes's "Highlanders and . . . [the Virginia troops] are become one People, shaking each other by the hand wherever they meet."[38]

In fact, during the Forbes expedition Washington had finally operated with a full regiment. He was able to do so because Virginia, promised subsidies by William Pitt, abandoned conscription, "the cornerstone" of its defensive policy since 1754; instead, it offered liberal bounties for voluntary enlistments in 1758 and thereafter. As the Reverend Samuel Davies approvingly stated in a sermon, Virginians were no longer coerced into taking up arms but could now make their own choice as free men.[39]

Yet it would do an injustice to Washington—and to his soldiers—to deny that his own persuasiveness had bound some of the rank and file to the regiment before enlistments or reenlistments became more financially attractive in 1758. Regardless of their social backgrounds or their perception of Virginia's war aims, some of the men voluntarily stayed with Washington. They persevered in spite of conditions, and in doing so they maintained the integrity of the regiment. If these "blues" were as poor and devoid of property as contemporaries claimed, and if the conflict stemmed from expansionist impulses of a portion of the elite, then Washington could hardly press upon them the notion that theirs was a "glorious cause," as he did quite justifiably in his exhortations to Continental troops in the Revolution. He and the other officers could stress what might be termed a professional ethic, an idea which requires elucidation at this juncture. Such an ethic seems to have been a factor in the steady improvement of the regiment in the year before the Forbes campaign. When two companies were temporarily dispatched to Charleston, South Carolina, in 1757, they found—according to Captain George Mercer—that they were "looked upon in quite another Light by all the [British] Officers than we were by Genl Braddock. . . . we have been told by the Officers that nothing ever gave them such Surprise as our Appearance . . . . , for expecting to see a Parcel of ragged disorderly Fellows headed by Officers of their own Stamp (like the rest of the Provincials they had seen) behold they saw Men properly disposed who made a good & Soldier like Appearance and performed in every Particular as well as could be expected from any Troops." And as for the Virginia officers, their royal counterparts were impressed by their appearance as well as by their leadership, possessing as they did "Sash & Gorget with a gentell Uniform, a Sword properly hung, [and] a Hat cocked." Lieutenant Colonel Adam Stephen was equally proud of the

Charleston-based contingent, which he commanded. His comments about their tactical abilities indicate that Washington's training—a combination of European and American methods—had paid off. His troops were as "well disciplin'd" as any regular units in North America. Furthermore, they knew "parade [formations] as well as prussians, and the fighting in a Close Country as well as 'Tartars'."[40]

Stephen might have added that a unit whose performance improves because of its training will in turn bring out the best in its members as individuals, including a sense of pride in being part of a respected fighting force. That, in brief, is a professional ethic. Washington would have concurred had Stephen simultaneously acknowledged that noncommissioned officers also contributed substantially to unit cohesion. There were sergeants who put in years with the regiment and in time became officers themselves. One should eschew easy generalization about military behavior and socio-economic status, an opinion confirmed by a recent study showing that many Massachusetts recruits in the French and Indian War whose names did not turn up in tax and property records nonetheless made good soldiers.[41]

The Virginia Regiment continued to give a good accounting of itself in the years before it was disbanded in 1762. Brigadier General Robert Monckton, heading British forces in the Southern colonies, assured his superior General Jeffery Amherst that the Virginia Regiment performed its "Duty as well as any old Regiment" on the royal establishment. The credit for its "distinguished character," according to Captain Stewart, was owing to Washington's "Military Talents," even though Washington had retired from the profession of arms. The former colonel continued to follow the regiment's campaigning with understandable pride, as his correspondence reveals.[42]

There is irony in the awareness that some Englishmen and Virginians probably considered Washington's retirement no severe loss either to Britain or to America. Since he had demonstrated fine ability under arms, that might seem like an unfair opinion. However, he had evinced scant sympathy or understanding for the problems of his superiors, both civilian and military. Washington was too quick to blame others for obstacles not easily overcome in a backwoods conflict marked by human and material shortages, home-front discord, inadequate governmental machinery, and jurisdictional conflicts between the colonies themselves and between the provincials and the home government.

Washington the soldier became exceedingly political in his behavior. Once close to Governor Dinwiddie, who had boosted his career at every opportunity, Washington was mainly responsible for the chill that enveloped their relationship. When the colonel did not get satisfaction from the governor—when he felt Dinwiddie did not respond properly to his difficulties—he circumvented him by dashing off letters at times critical of the chief executive to leaders of the General Assembly, including Councilor William Fairfax and House Speaker John Robinson, who was also treasurer of the colony.[43]

Up to a point, Washington's epistolary energies might have been defensible, for in reality war-making authority was divided in colonial Virginia, just as it has been in the United States under the federal Constitution. Such divisions have always generated conflicts over control of military matters and the overall governmental war powers. In Virginia and the other colonies, however, the military role of the legislatures grew in an evolutionary manner, the result of protracted and expensive eighteenth-century imperial conflicts. As governors requested swollen sums for militias and semiprofessional forces such as Washington's regiment, American provincial legislatures demanded in return a hand in scrutinizing campaign expenditures and insisted on a voice in still other areas that London officials had considered the preserve of royal executives. In Virginia, these precedents were firmly implanted before the governorship of Dinwiddie, who reluctantly agreed to a joint committee of the Council and the Burgesses overseeing appropriations.[44] Therefore, it was not unreasonable, in the absence of any instructions to the contrary from Dinwiddie, for Washington to keep powerful provincial leaders abreast of military developments and his regiment's requirements.

Doubtless Washington himself realized that the balance of power in Virginia had shifted to the lower house of assembly. Likewise, he must have concluded early in the conflict that his regiment had no political constituency, as did the militia, composed as it was of the electorate. Given those circumstances, he could hardly avoid being a lobbyist for his command along with executing his overwhelming responsibilities in the field.

Furthermore, most of the concerns that Washington penned to Fairfax and Robinson were addressed to Dinwiddie as well. But the colonel was sorely at fault in casting aspersions on the governor's character and ability in communicating to the legislative chieftains. He asserted that Dinwiddie's unresponsiveness was partly personal in nature—that the governor appeared to wish to discredit him. To the speaker he confided on December 19, 1756, "My Orders are dark, doubtful, and uncertain; *to day approved, to-morrow condemned:* Left to act and proceed at hazard: accountable for the consequences; and blamed, without the Benefit of defense!"[45] We can, of course, endeavor to find some extenuating circumstances in this situation. The governor and the colonel were separated in more ways than one: by a thirty-nine-year age difference and by the perspectives of frontier Winchester and tidewater Williamsburg. Still, one must conclude that Washington's behavior was far from admirable.

Equally indefensible were his behind-the-back barbs at both executive and legislative branches. Military men in free and open societies are not infrequently provoked by the slowness and awkwardness of what has become known as the democratic process, even when they acknowledge—in theory, at any rate—their commitment to civil control. Washington displayed this irritation in what he might have styled a soldier-to-soldier letter to Lord Loudoun in 1757. He complained of the dearth of military know-how on the part of his political masters in Williamsburg, where, he might have added, he was required to journey periodically to explain and justify his accounts and other matters, where too he had been on the receiving end now and then of harsh and probably unfair remarks about his own performance and about the conduct of certain of his officers and men.[46] These "Chimney Corner Politicians," as he labeled them, were cautious to a fault, having given "no regard hitherto . . . to my remonstrances" on various issues. Even in extreme emergencies, the lawmakers had bowed to the people's insistence on putting their personal freedom ahead of the order and regimentation essential to choke off the Franco-Indian peril. Only stern, far-reaching legislation dealing with the military's sometime need to impress goods, quarter troops on civilians, and augment the authority of courts-martial could bring victory. Without such laws, he had reluctantly and as a last recourse taken extralegal measures in the defense of the colony; but the lawmakers, excessively "tenacious of Liberty," were "prone to Censure; [and] condemn all Proceedings that are not strictly Lawful, never considering what Cases may arise to make it necessary and excusable."[47]

Since Loudoun himself had been accused by provincial legislatures of imperious and dictatorial conduct, he likely had some feeling for Washington's view of political bodies. In any event, the colonel found a defender of what might be called his less-than-respectful attitude toward civil control in the person of Richard Bland, a highly regarded veteran legislator and prolific essayist from Prince George County. Bland evidently expressed himself in a now-missing issue of the *Virginia Gazette* in 1756, his remarks prompted by criticisms of Washington appearing previously in that same newspaper. Bland voiced an opinion of civil-military relations that would occasionally surface in the course of American history, though never gaining wide acceptance. In moments of crisis, he warned, "Generals and Commanders of Armies must be left to act as they find it most expedient for their Country's Interest." Whatever the merits of "shake[ing] off all restraints," as Bland phrased it, the legislature failed to adopt the more aggressive measures that he advocated, with the result that he wrote Washington the following year of his continued displeasure with his fellow burgesses.[48]

Judging from the openness with which Washington's own staff revealed to him their hostility toward their civilian superiors, it seems reasonable to assume that the colonel scarcely discouraged what at a later time would be seen as both potentially dangerous and unethical behavior. "How infatuate are our Assemblies!" exclaimed his secretary John Kirkpatrick, "heedless to the reports of Danger, and indifferent in their measures for the General safety."[49]

Yet Washington also exhibited the ability of cozying up to Virginia politicians at the expense of a British general—in this instance, John Forbes, whom Washington indiscreetly faulted to Dinwiddie's successor, Governor Francis Fauquier, and Speaker Robinson for electing to build a new road through Pennsylvania to the confluence of the Ohio rather than follow the old Braddock path from the Potomac. Perhaps there were legitimate arguments for either approach, but it was the general's decision and not Washington's. He accused his superior of being hoodwinked by selfish Pennsylvanians panting to construct an artery that would enable them to corner the Ohio Valley trade at the expense of the Old Dominion. He encouraged Virginia officials to go over Forbes's head and even appeal directly to the king: "Let him know how grossly his Hon'r and the Publick money have been prostituted." Fortunately for Washington, Forbes proved to be a bigger man than the hotheaded colonel. He could still respect his adversary and employ him to good advantage, though stating sadly that "his Behaviour about the roads was no ways like a Soldier."[50]

In the last analysis, what can we say about George Washington in 1758, at the end of this first career in arms, beyond the very notable fact that he had encountered problems and controversies that would long constitute important features of the American military tradition? Highly educated at the war academy of hard knocks, he was a first-rate administrator and combat officer, a leader of men in action; he was tough, tenacious, brave, perhaps even inspirational. But a splendid field-grade officer does not always see his wartime role in broad perspective, nor is he usually required to. Much less is he likely to hold a colonelcy and to have such enormous responsibilities thrust upon him in his early-to-middle twenties. After all, he had not yet turned twenty-seven when he retired to Mount Vernon.

The irony mentioned previously refers to more than the realization that there were those who shed no tears over his departure from active duty— he who would one day rank among the great captains. The more significant irony is this: his most glaring weaknesses as a field-grade officer were to be corrected in time and were to become the sources of his greatest strength. His respect for and understanding of superior authority—that is to say, civil control of the military *and all that it meant*—became his most admirable soldierly quality in the War of Independence and his foremost contribution to the American military tradition.

Notes

1. Freeman, *Washington* 3:292.

2. *PGW: Col. Ser.* 1:336; "The Journal of Captain Robert Cholmley's Batman," in *Braddock's Defeat,* ed. Charles Hamilton (Norman, Okla., 1959), 29. GW recorded accounts of Braddock's disaster in letters to Mary Ball Washington, to Robert Dinwiddie, and to John Augustine Washington, all dated July 18, 1755, *PGW: Col. Ser.* 1:336–45. For GW's later reflections, see "Biographical Memorandum," Oct. 1783, *GW: Writings* 29:42–45.

3. *PGW: Col. Ser.* 1:336, 339. Captain Cholmley's servant would seem to confirm GW's view of the provincials. He declared, "I believe there might be two hundred of the American Soldiers that fought behind Trees and I believe they did the moast Execution of Any" ("Journal of Captain Robert Cholmley's Batman," 29). See fuller praise of the Virginians in Joseph Ball to GW, Sept. 5, 1755, *PGW: Col. Ser.* 2:15.

4. John Bolling to Robert Bolling, Aug. 13, 1755, quoted in *PGW: Col. Ser.* 2:2n. For reference to our "Brave Blues," see John Martin to GW, Aug. 30, 1755, ibid., 11.

5. Thomas Nairne, "A Letter from a Swiss Gentleman to His Friend in Bern," *North Carolina University Magazine* 4 (1855): 297.

6. *Boston Gazette,* Sept. 19, 1755; *Boston Weekly News-Letter,* Aug. 21, 1755; Charles Chauncy, *A Letter to a Friend, Giving a Concise, but Just Account . . . of the Ohio-Defeat* (Boston, 1755), 7–8.

7. Douglas E. Leach, *Arms for Empire: A Military History of the British Colonies in North America, 1607–1763* (New York, 1973), 507.

8. *Boston Evening Post,* Dec. 6, 1773. While in England, Franklin in February 1775 published a letter in the London *Public Advertiser* in which he reminded his readers that colonial soldiers had "covered the Retreat of the British Regulars and saved them from utter Destruction in the Expedition under Braddock" (Verner W. Crane, ed., *Benjamin Franklin's Letters to the Press, 1758–1775* [Chapel Hill, N.C., 1950], 279–82).

9. Quoted in John E. Ferling, *A Wilderness of Miseries: War and Warriors in Early America* (Westport, Conn., 1980), 16. GW's superior, Governor Robert Dinwiddie, would have scarcely disagreed. "On my arrival at my Gov't, I found the Militia in very bad Order," he informed the Board of Trade on Feb. 24, 1756 (R. A. Brock, ed., *The Official Records of Robert Dinwiddie ... 1752–1758*, 2 vols. [Richmond, 1883–84], 1:344). A decade or so earlier, an English visitor wrote of the Virginia militia: "Alas! to behold the Musters of their Militia, would induce a Man to Nauseate a Sash and hold a Sword forever in Derision. Diversity of Weapons and Dresses, Unsizeableness of the Men, and Want of the least Grain of Discipline in their Officers or them, make the whole Scene little better than Dryden has expressed it: And raw in fields the rude militia swarms; ... Of seeming arms, they make a short essay, then hasten so get drunk the bus'ness of the day" ("Observations in Several Voyages and Travels in America," reprinted from the *London Magazine* for July 1744, WMQ, 1st ser., 15 [1907]: 47–48).

10. For the raising of provincials for the Cartagena expedition, see H. C. McBarron et al., "The American Regiment, 1740–1746," *Military Collector and Historian* 21 (1969): 84–86. For the companies of Virginians serving with Braddock, see Dinwiddie to Thomas Robinson, March 17, 1755, in Brock, *Dinwiddie Papers* 1:525; Franklin T. Nichols, "The Organization of Braddock's Army," *WMQ* 4 (1947): 130–33.

11. "Commission," Aug. 14, 1755, *PGW: Col. Ser.* 2:3–4.

12. References to GW's enthusiasm for military service are in ibid., 1:226, 278, 243. See Freeman, *Washington* 1:77, on Lawrence Washington. As Douglas Leach says, "Cartagena soon became a tradition in the American colonies, and those who had been there and returned were looked upon as heroes" (*Arms for Empire*, 218). GW's description of Fort James is in *PGW: Diaries* 1:36, 75; Freeman, *Washington* 1:250–51. GW's friend and mentor William Fairfax subsequently assured him that his familiarity with the writings of military authors should enable him to bear up better under the burdens of command (Fairfax to GW, May 13–14, 1756, *PGW: Col. Ser.* 3:125).

13. *PGW: Col. Ser.* 1:348n; *GW: Writings* 29:45. For GW's opinion of Braddock during the campaign, see his letters to John Augustine Washington, May 6, 1755, and to William Fairfax, June 7, 1755, *PGW: Col. Ser.* 1:266–67, 298–300. GW's fencing is mentioned in Freeman, *Washington* 2:204.

14. "Orders," Jan. 8, 1756, *PGW: Col. Ser.* 2:257.

15. Ibid.

16. "Orders," Oct. 26, 1755, ibid., 136.

17. "General Instructions to all the Captains of Companies," July 29, 1757, ibid., 4:341–45. As to his differences with Braddock, GW wrote: "The General, by frequent breaches of Contracts, has lost all degree of Patience; and for want of that consideration, & moderation which should be used by a Man of Sense upon these occasions, will, I fear, represent us home in a light we little deserve; for instead of blameing the Individuals as he ought, he charges all his Disap-

pointments to publick Supineness; and looks upon the Country, I believe, as void of both Honour and Honesty" (GW to William Fairfax, June 7, 1755, ibid., 1:298–99). The fullest account of British difficulties concerning quartering, impressment, and recruitment is Alan Rogers, *Empire and Liberty: American Resistance to British Authority, 1755–1763* (Berkeley, Los Angeles, and London, 1974), chaps. 4, 5, 7.

18. Stanley M. Pargellis, "Braddock's Defeat," *American Historical Review* 41 (1936): 253–69; Lee McCardell, *Ill-Starred General: Braddock of the Coldstream Guards* (Pittsburgh, 1958), chap. 12, esp. 229; Paul E. Kopperman, *Braddock at the Monongahela* (Pittsburgh, 1977), 13–14, 16–17; John Shy, *Toward Lexington: The Role of the British Army in the Coming of the American Revolution* (Princeton, N.J., 1965), 127; Lawrence H. Gipson, *The British Empire before the American Revolution*, 15 vols. (Caldwell, Idaho, and New York, 1936–70), 6:86, 94. British flexible responses in both Europe and America are discussed in Peter E. Russell, "Redcoats in the Wilderness: British Officers and Irregular Warfare in Europe and America, 1740–1760," *WMQ* 34 (1978): 629–52. Peter Paret also places early American warfare within the context of military developments in the Western world in "Colonial Experience and European Military Reform at the End of the Eighteenth Century," *Bulletin of the Institute of Historical Research* 37 (1964): 49–56, and in "The Relationship between the Revolutionary War and European Military Thought and Practice in the Second Half of the Eighteenth Century," in *Reconsiderations on the Revolutionary War*, ed. Don Higginbotham (Westport, Conn., 1978), 144–57.

19. *PGW: Col. Ser.* 2:257, 23, 4:344; J. A. Houlding, *Fit for Service: The Training of the British Army, 1715–1797* (Oxford, 1981), 195–99 passim.

20. *PGW: Col. Ser.* 4:344, 343, 2:76, 124, 135.

21. "Biographical Memoranda," Oct. 1783, *GW: Writings* 29:37; GW to Dinwiddie, April 16, 1756, Stephen to GW, March 29, 1756, *PGW: Col. Ser.* 3:1–2, 2:325.

22. William H. Browne, ed., *Correspondence of Governor Horatio Sharpe*, 3 vols. (Baltimore, 1888–95), 1:416.

23. GW to Dinwiddie, March 10, 1757, Memorial to Lord Loudoun, March 23, 1757, *PGW: Col. Ser.* 4:112–14, 120–21.

24. Freeman, *Washington* 2:407–8; William Henry Fairfax to GW, Dec. 9, 1757, in Stanislaus M. Hamilton, ed., *Letters to Washington*, 5 vols. (Boston and New York, 1892–1902), 2:252–54; William Fairfax to GW, July 17, 1757, *PGW: Col. Ser.* 4:309–10 and note.

25. Freeman, *Washington* 2:204; GW to Robinson, Aug. 5, 1756, to Dinwiddie, Oct. 11, 1755, *PGW: Col. Ser.* 3:330, 2:102.

26. Brock, *Dinwiddie Papers* 2:425, 345, 346. For the fluctuations in GW's troop strength and the reduction in number of frontier posts, see Bernhard Knollenberg, *George Washington: The Virginia Period, 1732–1775* (Durham, N.C. 1964), chaps. 7, 9, and esp. notes, which are a mine of statistical information. See

also "Return of the Virginia Regiment," Oct. 9, 1756, Jan. 1, 1757, *PGW: Col. Ser.* 3:428–29, 4:76–77.

27. "Memorandum respecting the Militia," May 9, 10, 1756, *PGW: Col. Ser.* 3:106, 111. As for a later turnout from Culpeper: "Out of the hundred that were draughted, seventy-odd arrived here; of which only twenty-five were tolerably armed" (GW to Dinwiddie, May 27, 1757, ibid., 4:264). According to Dinwiddie, "The Militia are not above one-half arm'd, and their Small Arms of different Bores making it very inconvenient in time of Action" (to the Board of Trade, Feb. 24, 1756, in Brock, *Dinwiddie Papers* 2:344).

28. *PGW: Col. Ser.* 3:432, 4:1–2, 12–13, 1:289; Freeman, *Washington* 2:216, 257–58; Brock, *Dinwiddie Papers* 1:387.

29. *PGW: Col. Ser.* 1:192n, 2:172, 174n, 3:66, 145–46; Freeman, *Washington* 2:189.

30. "Memorandum respecting the Militia, May 8, 1756, *PGW: Col. Ser.* 3:99.

31. GW to Dinwiddie, Nov. 9, 1756, ibid., 4:2. See also GW to Robinson, Nov. 9, 1756, ibid., 11–13.

32. Hening, *Statutes* 7:70–71; *PGW: Col. Ser.* 1:73. It is hazardous to generalize about the Virginia militia laws, which might be changed once or twice a year. Freeman, *Washington* 1:330n, discusses the statutes in force at the beginning of the French and Indian War. See also John Shy, *A People Numerous and Armed* (New York, 1976), 30. A number of the statutes are described in Richard L. Morton, *Colonial Virginia*, 2 vols. (Chapel Hill, N.C., 1960), 2: chaps. 20–23.

33. GW to Loudoun, Jan. 10, 1757, *PGW: Col. Ser.* 4:79–80; Ann Maury, ed. and trans., *Memoirs of a Huguenot Family: Translated and Compiled from the Original Autobiography of the Reverend James Maury* (1833; Baltimore, 1967), 404.

This paragraph draws on an important study by James W. Titus, *The Old Dominion at War: Society, Politics, and Warfare in Late Colonial Virginia* (Columbia, S.C., 1991), particularly chap. 1. Titus also suggests that the use of the disadvantaged and disfranchised proved attractive, because it would preserve the harmonious relationship that existed between the colony's elite and its "middling" social orders. Besides, he notes, the government lacked the police power to carry out effectively what would have been the extremely controversial step of large-scale mobilization of the yeoman-planter militia (ibid., chap. 5). Another study that reaches somewhat different conclusions about the social composition of GW's Virginia Regiment is John E. Ferling, "Soldiers for Virginia: Who Served in the French and Indian War?" *VMHB* 94 (1986): 307–28.

34. GW to Stanwix, April 10, 1758, to Gage, April 12, 1758, *GW: Writings* 2:173, 177.

35. Forbes to Pitt, Sept. 6, 1758, in A. P. James, ed., *Writings of General John Forbes* (Menasha, Wis., 1938), 205; GW to Forbes, Oct. 8, 1758, *GW: Writings* 2:295–98.

36. Freeman, *Washington* 2:213.

37. "The Humble Address of the Officers of the Virginia Regiment," in Hamilton, *Letters to Washington* 3:143–46. For other expressions of the officers' opinions of GW, see *Theodorick Bland Papers,* 2 vols. (Richmond, 1840), 1:10; and various letters to GW, particularly those of Adam Stephen, Hugh Mercer, and Robert Stewart, in Hamilton, *Letters to Washington* and *PGW: Col. Ser.* Consult as well Freeman, *Washington* 2:369–71.

38. Stewart to GW, Jan. 25, 1769, in Hamilton, *Letters to Washington* 3:335. Dinwiddie's lament about the lack of serious officers is in Brock, *Dinwiddie Papers* 1:94, 120. The attitudes of Forbes and his men toward the Virginians are described in GW to Fauquier, Sept. 25, 1758, *GW: Writings* 2:290–91; GW to George William Fairfax, Sept. 25, 1758, "George Washington and the Fairfax Family: Some New Documents," ed. Peter Walne, *VMHB* 77 (1969): 455.

39. Samuel Davies, *Sermons on Important Subjects . . . ,* 5 vols. (Philadelphia, 1818), 5:277; George W. Pelcher, *Samuel Davies: Apostle of Dissent in Colonial Virginia* (Knoxville, Tenn., 1971), chap. 9, esp. 166–67.

40. Mercer to GW, Aug. 17, 1757, Stephen to GW, Aug. 20, 1757, *PGW: Col. Ser.* 4:372, 375.

41. Fred Anderson, "A People's Army: Provincial Military Service in Massachusetts during the Seven Years' War," *WMQ* 40 (1983): 500–527, and *A People's Army: Massachusetts Soldiers and Society in the Seven Years' War* (Chapel Hill, N.C., 1984), chap. 2.

42. Monckton to Amherst, July 9, 1760, quoted in Titus, *Old Dominion at War,* 133, 196n; Stewart to GW, Jan. 25, 1769, in Hamilton, *Letters to Washington* 3:335.

43. For the GW-Dinwiddie relationship, see Knollenberg, *Washington,* chap. 9 and notes; Freeman, *Washington* 2:248, 260, 267, 270–75; John R. Alden, *Robert Dinwiddie: Servant of the Crown* (Charlottesville, Va., 1973), 90–110.

44. Jack P. Greene, *The Quest for Power: The Lower Houses of Assembly in the Southern Royal Colonies, 1689–1776* (Chapel Hill, N.C., 1963), chap. 15, esp. 303–6 for Dinwiddie's Virginia.

45. GW to Robinson, Dec. 19, 1756, *PGW: Col. Ser.* 4:68. While Councillor Fairfax wished to smooth things over (he had a good relationship with Dinwiddie), Speaker Robinson (who did not) seems to have encouraged such correspondence. See also GW to Robinson, Aug. 5, 1756, June 10, 1757, ibid., 3:323–30, 4:198–99; GW to Robinson, Oct. 25, 1757, *GW: Writings* 2:153–56; Fairfax to GW, May 13–14, 1756, *PGW: Col. Ser.* 3:131.

46. GW was particularly incensed by a Sept. 3, 1756, essay, "The Virginia-Centennial No. X," in the *Virginia Gazette* (Hunter), that referred to some regimental officers as "dastardly Debauchees" who idled their time "skulking in Forts." Portions relating to the Virginia Regiment are quoted in *PGW: Col. Ser.* 3:410–11n. GW himself, according to rumor, was thought by some in Williamsburg to have fabricated news of a likely Indian raid in the spring of 1757 in order to jolt the legislature into providing him with more men and necessaries. But Dinwiddie told

GW that he had not even heard the story until the colonel had brought it to his attention (GW to Dinwiddie, Sept. 7, 1757, Dinwiddie to GW, Sept. 24, 1757, ibid., 4:411–12, 422). The legislators raised various questions about regimental expenditures, including GW's "extraordinary" idea that he needed both an aide and a secretary (William Fairfax to GW, April 14, 1756, ibid., 2:351–52).

47. GW to the earl of Loudoun, Jan. 10, 1757, ibid., 4:79–90 (quotations on 83, 85).

48. Bland's eleven-page manuscript essay, signed "Philo patria," was endorsed by GW, who evidently received a copy from the author: "Written it is supposed by Richard Bland Octo. 1756." The editors of the *Papers of George Washington* note that the manuscript "is misfiled" in the Library of Congress's GW collection "after the incoming letters of 1757" (ibid., 3:437n). For Bland's continued support, see his letter to GW, June 7, 1757, ibid., 4:187–88.

49. Kirkpatrick to GW, June 19, 1757, ibid., 237–38.

50. *GW: Writings* 2:277–83, 290–91, 294–95, 299–300 (quotation on 278); James, *Forbes Writings,* 199, 219.

3. George Washington, the British Tobacco Trade, and Economic Opportunity in Pre-Revolutionary Virginia

BRUCE A. RAGSDALE

Washington's years as a tobacco grower in Virginia taught him important things that lasted a lifetime. He learned to hate extravagance and dependence. He sought and secured his independence from the grip of a system of producing second-rate crops on marginal lands. He did so by being one of the first Virginians to turn to wheat and other diversification such as fisheries and to use his increasing income to emerge from the kind of indebtedness to his London factor that continued to plague other Virginia husbandmen. In all this he showed himself to be bold and creative, just as he had fashioned his Virginia Regiment into something far better than the quality of most provincial military units in the French and Indian War. Historians have debated whether Virginia planters sought political independence from Britain as a way to avoid paying their mounting obligations to metropolitan business houses. Since Virginians hardly rushed to separate from the empire, that is a dubious contention. It certainly does not apply to Washington, who had already escaped from his financial straitjacket. In yet another respect Washington proved different from most Virginia planters of his age, by eschewing narrow rural predispositions. His advocacy of economic diversification in time came to include an appreciation of a balanced economy and a society that included centers of commerce and industry. For these reasons, we can better understand his siding with Hamilton over Jefferson during his presidential years in formulating a vision of economic diversity in order to ensure America's independence in a world of nations.

Author of A Planters' Republic: The Search for Economic Independence in Revolutionary Virginia, *Bruce A. Ragsdale is chief historian, Federal Judicial History Office at the Federal Judicial Center in Washington, D.C. His essay first appeared in the* Virginia Magazine of History and Biography *97 (1989): 133–62 and is reprinted by permission of the Virginia Historical Society.*

FOR A DECADE AND A HALF preceding the American Revolution George Washington devoted nearly undivided attention to the management and expansion of his estate. As the proprietor of extensive holdings on the Potomac and York Rivers and in the Shenandoah Valley, he controlled the resources necessary for financial independence and prosperity in Virginia's colonial economy. Like all Virginians who produced tobacco and other crops for export, Washington knew his success in employing these resources ultimately depended on access to the best markets for agricultural goods. The principal challenge facing Washington in the 1760s was to secure a steady profit from tobacco shipped for sale in Great Britain. His increasing dissatisfaction with the London tobacco trade and his difficulty in replacing the essential services of the metropolitan merchants had implications far beyond the organization of his estate. As an ambitious planter confronting the complicated Atlantic economy, Washington faced problems of the tobacco trade that provided him a context within which to view imperial relations, the economic development of Virginia, and his own position in provincial society. By the opening of the American Revolution, Washington had abandoned tobacco as part of a broader effort to achieve economic independence for himself and for Virginia.

When he returned from the Forbes expedition in December of 1758, the young colonel of the First Virginia Regiment was eager to secure his position as a planter of the first rank in Fairfax County. He already possessed a sizable estate, and if his family appeared less prosperous than the wealthiest Virginia dynasties, he was thoroughly familiar with the world of the great planters. Following his marriage to Martha Dandridge Custis in January 1759, Washington assumed the administration of the Custis estate, among the most valuable in the colony, including some 18,000 acres on the York River. Through his half-brother Lawrence and his friendship with the Fairfax family, Washington knew the leading men of the Northern Neck.

His position in the Virginia Regiment and his election to the House of Burgesses in 1758 brought him into further contact with influential men throughout the colony. When he first took his seat in the assembly in the spring of 1759, his fellow burgesses already held him in high esteem for his service in the French and Indian War. With his military duties behind him, Washington prepared to emulate the great tobacco planters who dominated the economic and political life of Virginia.

To a young Virginian of means in 1759, the path to success appeared obvious and well tested. For most of the eighteenth century tobacco offered a lucrative if narrow opportunity for planters able to produce large, quality crops. Tobacco continued to dominate the colony's economy despite internal diversification of agricultural production and expansion of settlement well beyond the Tidewater. By the established standards of tobacco cultivation, Washington was in good position to emerge as a leading planter. In 1758 he leased or owned over 4,700 acres and held close to fifty slaves on his Potomac estates. Upon his return to Mount Vernon, Washington steadily added to his landholdings through the purchase of neighboring tracts in Fairfax County. Once he established a regular correspondence with a consignment merchant in London, he had every reason to expect a profitable return for his tobacco.[1]

Washington had made his first venture in the British tobacco trade during the years of his military service on the frontier. Beginning in 1754 he directed his brother-in-law, Fielding Lewis, and John Carlyle, the leading merchant of Alexandria, to manage the sale of tobacco from his estates and the purchase of provisions needed at Mount Vernon. Carlyle, who as commissary of the Virginia Regiment regularly corresponded with Washington, provided the initial introduction to British merchants. In 1755 Washington received goods that Carlyle had ordered for him from Anthony Bacon, a London tobacco merchant who previously had sailed as a ship captain in the Chesapeake and continued in partnership with several Virginians. Later that year Washington offered Bacon two hogsheads of the first tobacco he shipped to Great Britain. In 1757 he shipped eighteen hogsheads to the same merchant.[2]

While home at Mount Vernon in December of 1755, Washington began what he hoped would be his principal correspondence with the London tobacco market. He could offer only three hogsheads to Richard Washington (no relation), although he promised regular shipments and requested a return shipment of goods that he knew would cost more than the expected proceeds from the sale of the tobacco. During the next three years George Washington shipped the Londoner whatever tobacco he could and relied on him to supply many of the imported goods used at Mount Vernon. Carlyle opened a third correspondence in January 1756 with a small shipment of Washington's tobacco to the Bristol merchant Thomas Knox. Washington subsequently ordered some coarse goods from Knox and shipped further tobacco in order to compare sales at Bristol with those at London.[3]

Washington expected these early trading partners, particularly Richard Washington, to offer the services and advantages that were central to the consignment trade. Beginning in the late seventeenth century many Virginia planters chose-to consign their tobacco crop to individual merchants in England, most commonly London. Planters maintained ownership of the tobacco until the final sale in England and thus were responsible for all charges incurred in the shipping and storage of their hogsheads. In return, planters received the personal supervision of their shipment by merchants who watched for the best market. This form of marketing dominated the Virginia tobacco trade from 1690 until the 1720s. At the time Washington assumed management of Mount Vernon the consignment system remained the favored trading arrangement for larger planters in the Tidewater.

In addition to seeking out the best markets for quality leaf, the consignment merchants offered a variety of services prized by the owners of large estates in Virginia. The merchants regularly acted as bankers and allowed planters to draw bills of exchange on the proceeds of tobacco sales or in expectation of future shipments. These bills were a principal medium of exchange in the colony as well as a source of credit. Merchants also extended credit in the form of British goods shipped on a planter's account. Planters were able to purchase from London fashionable articles unavailable in the colony and plantation supplies in quantities that local storekeepers hesitated to sell on credit. In many of the long-established correspondences between planter and merchant, the consignment merchant became the Virginian's personal agent in legal matters or family business in London. What began as a strictly commercial relationship had by the time of Washington evolved into a tie to the metropolitan center that secured many of the advantages that defined the great planters' distinction in provincial society.[4]

By sending his modest shipment of tobacco to Richard Washington in 1755, Washington hoped to gain access to British goods as much as find a new market for his crop. In his request for two suits of livery and personal furnishings, Washington urged the merchant to "choose agreeable to the present taste, and send things good of their kind." After shipping Richard Washington more tobacco in 1757 and transferring to him the proceeds from tobacco shipped to Anthony Bacon, Washington submitted from his post at Fort Loudoun an order for the kind of British goods found only in the wealthiest Virginia households. The order made clear Washington's intent to transform his home into a display of refinement and English taste. The shipment he received from Richard Washington in March 1758 included a wide variety of tools necessary for the enlargement of the house at Mount Vernon. The bachelor colonel also ordered a range of decorations, including Wilton carpets, papier-mâché ceiling ornaments, and the "Neat Landskip" still in place above the mantel in the west parlor. To furnish the enlarged house, Washington ordered fine china, glassware, and a selection of mahogany furniture that included a bed Richard Washington obtained at auction for £25. In the first few years of his correspondence with Richard Washington and Thomas Knox, Washington relied on the merchants to supply common English manufactures as well as luxury goods. Coarse cloth for the use of slaves, inexpensive stoneware, grubbing hoes, and great quantities of nails all arrived at Mount Vernon from Great Britain.[5]

Washington's initial entry into the British tobacco trade provided the ambitious planter an opportunity to sell his crop on the most select English markets and a source for the kind of goods that marked the households of Virginia's great planters. These early correspondences, however, proved to be a far-from-satisfactory introduction to the commerce between Great Britain and the colony. Between 1755 and 1759, the war that kept Washington away on the frontier and disrupted Atlantic shipping prevented both planter and merchant from fulfilling their mutual obligations. Even with the assistance of John Carlyle, Washington found it difficult to manage affairs on his estate. French seizure of ships compelled British merchants to charge insurance rates so high that Washington decided to risk a safe passage for his tobacco.[6]

Other problems suggested difficulties that persisted long after peace returned. Sales of tobacco proved disappointing, and many of the goods ordered never arrived or came damaged. In his efforts to favor trade with Richard Washington, the Virginia Washington discovered the difficulties inherent in dealing with a merchant who concentrated his colonial shipping along the York and James Rivers. Many of the ship captains who frequented the Potomac accepted tobacco only for consignment to their partners in England. As long as Richard Washington failed to send a ship to the Potomac, George Washington sought out ships that might carry a few hogsheads on liberty of consignment or transferred the proceeds from sales of tobacco consigned to other merchants.[7]

By the time Washington returned to Mount Vernon in the spring of 1759, his marriage to Martha Custis had opened up a new range of opportunities in the British tobacco trade. In addition to his dower rights to the Custis estate, Washington gained access to that family's correspondence with several of the leading merchant houses of London. He could ship tobacco from his own and the dower estate's lands to the same merchants who traded with the largest planters in the highly regarded York River area. He soon closed out his account with Thomas Knox, of Bristol, and sharply curtailed consignments to Richard Washington before ending all contact with the latter merchant following a dispute in 1765.[8]

The principal agent for Washington's London business after 1759 was Robert Cary & Co., a large mercantile firm with long-standing connections in Virginia. The Cary house, representing a partnership of Robert Cary, John Moorey, and Wakelin Welch, had received consignments from the Custis family. After the death of Daniel Parke Custis in 1757, his widow Martha promised to continue to send the firm the largest share of the estate's tobacco. In May 1759 Washington announced his intent to continue this practice and to consign all of his Potomac tobacco to the house as well. Washington expected this prestigious firm would be better able to sell his crop to advantage and to meet his growing demand for British goods.[9]

Washington opened his trade with Robert Cary & Co. at a time when he could assume personal supervision of every stage in the production of tobacco at Mount Vernon. While on his trips to the sessions of the House of Burgesses in Williamsburg and in correspondence with his estate steward on the Custis lands in King William County, Washington managed tobacco cultivation, albeit less effectively, on his York River land as well. Washington generally shipped his annual crop during the spring or summer of the year following the harvest. In the intervening months slaves cured the tobacco and prized it into hogsheads that Washington delivered for inspection. At the warehouses at Hunting Creek on the Potomac or at various locations along the York River officials appointed under the terms of the Inspection Act of 1730 approved all tobacco to be exported.[10]

Washington shipped the tobacco from his Custis lands on a chartered ship that Robert Cary & Co. regularly sent to the York River. The annual Cary ship collected an entire cargo from the firm's clientele along that river, noted in London for the highest quality leaf. After consulting with the London merchants, Washington decided to continue shipping his York River crop under the Custis mark "DPC" that was recognized by British purchasers. For his Potomac crop, Washington sought out ships that accepted hogsheads on liberty of consignment. During the 1760s John Johnstoun, captain of a ship owned by London merchant James Russell, frequently carried the tobacco from Mount Vernon.[11]

Once the tobacco was loaded for shipment to Robert Cary & Co., Washington sent word to London by separate conveyance and requested insurance against loss of the cargo at sea. Rates for insurance varied according to states of war and peace or the conditions under which a ship sailed; even during war vessels armed or sailing in a convoy received lower rates. The costs of the insurance premia purchased by Cary, like all payments involved in the shipping and marketing of the tobacco, were charged against Washington's account with the firm.

The greatest charges on the tobacco were the various duties in place after 1759. The country duty of two shillings per hogshead applied to all tobacco exported from Virginia. The ship captain paid this initial duty and received compensation from Cary & Co. Once the tobacco arrived in England, the merchant paid the sum required under a complicated system of duties. The crown repeatedly added to the original Old Subsidy duty of one penny per pound of tobacco until by 1759 the total due often represented 80 percent of the final sales price. Merchants never paid this amount in full because they received a discount for cash payments on the Old Subsidy and a further discount for payment in bond for the remaining duties. Tobacco firms like Robert Cary & Co. received an additional discount if they paid all duties in cash.[12]

Robert Cary & Co. also paid the freight charges, which varied according to market conditions, shipping hazards, and the length of time a ship spent in Virginia. During the Seven Years' War freight rates on Cary's ship to the York River reached as high as £16 per ton. After the return of peace they remained steady at £8 per ton. Washington negotiated the freight rates with the various carriers who loaded his tobacco along the Potomac. According to custom, ship captains reckoned four hogsheads equaled one ton, regardless of the actual weight of the hogsheads. By Washington's time, planters routinely prized a thousand or more pounds of tobacco into each hogshead to save on freight charges.[13]

Robert Cary & Co. negotiated all or a portion of Washington's consignment with London brokers who bought for domestic tobacco manufacturers. The brokers' fee cost the planter two shillings per hogshead. Occasionally a depressed domestic market forced Cary to sell part of the crop on the reexport market, where 85 percent of Virginia's crop sold but at much lower prices. Reexport allowed a drawback on all duties but provided little compensation for Washington, who could have received an equal or better price from cash purchasers in Virginia. The final cost for marketing the tobacco was Cary's commission of 3 percent on the sales price, up from the 2 1/2 percent that had prevailed through the first half of the eighteenth century.[14]

In the years following his marriage to Martha Custis, Washington delivered only occasional shipments of tobacco to merchants other than Robert Cary & Co. He offered Capel and Osgood Hanbury several small consignments of Custis tobacco but was disappointed by the sales from this firm that was among the oldest Virginia traders and that had carried on an extensive business with the Custis estate. Another Custis correspondent, James Gildart, of Liverpool, received small tobacco shipments from Washington in return for salt, which was cheaper in that outport. Isolated consignments to merchants in Bristol and Liverpool offered Washington a means of paying off debts or purchasing special goods in the outports. As guardian of Martha's two children, John Parke Custis and Martha Parke Custis, Washington managed the production and marketing of all tobacco produced on Jackie Custis's portion of the estate. Washington generally divided the valuable leaf from Jackie's land between Robert Cary & Co. and the Hanburys.[15]

By concentrating his tobacco shipments with Robert Cary & Co., Washington established the kind of account that provided the full range of services available from a leading consignment merchant. In return for his annual shipments of tobacco after 1759, Washington received from the Cary firm nearly all of the imported goods consumed at Mount Vernon and on the Custis lands. Each year, often at the time he sent notification of his tobacco shipment, Washington submitted an order with explicit details of the goods he wanted from Great Britain. An agent of the Cary firm, probably John Moorey, contacted tradesmen, artisans, and warehousemen in London, who filled the various parts of Washington's order. The large orders sent from Mount Vernon in the 1760s required purchases from as many as forty-five tradesmen. The merchants purchased the goods on twelve months' credit and included the cost of the credit in the price charged Washington. Merchants frequently increased their profit by paying for the goods before twelve months expired, thereby receiving a discount.[16]

Washington's costs for the goods also included fees for primage (loading the cargo), clearing the ship out of London, freight to Virginia, insurance, and Robert Cary & Co.'s commission of 2 1/2 percent on the total charges. As with tobacco shipments, insurance on goods varied according to shipping conditions, with premia ranging from 12 guineas per £100 of goods in 1761 to a standard 2 1/2 percent ad valorem in peacetime. The actual shipping time for London goods was two to three months, but because Cary & Co. sent the goods with the spring tobacco ships, Washington often waited ten months or more between ordering and receiving a cargo.[17]

In the range of goods received and in the costs of the shipments, Washington's invoices from Robert Cary & Co. exceeded anything the planter had ordered before his marriage. Washington's most expensive shipment before 1759 had cost £277, and the next largest was £111. During the first five years of trade with Robert Cary & Co., Washington's annual orders for Mount Vernon alone averaged more than £350. The costs in part reflected the couple's pursuit of a standard of living that had come to characterize Virginia's most prominent planters. Fine china and silver, fashionable clothing, furniture, books, decorative porcelains, statuary, and paintings all were found in the shipments from Robert Cary & Co. The latest London fashions appeared at Mount Vernon within months of their introduction on the London market.[18]

Side by side with these luxury goods came the basic necessities upon which Washington's plantations depended. London tradesmen supplied not only the Washingtons' clothing but also almost everything worn by slaves on the estate. The annual shipments contained bolts of coarse woolens and cotton, hosiery, and felt hats worn by field hands. The tools used by the slaves also came from Britain. All sorts of ironware, including the hoes used in field work and thousands of nails, arrived with the shipments from Robert Cary & Co. London craftsmen made the seines used at the fisheries at Mount Vernon and the still for the plantation's distillery. Seeds for Washington's experiments with lucerne, St. Foine, rye, and hops came from London stores. Apothecaries in London answered Washington's regular call for the drugs and herbal remedies used to treat illness within the family and among slaves. Washington even relied on London merchants to supply such foodstuffs as cheeses, pickles, tea, wine, and beer.[19]

Washington annually furnished Robert Cary & Co. a separate order for the supplies in demand on the dower lands in King William County. These shipments consisted exclusively of agricultural tools and materials for slaves' clothing. The Cary firm delivered the goods for the York River in a separate ship that also carried supplies for John Parke Custis's land along that river. At the same time that Washington made out his orders for Mount Vernon, he sent to London instructions for goods to be shipped to the Custis children. These goods usually arrived on the same ship that carried Washington's supplies, but Robert Cary & Co. charged them to individual accounts and shipped them under separate invoices.[20]

Within the first year of his correspondence with Robert Cary & Co.,

Washington took advantage of the firm's credit resources by drawing sterling bills as well as expanding his orders for British manufactures. In June 1760 he drew two bills of exchange, totaling more than £669, to help pay for nearly 2,000 acres across Little Hunting Creek from the original Mount Vernon tract. Three months later, a bill of exchange for £200 in favor of George Brent paid for another 238 acres adjoining the estate. In the summer of 1761 Washington drew on Robert Cary & Co. for £259 to cover the costs of a recent purchase of slaves. Washington also relied on the firm's management of bank stock that had been part of the Custis estate and that made up a considerable portion of Patsy Custis's inheritance. These financial services of Robert Cary & Co., like the marketing of sweet-scented tobacco and the purchase and shipment of British goods, brought Washington the full range of advantages enjoyed by other great planters, including William Byrd, Robert Carter, and Philip Ludwell Lee, who also traded with the firm.[21]

In many ways, Washington achieved striking success as a planter during the fifteen years following his service in the Virginia Regiment. His marriage to Martha Custis brought him control of one of the richest estates in Virginia and provided an introduction to the leading merchants in the London consignment trade. He also expanded his land- and slaveholdings in northern Virginia. Between 1759 and 1775 Washington established the foundation of the fortune that supported him through the long years when he was unable to supervise the operation of his estates.

Yet, within a few years of his return to Mount Vernon, Washington recognized that the traditional management of a Virginia plantation no longer ensured the personal independence upon which rested the social and economic influence of the great planters. His tobacco shipments to London frequently sold for less than the prices offered by direct traders in Virginia, and the goods shipped in return from England were overpriced and inferior in quality. To Washington's dismay, the consignment trade that offered essential services to the large planters no longer stood at the center of the tobacco trade. Washington's residence in the Northern Neck further restricted his advantages in the consignment trade.

Washington's initial dissatisfaction with the tobacco trade centered on the personal services of his London merchants rather than the declining opportunities within the consignment system. His complaints to Robert Cary & Co., the Hanbury brothers, and James Gildart, like those to Richard Washington, echoed language common to the correspondences between Virginia planters and consignment merchants. In a typical response to Cary & Co. Washington protested that his own tobacco sold in London for only a fraction of the price that merchant Samuel Athawes had obtained for similar leaf grown on Fairfax's neighboring plantation. Insisting that he supervised his crop as carefully as any planter in the colony, Washington demanded an explanation of "why Mr. Wormeleys, and indeed some other Gentlemen's Tobacco's shoud sell at 12d last year and mine . . . only fetch 11 1/2." To Gildart he expressed astonishment that a hogshead shipped to Liverpool sold for less than half the price obtained by Cary in London. At no time did Washington acknowledge that tobacco sales met his expectations.[22]

This near-formulaic objection to tobacco prices was one of the few defenses to which Washington and other consigning planters had recourse. From a distance of 3,000 miles a planter could only make clear that he was aware of prices received by other Virginians and threaten to discontinue shipments if sales did not match those from comparable estates. At the opening of his correspondence with Robert Cary & Co., Washington agreed to continue shipments only if the firm was able "to render such Sales as will not only justifie the pres[en]t Consignment to you but encourage my enlarging them." This exact threat was repeated to the Hanburys, as was a caveat that Washington's duty as administrator of the Custis estate and his own self-interest compelled him to favor that merchant who provided the highest tobacco sales and the cheapest goods. The cessation of shipments to the Hanburys made good Washington's threat at the same time that it diminished his bargaining power with Cary.[23]

Washington's resumption of the management of Mount Vernon coincided with a sharp decline in tobacco prices in Great Britain following a wartime high in 1759. As tobacco flooded European markets, the returns for Washington's own crops fell steadily during the first four years of the 1760s. Prices recovered slightly during the middle of the decade, but Washington found no marked improvement until 1767.[24]

In the face of this broad decline in tobacco markets, Washington could make only limited efforts to protect his interests in transactions with the consignment merchants. From the outset of his correspondence with the merchants associated with the Custis estate, Washington carefully demonstrated his knowledge of the tobacco trade in an attempt to secure their most favorable treatment. As long as the account of the Custis estate enjoyed a favorable balance with Robert Cary & Co., Washington expected the firm to pay all duties in cash and to credit the estate with the discount. He also asked the merchant houses to send an account current so that he might compare their annual statements with his own ledgers. Washington's frequent reports of tobacco prices in Virginia and predictions regarding the next crop provided the merchants with an estimate of the return he expected as well as helped them gauge sales.[25]

Washington quickly demanded redress whenever his merchants failed to abide by the accepted practices of the consignment trade as he understood them. In 1767 he discovered that Robert Cary & Co. paid Jackie Custis 4 percent interest on his favorable account with the firm at the same time that they charged Washington 5 percent on the debt he owed the company. Declaring "it must seem strange if his money is not equal of value with yours," Washington threatened to withdraw his ward's money if Cary did not offer 5 percent or apply the difference to the payment of tobacco duties in cash. Cary acquiesced and credited Jackie's account with an additional 1 percent interest. Soon after his return from a trip to the York River, Washington informed Robert Cary & Co. of reports that the firm's annual ship to Virginia was loading tobacco from regular clients at a freight rate of £8 per ton and then completing the load with tobacco on liberty of consignment at £6. Although he could not confirm "that this information is literally fact," he assured Cary that such a practice would damage the firm's ability to attract consignments.[26]

Following the disappointing sales of his first shipments to Robert Cary & Co., Washington sought to improve his own management of the tobacco crop. He assured the firm that he "was more anxious about the quality than quantity of what I Ship" and asked for advice on preparing tobacco for the best markets. After receiving Cary's directions for stemming tobacco before packing it, Washington in 1762 divided his shipment into three parcels, each prepared in a different fashion. The returns, he hoped, would determine his future management as well as the wisdom of the extra expense involved in stemming. Careful handling of the crop, however, could be self-defeating. In an effort to prevent damage to his shipment of 1766, Washington prized the tobacco so lightly "that the Freight and other Incident charges swallowed up the Sales and rendered me very unprofitable returns."[27]

Washington's orders for British goods often proved as unsatisfactory as the sale of tobacco and acted as a particularly frustrating reminder of the colonists' dependence on British traders. The first shipment gathered by Robert Cary & Co. disappointed Washington in both quality and cost. Drawing on records of his earlier imports of British goods, Washington projected the costs of his order of 20 September 1759, only to find that Cary's invoice of 15 March 1760 exceeded his calculations by more than 25 percent. The quality of the goods in no way compensated for the exorbitant prices. Linens, woolens, even nails, were of the meanest sort. Articles meant to be fashionable were instead of a style "that could only have been usd by our Forefathers in the days of yore." Washington suspected that the tradesmen of London selected inferior goods and advanced the price as much as 20 percent if they knew the destination to be the colonies. When he ordered a chariot for Fielding Lewis in 1762, he forwarded instructions that the tradesman not be told it was for a Virginia customer.[28]

Robert Cary & Co. displayed remarkable efficiency and accuracy in filling Washington's order despite complicated instructions and the necessity of dealing with a variety of tradesmen. Any error, however, might interrupt the work of Washington's estate. Washington depended so heavily on the annual shipments that in the final years of the French and Indian War he instructed his merchants immediately to dispatch a replacement cargo in the event that the enemy captured the first ship. The planter in Virginia had little recourse when the goods arrived damaged or useless. To Cary's suggestion that such goods be returned, Washington replied that "a moments reflection points out the Inconveniencies of such a measure unless . . . we coud have a years stock before hand." Although Washington in 1772 returned wheat riddles not made according to instructions, he generally accepted inferior goods and waited for the next year's shipment.[29]

The risks of the consignment trade became alarmingly evident in 1764, when Robert Cary & Co. informed Washington that he had fallen more than £1,800 in their debt. In an apology that Washington knew was all too familiar to the merchants, he explained how tobacco markets and his own credit demands combined to put him in arrears. Three successive years of poor crops had coincided with low prices on the London market. During the same years Washington had drawn bills on Cary for the purchase of land and slaves. These purchases also had absorbed much of the Virginia currency owed to the Custis estate and forced Washington to draw £1,400 from Cary in order to provide Jackie Custis his share of the estate. The final injury to Washington's credit came when four bills of exchange he submitted to Cary were returned protested.[30]

The debt of £1,800 required annual interest payments of 5 percent. Washington accepted this standard lending practice for long-standing debts and promised to ship his crop to Robert Cary & Co. until the debt was paid. He greatly resented, however, what he interpreted as pressure to pay the full amount at once. He had expected a firm that received his greatest favor in trade would be tolerant of a temporary debt. If Cary insisted on immediate payment, Washington intended to find a way, however difficult, and end the matter there. Washington assumed that the merchants would allow him to make remittances of tobacco "without distressing myself too much." He already had stopped drawing bills on Cary & Co. and assured the merchants that future orders for goods would be more modest. In the following years he sent the firm almost his entire annual crop and paid the interest on a steadily decreasing debt. In the aftermath of his dispute over the debt owed Robert Cary & Co., Washington remained protective of his credit reputation. When Osgood Hanbury mistakenly protested a bill Washington drew on the account of Jackie Custis, Washington closed out his ward's account with the London merchant and refused Hanbury the opportunity to explain his error.[31]

Within a few years of opening his correspondence with Robert Cary & Co. Washington recognized that neither personal misjudgment nor the conduct of individual merchants offered sufficient explanation for his misfortunes in the tobacco trade. Throughout the decade following his return to Mount Vernon, Washington confronted the effects of a restructuring of the tobacco trade that had been under way since the 1730s. While British consumption of tobacco remained steady, the opening of new markets on the Continent, particularly in France, prompted the establishment of a new type of merchant firm designed to meet the growing demand in Europe. Continental buyers shunned the sweet-scented tobacco grown by large planters and preferred instead the cheaper oronoco variety that grew easily in the Piedmont as well as the Tidewater and was widely available from small planters who produced only a few hogsheads a year. Merchants who catered to the Continent sent factors to the Chesapeake, where they purchased the cheaper tobacco directly from the growers and returned the cargo to Great Britain for bulk sales on the reexport market.[32]

As the direct trade expanded, British merchant firms established chains of stores at which resident factors offered British goods on credit or in exchange for tobacco. The store system succeeded so well that direct-trade merchants offered the highest tobacco prices available in the Chesapeake and thereby encouraged production of the type of leaf they desired. Tobacco production in Virginia after 1730 expanded greatest in those areas with the highest concentration of direct traders. Glasgow firms with the necessary capital and superior contacts in the French market led the way in the development of the store system and the direct trade. By 1770 Scottish merchants accounted for fully half of the tobacco imported from the Chesapeake. The direct trade proved so successful during the second third of the eighteenth century that London firms commonly followed the Scottish model by the 1760s. On the eve of the American Revolution, direct traders handled as much as four-fifths of the tobacco shipped to Great Britain from the Chesapeake.[33]

Despite their role in the growth of tobacco production and the competitive prices they paid for Virginia leaf, direct traders offered few opportunities for such large planters as Washington, who annually marketed as many as fifty or even sixty hogsheads of sweet-scented tobacco. These firms that depended on a heavy volume of trade provided no personal agent to manage the sale of an individual's crop, regardless of quality. The more strictly business relationship between factor and planter in the direct trade precluded the kind of personal services that attracted Washington to the London merchants. The direct-trade merchants refused any one individual the level of credit extensions and banking services that allowed Washington to expand his landholdings or to import several hundred pounds' worth of British goods. The factors' stores carried few of the luxury goods desired by Washington. Moreover, some of the direct-trade firms discouraged extensive dealings with the great planters, who had come to expect generous credit terms and attentive service. One of the largest Glasgow firms, William Cunninghame & Co., instructed its Virginia agent to deal with middling planters who were seldom in debt rather than with the "first crop masters who are continually so." If the Cunninghame factors ever bought tobacco from the "Great Men," the transaction was supposed to be in cash.[34]

The rise of the direct trade and the diminishing share of the market controlled by consignment merchants made it particularly difficult for growers in the Northern Neck to follow the form of plantation management associated with the great planters along the York River. Throughout the eighteenth century the Potomac River district maintained its proportional share of tobacco exported from Virginia to Great Britain, but the character of the tobacco trade in the area changed. Soil conditions less favorable to sweet-scented tobacco, the distance from the highly regarded York River, and the added costs of shipments to the Potomac persuaded consignment merchants to restrict their trade in the area. At the same time direct traders found that oronoco tobacco grown along the Potomac met the demands of the reexport market. Factors from Scotland and independent purchasers from England soon carried the bulk of the tobacco produced in the region. Unlike the Upper James district, where factors also dominated the tobacco trade, the Northern Neck was home to some of Virginia's largest landholders and wealthiest planters. These great planters, among whom Washington ranked by the 1760s, were the first in Virginia to confront the challenge of the direct purchasers and to search for new ways to secure the advantages traditionally offered by consignment merchants.[35]

Soon after he began to grow tobacco at Mount Vernon, Washington discovered that the Potomac River lay beyond the reach of many of London's leading consignment merchants. After several years of searching out ships to carry his tobacco on liberty of consignment and paying to retrieve goods delivered to the wrong river, Washington encouraged Robert Cary & Co. in their proposal to send their own ship to the Potomac. Although Cary hoped at the end of the French and Indian War to dispatch a ship for the tobacco of Washington and such important correspondents as Robert Carter and Philip Ludwell Lee, consignments from the area were never sufficient to justify a charter.[36]

Throughout his correspondence with Robert Cary & Co. Washington complained of the inconvenience of dealing with merchants who refused to ship directly to his river. "I had almost as soon have Goods in any part of Great Britain as in any River except the one on which I live," he protested in 1762. Nine years later he continued to remind Cary that a ship on the York, James, or even the Rappahannock was as removed from Mount Vernon as a vessel in Whitehaven or Bristol would be from London. Months might pass before Washington learned his goods had arrived along another river, and the cost of recovering them was almost as great as the freight charges from England.[37]

Washington's repeated disappointment in the sale of tobacco consigned from the Potomac aggravated the inconvenience of shipping from that river. During the six years that Washington kept separate accounts for Potomac and York exports, the return on Potomac tobacco was generally 2 to 3 shillings less per hundredweight than that received for the crop from King William County. From the beginning of his trade with Robert Cary & Co., Washington recognized that direct purchasers "in the country" frequently offered prices superior to his returns for Potomac tobacco sold on the London market. In the spring of 1759 "the Scarcity of the last years Crop, and the high prices of Tobo consequent thereupon" nearly convinced him to sell in Virginia. Washington shipped his fifteen hogsheads to Cary only out of a desire to continue the long correspondence of the Custis family with that merchant. The following year, rather than ship to Richard Washington the twenty hogsheads of tobacco collected from tenants, Washington sold the rent tobacco to Harry Piper, an independent factor in Alexandria who bought for the Whitehaven market. The leaf produced by tenants was generally inferior in quality to that grown under Washington's supervision and suited well the demands of buyers in the British outports. Washington again chose to sell rent tobacco to Piper in 1765.[38]

The returns for even the most carefully grown tobacco often raised doubts about the wisdom of consigning. The tobacco shipped to Cary in

1761 from the Custis lands along the York River sold for export at 3 1/2 pence per pound, "a practise and price never known till now." The returns for consignments from Mount Vernon, grown under Washington's direct supervision, compared even less favorably with the direct trade. Although soil conditions may have presented particular problems for tobacco cultivation at Mount Vernon, Washington blamed the metropolitan merchants. By 1765 he complained that his friends along the Potomac regularly received better prices for tobacco shipped to the outports than he got in London. He was convinced that in at least four out of five years he lost by shipping to London rather than selling in Virginia, where he might have received a bill of exchange for as much as £10 sterling per hogshead. The relative advantages of selling in the country became more apparent in the late 1760s and early 1770s, when a surplus of credit in Great Britain and a booming tobacco market on the Continent prompted the direct traders to offer premium prices for Virginia leaf.[39]

At the outset of Washington's trade with the British merchants, the importation of goods appeared to be an obvious advantage of the consignment trade. When Thomas Knox failed to ship the complete order for British goods in 1757, Washington feared that he would have to purchase the missing items from local traders "at exorbitant prices." In the latter half of the 1760s, however, with freight rates at a peacetime low and wholesalers' credit to the direct traders on the rise, Washington discovered that the factors' stores in Virginia sold many imported goods as cheaply as or more cheaply than those he ordered through Robert Cary & Co. He offered Cary specific examples of ordinary goods such as clover and turnip seed that sold in Virginia for a fraction of the cost charged Washington. By 1770 and 1771, when the influx of British credit and record importations of British goods further reduced prices at the factors' stores, the cost of goods selected and shipped by a consignment merchant seemed to Washington to outweigh the advantages of personal service.[40]

Washington did not understand why the linens and woolens that he ordered from London shops were comparable in price to the cloth in Virginia stores, where the imports presumably carried the mark-up, or "advance," necessary for the merchants' profit. Certainly Robert Cary & Co. purchased goods in sufficient quantities to receive a wholesaler's discount. Why, Washington asked, did their correspondents not receive the benefits of those savings? Even if he lacked the cash to take advantage of Cary's discount, "the heavy charges upon our Tobacco and the ample and uncommon Commissions which are drawn upon the Sales of it" ought to bring the consigning planter "every advantage which can be procured in the purchase of our Goods." "Otherwise," Washington concluded, "I should be glad to know to what end we Import them."[41]

A comparison of his experience in the consignment trade and the opportunities in the direct trade, Washington admitted in 1768, was "not only discouraging but almost sufficient to bring about a change in the System of my management." In fact, Washington by that time had diversified his agricultural production and sought alternatives to the services provided by Robert Cary & Co. and other consignment merchants. Since the early 1760s Washington had grown wheat alongside tobacco and gathered further income from the fishery and mill at Mount Vernon. His debt to Cary in 1764 and the disappointing tobacco markets following the French and Indian War further encouraged Washington to limit his dependence on tobacco production. At the same time he recognized that continued shipment of tobacco provided the only sure means of reducing his debt and paying for the annual shipments of British goods.[42]

During the second half of the 1760s, as the differences between the consignment and direct trades became more obvious and political tensions increased, Washington came to regard his restricted opportunities in the tobacco trade as part of a larger problem resulting from Virginia's economic dependence on Great Britain. His own plantation management or the actions of any one merchant firm could not fully explain the problem. Rather, the colony's reliance on a single export to the mother country and the absence of an alternative source of manufactures or credit within Virginia created a cycle of overproduction and cultivation of unsuitable lands followed by depressed tobacco prices and renewed indebtedness.

The turning point of Washington's involvement in the British tobacco trade came in response to the Stamp Act, which forever altered so many aspects of relations within the empire. The demand for greater revenue from a colony that already provided a lucrative trade for the mother country politicized the trading problems that Washington and other planters previously considered a matter of private business. Several weeks before the Stamp Act went into effect, Washington warned Robert Cary & Co. that the British ministry would be disappointed if it expected to extract greater wealth from Virginia, "for certain it is, the whole produce of our labour hitherto has centered in Great Britain—what more can they desire?"[43]

Noting the popular interest in domestic manufactures that followed announcement of the Stamp Act, Washington predicted that British demands for additional revenue would undermine the mother country's commercial authority over the colony. He recognized that nonimportation and the success of local manufactures in Virginia would offer relief from the problems of commercial dependence and personal indebtedness as well as provide protection from the immediate threat of the revenue act. Once manufactures were established

> the Eyes of our People (already beginning to open) will perceive, that many of the Luxuries which we have heretofore lavished our Substances to Great Britain for can well be dispensed with whilst the Necessaries of Life are to be procured (for the most part) within ourselves. This consequently will introduce frugality and a necessary stimulant to Industry. Great Britain may then load her Exports with as Heavy Taxes as she pleases but where will the consumption be? I am apt to think no law or usage can compel us to barter our money supplied within ourselves upon the better terms.[44]

The reorganization of Mount Vernon initiated during the Stamp Act crisis indicated Washington's own hope of fulfilling his prediction of a more independent colonial economy. After the harvest of 1765, he abandoned all cultivation of tobacco along the Potomac. In September of that year he asked Robert Cary & Co. to advise him on the feasibility of shipping hemp and flax to British markets, where he also hoped to sell flour in place of tobacco. Beginning the following spring, Washington devoted his land and labor at Mount Vernon to the production of a variety of crops not dependent on one market or creditor. The increased production of grain and the expansion of the fishery at Mount Vernon provided Washington with opportunities in domestic markets as well as the West Indies. Beginning in the latter half of the 1760s Washington began converting his tenants' leases to payment in cash rather than tobacco, thereby encouraging diversification or forcing tenants to bear the risks of fluctuating tobacco markets. What tobacco he continued to receive from tenants he sold to Hector Ross in Colchester or offered in payment for local levies.

Curtailment of tobacco exports would be possible only if Washington found some way to reduce his reliance on British imports. In an order to Cary on 20 September 1765, he requested tools and equipment to convert hemp and flax into cloth for his own consumption. Within three years a full-time weaving operation at Mount Vernon annually produced more than 1,200 yards of homespun for use on the estate.[45]

When Americans responded to the Townshend Acts with new proposals for commercial resistance, Washington made clear his intention to reduce the colony's as well as his own dependence on British merchants and the tobacco trade. In April 1769 Washington proposed to George Mason that

Virginians endorse an association designed for the unique character of trade in the colony. Despite his doubts about the political effectiveness of such an agreement, Washington believed the private advantages of nonimportation would be worth the effort. He expected that by refusing British imports, Virginians could lower the level of indebtedness through which "many families are reduced, almost, if not quite, to penury and want." A popular nonimportation association would offer the great planters "a pretext to live within bounds" rather than continue extravagant purchases in a vain attempt to convince others of their wealth.[46]

At an extralegal session of the Virginia assembly in May 1769, the burgesses approved an association drafted by George Mason and presented in Williamsburg by Washington. The colony's extensive dependence on all manner of British manufactures forced the burgesses to make exceptions for coarse and cheap goods that could not be replaced in Virginia. Washington's close adherence to the agreement enabled him to reduce his annual order from Robert Cary & Co. to the lowest level ever. The cost of the goods he ordered during the second year of the association also fell well below his usual purchases. The nature of Washington's orders, however, illustrated the limitations of any nonimportation agreement in the colony as well as the difficulties faced by a planter who wished to curtail his trade with British merchants.[47]

The goods shipped to Washington in January 1770 and valued at £77 included nearly £50 in clothing supplies for the slaves at Mount Vernon. In his subsequent order that strictly observed the revised association of 1770, Washington requested goods worth £110. Inexpensive cloth again accounted for more than half the order, and much of the remainder consisted of basic tools unavailable from Virginia craftsmen. During each of the two years following the dissolution of Virginia's association, Washington imported more than £350 in British goods. These orders in 1771 and 1772 included items prohibited by the associations, but the greatest costs were for ordinary supplies that suggest the plantation suffered shortages during the period of nonimportation. Despite his efforts at diversification and the initiation of domestic manufactures, Washington, like most planters in Virginia, remained dependent on British merchants for the supply of basic goods.[48]

Washington's reliance on imported goods forced him to continue tobacco cultivation on the York River in the years after he ceased to grow any leaf at Mount Vernon. In 1768 he explained to the Hanburys that he would "make no more of that Article than barely serves to furnish me with Goods, this is the Reason therefore why I send it undivided to Messrs. Cary

& Co. as it is from that House I always get the necessaries wanted for my Family's use." In fact, it was the continued shipment of tobacco from the Custis estates in King William County that allowed Washington the luxury of establishing new trades from his Potomac estates. The proceeds from annual shipments of between eight and thirteen hogsheads after 1766 helped pay for the goods consumed at Mount Vernon and contributed to the reduction of Washington's debt to Robert Cary & Co. It was, however, only the death of Martha Parke Custis in 1773 and the subsequent division of her estate between Washington and John Parke Custis that provided Washington with bank stock sufficient to eliminate his debt to Cary & Co.[49]

In the wake of the collapse of the nonimportation association in 1771, Washington intensified his efforts to diversify his estate and to reduce the colony's dependence on the British tobacco trade. The construction of a new mill at Mount Vernon in 1771, the extensive cultivation of wheat, and his thriving fishery offered Washington opportunities to curtail his own commerce with Great Britain. His plans to settle western lands and his role in the scheme to open the Potomac to navigation promised a new era of growth for the regional economy. A Potomac canal, according to Washington, would make that river "the Channel of Commerce between Great Britain and that immense Territory which is unfolding to our view the advantages of which are too great & too obvious."[50] Yet the fortunes and interests of one planter were not sufficient to redirect the colonial economy. The severe credit crisis that began in Great Britain in 1772 and the renewal of imperial conflict following enactment of the Tea Act in 1773 reminded Washington and other Virginians that the chronic problems of commercial dependence on the mother country posed the greatest threat to the colony's prosperity.

In the face of British restrictions on Massachusetts, Washington again emerged as a leading advocate of commercial resistance. At a public meeting held in Fairfax County in July 1774, Washington helped draft a proposal for a wide-ranging nonimportation agreement to begin 1 September 1774, with nonexportation to follow a year later. Citizens of Fairfax agreed to suspend tobacco cultivation following the harvest of the current crop and to begin local manufactures in expectation of a complete boycott of British goods in 1776. The Fairfax Resolves served as the model for the association approved by the Virginia convention in August 1774 and subsequently for the Continental association endorsed by the Continental Congress in October.[51]

Washington's observance of the Continental association marked the effective close of his trade with the British tobacco merchants. He offered his last tobacco shipment to Robert Cary & Co. in 1773 and received his final invoice for British goods from the firm the following year. As Virginians joined in support of a revival of commercial resistance in the spring of 1774, Washington told Cary & Co. that "the whole of my Force is in a manner confind to the growth of Wheat and the Manufacturing of it into Flour." By the time the Continental association went into effect in December 1774, Washington's success in the grain and fish trades enabled him to replace his British imports with purchases from Philadelphia merchants. When trade with Great Britain resumed following the Revolutionary War, Washington's correspondence with Wakelin Welch, successor to the Cary firm, dealt with little more than the disposition of Bank of England stock and the long-delayed balancing of the account.[52]

The relative ease with which Washington recovered from the abandonment of tobacco and the cessation of trade with Great Britain belied the degree to which Virginia remained commercially dependent, whether it be on the centers of capital in Great Britain or the rising merchant cities of the North. Washington's residence in the Northern Neck, on the periphery of the consignment trade, hastened his realization of the need for diversification. His development of new crops for export during the decade preceding the Revolution helped him adjust to the shifts in trade following the war. The nature of Washington's transition from tobacco, however, indicated the limitations facing Virginia planters intent on preserving their influence in politics and society.

Washington had expected to guarantee his success in the tobacco trade by carefully following a pattern established by the great planters in the Tidewater. The expansion of his landed estate, purchase of additional slaves, personal supervision of tobacco cultivation, and careful attendance to financial records all appeared more decisive to Washington than an understanding of the market forces transforming the tobacco trade. He curtailed the growth of tobacco only after repeated disappointment with the sale of his crops in Great Britain. At the same time he reduced his orders for luxury goods and plantation supplies. Even then, Washington's investments in land and slaves and his commitment to a plantation system of agricultural production restricted the alternatives available to him. Despite Washington's intention to reduce the colony's dependence on British commerce, the reorganization of his estates and a close observance of the nonimportation associations offered only a measure of personal security, without providing any model by which Virginia might develop a more integrated and self-sufficient economy.

Notes

1. In 1770 the value of Virginia's grain exports was still only 10 percent of the value of tobacco exports (Jacob M. Price, "Economic Function and the Growth of American Port Towns in the Eighteenth Century," *Perspectives in American History* 8 [1974]: 165; "A List of Lands given to the Clerk of Fairfax County in the year 1758 To be Taxed" and "A List of Tithables in Fairfax County given in 1760" WPLC). GW's growing landholdings in the Northern Neck of Virginia are recorded in quitrents account, Ledger A, ff. 106, 199, 257, ibid.

2. Invoice of goods shipped by Anthony Bacon, Oct. [23], 1754, *PGW: Col. Ser.* 1:217–19; account with Anthony Bacon, Ledger A, f. 16, WPLC; GW to Richard Washington, April 15, 1757, *PGW: Col. Ser.* 4:132–34.

3. GW to Richard Washington, Dec. 6, 1755, John Carlyle to GW, Jan. 12, 1756, GW to Thomas Knox, Dec. 26, 1757, Jan. 1758, *PGW: Col. Ser.* 2:207–9, 275–76, 5:72, 87–88. Richard Washington had traded with GW's close friend George William Fairfax, who lived near Mount Vernon.

4. Samuel M. Rosenblatt, "The Significance of Credit in the Tobacco Consignment Trade: A Study of John Norton & Sons, 1768–1775," *WMQ* 19 (1962): 389–99; Robert Polk Thomson, "The Merchant in Virginia, 1700–1775" (Ph.D. diss, University of Wisconsin, 1955), chap. 2.

5. GW to Richard Washington, Dec. 6, 1755, April 15, 1757, March 18, 1758, to Anthony Bacon & Company, Sept. 10, 1757, invoice from Richard Washington, Aug. 20, 1757, invoice from Richard Washington, Nov. 10, 1757, invoices from Thomas Knox, Sept. 28, 1757, Aug. 18, 1758, *PGW: Col. Ser.* 2:207–9, 4:132–34, 5:105–6, 4:376–80, 400–401, 5:49–51, 4:427–28, 5:399–402.

6. GW to Richard Washington, Sept. 10, 1757, to Thomas Knox, Dec. 26, 1757, ibid., 4:401–2, 5:72–73.

7. GW to Richard Washington, April 1757, Sept. 1757, Dec. 26, 1757, ibid., 4:133–34, 401, 5:73–74.

8. GW to Richard Washington, May 7, 1759, to Robert Cary & Co., Aug. 10, 1760, ibid., 6:391, 448–50; accounts with Thomas Knox and Richard Washington, Ledger A, ff. 15–16, WPLC. The division of the Custis estate is described in Freeman, *Washington* 3:19–23, and Joseph Horrell and Richard W. Oram, "George Washington's 'Marble Colour'd Folio Book': A Newly Identified Ledger," *WMQ* 43 (1986): 252–66.

9. *Kent's Directory for the Year 1759* (London, 1759); Jacob M. Price, "Who Was John Norton? A Note on the Historical Character of Some Eighteenth-Century London Virginia Firms," *WMQ* 19 (1962): 400–407; Martha Dandridge Custis to Robert Cary & Co., Aug. 20, 1757, Custis Family Papers, Virginia Historical Society; GW to Robert Cary & Co., May 1, 1759, *PGW: Col. Ser.* 6:315–16.

10. See GW's correspondence with Joseph Valentine, 1760–71, WPLC; tobacco accounts, Ledger A, ff. 120, 148, 162, ibid.

11. GW to Robert Cary & Co., June 12, 1759, *PGW: Col. Ser.* 6:326–27. Captain Johnstoun is recorded regularly in GW's correspondence with Robert Cary & Co., 1759–74, WPLC.

12. Insurance charges in accounts with Robert Cary and Company, Ledger A, ff. 67, 154, 198, 284, WPLC; Lewis Cecil Gray, *History of Agriculture in the Southern United States to 1860,* 2 vols. (Washington, D.C., 1933), 1:241–46; Avery Odelle Craven, *Soil Exhaustion as a Factor in the Agricultural History of Virginia and Maryland, 1660–1860* (Urbana, Ill., 1926), 54–55; Rosenblatt, "Significance of Credit," 389–91.

13. Robert Cary & Co. accounts of sales for the sale of GW's tobacco do not survive. Cary's charges and commissions are recorded in numerous accounts of sales for John Parke Custis's tobacco (see, for instance, accounts of sales from Robert Cary & Co., May 31, 1762, May 18, 1763, Aug. 10, 22, 1764, Aug. 13, 1765; for freight rates, see also charges on tobacco shipped to Robert Cary & Co. by the estate of Daniel Custis, March 1, 1758, and ship manifest for tobacco shipped to Robert Cary & Co. by Martha Dandridge Custis, Aug. 28, 1758, all in Custis Family Papers). The net weight of GW's hogsheads is found in his tobacco accounts, Ledger A, WPLC.

14. Rosenblatt, "Significance of Credit," 387–91; accounts of sales for tobacco shipped on account of John Parke Custis, Custis Family Papers.

15. GW to Capel and Osgood Hanbury, Nov. 25, 1769, *PGW: Col. Ser.* 6:373; account with Capel and Osgood Hanbury, GW's correspondence with James Gildart and account with Gildart, isolated shipments recorded in account with Farrel and Jones, and account with Crosbies and Trafford, Ledger A, ff. 66, 107, 94, 212, WPLC; GW's guardianship account book, 1760–75, 2 vols., Washington Papers, Virginia Historical Society.

16. See GW's correspondence with Robert Cary & Co., 1759–74, and invoices for goods shipped from English merchants, 1754–66, 1766–73, WPLC; Jacob M. Price, *Capital and Credit in the British Overseas Trade: The View from the Chesapeake, 1700–1760* (Cambridge, Mass., 1980), 96–123.

17. Invoices for goods shipped from English merchants, 1754–66, 1766–73, WPLC.

18. Ibid. For a complete description of GW's purchases of English chinaware, see Susan Gray Detweiler, *George Washington's Chinaware* (New York, 1982).

19. Invoices for goods shipped from English merchants, 1754–66, 1766–73, WPLC. See esp. invoices of March 31, 1761, April 10, 1762, and Feb. 13, 1764.

20. Ibid.; John Parke Custis and Martha Parke Custis accounts with Robert Cary & Co., Custis Family Papers.

21. GW accounts with Robert Cary & Co., Ledger A, f. 67, WPLC; GW to Robert Cary & Co., June 20, Sept. 28, 1760, *PGW: Col. Ser.* 6:437–38, 459–61; GW to Robert Cary & Co., Aug. 1, 1761, WPLC.

22. GW to Robert Cary & Co., May 28, 1762, April 3, 1761, to James Gildart, April 3, 1761, WPLC.

23. GW to Robert Cary & Co., June 12, 1759, to Capel and Osgood Hanbury, June 12, 1759, *PGW: Col. Ser.* 6:326–27, 322–23.

24. Allan Kulikoff, *Tobacco and Slaves: The Development of Southern Cultures in the Chesapeake, 1680–1800* (Chapel Hill, N.C., 1986), 119–22; Gray, *History of Agriculture* 1:273–74. Robert Cary & Co.'s accounts of sales for the sale of GW's tobacco do not survive, thus making it impossible to determine the exact price for which the tobacco sold in London. GW's surviving accounts with Cary & Co., combined with his tobacco accounts, allow a calculation of the return GW received following the deduction of all charges by the merchants.

25. GW to Robert Cary & Co., June 12, 1759, to Capel and Osgood Hanbury, June 12, 1759, to James Gildart, June 12, 1759, *PGW: Col. Ser.* 6:326–27, 348–50, 322–25.

26. GW to Robert Cary & Co., July 20, 1767, June 23, 1766, WPLC; John Parke Custis account with Robert Cary & Co. in GW guardianship account book, Washington Papers, Virginia Historical Society.

27. GW to Robert Cary & Co., Oct. 12, 1761, May 28, 1762, July 20, 1767, WPLC.

28. GW to Robert Cary & Co., Aug. 10, Sept. 28, 1760, Sept. 20, 1759, *PGW: Col. Ser.* 6:448–50, 459–64, 348–55; GW to Robert Cary & Co., March 16, 1762, WPLC; invoice from Robert Cary & Co., March 15, 1760, *PGW: Col. Ser.* 6:392–402.

29. GW to Robert Cary & Co., July 5, 1761, Sept. 20, 1765, July 15, 1772, WPLC; for Cary's shipment of goods, see invoices in ibid.

30. GW to Robert Cary & Co., May 1, Aug. 10, 1764, WPLC; accounts with Robert Cary & Co., Ledger A, ff. 67, 154, 198, ibid. Robert Cary & Co.'s letters to GW on Feb. 13 and March 28, 1764, are not extant.

31. GW to Robert Cary & Co., May 1, Aug. 10, 1764, GW to Osgood Hanbury, Aug. 4, 1774, WPLC; accounts with Robert Cary & Co., Ledger A, ff. 198, 284, ibid.

32. See the work of Jacob M. Price, esp. *France and the Chesapeake: A History of the French Tobacco Monopoly, 1674–1791, and of Its Relationship to the British and American Tobacco Trades* . . . , 2 vols. (Ann Arbor, Mich., 1973); "The Rise of Glasgow in the Chesapeake Tobacco Trade, 1707–1775," *WMQ* 11 (1954): 179–99; and "The Economic Growth of the Chesapeake and the European Market, 1677–1775," *Journal of Economic History* 24 (1964): 496–511.

33. Price, "Rise of Glasgow"; Price, "Economic Function and the Growth of American Port Towns," 168.

34. J. H. Soltow, "Scottish Traders in Virginia, 1750–1775," *Economic History Review,* 2d ser., 12 (1959): 83–98; William Cunninghame & Co. to James Robinson, May 16, 1772, Cunninghame of Lainshaw Muniments, 1761–78, Scottish Record Office, Edinburgh.

35. Peter V. Bergstrom, "Markets and Merchants: Economic Diversification in Colonial Virginia, 1700–75" (Ph.D. diss., University of New Hampshire,

1980), 141; Robert Polk Thomson, "The Tobacco Export of the Upper James River Naval District, 1773–1775," *WMQ* 18 (1961): 393–407; Freeman, *Washington* 3:117.

36. GW to Robert Cary & Co., May 28, Nov. 15, 1762, WPLC; Robert Cary & Co. to Richard Lingan Hall, Sept. 16, 1761, Peckatone Papers, Virginia Historical Society.

37. GW to Robert Cary & Co., Nov. 30, 1759, Aug. 10, 1760, June 20, 1762, July 20, 1771, WPLC.

38. Price data drawn from accounts with Robert Cary & Co., Ledger A, ff. 67, 154, 198, 284, ibid.; tobacco accounts, ibid.; account with Harry Piper, ibid., f. 103; GW to Robert Cary & Co., May 1, 1759, to Richard Washington, Aug. 10, 1760, *PGW: Col. Ser.* 6:315–16, 452–53.

39. Account with Robert Cary & Co., Ledger A, ff. 67, 154, 198, WPLC; tobacco accounts, ibid.; GW to Robert Cary & Co., Sept. 18, 1762, Sept. 20, 1765, May 5, 1768, June 20, 1768, ibid.; Freeman, *Washington* 3:117; Price, "Capital and Credit," 128–29.

40. GW to Thomas Knox, Dec. 26, 1757, *PGW: Col. Ser.* 5:72; GW to Robert Cary & Co., June 23, 1766, Aug. 20, 1770, July 20, 1771, WPLC; Price, *Capital and Credit,* 128–29.

41. GW to Robert Cary & Co., July 20, 1771, WPLC.

42. Ibid., June 20, 1768; Freeman, *Washington* 3:117, 125–27, 145–46.

43. GW to Robert Cary & Co., Sept. 20, 1765, WPLC. For Virginia's commercial resistance to the Stamp Act, see Bruce A. Ragsdale, *A Planters' Republic: The Search for Economic Independence in Revolutionary Virginia* (Madison, Wis., 1996).

44. GW to Robert Cary & Co., Sept. 20, 1765, WPLC.

45. Ibid.; weaving account, Mount Vernon, ibid.; Freeman, *Washington* 3:152–53, 176, 179–80; tobacco account, Ledger A, f. 289, WPLC; account with Hector Ross, ibid., ff. 111, 276.

46. GW to George Mason, April 5, 1769, WPLC.

47. Text of the association of 1769 in William J. Van Schreeven, Robert L. Scribner, and Brent Tarter, eds., *Revolutionary Virginia: The Road to Independence,* 7 vols. (Charlottesville, Va., 1973–83), 1:73–77; invoices for goods shipped by Robert Cary and Co., Jan. 23, Nov. 13, 1770, in invoices for goods shipped from English merchants, 1766–73, WPLC.

48. Invoices from Robert Cary & Co., Nov. 13, 1770, Dec. 3, 1771, Sept. 29, 1772, in invoices for goods shipped from English merchants, 1766–73, WPLC.

49. GW to Capel and Osgood Hanbury, May 5, 1768, WPLC; GW accounts with Robert Cary & Co., Ledger A, ff. 198, 284, Ledger B, f. 26, ibid.; GW to Robert Cary & Co., Nov. 10, 1773, ibid. For the final settlement of GW's account with Robert Cary & Co., see note 52 below.

50. Freeman, *Washington* 3:263–338; GW to Thomas Johnson, July 20, 1770, *GW: Writings* 3:17–21.

51. Ragsdale, *A Planters' Republic*, 191–216.

52. GW to Robert Cary & Co., July 10, 26, 1773, WPLC; GW to Robert Cary & Co., June 1, 1774, *GW: Writings* 3:219–21; account with Wakelin Welch, account with William Milnor, cash account, Ledger B, ff. 234, 123, 125, WPLC. Despite GW's instructions to Robert Cary & Co. on Nov. 10, 1773, the London firm did not sell the Bank of England stock or settle GW's account before the Revolution. GW's final settlement is discussed in GW to Wakelin Welch, Oct. 30, 1783, July 27, 1784, July 1786, *GW: Writings*, 27:211–13, 450–51, 28:496–98.

4. Interpreting George Washington's Mount Vernon

ROBERT F. DALZELL JR. AND
LEE BALDWIN DALZELL

Elite Virginians called their dwellings "the great house." Some structures, like Mount Vernon and Jefferson's Monticello, evolved over decades to appearances far different from the time of their construction, a reflection of new needs and, more significant, of elevated social status. A part of that distant world is recaptured by visits to Mount Vernon and to the surviving great houses of Washington's friends and neighbors in the Northern Neck, between the Potomac and Rappahannock Rivers—to George Mason's Gunston Hall, to Thomas Lee's Stratford Hall, to John Tayloe's Mount Airy, to Landon Carter's Sabine Hall, or by reading accounts of once-flourishing rural seats such as Robert Carter's Nomini Hall and William Fairfax's Belvoir.

But those imposing edifices were only one emblem of station, albeit the most visible one. Other physical declarations of planter hegemony were the courthouses and Anglican churches that dotted the landscape. So was Williamsburg, the home of provincial government, with its Governor's Palace and Capitol. The gentry's opportunities for political office, often beginning as a justice of the county court, peaked with either appointment to the council or election to the House of Burgesses, to say nothing of years along the way performing the parish vestry duties. Important too was high rank in the militia or in a provincial regiment. It is no accident that the first Washington countenance on canvas, the work of Charles Willson Peale in 1772, shows Washington in his Virginia regimentals, or that the sole surviving painting of his brother Lawrence (Washington displayed it in his office or study, the only portrait on those walls, where it remains today) reveals him clad in his British army officer's uniform. People almost always addressed Washington in the preindependence years as Colonel Washington, and the same held true for countless Virginians who had obtained officer rank. A traveler in the Old Dominion observed wryly that surely Virginia must be a retreat for heroes, for he had never met a man who was not a captain, or a major, or a colonel and who did not feel insulted if not acknowledged by his title.

Robert F. Dalzell Jr. is Ephraim Williams Professor of History at Williams College. His books include Daniel Webster and the Trial of American Nationalism, 1843–1852, Enterprising Elite: The Boston Associates and the World They Made, *and, with Lee Baldwin Dalzell, head of the reference department of the Williams College Library,* George Washington's Mount Vernon: At Home in Revolutionary America.

THE DATE WAS AUGUST 20, 1775—barely a month after George Washington had arrived in Cambridge, Massachusetts, to take command of the Continental army. Whatever the future might hold, England and the colonies were at war, and the difficulties involved in molding the ragtag collection of patriot troops camped around Boston into an effective fighting force would have made a more sanguine individual than Washington quake with fear. It was an assignment he earnestly claimed he had not wanted, did not want. But the problems he faced at the front were not the only thing on his mind that day. His "mansion house" at home had been under renovation for the past sixteen months, and in spite of everything he was determined to have the work continue, as he wrote his kinsman, friend, and manager at Mount Vernon, Lund Washington: "I wish you would quicken Lamphere and Sears about the Dining Room Chimney Piece (to be executed as mentioned in one of my last Letters) as I could wish to have that end of the House completely finished when I return."[1]

That Washington could concern himself so intently, at such a moment, with a dining-room chimneypiece underlines what anyone who knew him understood: Mount Vernon was far more than simply his home. Signature and self-portrait, it was a tangible emblem of his character, his personality, his hopes, his dreams. Twice he all but completely rebuilt it, both times doubling it in size. As part of each rebuilding he also remade the grounds around the house, and over the years scores of smaller projects filled his thoughts and correspondence. For all of this work, too, Washington served as chief planner, architect, and landscape designer—roles he shared with no one, not even Martha Washington.

Considering how strongly—and intimately—Mount Vernon speaks of Washington, it is surprising that historians have not done more with the subject. What follows is an overview linking the major changes he made in the house and grounds. In broad terms, we see three distinct stages to the process. In the 1750s and 1760s Washington's choices in architecture and landscape design were those of a young planter self-consciously positioning himself in Virginia's elite. Then over the next two decades he reworked that design, making sweeping changes in it against the backdrop of the more intangible landscape of republican ideology. And finally, at the end of his life, he laid plans for revising the entire composition yet again, this time with an eye to undoing all it had taken so much time and energy to create.[2]

When Mount Vernon became George Washington's home, it was already a place rich with personal associations. The land on which it stood had been in his family since 1674 when John Washington, his great-grandfather, secured title to it. In those days it lay well beyond the line of settlement in Virginia. Even the name the family gave it—Little Hunting Creek— hinted of the wilderness and a not too distant past when Indians dominated the area.

John Washington was not alone in acquiring tracts of this sort. Land was the single most important avenue to riches in Virginia. In the Northern Neck, where Mount Vernon was located, Robert "King" Carter managed to patent over 200,000 acres for himself and his family by 1731.[3] To place the Washingtons in the social and political landscape of the time would be to note that though they did moderately well, they were hardly in the same league as the Carters.

John Washington's tract in the wilderness was inherited by his son, who in turn passed it along to his daughter, leaving his more valuable acreage to his two sons—the younger of whom, Augustine, or Gus, was George Washington's father. In 1727 Gus bought the tract from his sister and then, in a surprising move, installed his family there when George was still a toddler. A few years later the family moved again, and Lawrence Washington, George's older half brother, took over Little Hunting Creek, giving it its present name and building a new house on foundations probably built earlier by Gus. After Lawrence's death George leased the property from his brother's widow, and on her death he inherited it outright.

But if this was Washington's choice of where to make his home, not everyone who saw the area was struck by its promise. As late as 1814 someone traveling between Alexandria and Fredericksburg described passing "for a great part of the way through dreary forests of pine."[4] So swampy was the land that in rainy weather travelers were often compelled to cross the Potomac and proceed on the Maryland side.

In terms of human habitation, too, it was a rough and disorderly landscape. Most inhabitants did not own land themselves but were slaves, indentured servants, or tenants. The thin layer of topsoil was quickly exhausted by growing tobacco. Settlers treated properties as disposable, often moving to fresh land after only a few successive seasons. The usual means of clearing fields was to girdle the larger trees, letting them stand until they died and burning the underbrush or piling it at the edges of new patches. Neither practice escaped the attention of foreign travelers, one of whom deplored the "awful ruins [of] vast limbs."[5] Most people chose to fence only their crops, letting pigs, cows, and sheep forage randomly everywhere else.

In the general disorder the houses were no more prepossessing than the fields around them. In 1781 Jefferson, in his *Notes on the State of Virginia*, wrote: "Private buildings are very rarely constructed of stone or brick; much the greatest proportion being scantling and boards, plastered with lime. It is impossible to devise things more ugly, uncomfortable, and happily more perishable."[6] Still prevalent in the region were so-called Virginia houses that lacked the more complex English-style frames and permanent masonry foundations. With their sills attached to posts set directly in the ground, such houses often required so many repairs as to be uninhabitable after only a decade. When Washington took over Mount Vernon in the 1750s, the surrounding landscape was dotted with these disposable houses, most of them unpainted and in various stages of decay.

Houses also tended to be quite small. Between 1721 and 1730 twenty-nine of the thirty-four wealthiest families in Virginia lived in dwellings with only one or two rooms on the ground floor and a loft above, squeezed in under the eaves.[7] Typically, a two-room house had an outer room with direct access to the outside. This was the hall, which had multiple functions, including eating, cooking, other kinds of indoor work, and informal entertaining. The smaller of the two rooms was the parlor, accessible through the hall and used variously for sleeping or receiving guests more formally. A stairway in one of the rooms led to the loft.

Over time, as planter families organized interior space to better accommodate the pattern of their lives, the basic plan was enhanced by the addition of a passage between the two rooms. Because it generally contained both the door to the outside and the stairway, the passage controlled circulation within the house and made it possible to separate functions—and people—on a room-by-room basis. In time, the addition of another row of rooms behind the first further delineated the functions of spaces.[8]

Meanwhile, more and more of the workaday tasks of life were relegated to outbuildings. On large plantations these typically included not only kitchens but storerooms, dairies, stables, barns, tobacco sheds, corncribs, laundry houses, spinning houses, smitheries, quarters for slaves, laborers, and overseers, schoolhouses, privies, and even guest chambers. Whether the plantation was large or small, the outbuildings tended to surround the main house, in the words of a contemporary, "as a litter of pigs their mother"[9]—haphazardly, with little concern for order or symmetry.

It was in this landscape of small, dilapidated wooden buildings, scattered about amid dreary pine forests, burnt stumps, and wandering livestock, that Washington began to build. But the broader context also included developments in England, as well as some examples of housing in Virginia that departed dramatically from the norm.

"At home" across the ocean, an appropriate family "seat" had long been an essential badge of membership in the ruling class. Politically as well as socially the effect was to legitimize family power by simultaneously giving substance to its roots in the land and elevating it, on that foundation, to national political prominence. From the seventeenth century on, too, aristocratic houses and their appendages had increasingly reflected the taste for architectural classicism, with its emphasis on order and symmetry.

For the first hundred years of the colony's existence, none of this had much impact in Virginia. Society remained too fluid. But by the end of the first quarter of the eighteenth century, that had begun to change. A newly emergent gentry class was solidifying its power, and one of the ways its members chose to mark the new order of things was by building a different kind of house, one with clear antecedents in England. To be sure, the scale of things was different. There would be no tidewater Blenheims, no attempts to duplicate the enormous piles belonging to those in the premier ranks of Britain's aristocracy. Instead, it was the substantial sort of house favored by the prosperous British gentry that the "mansions" of the Virginia elite would most closely resemble. Still, in a world of one- or two-room earthfast houses, generally unpainted and often in poor condition, the houses of the colony's rising grandees, like William Byrd's Westover—

brick-built, foursquare, with symmetrically ordered facades, deep roofs, and flanking brick dependencies—spoke unmistakably of permanence and power.[10]

For the family of Gus Washington, however, there were to be no brick houses. In his hectic pursuit of the main chance, he had moved too often to establish a proper seat. He also lacked the means. At his death in 1743, none of his scattered ventures had reached maturity.

Therefore it fell to his heirs to do what they could, which explains Washington's decision to rebuild Mount Vernon and what underlay it—his relentless, uncompromising determination to rise above the rank his family had achieved. Before 1758, the year the rebuilding began, his dreams had all been focused on military glory, but his failure to win a commission in the regular British army had dashed those hopes. In a sense, then, settling at Mount Vernon meant settling for second best. But if that was the hand fate had dealt him, he meant to play it to the hilt.

His brother Lawrence's house—the one George started with—was a story-and-a-half clapboard building, with four rooms on the ground floor and a central passage containing a stairway to the chambers above. Washington's first major change was to raise the roof of this structure, giving it a full second story. He also refinished most of the spaces on the ground floor. The room in the northwest corner, a bedchamber previously, became his best room, or parlor. To mark its importance, its walls were completely paneled, and its doors were capped with projecting pediments supported by fluted pilasters. A newly carved chimneypiece was also added. Copied from an English pattern book, it featured an inset landscape painting done in the manner of Claude Lorraine, above which appeared a carved rendering of the Washington coat of arms. Only slightly less elaborate was the dining room across the passage, the walls of which were covered with imported crimson, embossed English-made wallpaper.

On entering the house, however, one would have encountered the passage first, and it too was reworked, becoming notably grander and more formal. As in the parlor, paneled walls were punctuated with doorways topped by triangular pediments. And as the pièce de résistance of the passage, Lawrence's simple staircase was replaced with a much wider one, sweeping in three stages up to the new second story and richly embellished with a curved railing, turned spindles, and, trimming the stairwell, a wide band of carving done in a Greek key pattern.

To keep pace with these interiors, the outside of the building was also redressed. Though still the kind of wooden house decried by Jefferson in his Notes on Virginia, it now had the added conceit of a surface completely covered by beveled wooden boards, with sand thrown on the paint while it was still wet to make them resemble rusticated stonework. Thus did Washington seek to enlarge and formalize the structure he had inherited from his brother. If still not quite in the same category as great brick mansions like Westover, it at least resembled them more closely than before. Certainly no one would have doubted that it was the house of some one of consequence.

But to cut a proper figure in the world, a house needed more than just a heightened silhouette, elaborately paneled rooms, and an imposing facade. As important as what people saw was how they saw it—the total sequence of experiences that began the moment the house first came into view—and over the next decade Washington worked continuously to embellish and extend the approach leading to Mount Vernon.

One major decision in this regard had already been made, and that was where the principal entrance of the rebuilt house would be. Lawrence's best rooms—his parlor and dining room—had been on the east, or river side, of the house, almost certainly where his main entrance was as well. Because most travel in Virginia was still by water when he was building, that made sense. Yet Washington completely reversed this orientation, putting his best rooms and main entrance on the opposite side of the house, facing west. By then there was at least a rough road leading from the new town of Alexandria to Mount Vernon, but the change may have been as much symbolic as practical. Lawrence Washington had been educated in England; George was not. Except for a brief trip to Barbados, he never left the country of his birth, and it was the land that captured his imagination, not the sea. With his surveyor's eye he would remain fascinated with, and almost frantically eager to acquire, rich river bottomlands reaching far into the interior. His military experience also had been grounded in the forest wilderness of the backcountry. How fitting, then, that his Mount Vernon should face the land, should face west.

And there is yet another sense in which the altered orientation of the house might have seemed appropriate. How much bitterness Washington harbored because of his failure to receive a proper commission in the British army he alone knew, but indications are that it ran deep. Deep enough to strain his fundamental loyalty to "home"—to England and the entire system that had proved so ungenerous in dealing with "provincial" claims of preferment? No doubt such a question would have shocked him, but perhaps unwittingly in turning Mount Vernon's back on the river and beyond it the sea, he answered it anyway.

All the more reason, too, to make sure the approach to the rebuilt, re-

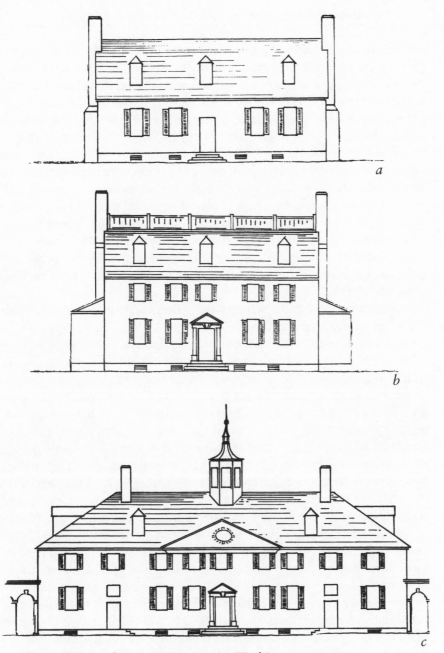

The evolution of Mount Vernon: *(a)* Washington spent part of his boyhood in this farmhouse, which he eventually inherited. *(b)* Washington began enlarging the house before marrying in 1759. *(c)* The final expansion, begun in 1774, was not completed until after the Revolution.

oriented house was properly done, and there the available models ran the gamut from the sublimely grandiose to the merely impressive. In France the landscape gardener Lenôtre had laid waste to entire villages and flattened the French countryside for miles around to provide Versailles with its huge parterres and geometrically precise allées radiating out from compasslike focal points. In England the gentry had compelled the land around their houses to conform to the prevailing taste for order and regularity with rigidly demarcated drives, gardens, fields, and parks. And the same ordering hand was evident on this side of the Atlantic, for example at Belvoir, the seat of the Fairfax family, which occupied the point of land just south of Mount Vernon. Although it burned down during the Revolution, archaeological evidence reveals a house thoroughly symmetrical in design, with an approach lined by brick walls connecting flanking dependencies, and elaborate gardens stretching in rectilinear uniformity to the edge of the bluff above the river.[11]

In each of these cases, compasses, rulers, and the surveyor's tools Washington had learned to use at an early age defined and organized the natural world, setting upon it the stamp of human will. But there was another model he could have turned to—one very different in conception. And as it happened, a book he had ordered from England soon after his marriage vigorously championed that model. The book was Batty Langley's *New Principles of Gardening*. Building on the work of landscape designer Lancelot "Capability" Brown and others, the "new principles" of Langley's title were in fact revolutionary, for they called for sweeping aside all those geometric, artificially delineated designs done in the French taste by Lenôtre et al. and putting in their place landscapes of rolling fields, random drifts of trees, meandering streams, and irregularly shaped ponds and lakes. The point was to have everything appear as natural as possible.

Even though Washington bought and owned Langley's book, in his initial landscaping efforts at Mount Vernon he chose to follow the more familiar models he knew from firsthand experience. Thus on either side of the rebuilt Mount Vernon, he added two symmetrically placed outbuildings to the two already there. Then in front of them he designed a pair of matching rectangular gardens, surrounded by palisaded brick walls, punctuated by octagonal wooden garden houses on brick foundations. And between the innermost garden walls, neatly bisecting the entire composition, ran the long drive up to the house.

Here was the geometry of symmetrically arranged rectangles, of straight lines intersecting at right angles, of space segmented and ordered axially. Carried throughout the house, this was the aesthetic that Washington chose

Mount Vernon, east front

Mount Vernon, west front

to project outward onto the land, forming a single, integrated composition—a wholly ordered, rational world—and one that spoke unequivocally of control, his control, over everything one saw moving up that long, straight drive to the house. Surprisingly enough, however, within a few years of finishing it all he was planning yet another set of changes—changes that would, in fact, radically alter the entire creation.

The immediate impetus for the new work seems to have been the death of Patsy Custis, Martha's daughter, which—as Washington interpreted the terms of the Custis estate—made it possible for him both to settle his debts with his London agent Robert Cary and to undertake what he described to Cary as "some repairs and alterations of my house."[12] Actually, the scope of the changes he had in mind went well beyond this rather modest description.

Once again he began with the house and moved outward from there. To the north and south large, two-story blocks would be added, extending the basic rectangular box of the building equally in both directions. The roofline above would terminate with sloping, "hipped" ends, and to dress up the west front of the house a central pediment would be projected outward from the main mass of the roof. The final flourish would be a cupola rising jauntily above the remade structure.

Taken together these changes seem to suggest Washington was intent on continuing as he had begun—on making a house he had already enlarged once larger still and endowing it even more emphatically with elements of order, symmetry, and classical style. Yet ultimately the changes he made moved in a very different direction.

The first hint would be evident as soon as one arrived at the west front of the house. In enlarging the central structure, Washington had no choice but to rebuild the outbuildings immediately adjacent to it. His solution was to construct a new kitchen to the south and what he called a "servant's hall" to the north, and connect them to the house with curving quadrant arms. This was a standard device in British neo-Palladian architectural design, and Mount Airy, a house Washington knew well, provided a memorable example of it in Virginia. But Washington did one thing with his quadrant arms, or "covered ways" as he called them, that none of the available models did. He reduced their sidewalls to a series of open arches, thereby minimizing their bulk and making of them something beguilingly light and airy.

The most interesting thing about the quadrant arms, however, is that in opening them up as he did, Washington provided glimpses of the river from the entrance front of the house, which otherwise masked the view to the east. Thus he was blending formal architectural structures with the natural landscape. Indeed, he was not just blending the two; he was fusing them, which represented a sharp departure from his strategy in the first rebuilding of the house, where architecture and a highly formalized landscape design had worked together to set the house and grounds apart from the surrounding natural world.

And the union of architecture and nature previewed in the covered ways would be even more strikingly evident in Washington's single greatest architectural innovation at Mount Vernon: the piazza. Formed by a flat extension of the roof supported by eight slender wooden pillars, the piazza rose a full two stories and rimmed the entire east or river front of the house. Porches were just beginning to be used in America at the time, but Washington could have seen nothing conceived on this scale, or at any rate diligent research has failed to uncover any even vaguely similar examples.

One thing the piazza was most definitely not was a classical-style portico, a temple front framing a grand entrance, which was the standard way architects used pillars and columns. Instead Washington placed his piazza at the rear of the house, where its primary function was to provide a vantage point from which to view Mount Vernon's greatest asset—the sweeping panorama of the Potomac as it rounded the promontory on which the house stood. Once again, in short, the purpose was to fuse architecture and nature. Unlike the controlled spaces in the interior of the house, too, the piazza was remarkably open in a social sense. One could come and go to it freely, either from outdoors or through any one of three doors leading from the house. All of which, in turn, made it ideal for informal entertaining. Indeed, for most visitors to Mount Vernon, the piazza would remain the most appealing, the most memorable part of the house.

The piazza also solved a problem created by the rapidly shifting currents in the fashionable taste of the day. In England after the first quarter of the eighteenth century, neo-Palladian architectural style reigned supreme, and the growing fashion for naturalistic landscape design of the Capability Brown school was thought by the tastemakers of the time to provide an appealing contrast to it when the two were used together. But in the mundane context of everyday life, the same contrast could become problematic. The formality of the architecture seemed to demand a corresponding formality of furniture and dress, whereas the informality of the landscape called for something quite different. Hence the odd, and to our eyes rather silly spectacle—when we discover it in eighteenth-century paintings—of aristocratic ladies and gentlemen sitting, dressed in silks and satins, in straight-backed chairs, in appropriately rustic landscapes, drinking tea or otherwise disporting themselves.[13] At Mount Vernon, on the other hand, the formal and the informal could and did meet comfortably on the piazza. Fusing architecture and nature, blending formality and informality, it was a uniquely accommodating space.

Like the covered ways, the piazza was part of Washington's second rebuilding of Mount Vernon, and considering the timing of that rebuilding— and the originality of such details compared with the rather conventional character of the first rebuilding—it is interesting to speculate on what might have been going through his mind at the time. Arguably, he had no pressing need for the additional space that would be created by the additions to the house. He and Martha had never had children of their own, and one of her two children had just died and the other was about to marry. Why, then, bother to rebuild at all?

One answer could have been that Washington wished to mark symbolically the end of his indebtedness to Robert Cary in London, which Patsy Custis's death had made possible. But even more to the point, perhaps, these were the years of the steadily deepening quarrel between England and its North American colonies, a conflict in which Washington's loyalties never wavered. Can houses substitute for rebellions—or become extensions of them? It is a tantalizing possibility, certainly, suggesting that once again, as he had in his first rebuilding of the house, Washington was using architecture to assert his control over the world around him. The terms of the assertion had changed, however. Dominion was now to be established not by imposing one's will on the landscape but by achieving harmony with it.

Yet Washington's second rebuilding of Mount Vernon also incorporated any number of thoroughly conventional details, including the typical borrowings from English pattern books evident in things like the Palladian window at the north end of the house, the oval window in the pediment, and the design for that dining-room chimneypiece he wrote home about at the start of the Revolution.[14] So exactly how much emphasis the new aesthetic deserves is unclear, at least at this point. After the Revolution, however, there could be no doubt about the direction in which Washington was moving. With the conflict over, he opted unequivocally for that blending of architecture and nature which the covered ways and the piazza had hinted at so enticingly. And the key was what he did to the landscape itself.

During the war Washington had written home from the front at one point ordering groves of trees planted at either end of the house. Significantly, he was careful to state that he wanted the planting done "without any order or regularity."[15] But it was only after his return from the war that a comprehensive plan for relandscaping the grounds materialized. At its heart was a completely reworked approach to the mansion house, which began with the elimination of the long, straight central drive put in twenty years earlier. In its place two serpentine drives, commencing at a gate several hundred feet to the west, would meander toward the house in undulating curves, through groves of trees and shrubs planted in the same naturalistic manner as those at the ends of the house. In the center would be a shield-shaped, close-clipped lawn referred to as the bowling green. The flanking gardens and garden walls would be retained, but the walls would be extended westward in broad, sweeping curves.

The change could hardly have been more dramatic. Where once the house had stood out starkly against the surrounding landscape, now, tucked among the trees, it slipped in and out of view as one moved toward it. Gone was the surveyor's relentless insistence on straight lines and right angles. Instead one was invited to come upon Washington's home nestled in a leafy bower, sparkling with dappled sunlight and glimpses of distant vistas.

All of which, as it happens, was the height of fashion in 1785. But it would have been just as fashionable twenty years earlier, as Batty Langley's book on gardening proves. In his initial landscape plan for Mount Vernon, Washington chose to ignore Langley's advice; now he appeared ready to embrace wholeheartedly the gospel of naturalistic landscape design. Why the change?

Timing seems to have been crucial. Between the first and second landscape designs at Mount Vernon, the American Revolution intervened, and the Revolution also inserted itself between the planning of the second rebuilding of the house and the planning of the new, more naturalistic landscape that eventually came to surround it. What these sequences appear to suggest is that the Revolution—as it did on so many other fronts—worked a kind of sea change in the way Washington saw Mount Vernon. As a young man he had wanted it to appear as imposing as possible. On the eve of the Revolution, his motivation in that regard might have moderated a bit, but it was still strong enough to require yet another major increase in the house's size. Then the change, and what became a singularly imaginative use of landscape design to draw the house into its surroundings instead of thrusting it forward into view.

It was almost as if Washington arrived home after the Revolution, looked at the rebuilding that had been accomplished in his absence, and decided that it was altogether too grand for the hero of a conflict fought—

among other things—on behalf of the proposition that all men were created equal. That he was capable of thinking in such terms he himself made clear in corresponding with his friend Samuel Vaughan about a marble chimneypiece Vaughan had given him for the large new room at the north end of Mount Vernon. Writing Vaughan to let him know that the ten separate packing cases containing the disassembled chimneypiece had arrived, he commented wryly that the number of cases suggested the gift might well be "too elegant & too costly by far . . . for my . . . room and republican stile of living."[16]

The room due to receive the chimneypiece was itself something of a problem for Washington. Obviously planned as a space for large-scale entertaining, it had no doubt been modeled on the ballroom in the Governor's Palace in Williamsburg, which in turn had been added to the Palace in response to the growing fashion for such rooms in England. But what possible use could the hero of the American Revolution have for such a thing? The interior of the room remained unfinished when Washington returned from the Revolution, and at first he delayed doing anything at all about it. Then, when he finally found an artisan to do the work, he was careful to specify that he wanted it done "in a plain neat style; which independently of its being the present taste (as I am informed) is my choice."[17] And taking his cue from Washington, perhaps, John Rawlins, the artisan in question, deftly incorporated into the plaster decorations of the room agricultural motifs to evoke Mount Vernon's rural character and its owner's favorite pastimes in retirement. In other words, whatever could be done to reconcile the room to Washington's republican consciousness and conscience was done. But to the end of his life he persisted in referring to the room simply as the "new room"—in effect denying what he had surely envisioned as its function when he planned it in the years before the Revolution.

To shape the landscape as he did, then—to use it to soften, even diminish, the impression Mount Vernon made—was of a piece with Washington's general desire to use his physical surroundings at home to objectify his commitment to republican principles. In the context of the life he led at Mount Vernon after the Revolution, too, such an effort must have seemed particularly appropriate. For a central feature of that life was the steady stream of visitors who found their way to his doorstep to see the great man in retirement. Some were merely curious, not a few were strangers, but Washington felt compelled to welcome them all. Convinced that the voluntary laying down of power—which his several retirements represented—

was an essential part of republican political life, he meant to demonstrate that he could indeed find contentment in the quiet pursuits of private life. His visitors were to carry that message to the world at large, and Mount Vernon provided the stage on which it was dramatized.

Nor is it easy to imagine a better one. The house was large, beautifully sited, and appropriately graced with classical detail. If built to impress, it nonetheless managed to avoid outright ostentation, and on the river front, with the piazza, it turned its face to the world in a strikingly open and airy way. Such was Washington's "vine and fig tree," under which, borrowing biblical imagery, he liked to picture himself in retirement. But if he had reason to be pleased with what he and Mount Vernon achieved together in retirement, there remained one persistent problem, which, try as he might, he seemed utterly unable to solve.

That problem was slavery. Washington had begun voicing privately his opposition to slavery during the Revolution, and his feelings on the subject grew stronger year by year. He objected to it on moral grounds; he also found it, as a system of labor, hopelessly inefficient. Among the earliest glimpses we have of him as plantation master is a diary entry in which he describes himself, pocket watch in hand, timing his slave carpenters while they hewed rough lumber out of poplar logs. By his calculation they produced four times as much when he was watching as they did when he was not.[18] As maddening as this seemed, over the years he worked out an explanation for the problem. Writing Arthur Young, the noted British agricultural reformer in 1792, he remarked that because slaves had no chance to earn "a *good* name," they cared too little about earning a bad one.[19] In other words, they worked poorly not because of any inherent incapacity but because they had no incentive to do otherwise.

Obviously the answer was to replace slave labor with free labor. But what would happen to the slaves if that were done? Washington was, as he described himself, "principled against selling Negroes, as you would cattle in the market."[20] And if the slaves were simply to be let go, where would the free labor needed to operate Mount Vernon come from? Was it even possible to imagine life there without slavery?

During Washington's years as president, these questions preyed on his mind with particular urgency, for he knew full well that when he had served his time in office he would be returning home, almost certainly for the remainder of his life. He even went so far as to try to find tenants to lease parts of the plantation and employ his slaves as free agricultural laborers.[21] But the tenants never materialized, leaving him when he finally returned to Mount Vernon in 1797 precisely where he had been eight years earlier when he left. As if he had never been away, too, the steady stream of visitors resumed, yet the servants who greeted them and waited on them at the table and the field hands who grew the food that they ate remained slaves. Plainly, if that was ever to change, only the boldest of measures would do it. Thus developed the third and final stage of Mount Vernon's evolution—the point, early in the summer of 1799, when, breaking his usual routine, Washington closeted himself in his study day after day, with no one to advise or assist him, drafting his will.

The result is as interesting and significant as anything he ever wrote. In the first place he did what he had long dreamed of doing: he freed his slaves. And he went further than simple manumission, carefully stipulating that those freed slaves too old or too young to be independent should be supported by the estate as long as necessary. The young were also to be provided with "some useful occupation," and they were to be taught to read and write.[22]

Unquestionably, the fact that Washington chose to free his slaves remains the most striking feature of his will. Yet precisely because it was such a dramatic step, it is easy to miss the extent to which that single act functioned as part of a larger design. For in freeing his slaves, Washington established a pattern, one he followed consistently throughout the will. It is this, finally, that makes the document so extraordinary.

Altogether he had close to a million dollars' worth of real estate and personal property to dispose of, a huge sum for that day. Even divided in two or three portions it would have made any person lucky enough to inherit one very rich. Washington had never fathered children of his own, but he and Martha had informally adopted two of her grandchildren. There were also some two dozen nieces and nephews of his own blood to choose from among. Yet in the end he settled the issue by singling out none of his prospective heirs to serve as primary beneficiaries. Instead he directed that the bulk of his property (mostly land in the West) should be sold, with the proceeds divided into equal shares to be distributed among all those nieces and nephews and step-grandchildren.

So at Washington's express direction there were to be no big winners. Rather he had chosen equality as his standard. To be sure, it could be argued that such a solution was only fair; that no one of his beneficiaries had more of a claim on him than the others. But giving fairness priority over everything else was hardly the norm in his society. Strategies for preserving family wealth had long since been raised to a minor art form in Virginia, and the usual pattern was to treat heirs unequally in order to achieve that goal.[23]

Almost certainly if Washington had had children of his own his will would have been different. But precisely because he was not constrained in that way he had the opportunity to make it, if he chose, something different—to make, in fact, a statement of principle. Did it represent, then, a settled conviction about the way things ought to be arranged in general: equality combined with freedom, as the touchstones of a new American social order? Surely this is the most fascinating possibility of all. And though we can never be sure what Washington was thinking, the way he chose to treat Mount Vernon in his will could well hold the key to the puzzle.

The provisions for Mount Vernon were different from those for the rest of the property. Washington's home was not to be part of the general division into equal shares. Yet that did not mean Mount Vernon would remain intact. Rather, there was to be another division, this time into three parts, to be distributed among five individuals. Bushrod Washington, one of the nephews, got the mansion house and half the land, but he was given no money—or slaves, of course—to maintain his inheritance. Nor was there any attempt made to keep the contents of the house together. On the contrary, Washington left express instructions for distributing all the items most intimately associated with him—his shaving mirror and dressing table, his desk and chair, his telescope, his pistols, his swords, the gold-headed cane Benjamin Franklin had left him in his will—each to a different person.

So piece by piece Mount Vernon was to be taken apart, its lands divided, its slaves freed, and its contents scattered. Today, thanks to the efforts of the Mount Vernon Ladies' Association, we know it as a hauntingly evocative monument to the man, with many of the crucial items back in place. But such a possibility seems to have been the farthest thing from Washington's mind. Or if it did occur to him, he did everything imaginable to prevent it from happening. Mount Vernon was his home; he had spent a lifetime improving and embellishing it. Still, when the time came he chose not to preserve it, just as he chose not to preserve his personal wealth and not to hold his slaves in bondage any longer. If he wanted a monument, apparently Mount Vernon was not the monument he wanted.

But the real issue here is not monument building, or even preservation. The real issue is perpetuation. With every opportunity to do so, Washington had chosen unequivocally not to project forward into the future his personal world, with all its intricately encoded emblems of status and power. Instead he had chosen to disassemble that world. This is where life under his vine and fig tree had ended; this was the final stamp he meant to leave on Mount Vernon. Knowing full well what it had taken to shape the place to suit his purposes, he now proposed to let it slip into decay—as surely it would, without land or labor to sustain it—amid that leafy bower of greenery he had caused to grow around it. His dominion no longer, it would become—once again, fully and finally—nature's.

Notes

1. GW to Lund Washington, Aug. 20, 1775, *PGW: Rev. Ser.* 1:337.
2. This summary and much of the ensuing analysis are drawn from the authors' *George Washington's Mount Vernon: At Home in Revolutionary America* (New York and Oxford, 1998). For an excellent brief account of the development of GW's home, see also Dennis J. Pogue, "Mount Vernon: Transformation of an Eighteenth-Century Plantation System," in *Historical Archaeology of the Chesapeake,* ed. Paul A. Shackel and Barbara J. Little (Washington, D.C., 1994), 101–14. More detailed information on design and construction can be found in the fine "Historic Structure Report," prepared for the Mount Vernon Ladies' Association by Mesick, Cohen, Waite, Architects, MSS (1993), MTVL.
3. Freeman, *Washington* 1:10–14.
4. "Observations Made during a Short Residence in Virginia in Letter from Thomas H. Palmer, May 31, 1814," quoted in Camille Wells, "The Eighteenth-Century Landscape of Virginia's Northern Neck," *Northern Neck of Virginia Historical Magazine* 37 (1987): 4224.
5. Thomas Anburey, *Travels through the Interior Parts of America,* quoted in ibid., 4225.
6. Thomas Jefferson, *Notes on the State of Virginia,* ed. William Peden (1955; New York, 1982), 152.
7. Dell Upton, "Vernacular Domestic Architecture in Eighteenth-Century Virginia," in *Common Places: Readings in American Vernacular Architecture,* ed. Dell Upton and John Michael Vlach (Athens, Ga., 1986), 317.
8. For the changing functions of rooms in eighteenth-century Virginia houses, see ibid., 313–35, and Fraser D. Neiman, "Domestic Architecture at Cliffs Plantation: The Social Context of Early Virginia Building," also in Upton and Vlach, *Common Places,* 294–307.
9. Benjamin Henry Latrobe, *The Journal of Latrobe,* quoted in Wells, "Landscape of Virginia's Northern Neck," 4230.
10. The most extensive treatment of eighteenth-century Virginia houses of the grander sort is Daniel D. Reiff, *Small Georgian Houses in England and Virginia: Origins and Development through the 1750s* (London, 1986). Other studies offering significant interpretive insights are Richard L. Bushman, *The Refinement of America: Persons, Houses, Cities* (New York, 1992); Mills Lane, *Architecture*

of the Old South: Virginia (New York, 1989); Dell Upton, *Holy Things and Profane: Anglican Parish Churches in Colonial Virginia* (New York and Cambridge, Mass., 1986); Rhys Isaac, *The Transformation of Virginia, 1740–1790* (Chapel Hill, N.C., 1982); Henry Glassie, *Folk Housing in Middle Virginia: A Structural Analysis of Historical Artifacts* (Knoxville, Tenn., 1975); William H. Pierson, *American Buildings and Their Architects: The Colonial and Neo-Classical Styles* (Garden City, N.Y., 1970); and Thomas Waterman, *Mansions of Virginia, 1706–1776* (Chapel Hill, N.C., 1946).

11. For a description and conjectural drawings of Belvoir, see Kenton Kilmer and Donald Sweig, *The Fairfax Family in Fairfax County: A Brief History* (Fairfax, Va., 1975), 30, and Waterman, *Mansions of Virginia,* 330–32.

12. GW to Robert Cary, Oct. 6, 1773, *PGW: Col. Ser.* 9:343.

13. See, for example, the works of Arthur Devis pictured in Ellen D'Oench, *The Conversation Piece: Arthur Devis and His Contemporaries* (New Haven, 1980).

14. Mesick, Cohen, Waite, "Historic Structure Report," provides a good general account of the use of printed architectural sources at Mount Vernon. For a more thoroughgoing analysis, see Scott Campbell Owen, "George Washington's Mount Vernon as British Palladian Architecture" (M.A. thesis, School of Architecture, University of Virginia, 1991).

15. GW to Lund Washington, Aug. 19, 1776, *PGW: Rev. Ser.* 6:84–85.

16. GW to Samuel Vaughan, Feb. 5, 1785, *PGW: Conf. Ser.* 2:326.

17. GW to John Rawlins, Aug. 29, 1785, ibid., 3:207–8.

18. *PGW: Diaries* 1:232–33.

19. GW to Arthur Young, June 18–21, 1792, *GW: Writings* 32:65–66.

20. GW to Alexander Spotswood, Nov. 13, 1794, ibid., 34:47–48.

21. See Dalzell and Dalzell, *George Washington's Mount Vernon,* 212–15.

22. For GW's will, see John C. Fitzpatrick, ed., *The Last Will and Testament of George Washington and Schedule of His Property, to Which Is Appended the Last Will and Testament of Martha Washington* (Mount Vernon, Va., 1939), and *PGW: Ret. Ser.* 4:477–511.

23. Holly Brewer, "Entailing Aristocracy in Colonial Virginia: 'Ancient Feudal Restraints' and Revolutionary Reform," *WMQ* 54 (1999): 307–46.

5. "That Species of Property"

Washington's Role in the Controversy over Slavery

Dorothy Twohig

Although both Jefferson and Washington were lifelong slaveholders, as were the previous generations of Washingtons in Virginia, the master of Mount Vernon has scarcely received a fraction of the criticism on the subject that has fallen on Jefferson since the 1960s. Jefferson spoke eloquently on the evils of the peculiar institution, especially in his Notes on the State of Virginia, *his only book. Washington said less about slavery, and what he said was expressed privately. There is no reason to think that either man thought that Africans, if free and given opportunities to advance, could have become the intellectual equals of whites. At least a handful of Americans saw that as a possibility, including Alexander Hamilton and Benjamin Franklin. Jefferson's critics rightly see inconsistency between his words and deeds, not only in his eloquent phrases about the evils of human bondage but, equally significant, in his efforts to promote his image as a champion of liberty. Washington never claimed to be a spokesman for human rights; besides, it was Jefferson who principally wrote the Declaration of Independence. Washington did free his slaves, as provided in his will. And there has never been, to date at least, creditable evidence that he fathered slave children at Mount Vernon. Although both the British during the War of Independence and the Republicans in the 1790s spread scurrilous stories about Washington's private life, the rumors died almost as quickly as they appeared. Jefferson, on the other hand, suffered genuine embarrassment over newspaperman James Callender's accusations that he had several children by his slave Sally Hemings. In the last twenty-five years, two scholars, Fawn Brodie in 1974 and Annette Gordon-Reed in 1996, produced serious if controversial books that pointed to the strong probability of Jefferson's paternity of the Hemings children. The year 1999 brought DNA testing to the subject. According to the results, Jefferson probably sired at least one of these offspring. And, of course, Jefferson's will provided only for manumitting Hemingses.*

Dorothy Twohig is former editor-in-chief of The Papers of George Washington *and editor of the one-volume edition of* George Washington's Diaries: An Abridgment. *She is associate professor emeritus at the University of Virginia.*

IN 1796 GEORGE WASHINGTON received a letter from Edward Rushton, a prominent English antislavery advocate. It was hardly the polite, respectful missive that the president of the United States normally received.

> It will generally be admitted, Sir, and perhaps with justice, that the great family of mankind were nevermore benefited by the military abilities of any individual, than by those which you displayed during the American contest. . . . By the flame which you have kindled every oppressed nation will be enabled to perceive its fetters. . . . But it is not to the commander in chief of the American forces, nor to the president of the United States, that I have ought to address. My business is with George Washington of Mount Vernon in Virginia, a man who not withstanding his hatred of oppression and his ardent love of liberty holds at this moment hundreds of his fellow being in a state of abject bondage—Yes: you who conquered under the banners of freedom—you who are now the first magistrate of a free people are (strange to relate) a slave holder. . . . Shame! Shame! That man should be deemed the property of man or that the name of Washington should be found among the list of such proprietors. . . . Ages to come will read with Astonishment that the man who was foremost to wrench the rights of America from the tyrannical grasp of Britain was among the last to relinquish his own oppressive hold of poor unoffending negroes. In the name of justice what can induce you thus to tarnish your own well earned celebrity and to impair the fair features of American liberty with so foul and indelible a blot.[1]

In his disillusion with what he regarded as Washington's lack of political courage, Edward Rushton spoke not only for his fellow opponents of slavery but for scores of later critics of the South's peculiar institution. To historians of succeeding generations not only Washington's ownership of slaves but his failure to speak out publicly against slavery in the face of his own growing opposition to the institution or to bring the weight of his enormous prestige to bear against it has sometimes eclipsed his reputation as the first man of his age. Why did he not from the platform of his enormous prestige and public veneration speak out publicly against a system that his private correspondence reveals he had gradually come to regard with distaste and apprehension? Virtually all of Washington's comments on slavery were expressed privately. On no occasion did he reveal publicly his own antipathy toward the institution or his privately expressed hopes that it would either wither naturally or be abolished by legislative action. On a less emotionally charged issue Washington's silence would call for little comment because he rarely expressed publicly his views on other controversial issues. His reticence in general on public matters was a matter of considerable discussion during his presidency. In fact, en route to his role of American icon Washington had developed a quality rare among American politicians of any era. He had learned from painful experience as early as his service in command of the Virginia Regiment during the French and Indian War that it would not be necessary to retract or explain or apologize later for what he had not said in the first place. By the time he reached the presidency, it had become habit. Washington remained throughout his career very conscious of the speed with which both public and private sectors could turn on their unsuccessful servants. John Adams noted that Washington had "the gift of silence." Whatever difficulties this attribute has created for historians, it contributed immensely to his reputation for wisdom. On slavery, as on many other matters, later generations can only interpret Washington's views from the meager private comments he made on the institution and conjecture the reasons for his public silence.

During the pre-Revolutionary years Washington's views toward slavery were conventional, reflecting those of a typical Virginia planter of his time. If he was perhaps more concerned than some planters with his slaves' welfare, his principal interest was still their contribution to the economic life of the plantation. His slave inventories indicate the number of slaves employed at Mount Vernon at various times: in 1759 he owned 24 slaves under the age of sixteen; in 1786 he owned slightly over 100 slaves on his own, with 113 dower slaves; in 1799 there were 164 Washington slaves and 153 dower slaves.[2] Partly because it was to his advantage to do so, he paid considerable attention to his slaves' welfare. Washington, like many Virginia planters, was deeply involved in their lives. "It is foremost in my thoughts," he wrote his Mount Vernon manager in 1792, "to desire you will be particularly attentive to my Negros in their sickness; and to order every Overseer positively to be so likewise; for I am sorry to observe that the generality of them, view these poor creatures in scarcely any other light than they do a draughthorse or Ox; neglecting them as much when they are unable to work; instead of comforting & nursing them when they lye on a sickbed."[3]

Scholarly research into the conditions of slavery on the Mount Vernon plantations is just beginning and may well reveal serious discrepancies between what Washington said and what actually happened. It appears, however, from his correspondence with his managers that as a matter of plantation policy, Washington did not want slaves worked when they were ill and provided competent medical care for them when they were ailing. Food, clothing, and housing seem to have been at least adequate; even though families often worked on separate plantations, they were not separated by sale or purchase. There are such occasional exceptions as Washington's acceptance in 1775, in settlement for a debt, of a slave in Maryland who put up a spirited resistance to being separated from his family.[4] Before the Revolution, Washington may have sold the occasional slave, but he had mixed feelings about the procedure. As he wrote his manager early in 1779, in spite of his "reluctance in offer these people at public venue . . . if these poor wretches are to be held in a State of Slavery I do not see that a change of masters will render it more irksome, provided husband & wife, and Parents & children are not separated from each other, which is not my intention to do."[5]

In both his military and political life, Washington adopted generally a hands-on policy, and this carried over to his management of Mount Vernon. Except for his long absences during the war and the presidency, Washington managed his own plantations and was well acquainted with the strengths and weaknesses of individual slaves. He was not impressed with them as a labor force. There are frequent comments in his correspondence with his managers on their irresponsibility and indolence, although he believed their poor work habits to be a result of the system itself. As early as 1778 his correspondence indicates his disillusion with the system. Writing his manager Lund Washington from White Plains during the Revolution, he expressed his hope to exchange slaves for land. "I had rather give Negroes—if Negroes would do. for to be plain I wish to get quit of Negroes."[6] It was, he felt, a system that prevented the best use of new farming methods and machinery and hindered agricultural progress. His correspondence with his white managers contains stern instructions concerning the role slaves were to play in specific aspects of the farming of the estate and on the dire consequences of dereliction of duty. But on his journeys home, especially during the presidency, it is evident that personal appeals and complaints from his slaves frequently mitigated his demands. Indeed, Washington's erratic mixture of sternness and indulgence inevitably created a certain amount of chaos in plantation management.[7]

Although he appreciated the inefficiency of the institution, there is little evidence that the moral and ethical considerations of slavery troubled Washington to any considerable degree before the Revolution. In 1772 he was a member of the House of Burgesses when it drafted a petition to the throne labeling the importation of slaves into the colonies from the coast of Africa "a trade of great inhumanity" that would endanger the "very existence of your Majesty's American dominions." And two years later he was certainly involved in the composition of the July 1774 Fairfax Resolves, one of which recommended that no slaves should be imported into the British colonies. The resolutions took the opportunity of "declaring our most earnest Wishes to see an entire Stop forever put to such a wicked cruel and unnatural Trade."[8] On the other hand, in 1772 Washington himself purchased five additional slaves for use on his plantations.

When he assumed command of the army at Cambridge in June 1775, Washington for the first time faced the necessity of creating some kind of public policy regarding slaves, free blacks, and the recruiting policies of the Continental army. Like most southerners he had strong objections to using blacks as soldiers. And, again like most southerners, he was too conscious of the possibility of slave revolts to look easily upon the distribution of guns into the hands of slaves. His initial reluctance was bolstered by a long colonial tradition of prohibiting slaves to bear arms. On November 12, 1775, he signed orders excluding blacks together with underage boys and old men as recruits for service because they would be "unfit to endure the fatigues of the campaign."[9] After Lord Dunmore's proclamation of November 7, 1775, encouraging indentured servants and free blacks to enlist in British service, Virginia blacks began to flee to British lines in the mistaken belief that British views on slavery differed from those of the slaves' Virginia masters. Most slaves and free blacks who fled to the British continued to be employed in a service capacity, chiefly working as military laborers.[10] The emergence of Dunmore's plan to enlist slaves and offer them their freedom and Washington's own desperate need for men in the aftermath of failed recruiting policies and massive desertions forced him and Congress to reconsider their initial positions at least in regard to free blacks. In fact, early in the war an important distinction came to be made in recruiting policies between slaves and free blacks. By the end of December 1775, Washington had altered his views to accommodate the situation, issuing orders that because "Numbers of free Negroes are desirous of inlisting, he gives leave to the recruiting Officers, to entertain them, and promises to lay the matter before the Congress, who he doubts not will approve of it."[11] By 1778 Washington went so far as to permit Joseph Varnum of Rhode Island to raise a battalion of African Americans. Washington continued to use former slaves in a number of more menial capacities during the course of the war. That he retained his prewar opinions on the unreliability of slave labor is indicated by his suggestion to Congress that although blacks should be hired to solve the difficulty of obtaining waggoners, the recruits should be freemen and not slaves, which "could not be sufficiently depended on. It is to be apprehended that they would too frequently desert to the enemy to obtain their liberty; and for the profit of it, or to conciliate a more favorable reception, would carry off their waggon-horses with them."[12]

In 1778 and 1779 John Laurens of South Carolina, one of Washington's aides-de-camp, with the qualified approval of his father, Henry Laurens, concocted a scheme to persuade the legislatures of South Carolina and Georgia to raise several battalions of slaves for service in the army, rewarding them with their freedom in exchange for their services. Washington, fond of his young aide, gave very guarded approval to the project. "The policy of our arming slaves is in my opinion a moot point, unless the enemy set the example," he wrote Henry Laurens. "I am not clear that a discrimination will not render Slavery more irksome to those who remain in it—Most of the good and evil things of this life are judged of by comparison, and I fear comparison in this Case will be productive of Much discontent in those, who are held in servitude—but as this is a subject that has never employed much of my thoughts, these are no more than the first crude Ideas that have struck me upon the occasion."[13] Washington was well aware of the dismay with which the plan would be received by southern slaveholders. That his reservations were justified is evidenced by the fact that the anger of South Carolina's leaders over the resolutions passed in Congress approving the scheme led to the threat that South Carolina would remain neutral during the war. When Laurens's scheme eventually failed, Washington was not surprised. "That Spirit of Freedom which at the commencement of this contest would have gladly sacrificed every thing to the attainment of its object has long since subsided, and every selfish Passion has take its place—it is not the public but the private Interest which influences the generality of Mankind nor can the Americans any longer boast an exception—under these circumstances, it would rather have been surprizing if you had succeeded."[14]

At the end of the war, Washington made halfhearted efforts to send back slaves who had run away from their masters to enlist and to order courts of inquiry for those who were now claimed by their masters. In 1783 when the British embarked from New York, he objected to British plans to take with them bondsmen who had served with the king's army, arguing that the provisional articles of peace prohibited such removal. He did on occasion exhibit some care that blacks enlisted in Continental and state regiments not be summarily repossessed by unscrupulous former owners. On the other hand, he approached one of the agents overseeing the embarkation of the British from New York, contending that some of his own slaves and those of his wartime manager Lund Washington might be in New York, and enlisted the agent's aid in seeking their return.[15]

Generally speaking, during the war Washington had taken great care to give the impression that he considered the military subservient to civilian authority in suggesting changes in policy. But if, at this stage of his career, he had entertained convictions about slavery strong enough to deviate from this position, his best opportunity presented itself when in his closing circular to the governors of the states—probably, except for the Farewell Address, his best-known public document—he abandoned his usual deferential posture toward civilian authority to issue what was in effect his final policy statement. In announcing to the states his resignation as commander in chief, he presented a vista of the limitless opportunities available to the new nation, advocated the establishment of an "indissoluble Union of the states under one Federal Head," and warned that according to the policies the states "shall adopt at this moment, they will stand or fall. . . . It is yet to be decided, whether the Revolution must ultimately be considered as a blessing or a curse . . . [and] not to the present age alone, for with our fate will the destiny of unborn Millions be involved." In the circular there is no mention of slavery per se or of its impact on the nature of the new Republic, except for a vague injunction that it was essential to the "well being" of the United States that its citizens forget their local prejudices and policies, make concessions necessary for the general good, and be willing, "in some instances, to sacrifice their individual advantages to the interest of the Community."[16]

Washington returned to Mount Vernon in time for Christmas in 1783, determined to enjoy a quiet life on his plantation. He was charmed with the idea that he had returned, as he said on more than one occasion, to his "vine and fig tree"—to the cultivation of his acres. "I am now a private

Citizen on the banks of the Potomac," he wrote in 1784, "meditating amidst Frost & snow . . . upon the structure of walks for private life."[17] Contemporary views of Washington were, as some of his biographers have noted, beginning to constitute a kind of secular religion. Although his incoming correspondence and the steady stream of foreign and domestic visitors to Mount Vernon in the postwar years kept him very well informed as to the state of the new nation (and his comments on political affairs, especially the need for a stronger union, are frequently frank and critical), he deliberately refrained from taking public positions on specific issues. But if Washington sincerely believed that he would be able to withdraw from public life, he underestimated the role he had been drafted to play in the new Republic.

Mount Vernon was always his passion, and he had endless plans for its improvement and adornment and for the increase of its acreage. When he returned to managing his plantations himself in 1784, his already low opinion of the deficiencies of the slave system were immediately confirmed. His own problems with slave labor at Mount Vernon made him well aware of the inefficiencies of the system, but at least some of his growing opposition is attributable to the principles of the Revolutionary War years, with their emphasis on the rights and responsibilities of men. One can only speculate how much this contributed to his meager comments on slavery during the 1780s. Occasional remarks reveal his changing attitudes toward the system. He wrote John Francis Mercer in September 1786, "I never mean (unless some particular circumstance should compel me to it) to possess another slave by purchase; it being among my first wishes to see some plan adopted by the legislature, by which slavery in this Country may be abolished by slow, sure & imperceptible degrees." In the same year he wrote of slavery to his friend Robert Morris, "I can only say, that there is not a man living who wishes more sincerely than I do, to see a plan adopted for the abolition of it—but there is only one proper and effectual mode by which it can be accomplished, & that is by Legislative authority; and this as far as my suffrage will go, shall never be wanting."[18] Oddly, in view of his obsession with the West, Washington seems not to have devoted much consideration to the possibility of expanding slavery to the frontier or to have regarded the abundance of land to the west as a solution to the wasteful results of slave cultivation in the East.

When Lafayette, an outspoken opponent of the system, wrote Washington from France in 1783 suggesting they cooperate in an experimental settlement for freed slaves, Washington responded cordially, as he always did to Lafayette, but without committing himself to any course of action.

Lafayette proposed that he and Washington "Unite in Purchasing a Small Estate Where We May try the Experiment to free the Negroes, and Use them only as tenants. Such an Example as Yours Might Render it a General Practice." In February 1786 Lafayette informed Washington that he had bought a plantation in Cayenne for a "Hundred And twenty five thousand French livres . . . and am going to free my Negroes in order to Make that Experiment which you know is My Hobby Horse." Washington praised the project, writing, "Would to God a like spirit would diffuse itself generally into the minds of the people of this country, but I dispair of seeing it. . . . To set them afloat at once would, I really believe, be productive of much inconvenience & mischief; but by degrees it certainly might, & assuredly ought to be effected & that too by Legislative authority." Yet in the end he lent Lafayette only moral support.[19] Washington seems to have been little impressed by the embryonic colonization movement. His lack of enthusiasm may have resulted partly from the fate of the settlement of free blacks in Nova Scotia after the Revolution and in Sierra Leone on the West African coast during the 1780s and 1790s.[20]

It is evident that Washington expressed his private opinions rather widely. Francis Asbury, first bishop of the Methodist Church in America, for example, visited Mount Vernon in 1785 and noted in his diary that General Washington had given his visitors "his opinion against slavery."[21] But whatever his changing views, Washington, like many of his antislavery contemporaries, still let his own economic interests rule when they interfered with his principles. Not only did he still need slaves to work his own plantation, he must have been at least somewhat aware that much of the golden age of economic and social expansion in the Chesapeake had rested on black bondsmen. Washington himself was an avid partaker in the anglicization of Chesapeake society with its emphasis on creature comforts and the acquisition of consumer goods, much of which was dependent on a slave economy.[22] In fact, it is difficult to discern from his meager comments whether Washington's disgust with slavery rested on moral grounds (although there are some indications that this was so) or primarily on the grounds of the institution's economic inefficiencies. Although he probably never exposed his sentiments to the wrenching self-examination that Jefferson did, it is reasonable to project to Washington at least some of Jefferson's painful attempts to justify the inconsistencies of preaching freedom for the rebelling colonies and still defend the fetters that kept another race enslaved. Jefferson's moral struggles, even if, as Bernard Bailyn suggests, they led him into a reluctant and apologetic racism, are more enlightening than Washington's, if only because we know more about them.[23] Washington cut back sharply on his purchases of slaves during the Confederation years, but he occasionally continued to acquire them. In 1786 he accepted five slaves in payment for a debt owed him by the Mercer family, even though, as he wrote Mercer, "I have great repugnance to increasing my slaves by purchase." A little later he wrote Henry Lee requesting that he purchase a bricklayer for him because "I have much work in this way to do this Summer."[24]

On April 16, 1789, Washington left Mount Vernon to begin his journey to New York City to assume the presidency. He went, he said, "to the chair of government" with "feelings not unlike those of a culprit who is going to the place of his execution, so unwilling am I, in the evening of a life nearly consumed in public cares, to quit a peaceful abode for an Ocean of difficulties."[25] Over the preceding months he had conducted an extensive correspondence with friends, countering their unanimous urging that he accept the presidency with his own agonizing reluctance to risk his hard-won reputation on the uncertainties of the new government.[26] All along the route to the capital, he passed through cheering throngs to whom he seemed the embodiment of the patriot leader. Gouverneur Morris probably echoed the views of most Americans when he wrote Washington in 1788 that "You alone can awe the Insolence of opposing Factions & the greater Insolence of assuming Adherents. . . . You will become a Father to more than three Millions of Children."[27] Washington brought with him from his service in the Revolution an unblemished reputation for honor and integrity, for being above the struggles of political life, for dedication to duty and to the state.[28] Both at home and abroad he was the man of the century.

Critics of Washington have insisted that if there was a time before the Civil War when slavery as an institution might have been successfully attacked, Washington could have seized this moment if he had given leadership to the antislavery forces. There is no indication that he ever considered any such course. No one understood better than he the fragility of the framework that bound the states together. During the Confederation years his faith in the new nation he had given almost ten years of his life to create had faltered. "I see," he wrote Lafayette, "one head gradually changing into thirteen." He confided to John Jay in 1786 that in his opinion virtue had "in a great degree, taken its departure from our Land." "We have probably had too good an opinion of human nature in forming our confederation," he wrote in the mid-1780s, adding that men would not "adopt & carry into execution, measures the best calculated for their own good without the intervention of a coercive power."[29] The convention of 1787 restored his optimism. "I begin to look forward," he wrote Sir Edward Newenham in 1788, "with a kind of political faith, to scenes of National happiness, which have not heretofore been offered for the fruition of the Most favoured Nations. The Natural, political, and Moral circumstances of our Nascent empire justify the anticipation."[30]

But Washington was a political realist. Presiding over the Constitutional Convention left him fully aware of the specter that slavery had presented at the convention. Although it had not seemed an important factor when sessions began in Philadelphia, by the end of the summer it had permeated every phase of the deliberations. In the convention the strongest supporters of the Constitution were willing to take a stand on matters they felt essential to the success of the enterprise—to the making of a new government; but, as Washington had observed, they were not willing to sink their ship by taking on North and South Carolina and Georgia on the subject of slavery. In many of the debates the delegates trod so delicately that they employed euphemisms to avoid even the use of the word; slaves were disguised as "persons" or "persons held to Service or Labour"; the slave trade became "migrations." Day after day Washington sat in the president's chair listening attentively to the debates, although there is no evidence he spoke out on slavery or indeed on many other matters.[31] The reception given to the strong antislavery speeches of Gouverneur Morris of New York and the diatribes against slavery by George Mason of Virginia were not lost on Washington. Delegates such as Charles C. Pinckney contended that "the property of the Southern States was to be as sacredly preserved, and protected to them, as that of land, or any other kind of property in the Eastern States were to be to their citizens." Property in slaves should not be exposed to danger under a government instituted for the protection of property. Even staunch supporters of the Constitution like Pierce Butler of South Carolina retrenched when slavery was threatened. "The security the Southern States want," Butler said, "is that their negroes may not be taken from them, which some gentlemen within or without doors have a very good mind to do."[32]

The experience of the convention may well have shown Washington that there would be little substantive support from antislavery spokesmen if he had decided to take a vigorous position on the question. As William Lee Miller has observed, when the New Englanders were needed at the convention to inject fortitude into the discussions on slavery, "New England was in the backrooms of the taverns making deals, and then on the floor of the convention prefacing its part in those deals by saying that of course it had never owned slaves and disapproved of the slave trade and knew slavery to be a moral evil."[33] In return for their support of the new government, the slave-owning southerners got most of what they wanted in the convention. The three-fifths clause gave them extra representation in Congress; the electoral college gave their votes for president more potency than the votes from the North; the prohibition on export taxes favored the products of slave labor; the slave trade clause guaranteed their right to import new slaves for at least twenty years; the fugitive slave clause gave slave owners the right to repossess runaway slaves in free states; in the event of a slave rebellion, the domestic violence clause promised the states federal aid. As Charles C. Pinckney pointed out in the South Carolina Ratifying Convention, "Considering all circumstances, we have made the best terms for the security of this species of property it was in our power to make. We would have made better if we could, but, on the whole, I do not think them bad."[34]

The climate of the presidential years proved equally unpromising. By the mid-1780s it was evident that the idealism of the 1770s had turned out to be an illusion. As Washington well knew, the last decades of the century witnessed a reversal in states like Virginia, where during the war there had been widespread public attacks on slavery and embryonic plans for the abolition of the institution. Proslavery petitions proliferated in Virginia; over twelve hundred signatures appeared in such petitions to the assembly, testifying to considerable opposition to manumission and to deepening hostility toward the antislavery activities of the Quakers, Methodists, and others. The Deep South tightened legislation regarding slaves. There were sporadic objections to slavery on moral grounds, some northerners pointing out as early as 1790 the immorality of aristocrats living off the sweat of their slaves. On occasion northern intellectuals may have espoused a free-labor ideology, but they failed to advance their cause by overt action. Even the North profited by slavery in terms of its economic connections with the South, and except for occasional lip service from societies to promote manumission, there was little mainstream opposition from that quarter.[35] In considering ratification of the Constitution, not one state which held a convention in the late 1780s introduced any amendment concerning slavery. And in fact there was little vocal support for the antislavery movement. Among Washington's peers, critics of slavery like Hamilton and Jay were active in manumission societies but offered few public comments. Madison, a lifelong opponent of the institution, confined his musings on the contradictions between the ideals of the Revolution and the existence of slavery to his memoranda. Jefferson made relatively few public statements on the institution, except for his agonized soul-searching concerning the eligibility of blacks for full citizenship.[36] Benjamin Franklin, especially through the Pennsylvania Abolition Society, gave more impressive leadership. Patrick Henry opposed slavery but kept his own slaves because, as he said, of the "general Inconvenience of living here without them."[37]

Washington was aware that organized opposition to slavery had never come from a wide spectrum of the population. Postwar clerical arguments against slavery had made little headway and less impact on southern owners. Certainly such mainstream questioning of the validity of the institution as did exist tended to center on the contention that slavery had been foisted by Great Britain on unwilling colonies who now had to deal with the resulting evils. Washington, like many others of his post-Revolutionary generation, still blamed Britain for hanging slavery around colonial necks.[38] Even the opposition itself was fragmented. Most of the opponents of slavery were Quakers and members of other benevolent religious groups, and slavery was only one of their interests. Early in the eighteenth century Quaker opponents of slavery had concentrated their efforts on the conditions of slavery and on the sect's religious duties toward the slaves. Not until the late 1760s and early 1770s was there strong opposition to the foreign and domestic slave trade, and recent research has suggested serious conflicts among Quakers regarding the freeing of slaves. Quakers generally shared Washington's strongest objection to the institution—that the buying and selling of slaves broke up families. The fact that by the end of the Revolution slaveholders had an enormous economic stake in the preservation of the institution while advocates of abolition had nothing to lose was certainly not lost on Washington.[39]

Washington shared the determination of most of his own generation of statesmen not to allow slavery to disturb their agenda for the new Republic. Antislavery sentiment came in a poor second when it conflicted with the powerful economic interests of proslavery forces. To Washington as to many Americans, even some whose opinions on slavery were far more radical than his own, the institution had become a subject so divisive that public comments were best left unsaid. Washington himself was far from being an egalitarian. In spite of the Revolution's rhetoric, the United States was still a society of deference, and Washington never seriously questioned the political and social validity of the prevailing ideas of rule by an elite any more than he questioned his own position in such a society. Publicly no comments came from him on slavery. For Washington, as for most of the other founders, when the fate of the new Republic was balanced against his own essentially conservative opposition to slavery, there was really no contest. And there was a widely held, if convenient, feeling among many opponents of slavery that if left alone, the institution would wither by it-self. Ironically, the clause of the Constitution barring the importation of slaves after 1808 fostered this salve to the antislavery conscience by im-parting the feeling that at least some progress had been made.

A major factor in Washington's failure to put his growing opposition to slavery into practice in the 1790s was his own conception of his presi-dential role. He assumed the office on a wave of bipartisan support and reverence. Even the meager criticism his support of the Constitution had evoked from its detractors—one critic had called him the Trojan horse in which the designs upon the liberty of the nation were being smuggled into the new Republic—redounded to his credit as a man willing to risk his rep-utation for the good of his country. But he went into office with scarcely a specific blueprint for his presidency. At the convention none of the del-egates except possibly Hamilton, James Wilson, and Gouverneur Morris had clearly formulated ideas as to the kind of executive that would emerge. Washington was certainly aware of—and to a certain extent shared—the general whig bias of the Revolutionary generation against the concentra-tion of power in the executive. To many of the delegates at the convention in Philadelphia, the provisions of Article II were based on the assumption that Washington would accept the office of president. Pierce Butler noted that presidential powers were "full great and greater than I was disposed to make them," and that members would not have expanded Article II had they not "cast their eyes toward General Washington as President, and shaped their Ideas of the Powers to be given to a President, by their opin-ions of his virtue."[40] Washington was well aware of the general public un-easiness concerning executive power and other aspects of the new gov-ernment. He had carefully created his role of a national icon—John Adams called him "the best actor of the presidency that we have ever had"—and he had an extraordinary grasp of the symbolic function of his office as a unifying force for the new nation.[41] Even the most cursory examination of the political correspondence of the period indicates how important Wash-ington was in holding the fabric of the new nation together. At some point in his journey he had become a precarious symbol for a chimerical Amer-ican consensus. He was not about to risk this role in what he certainly re-garded as a quixotic attempt to challenge the South's peculiar institution.

As president, Washington proceeded tentatively and with his custom-ary caution. "To form a new government," he had written John Washington in 1776, "requires infinite care & unbounded attention; for if the foun-dation is badly laid the superstructure must be bad. . . . A matter of such moment cannot be the Work of a day."[42] He felt even the slightest decision had implications for the future of his office and for the new government. "In our progress toward political happiness," he wrote Catharine Macaulay Graham early in his first administration, "I walk on untrodden ground." He believed, as he wrote Rochambeau in the summer of 1790, that "in a government which depends so much in its first stages on public opinion, much circumspection is still necessary for those who are engaged in its administration."[43] He cherished the approval of his peers and of the public; he had worked hard to deserve it. But probably more than any other of the Founders, he was acutely aware how fragile it all was and how easily the slavery controversy could destroy it. Through both of his administrations he feared the new Republic was still on experimental ground.

Washington's few private comments during the presidential years regarding slavery have been widely quoted. Clearly his own economic necessities seconded his political caution. He wrote Tobias Lear in 1794 giving elaborate instructions on the sale of land to put his financial affairs in order. "I have no scruple to disclose to you, that my motives to these sales . . . are to reduce my income, be it more or less, to specialties, that the remainder of my days may, thereby, be more tranquil & freer from cares; and that I may be enabled . . . to do as much good with it as the resource will admit; for although, in the estimation of the world I possess a good, & clear estate, yet, so unproductive is it, that I am oftentimes ashamed to refuse aids which I cannot afford unless I was to sell part of it to answer the purpose." Washington added a coda to the letter, which, ever cautious, he marked "Private": "Besides these, I have another motive which makes me earnestly wish for the accomplishment of these things, it is indeed more powerful than all the rest. namely to liberate a certain species of property— which I possess, very repugnantly to my own feelings; but which imperious necessity compels . . . until I can substitute some other expedient, by which expences not in my power to avoid (however well disposed I may be to do it) can be defrayed."[44] In the same year he told Alexander Spotswood: "With respect to the other species of property, concerning which you ask my opinion, I shall frankly declare to you that I do not like even to think much less talk of it. However, as you have put the question, I shall, in a few words, give you my ideas of it. Were it not then, that I am principled agt selling Negroes, as you would Cattle in the market, I would not, in twelve months from this date, be possessed of one as a slave."[45] Most frequently quoted is his remark to David Stuart after the failure of one of the myriad Quaker petitions to Congress: "The memorial of the Quakers (& a very mal-apropos one it was) has at length been put to sleep, from which it is not [illegible] it will awake before the year 1808." Stuart had reported to Washington the growing feeling in Virginia that a "Northern phalanx" was bearing down on the state and that it was said that "many who were warm Supporters of the government, are changing their sentiments, from a conviction of the impracticability of Union with States, whose interests are so dissimilar with those of Virginia." The Quaker petitions to Congress, Stuart contended, had given "particular umbrage" in Virginia as had the fact that the "Quakers should be so busy in this business. That they will raise up a storm against themselves, appears to me very certain."[46]

On a personal level, Washington, with his passion for order, feared the element of anarchism in the antislavery movement. In general he did not give a warm reception to gadflys—especially Quaker gadflys—and the tone of many of the antislavery appeals with which he was deluged in the 1780s and 1790s, combining imperious demands with evangelical piety, was not likely to incline him in their favor. Edward Rushton's was not the only castigation that he received in these years from antislavery sources. One of Washington's weaknesses as a politician was the fact that he was extraordinarily thin-skinned and criticism of either his personal or political behavior often troubled him far out of proportion to the event. The copy of Edward Rushton's polemic bears a notation in a contemporary hand, dated Liverpool, February 20, 1797, that the letter was transmitted to Washington in July 1796 and "a few weeks ago it was returned under cover, without a syllable in reply."[47]

Even in a private capacity Washington's achievements in regard to slavery during the presidency were not impressive. In April 1791, fearing the impact of a Pennsylvania law freeing slaves after six months' residence in that state, he instructed his secretary Tobias Lear to ascertain what effect the law would have on the status of the slaves who served the presidential household in Philadelphia. In case Lear believed that any of the slaves were likely to seek their freedom under Pennsylvania law, Washington wished them sent home to Mount Vernon. "If upon taking good advise it is found expedient to send them back to Virginia, I wish to have it accomplished under pretext that may decieve both them and the Public." When one of his slaves ran away in 1795, Washington told his overseer to take measures to apprehend the slave, "but I would not have my name appear in any advertisement, or other measure, leading to it."[48]

To Washington, factions were the death knell of republics, introducing party squabbles and leading to the divisiveness that would destroy his dream of creating a republic with a responsible citizenry, free of political strife. He exhibited great skill in defusing potential domestic crises during his first administration, and like Bolingbroke's patriot king, he hoped to remain above the fray. When party faction and internal strife developed during the second administration—the neutrality crisis in 1793, the fight over the Jay Treaty, the Whiskey Insurrection in western Pennsylvania— Washington took it as a personal defeat of his view of the Republic. And the slavery question, he well knew, dwarfed the other controversies that troubled his administration. Many southerners had already come to regard opposition to slavery as a symbol for the mistrust and disillusion with which they regarded the new government. And there are strong indications in the correspondence of many that they still considered Washington as their only bulwark against ravishment by northern politicians.

If Washington still had any doubts concerning reaction in the United States to the specter raised by the question of emancipation, public reaction toward the slave revolt in the French colony of Saint Domingue in 1791 would have confirmed his determination to avoid pursuing the issue at all costs. The horrors of the revolt of the slaves on Saint Domingue against their French masters were immediately apparent, although less understood in the United States were the appalling conditions that had inspired the revolt. Daily reports appeared in American newspapers on the insurrection. The revolution struck Americans on two fronts. It played to their views of the sanctity of property, which to most Americans was part of the basic natural rights for which they had fought Britain for eight and a half long years, and it fed fear, in the Deep South, of slave insurrections. Southern slaveholders were understandably most vocal in support of their Saint-Domingan counterparts. But nationwide sympathy, even among antislavery supporters, swung immediately to the planters, many of whom were important, both financially and politically, and many of whom had major economic connections in the United States. Washington wrote Jean Baptiste de Ternant, the French minister, in September 1791, promising to lose no time in dispatching orders to furnish money and arms requested by the French government to quell the revolt. "I am happy in the opportunity of testifying how well disposed the United states are to render every aid in their power to our good friends and Allies the French to quell 'the alarming insurrection of the Negros in Hispanola' and of the ready disposition to effect it, of the Executive authority thereof." The administration bowed immediately to French requests that portions of the Revolutionary War debt still owed to France by the United States be used to aid French efforts to put down the revolt and provision the colony.[49] Strongly supported by the Washington administration with money and arms and by public opinion in the United States, thousands of refugees fled to America, settling in seaboard cities, where their tales of the death and destruction left in the path of the rebelling slaves appalled Americans in the North and fed southern paranoia.[50]

No one was more aware than Washington of the potential the slavery issue had for the destruction of the Republic. As he had written to Alexander Spotswood in 1794, "I shall be happily mistaken if [slaves] are not found to be a very troublesome species of property ere many years pass over our heads."[51] From Washington's occasional comments on slavery expressing his desire to see it disappear from the new American nation it is difficult to decipher how deep his sentiments ran. It is likely that he had come to disapprove of the institution on moral grounds and that he considered it a serious impediment to economic development. Although he did not make sufficient comments on the institution of slavery for us to be certain, it appears that his opposition dealt more with the immorality of one man holding ownership over another than with the cruelty and abuse to individuals that slavery might engender. But there is no indication in his correspondence that he advocated any immediate policy of abolition. Obsessed with order both in his personal life and in politics, he would hardly have contemplated saddling the fragile new nation with the enormous problems resulting from immediate abolition—the disruption in the labor market, the care of blacks too old or too sick to work. In the eighteenth century immediate abolition found few supporters except among antislavery radicals. Many of the founding generation feared the idle poor of whatever color, and the anticipation that emancipation would contribute to a vast idle population made, even for such statesmen as Jefferson, foreign settlement of freed slaves a corollary to emancipation. "Justice is in one scale," Jefferson observed, "and self preservation is in the other."[52] Such apprehensions were not confined to the South. A New York law of the colonial period contended that "it is found by Experience, that the free Negroes of this colony are an Idle slothful people and prove very often a charge on the place where they be."[53] When Washington freed his own slaves at his death, he made relatively elaborate arrangements to prevent them from becoming a liability to the community. Washington specified that those of his slaves who were too old, too young, or too infirm to support themselves should be "comfortably cloathed & fed by my heirs while they live." Young slaves were to be taught to read and write.[54] Like most of his peers, Washington regarded stability and the sanctity of property as basic tenets of the new Republic.

It is likely, also, that Washington subscribed to the widely held belief that slavery would die a natural death, debilitated by the prohibition of importation of slaves after 1808, although that argument was weakened by the extensive natural increase among the slave population along the Chesapeake after 1730.[55] To his credit Washington, unlike most of his peers, did free his slaves in his will, and during much of his public life he gave at least private support to the idea of emancipation. But given his accurate conception of his own great and pivotal role in the infant country and his fears for the survival of the Republic itself, it is far from likely that he was ever sorely tempted to open as a national issue the Pandora's box that the Constitutional Convention appeared to contemporaries to have closed for the next twenty years.

Notes

1. Edward Rushton to GW, July 1796. The quotation is taken from a contemporary copy in the Rhode Island Historical Society. Rushton, a prominent English antislavery advocate, later published in England his "Expostulatory Letter to George Washington on his continuing to be a Proprietor of Slaves."

2. Memorandum, 1758–59, *PGW: Col. Ser.* 6:183–84; *PGW: Diaries* 4:277–83; *GW: Writings* 37:268. The dower slaves were those slaves that had originally belonged to the estate of Martha Washington's first husband, Daniel Parke Custis. Custis had died intestate, and by law his widow acquired ownership of one-third of her husband's personal property and a lifetime right to the use of one-third of his land and slaves. Her two young children by Custis each received one-third of Custis's personal property. Upon his marriage in 1759 to Martha Dandridge Custis, GW assumed control not only of her dower rights in the Custis estate but also of a considerable number of slaves. Martha Washington's son, John Parke Custis, inherited immediately two-thirds of his father's land and slaves. The remaining third would devolve upon him or his estate on the death of his mother. During his stepson's minority GW was able to use John Parke Custis's slaves as if they were his own, as he did Martha Washington's dower slaves. Because upon his wife's death the dower slaves would go to the Custis heirs, any plans GW had for disposing of his own slaves could not include those belonging to the Custis estate. By the time of GW's death, the two groups had extensively intermarried. For a detailed account of the distribution of the Custis property, see "Settlement of the Daniel Parke Custis Estate," in *PGW: Col. Ser.* 6:201–313. A list of the dower slaves by name, c. 1760–61, is in ibid., 311–13.

3. GW to Anthony Whitting, Oct. 14, 1792, WPLC.

4. See Daniel Jenifer Adams to GW, March 15, 1775, *PGW: Col. Ser.* 10:302–4. The slave proved so recalcitrant that he was eventually returned to Maryland. See also Lund Washington to GW, Dec. 3, 17, 1775, Jan. 25, Feb. 8, 1776, *PGW: Rev. Ser.* 2:477–82, 569–72, 3:187–89, 229–72.

5. GW to Lund Washington, Feb. 24, 1779, WPLC. GW would undoubtedly

have characterized his role as paternalistic. See Howard McGary, "Paternalism and Slavery," in *Subjugation and Bondage: Critical Essays on Slavery and Social Philosophy*, ed. Tommy L. Lott (Lanham, Md., 1998), 187–208.

6. GW to Lund Washington, Aug. 15, 1778, WPLC.

7. At least some of GW's derogatory comments on slaves and their labor must be considered in the light of his perennial dissatisfaction with the performance of other subordinates, from general officers to relatives to farm managers. See also Robert W. Fogel et al., *Without Consent or Contract: The Rise and Fall of American Slavery, Evidence and Methods* (New York, 1992), 58–61; Philip D. Morgan, *Slave Counterpoint: Black Culture in the Eighteenth-Century Chesapeake and Low Country* (Chapel Hill, N.C., 1998), 172, 191, 192.

8. H. R. McIlwaine and John P. Kennedy, eds., *Journal of the House of Burgesses of Virginia*, 13 vols. (Richmond, 1905–15), 1770–72: 283–84; *PGW: Col. Ser.* 10:119–28.

9. General Orders, Nov. 12, 1775, *PGW: Rev. Ser.* 2:353–55. Almost all colonies had exclusionary legislation barring slaves from serving in the militia and owning weapons. But all colonies also made occasional exceptions. See, for example, Hening, *Statutes* 2:481, 3:459. See also Benjamin Quarles, "The Colonial Militia and Negro Manpower," *Mississippi Valley Historical Review* 45 (1959): 643–52.

10. Virginia enacted stringent regulations to prevent defection by slaves, ranging from execution to transportation to the West Indies. Because the state was required by law to compensate the owners of executed slaves, a more convenient punishment was a sentence to labor in the lead mines of remote Fincastle and Montgomery counties, serving the dual purpose of removing rebellious slaves and contributing to the war effort. See Sylvia R. Frey, "Between Slavery and Freedom: Virginia Blacks in the American Revolution," *Journal of Southern History* 49 (1983): 383–85. Indeed, the appalling indifference to the plight of former slaves, hit by devastating epidemics of smallpox and by overwork and exposure in British service, should not have encouraged enlistment on either side. Rumors, often unsubstantiated, persisted of slaves offered for sale by the British. In Virginia at least slaves were used by the British "as a tool instead of as a weapon" (ibid., 394–95, 398).

11. General Orders, Dec. 30, 1775, *PGW: Rev. Ser.* 2:620.

12. Pete Maslowski, "National Policy toward the Use of Black Troops in the Revolution," *South Carolina Historical Magazine* 73 (1972): 2–6; Varnum to GW, Jan. 2, 1778, WPLC. For GW's reservations on enlisting slaves, see GW to Henry Laurens, March 20, 1779, Laurens Papers, South Carolina Historical Society. See also GW to Committee of Congress with the Army, Jan. 29, 1778, WPLC.

13. GW to Henry Laurens, March 20, 1779, Laurens Papers. For details on the evolution of the Laurens plan, see Maslowski, "National Policy toward the Use of Black Troops in the Revolution," 6–17. See also Worthington C. Ford et al., eds., *Journals of the Continental Congress, 1774–1789*, 34 vols. (Washington, D.C., 1904–37), 8:385–87.

14. GW to John Laurens, July 10, 1782, WPLC. Writing to his son in early 1778, Henry Laurens had pointed out effectively the obstacles to the younger man's agenda. "If any good shall arise from a prosecution of it, the merit will be solely yours. For now, I will undertake to say there is not a Man in America of your opinion" (Henry Laurens to John Laurens, Feb. 6, 1778, in Paul H. Smith et al., eds., *Letters of Delegates to Congress, 1774–1789*, 26 vols. (Washington, D.C., 1976–98), 9:38–40. For John Laurens's description of the eventual demise of the plan in the South Carolina council and assembly, amid "the howlings of a triple-headed monster in which Prejudice Avarice & Pusillanimity were united," see his letter to GW, May 19, 1782, WPLC. The plan was equally unsuccessful in Georgia.

15. GW to Daniel Parker, April 28, 1783, Boston Public Library; GW to Benjamin Harrison, April 30, May 6, 1783, Conference between GW and Lord Carleton, May 6, 1783, GW to Rufus Putnam, Feb. 4, 1783, WPLC; GW to Rufus Putnam, Feb. 2, 1783, Marietta College. See also Walter H. Mazyck, *George Washington and the Negro* (Washington, D.C., 1932), 82–84; Sylvia R. Frey, *Water from the Rock* (Princeton, N.J., 1991), 192–93.

16. "Circular to the Governors of the States," June 8, 1783, WPLC.

17. GW to the duc de Lauzun, Feb. 1, 1784, *PGW: Conf. Ser.* 1:90–91; Garry Wills, *Cincinnatus: George Washington and the Enlightenment* (Garden City, N.Y., 1984), 3.

18. GW to John Francis Mercer, Sept. 9, 1786, to Robert Morris, April 12, 1786, *PGW: Conf. Ser.* 4:15–16, 243–44. GW's comments to Morris were elicited by *Pirate, alias Belt, v. Dalby,* one of the first cases heard by the Pennsylvania Supreme Court concerning Pennsylvania's 1780 and 1788 laws dealing with slavery. For the case and the background to GW's comments, see Paul Finkelman, *An Imperfect Union: Slavery, Federalism, and Comity* (Chapel Hill, N.C., 1981), 50–51. See also the *Virginia Journal and Alexandria Advertiser,* March 30, 1786.

19. Lafayette to GW, Feb. 6, 1786, GW to Lafayette, May 10, 1786, *PGW: Conf. Ser.* 3:544, 4:41–45. After his purchase of "La Belle Gabrielle," Lafayette acquired additional lands in Cayenne and instituted a program of limited education, reimbursed labor, and gradual emancipation. The scheme and the plantation itself perished in the early days of the French Revolution. After Lafayette was arrested and imprisoned in 1792, the Cayenne property was seized by the French Revolutionary government, and the slaves were sold.

20. His contacts with Granville Sharpe and his circle may well have given GW considerable information on the difficulties in the Sierra Leone settlements. See Frey, *Water from the Rock,* 193–94; *PGW: Diaries* 4:78. GW's library contained over fifteen of Sharpe's works, including several treatises on slavery. See Franklin Osborne Poole, *Index to A Catalogue of the Washington Collection in the Boston Athenaeum* (Boston, 1900), 58–59.

21. Francis Asbury, *The Journal of the Rev. Francis Asbury,* 3 vols. (New York, 1821), 1:385. Asbury and Thomas Coke were at Mount Vernon in a vain attempt to persuade GW to support the antislavery petition pending in the Virginia House

of Burgesses. For an account of the fate of the unsuccessful petition, see William T. Hutchinson et al., eds., *The Papers of James Madison: Congressional Series,* 17 vols. (Chicago and Charlottesville, Va., 1962–91), 8:403–5. See also Madison to GW, Nov. 11, 1785, *PGW: Conf. Ser.* 3:355–58.

22. See Lois Green Carr and Lorena S. Walsh, "Changing Life Styles and Consumer Behavior in the Colonial Chesapeake," in *Of Consuming Interests: The Style of Life in the Eighteenth Century,* ed. Cary Carson et al. (Charlottesville, Va., 1994), 59–166; Timothy H. Breen, "An Empire of Goods: The Anglicization of Colonial America, 1690–1776," *Journal of British Studies* 25 (1986): 467–99.

23. Jean Yarbrough, "Race and the Moral Foundation of the American Republic: Another Look at the Declaration and the Notes on Virginia," *Journal of Politics* 53 (1991): 90–105; Bernard Bailyn, "Jefferson and the Ambiguities of Freedom," *Proceedings of the American Philosophical Society* 137 (1993): 498–515.

24. GW to John Francis Mercer, Nov. 6, 1786, to Henry Lee, Feb. 4, 1787, *PGW: Conf. Ser.* 4:336–38, 5:10–11.

25. GW to Knox, April 1, 1789, *PGW: Pres. Ser.* 2:2–3.

26. See, for example, Benjamin Lincoln to GW, Sept. 24, 1788, Alexander Hamilton to GW, Sept. 1788, GW to Hamilton, Oct. 3, 1788, to Lincoln, Oct. 26, 1788, Gouverneur Morris to GW, Dec. 6, 1788, ibid., 1:5–8, 23–25, 31–33, 70–74, 165–66.

27. Gouverneur Morris to GW, Dec. 6, 1788, ibid., 1:165–66; Thomas Jefferson to GW, April 16, 1784, in Julian P. Boyd et al., eds., *The Papers of Thomas Jefferson,* 27 vols. to date (Princeton, N.J., 1950—), 7:105–10. See also Michael Gilmore, "Eulogy as Symbolic Biography," *Harvard English Studies* 8 (1978): 131; Barry Schwartz, "The Character of Washington: A Study in Republican Culture," *American Quarterly* 38 (1986): 204–20.

28. Rush to Thomas Ruston, Oct. 29, 1775, in L. H. Butterfield, ed., *Letters of Benjamin Rush,* 2 vols. (Princeton, N.J., 1951), 2:91–94.

29. GW to John Jay, May 18, Aug. 15, 1786, *PGW: Conf. Ser.* 4:55–56, 212–13.

30. GW to Newenham, Aug. 29, 1788, The Rosenbach Foundation.

31. For slavery at the convention, see esp. Paul Finkelman, "Slavery and the Constitutional Convention: Making a Covenant with Death," in *Beyond Confederation,* ed. Richard Beeman et al. (Chapel Hill, N.C., 1987), 188–225. See also William L. Miller, *The Business of May Next: James Madison and the Founding* (Charlottesville, Va., 1992), 117–41.

32. Pinckney's speech in the House of Representatives, Feb. 14, 1820, quoted in Max Farrand, ed., *Records of the Federal Convention,* 4 vols. (New Haven, 1911–37), 3:439–44.

33. Miller, *Business of May Next,* 133.

34. Staughton Lynd, "The Compromise of 1787," *Political Science Quarterly* 81 (1966): 225–50; William W. Freehling, "The Founding Fathers and Slavery," *American Historical Review* 77 (1972): 81–93; William M. Wiecek, "The Witch

at the Christening: Slavery and the Constitution's Origins," in *The Framing and Ratification of the Constitution,* ed. Leonard W. Levy and Dennis J. Mahoney (New York, 1987), 167–84; Jonathan Elliot, ed., *The Debates in the Several State Conventions on the Adoption of the Federal Constitution,* 5 vols. (Philadelphia, 1861–63), 4:277–86.

35. James L. Hutson, "The American Revolutionaries, the Political Economy of Aristocracy, and the American Concept of the Distribution of Wealth, 1765–1900," *American Historical Review* 98 (1993): 1079–1105.

36. Examinations of Jefferson's views on slavery are legion. See esp. Bailyn, "Jefferson and the Ambiguities of Freedom," 506; John C. Miller, *Wolf by the Ears: Thomas Jefferson and Slavery* (New York, 1977); Paul Finkelman, "Jefferson and Slavery: Treason against the Hopes of the World," in *Jeffersonian Legacies,* ed. Peter S. Onuf (Charlottesville, Va., 1993), 181–221. Jefferson's reservations are somewhat explained by his fear of northern mercantilism and its spread to the South and to the new territories. GW, who had no such fears, has less excuse.

37. For the Pennsylvania Abolition Society, see Gary B. Nash and Jean R. Soderlund, *Freedom by Degrees: Emancipation in Pennsylvania and Its Aftermath* (New York, 1991), 115–36. For Henry's statement, see his letter to Robert Pleasants, Jan. 18, 1773, in William Wirt Henry, *Patrick Henry: Life, Correspondence, and Speeches,* 3 vols. (New York, 1891), 1:152–53.

38. Peter Augustine Lawler, "Tocqueville on Slavery, Ancient and Modern," *South Atlantic Quarterly* 80 (1981): 466–77. The charge had emerged during the debates over the Declaration of Independence, although the clause concerning the British role was struck out in compliance with the protests of South Carolina and Georgia. George Mason had observed at the convention that the trade originated "in the avarice of British merchants" (Farrand, *Records* 2:370). For the South's moral justification of slavery, see William W. Fisher III, "Ideology and Imagery in the Law of Slavery," in *Slavery and the Law,* ed. Paul Finkelman (Madison, Wis., 1997), 52–59.

39. See Jean R. Soderlund, *Quakers and Slavery: A Divided Spirit* (Princeton, N.J., 1985). For a conflicting view, see Jack Marietta, "Egoism and Altruism in Quaker Abolition," *Quaker History* 82 (1993): 123. See also Sydney V. James, *A People among Peoples* (Cambridge, Mass., 1963), 104, 126, 129–30; Herbert S. Klein, "Anglicanism, Catholicism, and the Negro Slave," *Comparative Studies in Society and History* 7 (1966): 322, 325; Howard Temperley, "Capitalism, Slavery, and Ideology," *Past and Present* 75 (1977): 97, 101; Gary B. Nash, "Slaves and Slaveowners in Colonial Philadelphia," *WMQ* 30 (1973): 255–56; Russell R. Menard, "From Servants to Slaves: The Transformation of Chesapeake Labor," *Southern Studies* 16 (1977): 355–90; Robert P. Forbes, "Slavery and the Evangelical Enlightenment," in *Religion and the Antebellum Debate over Slavery,* ed. John R. McKivigan and Mitchell Snay (Athens, Ga., 1998), 68–106; John R. McKivigan, "The Northern Churches and the Moral Problem of Slavery," in *The Meaning of Slavery in the North,* ed. David Roediger and Martin H. Blatt (New York, 1998), 77–94.

40. Butler to Weedon Butler, May 5, 1788, in Farrand, *Records* 3:301–4.

41. Adams to Benjamin Rush, June 21, 1811, in John A. Schutz and Douglass Adair, eds., *The Spur of Fame: Dialogues of John Adams and Benjamin Rush, 1805–1813* (San Marino, Calif., 1966), 181.

42. GW to John Augustine Washington, May 31–June 4, 1776, *PGW: Rev. Ser.* 4:411–12.

43. GW to Catharine Sawbridge Macaulay Graham, Jan. 9, 1790, to the comte de Rochambeau, Aug. 10, 1790, *PGW: Pres. Ser.* 4:551–54, 6:231–32.

44. GW to Lear, May 6, 1796, Huntington Library, San Marino, Calif.

45. Nov. 23, 1794, photocopy, MTVL.

46. GW to Stuart, March 28, 1790, Stuart to GW, March 15, 1790, *PGW: Pres. Ser.* 5:286–88, 235–38. Earlier in the month, while the Quaker petition was pending in Congress, Warner Mifflin, a prominent Quaker abolitionist, had visited GW to argue in behalf of the petition. The president responded to Mifflin by saying that "as it was a matter which might come before me for official decision I was not inclined to express any sentimts. on the merits of the question before this should happen" (*PGW: Diaries* 6:47).

47. Rhode Island Historical Society. The note continues: "As children that are crammed with confectionary have no relish for plain and wholesome food; so men in power who are seldom addressed but in the sweet tones of adulation, are apt to be disgusted with the plain and salutary language of truth. To offend was not the intention of the writer; yet the president has evidently been irritated."

48. Tobias Lear, *Letters and Recollections of George Washington* (New York, 1906), 38; GW to William Pearce, March 22, 1795, MTVL.

49. GW to Ternant, Sept. 24, 1791, Archives du Ministère des Affaires Etrangères, Mémoires et Documents, Etats-Unis, Paris. For French refugees influencing American public opinion, see Catherine Hebert, "French Publications in Philadelphia in the Age of the French Revolution," *Pennsylvania History* 58 (1992): 37–61, and Allan J. Barthold, "French Journalists in the United States, 1780–1800," *Franco-American Review* 1 (1937): 215–30. See also "Slavery in Virginia and Saint-Domingue in the Late Eighteenth Century," *Proceedings of the Annual Meeting of the French Colonial Historical Society,* 1990, 13–14; Carl A. Brasseaux, *The Road to Louisiana: The Saint Domingue Refugees, 1792–1809* (Lafayette, La., 1992). For the use of the American debt to France, see George Latimer to Alexander Hamilton, Jan. 2, 1793, introductory note, in Harold C. Syrett et al., eds., *The Papers of Alexander Hamilton,* 27 vols. (New York, 1961–87), 13:443–45.

50. For background to the slave revolt, see Carolyn E. Fick, *The Making of Haiti: The Saint Domingue Revolution from Below* (Knoxville, Tenn., 1990), esp. chap. 3.; Fick, "The French Revolution in Saint-Domingue," in *A Turbulent Time: The French Revolution and the Greater Caribbean,* ed. David Barry Gaspar and David Patrick Geggus (Bloomington, Ind., 1997), 51–75; Frances Sergeant Childs, *French Refugee Life in the United States, 1790–1800* (Baltimore, 1940), 11–16;

Thomas Fiehrer, "Saint-Domingue/Haiti: Louisiana's Caribbean Connection," *Louisiana History* 30 (1989): 426–27.

51. Nov. 23, 1794, photocopy, MTVL.

52. For the roots of these fears, see Edmund S. Morgan, "Slavery and Freedom: The American Paradox," *Journal of American History* 59 (1972): 12–26; Jefferson to John Holmes, April 22, 1820, in Paul Leicester Ford, ed., *The Works of Thomas Jefferson,* Federal Edition, 12 vols. (New York, 1904–5), 10:157.

53. Cited in William M. Wiecek, "The Statutory Law of Slavery and Race in the Thirteen Mainland Colonies of British America," *WMQ* 34 (1977): 278–79.

54. GW's will, July 9, 1799, *PGW: Ret. Ser.* 4:477–511; Ira Berlin, "The Revolution in Black Life," in *The American Revolution: Explorations in American Radicalism,* ed. Alfred Young (DeKalb, Ill., 1976), 368.

55. Allan Kulikoff, "A Prolific People: Black Population Growth in the Chesapeake Colonies, 1700–1790," *Southern Studies* 16 (1977): 394. For the concept that slavery would gradually disappear after importation ceased, see Jefferson to Jean Nicholas Demeunier, June 26, 1786, in Boyd, *Jefferson Papers* 10:62–64; Gary Nash, *Race and Revolution* (Madison, Wis., 1990), 3–20. William Cohen has pointed out that the natural increase during the latter part of the century on such Virginia plantations as Jefferson's Monticello, where between 1774 and 1778 there were at least 22 births to 12 deaths among his slaves, should have shown planters the fallacy of such arguments ("Thomas Jefferson and the Problem of Slavery," *Journal of American History* 56 [1969]: 509). The importation of slaves from Africa had dropped sharply after 1765, although the number of slaves through natural increase had grown in most of the southern states. In Virginia in particular the estimated number of slaves had increased from 189,000 in 1760 to 303,000 by 1780 (John J. McCusker and Russell R. Menard, *The Economy of British America, 1607–1789* [Chapel Hill, N.C., 1985], 136). See also Carr, *Colonial Chesapeake Society,* 12.

The American Nationalist

6. George Washington and Revolutionary Asceticism

The Localist as Nationalist

DON HIGGINBOTHAM

Washington, as this essay points out, possessed sound and steady personal characteristics, including good mental health, and was a leader hardly afflicted with cultural alienation, severe family problems, or dangerously inflated views of himself. But important as they were, these factors did not guarantee success as the foremost leader of the American Revolution. They did mean, and this fact is vital, that Washington, a man of enormous prestige and influence, posed no threat to the goals and ideals of the Revolution: an independent nation conceived in the name of individual liberties and republican self-government. Like revolutionaries elsewhere, he had drive, tenacity, and commitment. But he differed from some other would-be nation makers in that throughout his public career as military commander in chief, as advocate for the Constitution of 1787, and as president of the United States, he maintained a steady, unrelenting focus on American unity. So in the history of state formation he shares not only commonalties with certain revolutionaries in modern history but also similarities with such early modern European rulers as Gustavus Adolphus, Peter the Great, Frederick the Great, and Eugene of Austria. Indeed, we might bestow an appellation to his legal name to acknowledge his paramount achievement, the kind of recognition given either formally or informally to specific leaders of that age. Because of his ultimate achievement, we might call him Washington the Unifier. Washington's fellow American Revolutionary leaders would likely have echoed Voltaire's contention that the acts of great men inspire devotion to the fatherland. The Frenchman echoed Rousseau's assertion that the statesman "is the engi-

neer who invents the machine." And David Hume died without knowing the outcome of a prophecy: he had written that although republics flourished best in small geographic states, it was within the realm of possibility that someday a military man could be trusted to carve out a large, expansive republic without threatening the happiness and freedom of its citizens.

I have written extensively on George Washington and on the American Revolution. This essay originally appeared in George Washington and the Virginia Backcountry, *ed. Warren R. Hofstra (Madison, Wis.: Madison House, 1998), and is reprinted by permission of the publisher.*

To say that George Washington's pre-Revolutionary life in Virginia explains much about his character as a revolutionary figure is perhaps only to state the obvious. Even so, it seems that the subject is worth further exploration from the perspective of the study of comparative revolution. The Virginian was not an exile prior to the armed rebellion of 1775, as were the Kossuths, Lenins, Ho Chi Minhs, and Khoumanis of later revolutionary movements. Nor was his revolutionary persona in any way shaped by events in distant lands or by the reading of some seminal book or essay. He hardly planned or initiated a revolution against British rule. He was never a professional revolutionary, the kind one encounters in the nineteenth century, beginning with Blanqui, Buonarroti, Bakunin, Marx, and others. It is highly debatable whether Washington fits any of the definitions of a charismatic leader, a term loosely employed but usually emphasizing the revolutionary's dominating personality and ability to create political legitimacy in the absence of established governing institutions by his popularity and behavior.

Washington was, however, a hero of sorts long before the American Revolution. He had gained intercolonial recognition as Gov. Robert Dinwiddie's emissary to the French "intruders" in the Ohio Valley, as a military volunteer in the Braddock campaign, and afterward as commanding officer on the Virginia frontier during the Seven Years' War, fighting for his colony and for the British empire. But it was there, beyond the Blue Ridge, that his military accomplishments brought him his first tangible dividends. In 1758 the freeholders of Frederick County, that portion of the

Northern Neck which extended into the Valley of Virginia, had assembled at the courthouse in Winchester and elected him to the House of Burgesses. That same year Winchester's town fathers named a street after him. It was the first of such myriad honors and evidently the only one prior to the Revolution.[1]

These observations alone are enough to demonstrate that every revolution is unique, and therefore comparisons can be exaggerated or distorted, as the critics of such comparative historians as Crane Brinton and Robert R. Palmer have pointed out.[2] Even when these excursions result in discovering more contrasts than similarities, the undertakings can be beneficial for developing a broad interpretive framework in which to place Washington and the American Revolution. To Jefferson, writing soon after the treaty of peace that recognized American independence, the ultimate comparative question was what "prevented this revolution from being closed as most others have been by a subversion of that liberty it was intended to establish." His own answer was found in considerable part in "the moderation and virtue of a single character": Washington.[3]

Which of at least several different comparative approaches is most valid? Jefferson, with his rich classical knowledge, might well have been thinking of upheavals in the ancient world. Possibly he also had in mind Oliver Cromwell and the Puritan Revolution. For all their differences, Washington and Cromwell were both forty-three-year-old country squires when they turned to the most serious kind of soldiering. Still another leader from the early modern era could legitimately invite comparison with Washington, William the Silent. If the young Washington of Virginia adored Britain, the young William of Nassau-Dillenburg became a confidant of Charles V at Europe's foremost court. Both Washington and William went into opposition, renounced their royal ties, and became nation-makers; they were men of action rather than theory, talented at handling people.[4]

In any case, an examination of Washington's Virginia years within the context of themes developed by Bruce Mazlish in *The Revolutionary Ascetic* seems especially worth pursuing in a volume of essays that focuses on the Old Dominion.[5] According to Mazlish, a substantial number of revolutionaries in modern history have been ascetics. Drawing upon the studies of Max Weber and Sigmund Freud and their followers, Mazlish portrays many, but by no means all, revolutionaries as characterized by feelings of alienation from the dominant culture and by traits of self-denial, people principally unmindful of worldly, material pleasures associated with the comforts of home, family, and friends. Not only is this kind of revolutionary capable of cutting loose from past moorings—from kin, class, and province or region—but eschewing them enables the revolutionary more readily to oust from command and eliminate altogether old comrades in the cause and to risk the possibility of imprisonment or death.

Skeptics may assuredly argue that Mazlish casts his net too widely when he pulls in Robespierre, Lenin, Castro, and Mao together with Gandhi, and Arafat, even if they all share at least some forms of asceticism. Yet there have been revolutionaries who forsook the good life, and Mazlish demonstrates that total obsession with the revolution, sometimes including libidinal sublimation, has shown particular revolutionary leaders to be narcissists. They take themselves too seriously and, ultimately, see themselves as the revolution, without whom its values will erode and its cause will fail.

Does Washington fit the broad contours of Mazlish's revolutionary ascetics? Though the answer is clearly no, be it cultural alienation, or self-denial of familial and material wants, or narcissism, he certainly possessed the iron will and personal bravery that Mazlish discerns in his own revolutionary characters, to say nothing of his resolve to see his Potomac mansion go up in flames rather than have his plantation manager bargain with the British to save it.[6] In any event, a closer examination of Washington in relation to Mazlish's three categories may be helpful in understanding both his incorruptibility and the nature of his loyalties during the American Revolution. Though Washington has properly been hailed as the foremost nationalist of his age, both symbolically and as a relentless advocate of a strong American union, in critical respects he also remained throughout his life a committed localist, devoted to his roots—to people and place, which meant Virginia. For Washington, unlike some localists and nationalists—localists such as Patrick Henry of Virginia and Samuel Adams of Massachusetts, and nationalists such as Alexander Hamilton of New York—it was possible to be both.

Rather than expressing alienation from British culture, Washington, like other Tidewater planters, admired English ways. There were, of course, some differences between the country elites of England and Virginia—the English generally had greater wealth, which was not based on slavery or tobacco—but the similarities were more important to the Virginians, who felt they conformed closely to the Old World mold.[7] According to Edmund Randolph, whose own family was split by the Revolution, "almost every political sentiment, every fashion in Virginia, appeared to be imperfect unless it have a resemblance to some precedent in England." This "almost idolatrous deference" to things English, explained Randolph, was why Virginians before the Revolution had been more tolerant than other colonials when the mother country made mistakes.[8] Randolph might have added that cultural replication owed something to trans-Atlantic trade. Virginia, of all the mainland colonies, was "by far the most valuable to British interests. . . . The combined volume of colonial exports to, and imports from, Britain had grown to something more than a third of all British trade."[9]

That commerce had soared in volume and attendant riches for Virginians between Washington's youth and his manhood was abundantly evident to the planter John Wayles, Thomas Jefferson's father-in-law. He wrote in 1766 that "Luxury & expensive living have gone hand in hand with the increase of Wealth. In 1740 I don't remember to have seen such a thing as a turkey Carpet in the Country except a small thing in a bed chamber. Now nothing are so common as Turkey or Wilton Carpetts, the whole Furniture of the Roomes Elegant & every Appearance of Opulence."[10] William Eddis, in his *Letters from America,* also noted the change in colonial consumer patterns (even if he exaggerated somewhat) in claiming "that a new fashion is adopted earlier by the polished and affluent" Chesapeake planters "than by many opulent persons in the great metropolis."[11]

If Washington himself sought to become as English as his station and circumstances permitted, he sometimes encountered frustrations in his quest. First, there was the matter of his inadequate formal education. Over the generations his male clansmen had returned to England for schooling, and so had many other Virginians, such as the Blairs, Carters, Randolphs, Lees, George Wythe, and Thomas Nelson, their names on the rolls of a score or more institutions for the eighteenth century alone.[12] To do so was exceedingly expensive, and particularly for the first three generations of Washingtons, none of whom ever amassed the financial means to enter the upper ranks of the provincial notables. But their successful determination to send their sons abroad provides evidence for Louis B. Wright's contention that the rising gentry in Virginia was almost as concerned with passing on to its progeny the English cultural legacy as it was with the accumulation of wealth.[13]

Here, of course, Washington was an exception, explained by a shortage of family resources after the death of his father, when the boy was only eleven. Even out of the question for him was that more accessible institution, the College of William and Mary in Williamsburg, the colony's capital, where Robert Carter Nicholas, Thomas Jefferson, and the Harrisons broadened their horizons. But Washington particularly lamented his lost educational opportunity in the mother country and in his twenties spoke of "the longing desire, which for many years I have had of visiting . . . that Kingdom."[14]

Washington did, however, learn much about the glittering Georgian age from other family members. His Uncle Joseph Ball, son of a Lancaster County planter, had gone to England and eventually made it his home having studied at Gray's Inn and been called to the bar; but he was back in Virginia for some years during Washington's childhood. Later, from Stratford by Bow, near London, Ball advised George's mother, Mary Ball Washington, against permitting her son to take to the sea for a career. Free with instructions and eager to know of doings in the Old Dominion, Ball also entertained family and friends with stories about his life across the ocean. Other, more immediate sources of information for Washington were his British-educated older half-brothers, Lawrence and Augustine Jr. (Austin), especially the former, who was clearly his idol and in every way a polished Englishman.[15]

When Washington spoke of that "longing desire" of "many years" duration, he told us a good deal. Imagine, then, what a heady feeling it must have been for the young man to be in the company of English gentlemen in Virginia. His educational deficiencies in general and his inability to immerse himself personally in metropolitan life were partly overcome by those opportunities, which came as a result of spending much of his teenage life in the home of Lawrence Washington. Lawrence, in addition to his British schooling, had held a commission in the king's army and had afterward named his estate Mount Vernon, after his commander in the Cartagena campaign of 1740–1741. It is reasonable to assume that Washington absorbed much from his cultivated brother, who supervised his entry into provincial high society. As a thirteen-year-old, the fatherless George was diligently copying maxims of manners and deportment from a popular English courtesy book. Lawrence had married into the powerful Fairfax family, which had come over to the colony as major players in the land game. It is common knowledge that George visited frequently at nearby Belvoir, where Col. William Fairfax lived with his son George William and the latter's wife, the former Sally Cary.

Just as those years helped Washington wear off his rough edges and attain a measure of sophistication through mixing and mingling with his Belvoir neighbors and their influential friends and visitors—in their two elegant sitting rooms—so he also expanded his intellectual world by dipping into the books in their library. Washington would eventually have his own library with well over nine hundred volumes on a broad variety of subjects. While there has been disagreement about the extent of his reading and the range of his intellectual interests, Paul Longmore has recently argued convincingly that Washington's self-education was more extensive than has been acknowledged.[16] Assuredly Washington believed that any man possessed of a sizable estate needed to read works on mathematics and agricultural practices. He likewise considered "Philosophy, Moral, Natural, &ca . . . very desirable knowledge for a Gentleman" as was "Classical knowledge."[17] If, as a new survey of the Old Dominion's preindependence years avers, "the British Enlightenment reached its height in the eighteenth century," surely "Virginia shared tangentially in its triumphs."[18]

It is small wonder, then, that Washington's years on the frontier gave him a degree of cultural shock, eliciting from him unflattering comments about the lack of table manners, cleanliness, and creature comforts of the settlers beyond the Blue Ridge. Not infrequently disdainful of frontiersmen at various stages of his life, he talked of extending the values of his own Tidewater region to the West. The uncivilized life, with its crudities and dearth of amenities, was not for him. His Britishness made it difficult if not impossible for him to comprehend the values of the squatters on his transmontane lands or the backcountry militiamen who rejected his calls to arms because of their concerns about leaving their own families exposed. It is unlikely that he ever possessed the gift of understanding fully those who were very different from himself and his Tidewater circle. Actually, Washington's ambitious activities in the West as a surveyor, land speculator, soldier, and legislator were all designed to enhance his standing in the East, not in any sense to make him a westerner. Unlike Lord Fairfax, he never moved to the Shenandoah Valley or gave serious thought to doing so. In sum, his desire to enhance his Britishness drew him to the West, and his experiences there made him more of an Anglo-Virginian than ever.

Another dimension to Washington's Britishness, and a source of some further frustration as well, concerns his relationship with the British army. Both Lawrence Washington and Col. William Fairfax were British veterans with battlefield experience, and it takes little imagination to see Washington at Belvoir listening intently to their talk of campaigning in an age that still viewed war glamorously. He, too, wanted a British commission, and to that end between 1755 and 1757 he appealed to Generals Braddock, Shirley, and Loudoun, all to no avail, even though he was definitely worthy, given his combat record with Braddock and his impressive performance as colonel of the Virginia Regiment and commander of Virginia's frontier defenses during the most arduous period of the Seven Years' War.

It was European-style warfare that fascinated Washington, not backcountry tactics, which were already known as *guerrilla*, or *partisan*, methods and which were described in fascinating detail by contemporary chroniclers, especially Joseph Doddridge in his *Notes on the Settlement and*

Indian Wars of the Western Parts of Virginia and Pennsylvania and Samuel Kercheval in his *History of the Valley of Virginia*. Those frontier techniques were used effectively in the War of Independence by Gen. Daniel Morgan, from Frederick County in the Shenandoah Valley. If Morgan's experience as a teamster with Braddock and later as a Virginia ranger led him to dress in Indian garb, to employ the thin skirmish line, and to favor the backwoodsman's long rifle, Washington's service beyond the Blue Ridge only reinforced his learning at the feet of Lawrence Washington and Colonel Fairfax.[19] As a young Virginia officer, Washington read British army manuals, observed the practices of his crimson-clad superiors, and trained and disciplined his own provincial troops in such a manner that he could find some professional officers agreeing with his claim that his regiment was the equal of any British unit in America. His ideas remained fundamentally the same in 1775 when, as commander in chief of the Continental army, he drew upon British precedents to organize and train his own troops. Unlike many later revolutionaries, he was militarily conservative.

Washington was, in the decade and a half between his military commands, much like an English country gentleman, possessed as he was of the manners and deportment of his British counterparts, with their customary military title to boot; he was henceforth known to one and all as Colonel Washington. He ransacked the *Country Magazine* and other metropolitan periodicals and gazettes to determine the latest styles and fashions before ordering clothing, furniture, silver plate, and other interior adornments from London, not to mention his 1758 acquisition of "A Neat Landscape after Claude Lorrain," quite likely the first of a number of paintings of rural scenes he would eventually own.[20] He also wrote for seeds, cuttings, and bulbs to grow gardens and hedge rows in conformity with those of the English squirearchy. A year or so after placing such orders, Washington would watch eagerly at his plantation wharf as crates containing his shopping-list items were removed from a British vessel and unpacked.

If he had no ancient plantation house that served as a wellspring of family lineage, few Virginians did before the 1720s, from which time forward, with the tobacco wealth now available to them, they brought over skilled artisans from Britain to build such stately Georgian brick edifices as Stratford Hall, Westover, and Berkeley. Although Mount Vernon, which Washington acquired in the 1750s, was a modest frame structure, he added to it several times over the years, and he rusticated its siding so as to give the appearance of being constructed of stone.

In establishing his country seat, Washington accepted the responsibilities that Virginia planters, imitative of the English gentry, had long assumed. He and other landed magnates of the Old Dominion were familiar with the themes, if not always the specific passages, found in Richard Brathwait's *English Gentlemen,* which proclaimed that the greater one's station in life the greater one's obligation to society.[21] He became a justice of the peace, vestryman, and member of the House of Burgesses, the equivalent—in Virginians' eyes—of the British House of Commons.

Local elites in the rural realms of England and Virginia also had a responsibility to be patrons to lesser neighbors and to help the needy. In Washington's case, were these sincere concerns, or were they more a matter of acting a part required of his social station? Initially, it may well have been more the latter reason. His occasional high-flown expressions about the sufferings of frontier folk from Indian wartime depredations in the 1750s— "I could offer myself a willing Sacrifice . . . provided that would contribute to the peoples ease"—were inconsistent with his general attitude toward civilians incapable of making great sacrifices in areas where Washington's Virginia Regiment could hardly afford them protection.[22]

Quite likely Washington grew in his sense of real feeling and obligation for others. As a planter he came to realize that at times the patron's role could be a difficult one. His own father, Augustine, a justice of the peace, had discovered as much when farmer Job Shadrick sought his aid in obtaining redress after suffering abuse from Capt. John Bayes of the militia. When Augustine Washington demanded in writing an explanation from Bayes, the latter "flung the Letter in the fire and said that Col. Washington might kiss his backside."[23] As for Washington himself, in a quiet, unassuming way, he lent sizable sums to those in financial distress, even at the risk of his own solvency, as he explained to Capt. Thomas Posey, a small planter and old military companion, who repeatedly prevailed on Washington's liberality, notwithstanding his notoriously poor management of his own affairs.[24] And Washington accepted the burden of serving as executor or advisor for so many friends that he pictured himself in January 1775 as having had in the last year or two "scarce a Moment that I can properly call my own."[25] Whatever the demands on his physical and material resources, he reserved something for philanthropy. "Let the Hospitality of the House, with respect to the Poor, be kept up," Washington instructed Lund Washington. "Let no one go hungry away," and let some "money in Charity to the Amount of Forty or Fifty Pounds a Year" also be given to assist the indigent and afflicted.[26] It was easier to meet those public obligations because he had in 1764 employed Lund, his third cousin, as his business manager, a position similar to that of a steward on a spacious British estate.[27]

Washington nevertheless shared with his British gentry counterparts a desire to be a hands-on planter. Serious-minded agrarians in England and Virginia often preferred to call themselves farmers and boasted of their attention to the details of cultivating crops, raising livestock, and erecting storehouses and other dependencies. By birth and by habit, Washington was a true countryman, early to bed and early to rise but not without spare hours for the centuries-old English pastimes, particularly horse racing, riding, and fox hunts. In the mother country, only the great nobles such as the Bedfords, the Shelburnes, and the Rockinghams, like the West Indian sugar lords, could be habitual absentees and avoid the minutia of husbandry. Still, Washington and other Virginia gentlemen found opportunities to mix business with enjoyment on occasional trips to Williamsburg, Alexandria, and Annapolis, tiny urban enclaves where "long-tailed families" attended dinners, balls, and plays, to say nothing of indulging their "pleasures of the turf."[28]

Withal, Washington was not blinded by his Britishness. There is hardly a sense of deep regret, of wistfulness on his part, when the empire disintegrated in the War of Independence, as one finds in such Virginians as William Byrd III and Robert Carter Nicholas. This is not to say, however, that he was already deeply alienated from Britain by the mid-1760s, that his slights from the British army and his difficulties at getting an adequate return on his tobacco in London had made him bitter, suspicious of all that England did.[29] In fact, Washington never lost his affinity for the English country gentry, which, like its Virginia counterpart, was sometimes critical of the corruption of Hanoverian court life and the rapaciousness of London mercantile houses. His sympathies for the landed elite of the mother country were still much in evidence at the time of the French Revolution, for he saw in that segment of society the finest representations of British life.

Washington's recent biographer John E. Ferling maintains that the pre-Revolutionary "Washington who began his amazing ascent by carefully identifying with the habits and styles of the elite—and generally British—role models never abandoned the practice." Corresponding regularly after 1783 with prominent Englishmen, Washington sought their advice on a variety of subjects as "he made Mount Vernon into a grand English country manor house, carefully fashioned and furnished after its counterparts across the ocean, and had he had his way it would have been worked by English farmers not by American yeomen."[30]

Indeed, Washington's quarrel with Britain in the American Revolutionary crisis was principally with its political leadership and decidedly less with its cultural and institutional configurations. His criticisms of British imperial practices and policies evolved over a decade or so. The same pattern of disenchantment was probably also true of most of the Revolution's leaders. Doubtless there were some, however, whose alientation was cultural and was manifested relatively early, although they were not the Revolution's most influential helmsmen after 1776.[31]

As for self-denial, Washington certainly struck some contemporaries as distant and aloof. There was a reserve to the man, especially when in groups and in the presence of strangers and those he did not know well. Were he devoid of natural human feelings, he might have appeared indifferent to women. He did not take a wife as early as some men, and his marriage is often portrayed as one of convenience—-he needed a mistress for Mount Vernon, while Martha Custis sought a father and manager for her son and daughter and their properties.

If the above notions were wholly correct, a search for the causes of the impersonal Washington might go back to a preoccupation of some of his biographers—that of parental influences. One might theorize that the Washington who lost his father as a boy, who—in the opinion of some writers—was denied warmth and affection by his strong-willed mother, had turned cold, fearing that hurt might come to him in any intimate relationship.

Douglas Southall Freeman and other Washington scholars have turned to the same familial sources to account for what were admittedly aggressive qualities in the young man's makeup. But before his mother, in particular, is convicted for all his failings, a note of caution is in order. There is no learned consensus as to the roots of aggressive behavior. If domineering mothers—if that is what Mary Ball Washington was—may generate visible aggressions in their sons or daughters, they are just as likely to leave their offspring timid and straitlaced. Conceivably, too, Washington, were he severely damaged by his mother's influence, might have become effeminate, when in truth we know that he was strongly attached to the opposite sex and manly in all other respects as well. There are, one should add, multiple varieties of character, and to explain the grown man simply in terms of putative childhood determinants appears to leave small room for personal development.

In short, one may not weave together so easily the strands of Washington's personal life. Distant though he was at times, he had a healthy enjoyment of worldly pleasures. Whatever his reserve around some men, he was ever a gallant with women, once he passed his awkward teens. Did Washington speak from personal experience when in 1783 he observed to a female friend that "once the Woman has tempted us and we have tasted the forbidden fruit, there is no such thing as checking our appetites, whatever the consequences may be"?[32]

In any event, Washington could unbend in his letters in ways that would have surprised some of his contemporaries, let alone later generations. The Virginian expressed worry concerning certain performance responsibilities of elderly Col. Joseph Ward, a former army comrade who had lately taken a young bride. If the colonel had failed to "review his *strength*, his arms, and ammunition before he got involved in an action" then Washington would "advise him to make the *first* onset upon his fair del Tobaso, with vigor, that the impression may be deep, if it cannot be lasting, or frequently renewed."[33]

Despite the unceasing, titillating speculations about Washington's feelings for George William Fairfax's wife, Sally, with whom he carried on a flirtatious correspondence almost up to the time of his own nuptials, Washington's marriage to Martha Dandridge Custis seems to have been highly gratifying in every respect. To be sure, he and Martha had hardly the time to fall madly, deeply in love before their wedding, owing to his military duties—they seem to have become engaged during his second visit to White House, the Custis estate on the Pamunkey River in New Kent County. Doubtless he had not in his "contemplation of the married state," as he cautioned a relative in after years, "look[ed] for perfect felicity before consent[ing] to wed."[34]

Yet there is no reason to doubt that Washington considered Martha to be quite physically attractive at the time of their courtship. She was thought to be very handsome by the family of her first husband, Daniel Parke Custis.[35] Even if she may have been slightly plump when she gave her hand to Washington, that condition hardly resulted in the stigma that it would become for some people in a more recent period. Multiple pregnancies (she had had four), high-calorie diets, and negative attitudes about vigorous female exercise combine to explain why many upper-class women were somewhat heavy by today's standards. Her portrait by John Wollaston, completed a year or so before her engagement to Washington, shows a remarkably pretty face and an overall appearance consistent with what Lois Banner has described as the eighteenth-century ideal of femininity: "buxom, yet small and delicate," with "sensuality coy and indirect."[36]

Since Washington possessed healthy attitudes about romantic love and marriage, he was far different from the kind of revolutionary type portrayed by Erik Erikson: one who displays "special powers of sublimation" because of "passionate devotion and minute service to public causes."[37] Time and again Washington declared that he prized domestic felicity above all other pleasures and rewards. Just before the wedding of his nephew George Augustine to Martha's niece Fanny Bassett, Washington wrote that he had "always considered marriage as the most interesting event of one's life, the foundation of happiness or misery."[38] Unfortunately, only three of George and Martha's letters to each other are known to have survived,[39] but they bespeak a tenderness and sensitivity for his "dear Patcy" often lacking in an age when communications between husband and wife were not uncommonly formal. All three letters, two from him and one from her, begin with "My Dearest," what must have been their customary salutation. As commander in chief of the Revolutionary army, Washington urged Martha to join him in camp and stay as long as possible, and this she loyally and willingly did, although she confessed to a dislike of distant travel, unfamiliar places, and warlike activity. Though torn by a yearning to minister to a grieving Burwell Bassett over the loss of his wife and her own sister, Anna Maria (Nancy) Bassett, Martha in December 1777 explained to her brother-in-law that her greater obligation was to her husband, who was likely to call her north at any moment: "If he does, I must goe." Each year she usually set out from Mount Vernon in the autumn and returned—much to her husband's visible distress—in the spring with the opening of the next military campaign. "I was;" she recalled, "a kind of perambulator during eight or nine years of War." The prospect of ever undergoing such "fatiegue" again would be "too much for me to bear."[40]

The good life that Washington pursued to the fullest at Mount Vernon provides ample additional evidence that he manifested no zeal for self-denial. Martha Washington always presided over an abundant table, whether at camp or at home. Dinner, reported a French visitor, "was in the English fashion, consisting of eight or ten large dishes of meat and poultry, with vegetables of all sorts, followed by a second course . . . of 'pies and puddings'"[41] Although Washington lacked a facile tongue—he listened more than he talked—both he and Martha enjoyed leisurely dinner conversations with old friends, new guests, and various family members that sometimes stretched on for several hours into the late afternoon, concluding with apples, nuts, and with more wines.

There were swarms of Washington relatives who came to Mount Vernon, further indication that family was indeed meaningful to George Washington. (He would have derived little sense from the ongoing debate as to whether the American family, at various times and places, was nuclear or extended in its structure.) Relatives paraded in and out of his home throughout his entire married life or in other ways engaged his attention: Custises, Lewises, Dandridges, Bassetts, Washingtons, and more—perhaps as many as eighty-six of these kinfolk had some interaction with him. They often stayed for weeks, months, and longer—and sometimes remained in his employment as an overseer or secretary. One could say of his family (and many other planter clans then and later) that "its borders were permeable and its structure was elastic."[42]

Washington displayed a particular fondness for young people. He could scarcely have been more giving to his Custis stepchildren, John Parke (Jack) and Martha Parke (Patcy). Washington sought for Jack all the educational opportunities that had eluded him, composing detailed missives to tutors and teachers on his aspirations for Jack and traveling with him to enroll at King's College in New York City. The young man, no scholar and in love with a Maryland belle, soon dropped out of school in favor of marriage, much to Washington's distress. That pain could hardly be compared to his feelings when sixteen-year-old Patcy died of epilepsy. For three weeks thereafter Washington eschewed all business activity, and for three months—except for one occasion—he did not spend a night away from Martha. Several years later a more mature Jack Custis could better appreciate what Washington had meant to his mother and to him as well. "I am extremely desirious," he assured Washington, "to return you Thanks for your parental Care[,] which on all Occasions you have shewn for Me. . . . Few have experience'd such Care and Attention from real Parents as I have done."[43]

Washington was endlessly doing favors for his brothers, cousins, nephews, and nieces. He wrote long, avuncular letters to his younger relations on making their mark in the world, doubtless filled with the same maxims and principles that his own deceased older brother Lawrence had imparted to him years earlier and thoroughly typical of the concerns of Lord Chesterfield in his famous epistles to his son, published in the 1760s and constituting yet another popular form of courtesy literature. In his family letters, Washington frequently expressed "love" and "affection" for both male and female relatives, words hardly consistent with the marble image of the man and, for that matter, not even comfortable terms for many twentieth-century men to employ toward those of their own sex.

Although Washington gave more than he received, his kinfolk at times reciprocated. In his 1761 effort at reelection to the House of Burgesses, his brothers John and Samuel were the first two voters at the polls, followed shortly thereafter by his brother Charles, who joined them in voting for George. His cousin Lund faithfully managed his estates during his long eight and one-half year absence in the Revolutionary War. During his presidency his five nephews served in the federalized militia force that suppressed the Whiskey Rebellion. Before taking his leave of that army at Fort Cumberland, Maryland, Washington instructed his oldest nephew to set an example for his two brothers and two cousins. Washington later willed his swords to these same nephews, charging that they never "unsheath them for the purpose of shedding blood, except it be for self defence, or in the defence of their Country and its rights."[44]

Washington had a much healthier family relationship than some Virginia planters, such as William Byrd II and Landon Carter. Byrd fought with his wife over countless matters, including his marital infidelity and his cheating at cards. Carter considered his children unappreciative and disrespectful of their father and scarcely endeavored to avoid unpleasant domestic scenes. Even so, Washington's own deep commitment to kindred was hardly unique. Those ties seem generally to have been growing stronger within his social orbit in the second half of the eighteenth century; families appear to have become less patriarchal, authoritarian, and emotionally restrained. Assuredly those bonds were almost wholly unknown to Mazlish's revolutionary ascetics.[45]

Thus, it should not surprise us to learn that Washington was one of the few revolutionary helmsmen in modern history to be praised for his family life. The link between statecraft and domesticity was of the highest importance to Americans of the third quarter of the eighteenth century. Nothing could be more revealing in this respect than New York's advice in 1775 to its delegates in the Continental Congress on the appointment of a commander in chief. "On a General" for America, they declared, such a man should have "in his property, his kindred, and connexions . . . sure pledges that he will faithfully perform the duties of his high office, and readily lay down his power when the general weal shall require it."[46] It was widely perceived in the Continental Congress that Washington, a family man and large-scale cultivator, would make burdensome sacrifices in drawing his sword and would be eager to return to his former station in life at the earliest moment. John Adams, making the point graphically, spoke of this "gentleman of one of the first fortunes upon the continent, leaving his delicious retirement, his family and friends, sacrificing his ease, and hazarding all in the cause of his country!"[47]

Kenneth Silverman rightly says that Americans praised the nonmilitary dimensions of Washington more than his martial side, and they did not neglect his immediate family, during the war or afterward. Poets rhapsodized over his loving relationship with his wife, who prayed that

Heav'n give the angels charge, to protect my Hero George
And return him safe back to my arms!

Artists picked up the same themes. Congress early in the war expressed an interest in portraits of both George and Martha Washington. Charles Willson Peale, who had limned miniatures of the Washingtons, converted them into mezzotints entitled *His Excellency George Washington Esq.* and *Lady Washington.* At a later time Edward Savage's *Washington's Family* was quite popular in engraved form; it portrays George, Martha, and Martha's two grandchildren, whom the Washingtons adopted. Undoubtedly, Washington's countrymen saw him as a father figure not only because he was a nation-maker (and another George to replace George III?) but also because of his well-known domestic sensibilities.[48] That was definitely the opinion of Brissot de Warville, a French traveler in 1788, who, like other observers, declared that "Americans speak of him as they would of a father"; but not one who was austere or authoritarian, completely dehumanized, as would be the fate of Washington at the hands of nineteenth-century biographers.[49]

The Revolutionary generation's appreciation of close familial bonds may be hard for Americans in the late twentieth century to comprehend. David Potter, describing post-1960 American society, found it increasingly characterized by indirect and fragmented relationships compared with earlier periods when direct and integral relationships were more the rule than the exception. "Today," stated Potter, countless young people do not even "know their cousins and have no idea of clan."[50]

Washington's domestic orientation quite properly elicited the praise of his Northern Neck neighbor and fellow soldier Henry Lee of Stratford Hall. If Lee began the most quoted sentence of his famous Washington eulogy by saying that the soldier-statesman was "first in war, first in peace, and first in the hearts of his countrymen," he concluded it by asserting that "he was second to none in the humble and endearing scenes of private life."[51] Washington, himself, as Revolutionary chieftain, had said on countless occasions that his greatest desire was to spend the rest of his days back in Virginia, sitting "under my own vine and fig tree."

Yet not all in the Old Dominion felt that way after the onset of the Revolution, which there and elsewhere left some men restless and eager for new experiences on distant horizons. Generals Nathanael Greene of Rhode Island and Anthony Wayne of Pennsylvania both became planters in Georgia. In terms of Virginia's first families, those possessed of wanderlust were undoubtedly exceptions, but they included Henry Lee himself, the dashing ex-cavalryman who dissipated his energies and resources in one postwar speculative enterprise after another, dying far from his native acres. Lee's relative Richard Henry Lee also displayed little sign of missing home during his long departures in public service and came to visualize New England society as the prototypical ideal for a republican America.[52]

Washington's behavior regarding alienation and self-denial implicitly casts light on Mazlish's third category: that of the revolutionary's possible narcissism. There is simply no evidence that during Washington's generalship or later his mind turned to narcissistic thoughts, the kind that have been the undoing not only of certain revolutionary ascetics but also of a whole panoply of revolutionary types ranging from Latin American caudillos to Third World nation-makers such as the Nkrumahs and Sukarnos. And yet one might ask if Washington had earlier shown signs of narcissism in his intemperate carping to Dinwiddie and in his near-rebellious behavior toward Gen. James Forbes in the Fort Duquesne campaign. It is more probable that Washington, only in his early-to-middle twenties at the time, revealed marks of immaturity as he grappled with his own sense of worth and identity during a period in which he had far more responsibility than most men his age ever have.[53]

In his later public life, when there were moments for dreaming about his future, the mature Washington's attention turned to private concerns, to his Virginia world. He not only corresponded frequently with Martha but he wrote often to clansmen, friends, and business associates. He was saddened by the death of two brothers and a brother-in-law, and he worried about the orphans of his brother Samuel (several of whom became his responsibility). He carried on a voluminous epistolary exchange with Lund Washington, his manager.[54] Washington, at the time he assumed his military role in the Revolution, was already embarked on a course of economic diversification and a program of enlarging his house and gardens. They were activities that he watched as closely as possible from afar as they went forward under Lund's capable supervision. Indeed, throughout his adult lifetime Mount Vernon was growing and changing. Eventually, his estate, part of which had belonged to his great-grandfather, the immigrant John, numbered seventy-six hundred acres: his "Mansion House Farm" and four outlying farms. Displaying great creativity as a farmer, landscape designer, and architect, Washington in his minutely detailed directives to Lund and his subsequent managers (both during the Revolution and during his presidency) offers abundant evidence that he could hardly wait to return to take over the personal direction of what seemed to be a hundred and one enterprises.

Mount Vernon and all it meant to Washington ever remained the centerpiece of his life. Lionized by men of affairs, sought out by visiting dignitaries, all but deified by hosts of his countrymen, he kept his prewar values and priorities in place, something no narcissist could do. Still, he recognized that he had symbolic significance for the Revolution, both during the war itself and in the post-1783 years as well. As W. W. Abbot says: "We have only to look at the record of his willingness to sit for any artist who wished to paint his portrait, to correspond with any French, German, English, Dutch, Irish, Italian, Swedish, or American man or woman who wrote him a letter, and to open the doors of his house to any stranger, foreign or domestic, who came to pay homage or only to have a look."[55] What he did and said mattered to people and to himself, for he was a proud man, conscious of his honor and reputation for his own lifetime and for posterity. Although some historians have a different view, I believe that Washington was deeply reluctant to attend the Constitutional Convention in 1787 and to accept the presidency two years later.[56] He did so, of course, but only out of a sense of obligation and responsibility when confronted with the insistence of leaders throughout the country. Rather than seeking new opportunities to return to the limelight and reinforce his fame, he recognized that he could lose his hard-earned reputation along with the peace and tranquility of Mount Vernon if he returned to the national arena.

He was content for history to be the final judge of his record as it stood in 1787. He never, then or after his final retirement, wished to contribute to that judgment by penning a memoir or autobiography, but he did desire to do so in another way: by organizing and copying his papers for the benefit of future chroniclers, an undertaking he launched during the Revolutionary War, continued during the Confederation years, and returned to after his presidency. In fact, he considered erecting at Mount Vernon a building for their storage and preservation. On his deathbed he implored his secretary Tobias Lear to be sure his manuscripts were properly secured.[57]

If Washington's paramount concern was with documents bearing on his contributions to Virginia and the United States, this essay has endeavored to show that the public and private lives of statesmen are not easily separated. Washington's intention was to maintain some measure of his privacy, at least, at the expense of history. That explains why, for example, he singularly ignored the request of his former aide and secretary and would-be biographer, David Humphreys, for information about his family and early years.[58] Surely his attitude did not stem from a fear that he had more to hide which would reflect negatively upon his character than do most human beings. For other luminaries that has not always been the case. Even for leaders who maintain their public ideals in the face of acclaim, there has always been the temptation to compromise their family life. It has been true of some famous twentieth-century Americans, and it was also a temptation that men succumbed to in the Founders' generation.

How different in this respect was Washington from Benjamin Franklin, whose wife was probably no more educated and cultivated than Martha, and who seemed to consider his loyal, devoted Deborah Franklin to be an embarrassment, remaining apart from her for five- and ten-year stretches, even though, in the last case, he knew she was troubled by his broken promises to return and was gravely ill and longed to see him a final time.[59] It may tell us a good deal about Washington to say that Martha Washington hardly came across as a repressed or neglected spouse but rather as a happy, healthy, well-adjusted woman. Contemporary portrayals of her personality and character are notably consistent over a period of twenty years, beginning with the first known assessment by Mercy Otis Warren in April 1776. If Warren recorded Martha's openness and amiable disposition at that time, so did Abigail Adams—"her great ease and politeness" and "modest and unassuming" ways—in 1789, and so did the young English architect Benjamin Latrobe—her "good humoured free manner . . . was extremely pleasant and flattering"—in 1796.[60]

Had it been written then, Washington might well have called to mind the title of a song, although it would have involved changing the state. He would have called it "Virginia on My Mind." The Old Dominion does contain the key to why Washington was a safe man to lead a Revolution. We find it not only in his experiences as a Virginia officer in the Seven Years' War and in his seventeen-year career as a legislator in the House of Burgesses, subjects that have been addressed elsewhere.[61] But, even more important, we locate it in his domestic values and family life. This safe leader, a general and president who willingly, even eagerly, relinquished power, knew that in Virginia he found far more gratification than in any post or laurel ever bestowed upon him. It was, to recapitulate, the Virginia of deference and patriarchy, of well-born, well-connected friends and family, of Mount Vernon, and not the Virginia of the West, with its social fluidity and native cultures.

Washington said as much publicly and in his correspondence with quotable men of affairs. It was also what his countrymen wanted to hear—however much they pressed him to overcome his reluctance to serve. Theirs was a neoclassical age in which men took as warm and moving gospel the stories of Cato, who extolled the joys of rural retirement in the Sabine hills away from the pomp and corruption of Rome (Washington's friend Landon Carter named his home Sabine Hall), and of Cincinnatus, who relinquished his sword in favor of the plough. Washington was equally eloquent innumerable times to friends and family. And never more so than in his letter to Martha informing her that he had accepted the command of the Continental army in 1775: "I should enjoy more real happiness and felicity in one month with you, at home, than I have the most distant prospect of reaping abroad, if my stay was to be Seven times Seven years."[62] Sixteen years later, after accepting the highest civil office in the land, the pull of home had not diminished. To Dr. David Stuart, a family member, he wrote: "I can truly say I had rather be at Mount Vernon . . . than to be attended at the Seat of Government by the Officers of State and the Representatives of every Power in Europe."[63] Therefore, is it any wonder that he returned to his great house on the Potomac fifteen times during his presidency?

Paradoxical as it may seem, Washington was both a localist and a nationalist. His love of Virginia had led him to revolt and that same love kept his nationalism—powerful though it became owing to his service in the Continental Congress and his performance as commander in chief—within appropriate bounds.

Notes

1. Lucille Griffith, *The Virginia House of Burgesses, 1750–1774* (University, Ala., 1970), 94–96; Garland R. Quarles, *George Washington and Winchester,* Winchester–Frederick County Historical Society Papers, 7 (Winchester, Va., 1974), 38.

2. Even so, both scholars provide us with a starting point for comparative studies of the American Revolution (Crane Brinton, *The Anatomy of Revolution* [1938; New York, 1956]; R. R. Palmer, *The Age of Democratic Revolution: A Political History of Europe and America, 1760–1800,* 2 vols. [Princeton, N.J., 1959–64]). An illuminating dissection of earlier western European revolutions is Perez Zagorin, *Rebels and Rulers, 1500–1660,* 2 vols. (Cambridge, 1982).

3. Julian P. Boyd et al., eds., *The Papers of Thomas Jefferson,* 27 vols. to date (Princeton, N.J., 1950—), 7:106.

4. Michael Walser, *The Revolution of the Saints: A Study in the Origins of Radical Politics* (Cambridge, Mass., 1965); C. V. Wedgewood, *William the Silent: Prince of Orange, 1533–1584* (New Haven, 1944).

5. Bruce Mazlish, *The Revolutionary Ascetic: Evolution of a Political Type* (New York, 1976). Mazlish calls for more psychological studies of the American Revolution in his "Leadership in the American Revolution: The Psychological Dimension," in *Leadership in the American Revolution,* Library of Congress Symposia on the American Revolution, 3 (Washington, D.C., 1974), 113–33.

6. E. M. C. (Ellen M. Clark), "A Wartime Incident," Mount Vernon Ladies' Association of the Union, *Annual Report,* 1986, 23–25; Fritz Hirschfeld, "The

British Raid on Mount Vernon," *Naval History* 4 (1990): 7–9; Hirschfeld, "The Log of HMS *Savage* during a Raid up the Potomac River, Spring 1781," *VMHB* 99 (1991): 513–30.

7. In addition to the better-known studies of the Virginia elite, the following works have been helpful in seeing the similarities between the gentries: G. E. Mingay, *English Landed Society in the Eighteenth Century* (London, 1963); Mark Girouard, *Life in the English Country House: A Social and Architectural History* (New Haven, 1978); Daniel D. Reiff, *Small Georgian Houses in England and Virginia: Origins and Development through the 1750s* (London, 1986).

8. Edmund Randolph, *History of Virginia,* ed. Arthur H. Shaffer (Charlottesville, Va., 1970), 166, 176.

9. Warren M. Billings, John E. Selby, and Thad W. Tate, *Colonial Virginia: A History* (White Plains, N.Y., 1986), 253.

10. John M. Hemphill, "John Wayles Rates His Neighbors," *VMHB* 66 (1958): 305.

11. William Eddis, *Letters from America,* ed. Aubrey C. Land (Cambridge, Mass., 1969), 57.

12. T. Pape, "Appleby Grammar School and Its Washington Pupils," *WMQ,* 2d ser., 20 (1940): 498–501; Richard Beale Davis, *Intellectual Life in the Colonial South, 1585–1763,* 3 vols. (Knoxville, Tenn., 1978), 1:356–58.

13. Louis B. Wright, *First Gentlemen of Virginia: Intellectual Qualities of the Early Colonial Ruling Class* (San Marino, Calif., 1940).

14. GW to Richard Washington, Sept. 20, 1759, *PGW: Col. Ser.* 6:358.

15. Freeman, *Washington* 2:190–99. Joseph Ball's informative letter book for the years 1743–60 is in the Library of Congress.

16. Paul K. Longmore, *The Invention of George Washington* (Berkeley, Los Angeles, and London, 1988), esp. 213–26.

17. GW to Jonathan Boucher, Jan. 21, 1771, May 13, 1770, *PGW: Col. Ser.* 8:426, 335.

18. Billings, Selby, and Tate, *Colonial Virginia,* 216.

19. Don Higginbotham, *Daniel Morgan: Revolutionary Rifleman* (Chapel Hill, N.C., 1961).

20. Davis, *Intellectual Life* 3:1244.

21. Brathwaite's *The English Gentlemen* was an essential volume in the libraries of the rising Virginia gentry in the late seventeenth and early eighteenth centuries (Wright, *First Gentlemen of Virginia,* 15, 16, 32, 131, 185, 189, 231).

22. GW to Robert Dinwiddie, April 22, 1756, *PGW: Col. Ser.* 3:34.

23. A. G. Roeber, *Faithful Magistrates and Republican Lawyers: Creators of Virginia Legal Culture, 1680–1810* (Chapel Hill, N.C., 1981), 92.

24. For the GW-Posey relationship as "a particularly good example of the way that etiquette of debt operated between men of unequal social standing," see T. H. Breen, *Tobacco Culture: The Mentality of the Great Tidewater Planters on the Eve of the Revolution* (Princeton, N.J., 1985), 97–101.

25. *GW: Writings* 3:262.

26. *PGW: Rev. Ser.* 1:431.

27. Planter hegemony in Virginia was more fragile than used to be recognized. It depended on their fulfilling their manifold tasks well. The problem did not exist for the English rural elite (Keith Mason, "Localism, Evangelicalism, and Loyalism: The Sources of Oppression in the Revolutionary Chesapeake," *Journal of Southern History* 56 [1990]: 26, 27, and authorities cited therein).

28. GW's social activities in these regional centers are meticulously recorded in *PGW: Diaries.*

29. GW's difficulties with tobacco are treated in Curtis P. Nettels, *George Washington and American Independence* (Boston, 1951); Bruce A. Ragsdale, "George Washington, the British Tobacco Trade, and Economic Opportunity in Prerevolutionary Virginia," *VMHB* 97 (1989): 133–62 (see chap. 3 above).

30. John E. Ferling, *The First of Men: A Life of George Washington* (Knoxville, Tenn., 1988), 481, 482.

31. Pauline Maier, *The Old Revolutionaries: Political Lives in the Age of Samuel Adams* (New York, 1980).

32. *GW: Writings* 27:128.

33. Ibid., 28:15.

34. Ibid., 33:500–501.

35. Jo Zuppan, ed., "Father to Son: Letters from John Custis IV to Daniel Parke Custis," *VMHB* 98 (1990): 86; Freeman, *Washington* 2:292–94.

36. Lois W. Banner, *American Beauty* (New York, 1983), 46.

37. Erik H. Erikson, *Dimensions of a New Identity* (New York, 1974), 57–58.

38. *GW: Writings* 18:152.

39. The possibility of the existence of yet another surviving letter from GW to Martha is examined in Freeman, *Washington* 2:405–6.

40. Martha Washington to Burwell Bassett, Dec. 27, 1777, to Sally Fairfax, May 17, 1798, to Annis Stockton Boudinot, Jan. 15, 1784, in Joseph E. Fields, ed., *"Worthy Partner": The Papers of Martha Washington* (Westport, Conn. and London, 1994), 175, 314–15, 193. For Martha's wartime travels, see also Flexner, *Washington* 2:282, 517.

41. François Jean, marquis de Chastellux, *Travels in North America in the Years 1780, 1781, and 1782*, 2 vols., trans. Howard C. Rice Jr. (1786; Chapel Hill, N.C., 1963), 1:109.

42. Miriam Anne Bourne, *First Family: George Washington and His Intimate Relations* (New York, 1982), 207–9; Joan E. Cashin, "The Structure of Antebellum Planter Families: 'The Ties That Bound Us Was Strong,'" *Journal of Southern History* 56 (1990): 56.

43. Jack Custis to GW, June 10, 1776, *PGW: Rev. Ser.* 4:485.

44. *GW: Writings* 37:287–88.

45. Michael Zuckerman, "William Byrd's Family," *Perspectives in American History* 12 (1979): 255–311; Jack P. Greene, ed., *The Diary of Colonel Landon*

Carter of Sabine Hall, 1752–1778, 2 vols. (Charlottesville, Va., 1965), esp. Greene's introductory essay, 1:3–61; Daniel Blake Smith, *Inside the Great House: Family Life in Eighteenth-Century Chesapeake Society* (Ithaca, N.Y., 1980); Rhys Isaac, *The Transformation of Virginia, 1740–1790* (Chapel Hill, N.C., 1982); Jan Lewis, *The Pursuit of Happiness: Family and Values in Jefferson's Virginia* (New York, 1983).

46. Peter Force, ed., *American Archives* . . . , 4th ser., 6 vols. (Washington, D.C., 1837–46), 2:1281.

47. John Adams to Elbridge Gerry, June 18, 1775, in Paul H. Smith et al., eds., *Letters of Delegates to Congress,* 26 vols. (Washington, D.C., 1976–98), 1:504.

48. Kenneth Silverman, *A Cultural History of the American Revolution* (New York, 1976), 317, 361, 429–34, quotation on 602.

49. J. P. Brissot de Warville, *New Travels in the United States of America, 1788,* ed. Durand Echeverria (1791; Cambridge, Mass., 1964), 104, 344–45.

50. David M. Potter, *History and American Society,* ed. Don E. Fehrenbacher (New York, 1973), 313–15.

51. Albert Bushnell Hart, ed., *Tributes to Washington* (Washington, D.C., 1931), 16–17.

52. Charles Royster, *Light-Horse Harry Lee and the Legacy of the American Revolution* (New York, 1981); Maier, *Old Revolutionaries,* chap. 4.

53. For a cautionary note on the complexities of early manhood, see Lucian W. Pye, "Personal Identity and Political Ideology," in *Psychoanalysis and History,* ed. Bruce Mazlish (Englewood Cliffs, N.J., 1963), 150–73.

54. A sizable collection of Lund Washington letters to GW is in MTVL, along with a useful sketch of Lund. The editors of the *Papers of George Washington* note the bulk and diversity of GW's private wartime correspondence (*PGW: Rev. Ser.* 2:xvii).

55. W. W. Abbot, "An Uncommon Awareness of Self: The Papers of George Washington," *Prologue* 21 (1989): 10 (see chap. 11 below).

56. See, for example, Flexner, *Washington* 3: chap. 13; Barry Schwartz, *George Washington: The Making of an American Symbol* (New York, 1987); Ferling, *First of Men,* chaps. 13–14.

57. Abbot, "Uncommon Awareness of Self," 10, 12, 14–15, 17.

58. GW, however, provided Humphreys considerable information about his early public service (Rosemarie Zagarri, ed., *David Humphreys' "Life of General Washington" with George Washington's "Remarks"* [Athens, Ga., and London, 1991]).

59. Claude-Anne Lopez and Eugenia W. Herbert, *The Private Franklin: The Man and His Family* (New York, 1975), chap. 14.

60. Bernard Knollenberg, *George Washington: The Virginia Period, 1732–1775* (Durham, N.C., 1964), 72; Freeman, *Washington* 4:77; Stewart Mitchell, *New Letters of Abigail Adams, 1788–1801* (Boston, 1947), 13, 15, 30, 57–58 (quo-

tation on 13); Edward C. Carter II, *The Virginia Journals of Benjamin Henry Latrobe, 1795–1798* (New Haven, 1977), 168. Martha shared with GW a stoical attitude about making the most out of life's vicissitudes, including the need for personal sacrifice when duty called (Martha Washington to Mercy Otis Warren, Dec. 26, 1789, June 12, 1790, Fields, *"Worthy Partner,"* 223–26).

61. I, along with other historians, have examined GW's pre-Revolutionary public career (Don Higginbotham, *George Washington and the American Military Tradition* [Athens, Ga., 1985]).

62. GW to Martha Washington, June 18, 1775, *PGW: Rev. Ser.* 1:3–4.

63. *GW: Writings,* 31:54.

7. The Republican General

GLENN A. PHELPS

With the notable exception of Benedict Arnold, American generals displayed unfailing loyalty to the Revolution. They accepted the idea of civil supremacy, although they might grumble about Congress's sins of commission and omission, just as they realized that until the year of Yorktown that legislative body limped along as an extralegal forum. Even the ratification of the Articles of Confederation, the nation's first constitution, did not notably increase congressional jurisdiction but rather confirmed what the Philadelphia lawmakers had done on a de facto basis for six years. The problems that Washington encountered were also experienced by the heads of the regional military departments in New England, the West, and the South. They too had to deal directly with Congress and the states because Washington as commander in chief could hardly serve as the conduit for their needs and problems.

Under the Constitution of 1787, the president, the secretary of the army, and, much later, the secretary of defense would perform those functions. General Horatio Gates, who in the course of the conflict commanded both the Northern and Southern Departments, voiced the challenge of military leadership better than anyone else, even Washington. An American general, he complained, must be everything and do everything, and that was an impossibility. It is hardly surprising, given their painful confrontations with a weak central government and the sovereign states, that the former generals of the Revolution as well as countless lesser officers strongly supported the creation of a more muscular union in the 1780s and fought hard for the ratification of the Constitution in 1787. Their wartime experiences had nationalized them. To use contemporary expressions that character-ized their views, it was said that they had learned from the war to see things continentally or from a high ground.

Glenn A. Phelps is professor of political science at the University of North-ern Arizona. He is the co-author with Robert Poirier of Contemporary Debates on Civil Liberties: Enduring Constitutional Questions. *His essay originally appeared as chapter 2 of* George Washington and American Con-stitutionalism *(Lawrence, © 1993 by the University Press of Kansas. All rights reserved) and is reprinted, in slightly abbreviated form, by permis-sion of the publisher.*

THE WAR FOR AMERICAN INDEPENDENCE was a great influence on the development of George Washington's public philosophy.[1] One measure of the degree to which Washington was consumed by prosecuting and win-ning that war is that from June 15, 1775, when Congress selected him to serve as the Continental Army's commander-in-chief, until December 23, 1783, when he formally returned that commission to Congress, Washing-ton took not a single day off. That seemingly mundane observation tells us much about his dedication to the cause. It was common for his fellow officers to take extensive furloughs to look after private business, to recu-perate from injuries and fatigue, or sometimes just to remove themselves for a while from the dreary shabbiness of the army's encampments. Wash-ington was compelled to grant these furloughs, some of them coming even in the midst of critical military campaigns, in order to maintain the morale of the officer corps. But Washington never furloughed himself. For eight and a half years he stayed at the helm, dealing daily with the grinding frus-trations of leading a Patriot army, mediating the never-ending disputes over rank, pleading to Congress and the states for food and clothing for the army while imploring those same troops to be patient as they starved, re-viewing the verdicts of hundreds of general courts-martial, trying to settle squabbles between his troops and local civilians. Occasionally, he even fought the British. But for most of those eight and a half years Washing-ton was far more the administrative captive of headquarters routine than the daring field general of American legend.

Yet despite the camp drudgery and political infighting that caused most of his subordinates eventually to resign, Washington stayed on. When victory finally came, he was rewarded with honors far beyond those of even his great hero-ideal, Cato.[2] The merest rumor that Washington might be passing through town was sufficient to trigger spontaneous celebrations in Pennsylvania and New Jersey as enthusiastic and adulatory as any in Virginia. These sentiments toward Washington ran so deeply into every stratum of American life—rich and poor, farmer and shopkeeper, frontiersman and mechanic, Northerner and Southerner—that his critics (and there were still plenty who believed his military abilities were overrated and his politics suspect) felt it necessary to hold their tongues lest they be deemed unpatriotic.

This near-deification of Washington can be attributed in large part to his standing as the one national symbol of the struggle for independence. Other Americans were more central in leading the political movement toward independence. Indeed, while Washington was sympathetic to the movement's goals, he remained a peripheral player at best; his leadership of the army prevented any substantial involvement in revolutionary politics. Yet because he stood at the head of the one constant, visible symbol of the independence effort, the Continental Army, many Americans came to see Washington as the embodiment of all those complex aspirations that represented the Revolution.

Americans hailed Washington as the great soldier of liberty—a man whose exceptional patriotism and virtue assured final triumph over a corrupt king's mercenaries. Nor was his fame confined to unthinking Americans brainwashed by the propaganda of revolutionary pamphlets. Even many contemporary British accounts spoke favorably, if begrudgingly, of his character and military talents.[3] In short, his standing as the "Father of the Country" (and that phrase was already being widely used in pamphlets and sermons) derived from his wartime leadership, not from the popularity of his political beliefs. Few Americans were even aware that Washington was developing a distinctive vision of an American republic. For most it was enough to know that he was a Patriot.

Deference and Democracy

George Washington was a thoroughgoing republican both before and after the war. Unfortunately, that description does not tell us very much about his political ideas. By 1776 nearly everyone who supported independence (and even some who did not) called himself a republican.[4] Indeed, the term was virtually synonymous with the equally generic "patriot."[5] There were certain core values that all republicans shared: an aversion to hereditary and arbitrary power, government by popular consent, the promotion and protection of liberty (especially liberty in property), a commitment to constitutionalism and rule of law, a notion that government existed to provide for the common interest of the community, and the encouragement of public virtue. But endorsement of these general sentiments was not enough to bridge the ocean of political differences that separated republicans. Thomas Paine was a republican, but so was John Adams. Thomas Jefferson, Alexander Hamilton, Gouverneur Morris, John Dickinson, George Mason, Richard Henry Lee, Benjamin Rush: they all considered themselves republicans. There is a long tradition in American politics whereby the distinctive qualities between and even within ideological camps are blurred and intermingled. Republicanism in the late eighteenth century was no exception. It was something of a muddle even to its adherents.

The important question, then, focuses not on whether George Washington was a republican, but rather on what *kind* of republican he was. For example, republicans of all shadings believed that constitutional government could only be legitimated through the instrument of popular consent. But how much consent was required? By what means? And what were the instruments through which popular consent was registered?

Revolutionary-era republicanism was a house of many rooms; Washington was firmly situated within its conservative wing. If we compare Washington's republicanism with Abraham Lincoln's later model of democratic government ("of the people, by the people, and for the people") we can say that Washington readily acknowledged Lincoln's first principle—consent clearly had to come from the people. Even in class-conscious Virginia, Washington accepted the notion that the people's representatives had to be chosen by a broadly based electorate. And he most certainly endorsed Lincoln's third principle—republicans of almost all ideological shadings believed that public virtue was to be obtained by pursuing the interests of the whole community. Government was not to exist for the benefit of a privileged few. But the second of Lincoln's principles was anathema to Washington. He could never bring himself to accept the notion that all men were equally endowed with virtue, experience, and disinterestedness. Political liberty was a natural right and therefore held equally by all men; but political virtue was neither inherent nor held in equal measure by all men. Some men were clearly more virtuous than others and could more safely be entrusted with the people's business. Government by the self-interested, uneducated, propertyless masses might be democratic, but it could not be republican.

One of the best illustrations of his conservative republicanism can be seen in his relationship with his troops. He regularly made distinctions between his officer corps and the ordinary soldiers that underlined his hopes for the former and his fears about the latter. Popular mythology often portrays the American soldier as a receptacle for all of those virtues we wish to see exalted in times of national crisis. The American soldier (the "GI") is motivated by duty, loyalty, and patriotism. He is willing to sacrifice everything, including his life, to defend the principles underlying the "cause," whether it be independence, union, making the world safe for democracy, or rolling back the tide of communism. Washington harbored no such ideals about the capacities of the ordinary soldier. On the one hand, his addresses to his troops included the usual encomiums to the virtues of a Patriot army: men fighting for their liberty were morally superior to men who fought only for the king's silver; each soldier had the opportunity to earn the approbation of his fellow countrymen; the commander-in-chief was confident that every man would do his duty with great spirit. That was the official Washington.

Privately, and to Congress, he was far more skeptical of the virtues of the ordinary soldier. In a protracted war (and Washington was convinced early on that the conflict would be a long one) patriotism could go only so far in eliciting good behavior from soldiers. "When men are irritated, and the Passions inflamed, they fly hastely and chearfully to Arms; but after the first emotions are over, to expect, among such People, as compose the bulk of an Army, that they are influenced by any other principles than those of Interest, is to look for what never did, and I fear never will happen."[6] He believed that only a professional army under the firm discipline of competent officers could defeat the British in such a protracted war. Obtaining that discipline among liberty-loving American soldiers would be no mean feat: "Men accustomed to unbounded freedom, and no controul, cannot brook the Restraint which is indispensably necessary to the good order and Government of an Army; without which, licentiousness, and every kind of disorder triumphantly reign."[7]

Upon his arrival in Boston in 1775 he was shocked at the behavior of the Massachusetts provincials. For an aristocrat reared in a culture of deference, these New Englanders seemed far too democratic and far too willing to erase the social barriers between gentlemen and the masses. He reported to some of his Virginia friends that the army was composed of "an exceeding dirty & nasty people."[8] They exhibited an "unaccountable kind of stupidity" that one could only expect from the "lower class of these people."9 He was astounded at the degree of "familiarity between the Officers and Men" in the New England regiments, convinced as he was that such leveling was incompatible with discipline and good order.10 And he took special exception to the common practice among New England units of having the enlisted men elect their officers. Washington's conservatism would not permit him to envision an army in which republican virtue was equally distributed among all citizens, especially among the rabble of the common soldiery.11

A good soldier, in Washington's view, was not necessarily one filled with the spirit of liberty. State militia units, objects of Washington's scorn for much of the war, often served as prime examples of this belief. He observed that militiamen were too "accustomed to unbounded freedom" and thus resentful of the kind of control and discipline necessary for a successful long-term campaign.12 Bravery and spirit were surely desirable, but in a soldier these qualities were a double-edged sword. The spirited soldier could as easily be turned to mutiny (a problem that nagged the Continental Army from 1779 until the end of the war) as to the defense of his country. Washington believed that only training and discipline could create an army for the long haul. To this end he encouraged the "Activity & Zeal" of his officers while asking only for "Docility & Obedience" from the common soldiery.13 Militiamen who bore arms when enemy troops approached their homes and farms but returned to their civilian lives as soon as British battle flags disappeared over the horizon could never be docile and obedient. They could never be the foundation of a permanent Continental Army. Washington wanted to command soldiers deferential to his vision of the common good, not a band of freedom-loving individualists bent on protecting their own interests.

Washington's hierarchical vision of military society becomes even more apparent when we contrast his attitudes toward the ordinary soldiers with his expectations for and treatment of his officer corps. While in his view enlisted men were crude, ignorant, and motivated largely by their immediate self-interest (poor metal indeed for the making of military steel), officers ought to be "men of character" actuated by "principles of honour, and a spirit of enterprize."14 The key word here is *ought*. Washington did not presume that rank alone endowed men with these virtuous qualities. New England's elected officers were his principle case in point: "Their Officers generally speaking are the most indifferent kind of People I ever saw. I have already broke one Colo. and five Captain's for Cowardice ... there is two more Colos. now under arrest, & to be tried for the same Offenses."[15] In Washington's estimation there could be no democracy in the organization of a republican army, for democracy took no account of the social values he most cherished: order, discipline, virtue, and most of all, deference.

Washington's idealized officer corps was to be composed principally of gentlemen. As in Virginia, gentlemen had the sort of social and economic independence that permitted them to look beyond their immediate self-interest toward the public good and freed them to pursue a more noble aspiration than wealth—glory. This did not mean that all gentlemen were inherently virtuous. Without appropriate inducements they could be just as susceptible to the allure of money and position as the privates under their command. The endless disputes over rank served to remind Washington of the capacity of some of his officers to act out of "interested" motives. He expressed profound disappointment over this unseemly behavior. Even when he pointedly questioned some of the complainants' commitment to the cause, words clearly intended to embarrass the aspirants, his appeals were usually futile.

Washington came to realize that virtue alone was too shaky a foundation upon which to construct a republican army; the notion of interest was too deeply imbedded in American character to simply wish it away. Experience taught Washington that virtue could only be promoted on a broad scale if it could be reinforced by interest. If there was one principle that Washington retained throughout the remainder of his political life it was this: *In republican government, virtue must always be tied to interest.*

To create this cadre of officers, then, Washington first had to recruit and retain the best sort of men—men whose military talents and political loyalty would bring honor upon them all. Rank (and its perquisites) was one means of announcing the public worth of his officers. The commander-in-chief regularly petitioned Congress to be frugal in giving out rank. Washington believed that for rank to be respected and pursued by men of character, it had to be scarce.[16] Appointing too many generals not only confused an already chaotic command structure, it devalued those who already held the rank. He also protested against the proliferation of foreign officers. Washington conceded that many of them were capable, especially as engineers and artillerists, in military specialties in which American officers had limited experience. However, he argued that these commissions limited the opportunities for American officers and pointed out that, in the long run, the republic would be better served by promoting "home-grown" officers.[17] In addition, he defended the practice of allowing officers to use soldiers as personal servants against criticisms that the practice was inconsistent with the egalitarian spirit of the Revolution.[18] Finally, whenever the military judgment or the character of any of his officers was assailed Washington came to their defense, even when he confided privately that, in a few cases, the public criticism was probably deserved. Washington did all of these in order to establish a sense of common cause and *elan* among his American officers.

But to have a republican officer corps one more thing was necessary. Washington had to attach the individual and collective interests of the officers to the success of the republic and its principal agent, the Congress; he had to somehow make the national interest congruent with their own. The usual appeals to high principle (e.g., patriotism, honor, duty, liberty) could only go so far. Officers had to be convinced that there was something in the war for them—that its successful conclusion would serve them individually at least as well as it served the larger community. As Washington put the problem to Congress: "The large Fortunes acquired by numbers out of the Army, affords a contrast that gives poignancy to every inconvenience from remaining in it. The Officers have begun again to realize their condition and I fear few of them can or will remain in the service on the present establishment."[19] Washington recommended several measures during the course of the war intended to improve the morale of his officers: pay increases for each rank that corresponded to pay scales in the British Army, a provision for a bounty to be paid in western lands, a pension for their wives and families, payment of all officers' wages in specie rather than the deflated, virtually worthless Continental currency, a promise of half-pay for life (a proposal that was later modified to provide a lump sum equal to full pay for seven years payable upon demobilization of the army). Washington believed that the more "respectable" the standing of an officer, the more he could be relied upon to act properly. "I have not the least doubt, that until Officers consider their Commissions in an honorable, and *interested point of view* [my emphasis], and are afraid to endanger them by negligence and inattention, that no order, regularity, or care, either of the Men, or Public property, will prevail."[20]

By contrast, Washington opposed giving economic incentives to the soldiery as a whole. He believed the practice tended to break down the distinctions between officers and enlisted men, strained public credit beyond the breaking point, and, perhaps most dangerously, raised the expectations of the soldiers without any real prospect of making good on those promises. "[Raising soldiers' pay] is a doctrine full of dangerous consequences, and which ought not to be countenanced in any way whatever. . . . All that the common soldiery of any country can expect is food and cloathing. . . . The idea of maintaining the families at home, at public expense is peculiar to us; and is incompatible with the finances of any government."[21] Washington was right, of course. The depleted national treasury could only have met the soldiers' demands with promises as worthless as its paper currency. Nevertheless, the anecdote again highlights the elitist, deferential quality in Washington's notion of republicanism. A republic could not long survive by relying solely on the virtue of its citizenry at large. It was likely to prosper only when the better sort of men could be induced to defend public virtue against a jealous, self-interested, liberty-loving people. Republicanism could only be constructed from the top down, not from the bottom up.

Republicanism and a Professional Army

A capable officer corps was also important because it was the principal instrument through which Washington could demonstrate the trustworthiness of a republican army. His problem was as much practical as it was political. Many Americans believed that the war could be effectively prosecuted by militia and by provincial troops loyal to the state governments. They envisioned the sort of conflict that has characterized many twentieth-century wars of liberation. In this model a large colonial army of occupation could be defeated not by a decisive set-piece engagement fought in traditional European fashion, but rather through continual harassment by small bands of irregulars who would skirmish with the enemy, destroy their lines of supply and communication, and then melt away into the forests and farms of the hinterland. These bands would avoid direct combat with the enemy's main forces whose advantage in discipline and firepower would probably overwhelm them. It was supposed that this guerrilla-style warfare would frustrate the British, both in the field and at home, and eventually bring them to the view that the war was unwinnable.[22]

Washington thought this scenario was absolutely wrongheaded. Guerrilla tactics might be appropriate for a peasant people who would have little to lose from a long, drawn-out conflict and the social upheaval that would inevitably ensue. But Americans were neither a peasant society nor a society that lacked indigenous social and political institutions worth defending. Once again revealing his conservative sentiments, Washington believed that Americans had more to lose from a long, populist war than did the enemy. In his view British troops could occupy the main commercial centers of America (New York, Philadelphia, Charleston, and Boston) almost at whim. Marauding by guerrilla bands might inconvenience the British, but it could never dislodge them. If this occupation went unchallenged by a concerted American effort, the effect on the American economy would be disastrous. As economic disruption deepened, American support for the war would falter. The treasuries of state and local governments, dependent on continued economic expansion, would be strained beyond their capacities. Patriot governments would be faced with a Hobson's choice—impose confiscatory and decidedly "unrepublican" taxes on the people in order to pay for a long *and* expensive war, or issue increasingly worthless paper currency, permanently undermining public confidence in the great republican experiment.

Washington believed that irregular forces simply lacked the military capability to remove the British. Pester them? Make life difficult for them? Inflict significant casualties on them?—Yes. But remove them?—No. He believed Britain's superior economic resources could outlast the states' in any war of attrition. "In modern wars the longest purse must chiefly determine the event. I fear that of the enemy will be found to be so. . . . Their system of public credit is such that it is capable of greater exertions than that of any other nation."[23] A long war, even one fought by small irregular units, would eventually pit an increasingly constricted American economy against this British leviathan and so impoverish the states that either the war effort would collapse or the newly emerging republican governments would be transformed into something far less worthy of defending. Washington believed that only the defeat of British arms in the field could induce Parliament to consider peace; only an army built on a permanent establishment under centralized leadership could pose that credible threat to the British forces. For more than six years his entreaties to Congress, often delivered in the midst of mutiny and starvation, carried the same urgent message: Stop dissipating valuable resources for temporary expedients (e.g., bounties for state militia); raise funds sufficient to establish and maintain a professional national army large enough to drive the British Army from American soil once and for all. Not only would the war be won more quickly, it would be less expensive in the long run. Moreover, a quick victory would not jeopardize nascent political institutions or existing American social structures—a matter of no little consequence to a conservative revolutionary like Washington.

Washington's formula for victory seems orthodox enough today. Use a superior, well-trained army to destroy the enemy's military capabilities and peace will quickly follow. Yet many Americans feared their own army nearly as much as they feared the British; opposition to Washington's insistence on a professional national army was widespread. The very idea of such an army ran counter to widely accepted republican principles. Ironically, suspicion of the Continental Army was particularly deep-rooted among the same Country ideologues who had so influenced Washington's early political views.[24]

After an early period of enthusiasm for the notion of a national army, these older suspicions reemerged.[25] First, a standing army would have to be fed. Moreover, because it was a permanent establishment the army would have to be fed and clothed even when not fighting—a condition more common to the life of the Continental Army than even Washington would have liked. Some republicans feared that provisioning such a large body for an extended period inevitably would strain the public treasury. As the gap between the soldiers' expectations and the public's pockets widened, the army would be tempted to extort satisfaction from the government, e.g., "Tax yourselves to feed us adequately or we will take what we need from the property of the citizens." Republican government thus would be lost to the predations of its nominal defenders.

A second republican concern about a professional army focused on the "loaded gun" scenario. Many Americans believed that armies were blunt instruments capable of directing their force against whatever objects were chosen for them by their officers. Well-trained, well-disciplined troops loyal to their military commanders might prove an irresistible temptation to a clique of officers bent on pursuing their own political agenda. Cromwell's army was still near enough in the historical memory of most Americans to make them cautious about a permanent military establishment. In addition, many of these critics believed that there were always enough corruptible men in government, even in a republic, capable of enlisting the army as leverage for obtaining political advantage, thereby substituting force for the republic's commitment to government by reason. State leaders were especially concerned that the Continental Army would look to Congress for support, thereby strengthening the hand of centralist elements within the Confederation.[26]

Washington was thus faced with a war on two fronts. He not only would have to defeat the British, he would also have to convince American skeptics that the army, and its commanding general, could be trusted to behave as good republicans. This was no simple task. Both publicly and privately he implored the army, and especially his officers, to be paragons of virtue, to prove their worth in the defense of liberty, and to show that a Patriot army could endure more hardships than mercenary troops. But Washington recognized that wishing for virtue was not enough.[27]

The Deferential Dictator

Washington could not guarantee the conduct of every one of his soldiers. The army was too scattered and command too decentralized to expect strict adherence to his orders. Yet his own thirst for fame and glory ("The approbation of my Country is what I wish. . . . It is the highest reward to a feeling Mind; and happy are they, who so conduct themselves to merit it."[28]) was inextricably tied to the army's behavior. Washington therefore tried to impress upon his fellow officers that deference to civil power would do as much to establish the army's reputation as any number of battlefield victories. If the army were found wanting politically, then no amount of military success could retrieve its honor, or Washington's.

Washington attempted to ensure that at least his own republican credentials were above reproach. If his conduct could serve as a model of republican rectitude and respect for civilian authority, then perhaps the army and its officers could be persuaded to govern their own behavior accordingly. As a standard for his political conduct (his military conduct was something on which he took no instruction) Washington looked to his commission from Congress. The commission stipulated that his office was awarded to him by "The Delegates of the United Colonies" and that he should "observe such orders and directions, from time to time, as you shall receive from this, or a future Congress of these United Colonies, or committee of Congress."[29] His authority was neither personal nor grounded in his military rank; it derived from Congress and the states—from the people's representatives.

The commander-in-chief went to great lengths to prove his republican reliability by deferring to civil authorities on many matters whose ambiguity might well have justified his own independent action. People submitted all manner of petitions to him, assuming that as commander-in-chief he had great political influence. Some asked for civil appointment to the army; some asked to pass through British lines; some sought to do business with the army. Even his own officers brought their personal and political grievances to him. In every instance in which even the remotest question of civil authority was raised, Washington passed the petitions on to Congress or to the appropriate state governor. The cumulative impact of

Washington's perspicacity in these matters was tremendous. Jealousies and suspicions toward Washington gradually melted away.

Disorder in the Ranks and the Doctrine of Civilian Supremacy

Congress came to trust Washington's republicanism. But their fears about the threat of a professional army were well-founded. As the war lumbered on, many soldiers came to believe that Congress deliberately starved them, that it refused to clothe them, that it failed to pay them on time, that it allowed their wives and families to be impoverished and dispossessed. Congress, they believed, did not trust its army and therefore avoided doing justice to its soldiers.

Many officers shared those resentments. But they added to them the sort of grievances brought on when men of means and social standing are subjected to unaccustomed slights and inconveniences. When they were paid at all (which was infrequently) the amount was often deemed insulting. Promised bounties of money and land seemed little more than congressionally summoned phantoms. The appointment and promotion of officers generated continual internecine squabbling, made worse in the eyes of some officers by the clumsy favoritism found in Congress and most of the states. Men and officers alike grew increasingly restive toward revolutionary political leadership, believing that it was unwilling or incapable of dealing with the army in good faith.[30]

By early in 1780 Washington was warning Congress that without redress of some of the army's grievances he could not guarantee its conduct. Men had not been paid for five months. There were widespread food shortages. The spirit of mutiny was in the air, and Washington pleaded with Congress to offer some sort of palliative. Without relief the army might disintegrate or, worse, loot the countryside.[31]

His warning was prophetic. On January 1, 1781, men of the Pennsylvania Line killed an officer, armed themselves, and began marching in the general direction of Philadelphia. The soldiers had the usual complaints: no pay, poor food, and resentments against some of their officers. They also believed that their enlistments, originally for three years but later extended by Congress for the duration of the war, had expired. Without more pay or a new enlistment bonus they believed they were free to go home. Why they chose to march in military formation toward the capital and not merely desert individually to their homes (a fairly common practice) is not clear. The soldiers seemed not to have had any explicit political agenda or plan of action. Their precise motives remain unknown even to this day, but their imminent arrival struck fear into Congress and the state legislature of Pennsylvania. Washington urged Congress to do what it could to address the mutineers' grievances (they were, after all, grievances common to most of the army). But he also assured the delegates that he and the other officers were firmly aligned with the constitutional government and would do what they could to suppress the fever of mutiny.[32] He exercised restraint in dealing with the Pennsylvanians and through the mediation of some of their officers eventually convinced them to give up their enterprise.

But within two weeks another mutiny erupted, this time in the New Jersey Line. Washington now reversed his course entirely. Rather than patiently letting passions subside, rather than using the event to underscore his own continued effort to secure a commitment from Congress for a resolution of the army's rightful complaints, rather than negotiating with the mutineers, Washington chose this time to suppress the uprising with decisive force. He authorized General Robert Howe, head of the detachment sent to quell the disturbance, to demand outright surrender by the mutineers and encouraged the summary execution of its leaders as an example to the troops.[33]

We might attribute Washington's iron-fisted reaction to panic. Perhaps he feared that he was losing control of the army, that once again unseen forces were seeking to undermine him and replace him as commander-in-chief. Perhaps he felt that the second mutiny was a sign that many troops had lost confidence in his ability to serve as their representative to Congress and were now prepared to make their case directly. Whatever his private thoughts, the mutinies provided Washington an opportunity to once again demonstrate his commitment to conservative republican principles.

As a conservative, he could not allow the army to violate every good order of discipline. The Revolution could not be permitted to descend into anarchy. Washington's decisive action, especially regarding the New Jersey mutiny, assured the political leadership in Congress and the states that Washington and his still-loyal officer corps could be trusted to keep the everworrisome soldiery on a short leash. As a republican, he could not allow the military to subvert civilian government. No republic could exercise genuine self-government while casting anxious glances over its shoulder at its military leaders. As sympathetic as Washington was to the genuine sufferings of the army he could never condone using it to undermine republican government and the rule of law. This would be a betrayal of his oath to Congress and also of his own reasons for supporting the Revolution in 1775.

Many of his officers shared similar sentiments. But not all. In 1782 Washington received a private letter from Colonel Lewis Nicola. In bemoaning the plight of the army Nicola wrote in terms much like those used by Washington in his own petitions and memorials to Congress and the states; Washington's headquarters received similar letters almost daily. But Nicola went further. He offered a proposal that so alarmed Washington he immediately struck off a reply. Nicola had argued that the government was in such disarray that Washington should, with the support of the army, seize control of the reins of power.

It was a quixotic gesture on Nicola's part. Washington had not the slightest intention, even in those moments when he most despaired over the weakness of America's governments, of being an instrument of republicanism's failure. He was unsure of the noble experiment's future (indeed, he was to be haunted at times throughout his public life with private fears that republicanism was an unattainable aspiration), but if it was to fail it would not be because of treason by himself or the army. But Washington feared that Nicola's offer cloaked a more widespread erosion of support for constitutional government among other officers. (Nicola, later seeking to salvage his reputation, admitted as much.) He enclosed his reply to Nicola the same day—an urgency intended to impress Nicola and whatever supporters he might have among other junior officers with Washington's unequivocal feelings. Washington invoked classical images of military virtue and honor sure to have an effect. Acknowledging their justifiable grievances he insisted that "no Man possesses a more sincere wish to see ample justice done to the Army than I do, and as far as my powers and influence, *in a constitutional way* [my emphasis] extend, they shall be employed to the utmost of my abilities to effect it, should there be any occasion." But he then implored that "if you have any regard for your Country, concern for yourself or posterity, or respect for me, to banish" any further discussion of such "painful," abhorrent, mischievous ideas.[34]

Washington's reply elicited a series of nervous, face-saving missives from Nicola, but we simply do not know whether Nicola shared the commander-in-chief's views with like-minded officers. We do know that dissatisfaction among the officer corps continued to ferment. Late in 1782 feelings were running so high that the officers, with Washington's tacit permission, were sending emissaries to Congress. (It is likely that Washington wanted to impress upon the delegates that he was not crying wolf, that the officers' discontents were, if anything, more profound than he had represented.) These discontents became so acute that by the following spring a conspiracy emerged against the republic so convoluted that, to this day,

we cannot be certain of the intentions of all of the players.[35] But it culmi
nated in a moment of high drama at Washington's Newburgh headquar
ters where the general made clear in one final gesture of republican hero
ism that no honorable army could permit itself to threaten, much les
replace, the duly constituted authority of the people.

Washington had long lobbied Congress to recognize the special situa
tion of the officer corps. Washington believed that most of these men ha
suffered severe economic hardship. Not only were they required to sup
port themselves and their retinue from insufficient salaries that were rarely
paid, they also resented the effects that service had on their private for
tunes and their hopes for future prosperity. A provision of half-pay for life
had been enacted by Congress in 1780, but by the winter of 1782–83 many
officers doubted Congress's capacity to raise the revenues necessary to pay
the pension. Peace was expected any day. What, the officers grumbled
would prevent Congress from dissolving the army and then, free of the
looming presence of an armed soldiery, reneging on the half-pay promise
Perhaps, some officers thought, the army ought *not* to stand down unless
concrete assurances were made. Many officers now insisted that a lump
sum payment be substituted for the less certain promise of half-pay for life
Washington thought the idea a good one, but he was reluctant to push Con
gress and the states too far. He had, after all, been a delegate to Congress
himself and understood the political difficulties that the national legisla
ture faced. He cautioned his officers to be firm, but patient.

In March came the spark that kindled the final crisis of the war. A ca
bal of younger officers, probably looking to Horatio Gates for leadership
circulated a letter written by John Armstrong, Gates's aide-de-camp. The
letter asked for a meeting of all field officers to discuss their standing griev
ances. Officers were encouraged to reject "moderation" and to consider
"bolder" measures for dealing with Congress. Among the boldest of these
measures was a suggestion that the army refuse to lay down its arms un
til its distresses were relieved: "What have you to expect from peace, when
your voice shall sink, and your strength dissipate by division? When those
very swords, the instruments and companions of your glory, shall be taken
from your sides, and . . . [you,] retiring from the field, grow old in poverty
wretchedness and contempt?" Soldiers should not shrink from tyranny even
if it cloaked itself in "the plain coat of republicanism." Make one last pe
tition to Congress, but if it were rejected the army should pledge: "If peace
that nothing shall separate them from your arms but death: if war, that
courting the auspices, and inviting the direction of your illustrious leader
[the recalcitrants still hoped to attract Washington's support], you will re

tire to some unsettled country, smile in your turn, and 'mock when their fear cometh on.'"[36]

Washington immediately sensed that something "irregular" was afoot and called his own meeting of officers for March 15.[37] This move would allow him to control the agenda and give him time to ferret out the motives of the conspirators, some of whom he suspected were political figures seeking to use the army for their own as yet unknown purposes. Washington insisted on speaking first at the meeting and, by doing so, completely disarmed the incipient conspiracy. After attacking the author of the Newburgh Address for appealing to the "feelings and passions" of the soldiers Washington proceeded to take the same tack. Responding to the veiled threat of armed resistance against Congress, Washington pleaded that

> this dreadful alternative, of either deserting our Country in the extremest hour of her distress, or turning arms against it, (which is the apparent object, unless Congress can be compelled into instant compliance) has something so shocking in it, that humanity revolts at the idea. My God! what can this writer have in view, by recommending such measures? Can he be a friend to this Country? Rather is he not an insidious foe? Some emissary, perhaps, from New York [British headquarters], plotting the ruin of both, by sowing the seeds of discord and separation between the Civil and Military powers of the Continent?[38]

But the passion that Washington now appealed to was not the anger and frustration of a hungry, unappreciated army. Instead, he drew on the classical republican images that had so instructed his own life. He argued that threats such as those suggested by the address would "lessen the dignity" and "sully the glory" of the army. He implored the officers "as you value your own *sacred honor* [my emphasis], as you respect the rights of humanity, and as you regard the Military and National character of America, to express your utmost horror and detestation of the Man who wishes, under any specious pretenses, to overturn the liberties of our Country, and who wickedly attempts to open the flood Gates of Civil discord." The officers' perseverance in these difficult times might, instead, "give one more proof of unexampled patriotism and patient virtue."[39]

At the end of this brief speech Washington attempted to read a letter from a member of Congress describing that body's most recent good-faith efforts. Before doing so Washington fumbled a bit and then said: "Gentleman, you will permit me to put on my spectacles, for I have not only grown gray, but almost blind, in the service of my country."[40] The moment, by most accounts, left many of the officers in tears. The cabal disintegrated, and the meeting returned to the orderly business of planning the next petition to Congress.

The conspiracy had an air of unreality about it from the outset. The army probably would have dissolved rather than march as a unit into the wilderness. The state militias might have posed an effective rejoinder to any effort by the Continentals to extort money from the states. But Congress thought the threat real. Therefore, Washington's firm stand against military interference in civilian government has enormous constitutional significance.

National Interest versus Local Interest

The War for Independence, however, did not merely serve to reaffirm the conservative republican views that Washington held in 1775. There was at least one profound, immensely significant change in his thinking that came about as a result of his wartime experience. Orthodox republican ideology presumed that only small republics could long retain their virtue and commitment to liberty. Republican governments had to guard against the centrifugal forces of corruption, power lust, and centralism. A carefully crafted constitution could serve republicanism as a partial bulwark against these disintegrationist forces. But most importantly, republicanism required a vigilant people prepared to defend their individual and corporate liberties against the slightest insult. By this criterion the notion of a large republic was an oxymoron. Only in a small republic where the customs and traditions of the people were relatively homogeneous could one hope to generate a consensus about the meaning of virtue and common interest strong enough to stand fast against corruption. The likelihood that a republic could maintain itself *as a republic* diminished as its territory enlarged, as its population became more diverse, and as the variety of interests its people pursued expanded. Small republics lived in constant peril; but large ones were doomed from birth.[41]

There are a few signs that Washington was not wholly comfortable with this conventional republican wisdom before his appointment as commander-in-chief. During the war with France he had come to see that the military theater of operations should be continental, not provincial, in scope. He subsequently campaigned unsuccessfully to convince his superiors to give him military command over the entire western frontier—an appointment that would have expanded his authority beyond the boundaries of Virginia.[42] In addition, his extensive land-holdings in the West, as well as his frequent surveying expeditions to the frontier, had placed him within a circle of Virginia politicians with somewhat more enterprising, expansionist, westward-looking interests than their tidewater brethren.[43] Finally, Washington's early enlistment in the revolutionary cause suggests that like many other Patriots he was able to conceive that *some* interests could be held in common by *all* American political communities. The Fairfax Resolves, after all, found Virginia making common cause with Massachusetts in defense of the great republican principle of liberty.

Still, in 1775 many republicans of Washington's generation looked to their states as their country. They conceded that some sort of voluntary, limited confederation of states might be necessary to coordinate the war effort. Republicans were practical men capable of realizing that thirteen separate wars for independence—wars on behalf of thirteen distinct political cultures—were doomed to fail against an integrated, administratively centralized enemy. Republican virtue alone was no match for the British Army. Nevertheless, many Patriots tolerated Congress only because it was an expedient instrument for defending the sovereignty of the newly independent republican state governments. They trusted Congress about as far as they trusted the Continental Army. So long as those bodies worked to protect the interests of the states, they elicited grudging support. But there was enough lingering distrust of corruption and centralism to make most "small republic" advocates suspicious of even the slightest misstep by either body.

By the late 1770s Washington had come to view the world quite differently from these localist republicans. Because these localists dominated government in most of the states, the breach widened to the point that Washington lost almost all confidence in the supposed advantages of small republics. The careful deference to the states that had characterized the early years of his command came more grudgingly as his army's sufferings increased. He placed more of the blame for his difficulties on the lassitude and self-interest of the state governments than on the military resources of the British.

A single-minded vision governed his actions during the war. Only military victory over the British could bring the war to a successful conclusion; only a well-disciplined national army could accomplish that victory; and only constant support by all patriotic Americans could maintain that national army. No half-measures could carry the day. Whatever the merits of other republican principles, Washington believed they were secondary to the achievement of this greatest of all public goods—independence.

Many Americans, especially many of his republican friends in the state gov
ernments, did not share his single-mindedness about the war and its purposes.[44] As their doubts increasingly obstructed Washington's goals, the
general abandoned the mildly unionist sentiments of his early revolution
ary days and became more and more an ultranationalist with a profound
skepticism toward the virtues of state sovereignty. His grievances against
the states read like a "long train of abuses."

He complained to Benjamin Harrison, governor of Virginia:

> the States separately are too much engaged in their local concerns, and have
> too many of their ablest men withdrawn from the general Council for the
> good of the common weal: in a word, I think our political system may, be
> compared to the mechanism of a Clock; and that our conduct should derive
> a lesson from it for it answers no good purpose to keep the smaller Wheels
> in order if the greater one which is the support and prime mover of the
> whole is neglected.[45]

He urged Harrison "to exert yourself in endeavouring to rescue your Country by . . . sending your ablest and best Men to Congress." Men of virtue
and talent "must not content themselves in the enjoyment of places of honor
or profit" in the states, "while the common interests of America are moul-
dering and sinking into irretrievable ruin."[46] But his pleadings went un-
heeded, and he was left to complain bitterly, "Where is Mason, Wythe, Jefferson, Nicholas, Pendleton, Nelson, and another I could name [Harrison
himself]?"[47]

The problem that most vexed Washington was supply. During the course
of the war Congress tried various methods for supplying the army. At first
Congress levied assessments on the states and supplemented those funds by
the issuance of Continental paper money. But the assessments fell short, and
the printing press currency became virtually worthless. Congress then
adopted a system of specific supplies. On its face, the system promised to
reintroduce sound republican principles to the army supply process. There
had been much criticism of the previous money-based system because it had
been rife with corruption and the profiteering of middlemen—two traditional bugbears in republican demonology. Under the system of specific supply each state was expected to provide a requisition of a commodity (e.g.,
shoes, beef, gunpowder) at a given time and place. Specific supply was good
republican theory, but it was bad military policy. When the requisitions were
fulfilled, which was infrequently, distribution was chaotic. The system broke
down in the periods between campaigns. Troops encamped for the winter

were never able to obtain even the marginal levels of support provided them when they were in the field. State politicians successfully justified these actions with the usual anti–standing army rhetoric; but Washington thought it utterly dishonorable and against the common national interest for state legislators, many of them far from the smoke and grapeshot of battle, to starve the army at pleasure:[48] "If the States *will* not, or *cannot* provide me with the means; it is in vain for them to look to me for the end, and accomplishment of their wishes. Bricks are not to be made without straw."[49]

Incidents of delay or noncompliance by the states kept Washington's army on the brink of disaster and dissolution for much of the war. But the states' perfidious conduct did not end there. A few states even "appropriated" supplies for their militia that were intended for the Continental Army. In one instance, New York troops seized twenty-six bales of clothing intended for Washington's army. The commander-in-chief was livid: "This I look upon as a most extraordinary piece of conduct, and what involves me just at this time in the greatest difficulties; for depending upon that cloathing, I have not applied elsewhere, and the troops in the field are now absolutely perishing for want of it."[50] These were strong words for a Virginia gentleman; in that era challenges to a person's honor less pointed than this often resulted in a duel.

Whatever the reality of the situation (and there is considerable evidence that most of the states strained mightily to meet their military obligations), Washington was convinced that state cooperation varied with the proximity of British battle flags. When enemy troops threatened the state, few efforts were spared to help the army. But when the British moved their operations elsewhere, local enthusiasm waned. Washington found himself in a curious, double-edged political game in which the army's status, and thus the national interest, was constantly jeopardized. State governors often failed to meet their supply obligations and recruitment quotas in large part because they feared the local political consequences of using their limited resources to benefit other states or a distant army.[51] Yet when the enemy posed an immediate threat to the state its leaders employed every art of persuasion to have Washington bring the Continental Army to its immediate defense.[52]

Even when the states sought to support the war effort Washington found their attempts inconsistent and meddlesome. Especially harmful to the cause, he believed, was the states' insistence on fighting the war as much as possible with militia. Washington was convinced that these "short-termers," raised by increasingly expensive bounties, were a detriment to the national interest. They were undisciplined, unreliable, and subject to recall by the states at times that made strategic planning extremely difficult for Washington and his staff. The militia, moreover, was usually better paid and better fed than the Continental troops—a condition that worsened the discontents already rampant within his army.[53] He also resented his lack of control over the militia. Although militiamen were nominally under his command, his options were constrained by state prerogatives and jealousies. He believed that militia could only be counted on to help in local campaigns; the merest inkling of a major campaign in a distant state sent many governors scurrying to recall their militia for the defense of "important local prizes."

The states also disrupted his unity of command. Authority, Washington believed, should be commensurate with responsibility. He complained of having "*powers* without the *means* of execution when these ought to be co-equal at least."[54] Because Washington was commander-in-chief of all the armed forces arrayed against the British, he naturally presumed that his authority would be fully competent to meet that enormous undertaking. He was wrong. He did not even have the authority to appoint his own officers or to recognize extraordinary merit with promotions. Washington often found himself saddled with generals too old, too independent, or too incompetent to do him much good, yet too politically well connected in their states for Washington to remove. This system caused endless wranglings and jealousies among the often better-qualified junior officers. Indeed, the seed of Benedict Arnold's treason is often attributed to his disappointment in not attaining a rank suitable to his military deeds in the war—a rank that Washington lacked the authority to give. Without political control over his most responsible lieutenants, how, Washington complained, could he be held responsible for the army's failures?[55]

Republicanism on a Large Scale

Washington's unique vantage point during the War for Independence (he was, after all, the *only* commander-in-chief) provided him with an opportunity to assess, firsthand, confederation politics. No other American of his time—not Adams, not Jefferson, not Franklin—witnessed the birth of thirteen infant republics and a national Congress from a perspective remotely like Washington's. As commander-in-chief he was subject to the authority of a curious array of departments, committees, secretaries, and boards at the national level, while simultaneously having to assuage the local concerns of thirteen very independent, very different constitutional republics. As the eight years of his commission dragged on, much of this constitutional infancy must have seemed to Washington as painful and as troublesome as a breech birth.

Washington emerged in 1783 still very much the republican, but his republicanism had taken on deeper hues as a result of his wartime experiences. He was still the Virginia gentleman, but his willingness to consider a republic on a national scale forced him to jettison much of the oppositionist Country ideology that had characterized his early political career in Virginia. He was still a political and social conservative, but the war had convinced him that conservatism was best served by a national government sufficiently energetic to instill its special brand of public virtue on the widest scale possible. He still harbored a vision of a continental America stretching to the Mississippi, but he now believed that only a national government could safeguard the interests of the West from Europe and the predations of the Eastern states.

In short, the war had caused Washington to rethink his notions of what a constitutional republic should look like. Reluctantly at first, then with increasing vehemence, Washington began to see a *national* political system— a stronger union of some sort, though he still lacked a specific point of reference—as the only salvation for America's political, economic, and military troubles. Washington was certainly not the first American nationalist, but he became the first great national symbol of the nationalist cause.

To get to that point required him to radically rethink the nature of public virtue. Like most republicans, Washington believed that there could be only one true public interest. The common welfare had to be something more than just the result of an open competition between numerous interests within the community. Such a competition, he thought, would surely give sway to private interests rather than the genuine common interest. Moreover, harmony, not conflict, was essential to a virtuous community. This understanding explains why most republicans believed that good government could emerge only in a small republic—large, diverse populations would inevitably diverge over the question of what was in the public interest and would succumb, whatever the formal constitutional arrangements, to powerful partisan interests.

Such partisanship and division were anathema to a good republican. So it was with Washington early in the war. After his early, impolitic criticisms of New England soldiers, Washington tried to create a truly national army organized around the common goal of defeating the British and protecting the liberties of all Americans. But partisan bickering among the officers, especially disputes over the relative contributions of various states' regiments, interfered with that goal. To one brigadier he wrote, "How strange it is that Men, engaged in the same Important Service, should be eternally bickering, instead of giving mutual aid! Officers cannot act upon proper principles, who suffer trifles to interpose to create distrust and jealousy. All our actions should be regulated by one Uniform plan, and that Plan should have one object in view, to wit, the good of the Service."[56] This same notion informed his analysis of national politics. For Washington there was a clear public interest held in common by all patriotic Americans—winning the war. There was no room for ambiguity or legitimate differences of opinion on this goal. All else that was of value to the community—constitutional government, liberty, republicanism, prosperity—depended on winning the war. To Washington it was inconceivable that there could be any dissent to the idea that military victory was genuinely in the public interest.

To Washington, then, virtue was wedded to one's willingness to sacrifice private interest in service to the pubic interest. Once the public interest was determined, a desire for fame should lead honorable men only to unanimity and unity of purpose. "If we would pursue a right System of policy, in my Opinion, there should be none of these distinctions. We should all be considered, Congress, Army, &c. as one people, embarked in one Cause, in one interest; acting on the same principle and to the same End."[57]

It came as a rude shock when Washington found that many politicians in state and national government could not agree on what was genuinely in the public interest. He was particularly upset with the behavior of the state governments, many of which could not fully embrace any notion of the public interest that emanated from Congress or the army. Their particular view of republicanism taught them to be wary of centralism (a traditional enemy of true republicanism) masquerading as public virtue. Thus, it was more than narrow self-interest and petty partisanship that led many state governments to withhold wholehearted support from Congress and the army. For many Pennsylvanians and Marylanders and Rhode Islanders there was more to the public interest than winning the war. State citizens also shared a common interest in preserving their local republics against the centralizing impulses of Congress and the Continental Army. These "small scale" republicans feared an American "court" as much as a distant Parliament. Each was an instrument for undermining liberty and independence. Winning the war, though clearly in the common interest of all the states, should not come at the expense of devaluing state governments and state constitutions.

When he realized that this local support would never materialize in the way he envisioned, Washington began to take a more active role in the promulgation of a new version of republicanism. Beginning in the winter of 1779–1780 Washington used his political influence on behalf of three goals inherently incompatible with the older, "small scale" republicanism. First, he argued that the Congress should be granted greater powers to act on matters of general interest to the confederacy. Second, he maintained that in those matters of general interest the power and authority of the national government should be supreme over any state interests. Finally, in order to more effectively meet these new responsibilities, Congress should establish a strong executive branch, preferably with individual executives capable of accepting and exercising political responsibility.

There is a spirited debate among historians as to whether the Revolution established national sovereignty or the sovereignty of the several states.[58] For the most part, Washington tried to distance himself from that issue, which was debated by his contemporaries as well. But starvation and mutiny among his troops and the prospect of military disaster forced him off the fence. When a nationalist faction arose within Congress and many of the states in 1780, especially among veterans of the war, Washington abandoned his carefully constructed policy of deference to the states and indicated his unequivocal support for the nationalists.[59] He laid out his principal objections to "politics as usual" in a long letter to a former member of Congress:

> In a word, our measures are not under the influence and direction of one council, but thirteen, each of which is actuated by local views and politics, without considering the fatal consequences of not complying with plans which the united wisdom of America in its representative capacity have digested, or the unhappy tendency of delay, mutilation, or alteration. I do not scruple to add, and I give it decisively as my opinion, that unless the States will content themselves with a full, and well chosen representation in Congress, and vest that body with absolute powers in all matters relative to the great purposes of war, and of general concern . . . we are attempting an impossibility, and very soon shall become (if it is not already the case) a many headed Monster, a heterogenious Mass, that never will or can, steer to the same point. The contest among the different States *now*, is not which shall do most for the common cause, but which shall do least.[60]

This letter is one of Washington's most bitter; other parts of it are even more strident and accusatory. But it lays out the parameters of his nationalist thinking. His criticisms of confederation politics were both structural and ideological. He was outraged at the timidity of Congress and by its practice of merely recommending measures to the states. Rather than a Congress with authority to match its responsibilities Washington saw a system in which "each State undertakes to determine, 1st. whether they will comply or not 2d. In what manner they will do it, &ca. 3dly. in what time."[61] Blame for this political timidity was placed entirely at the doorstep of the states. Their local views, jealousy of the national government, unjustified fear of the army, and self-interest combined to make them the greatest obstacle to attaining the unity necessary for winning the war. Washington usually spoke in rather broad terms on the subject of expanded congressional powers, calling for Congress to act in matters of "general concern." Beyond a suggestion that Congress be granted the authority to lay taxes, borrow money, and provide for the army, he offered few specific recommendations as to what those powers ought to be. In truth, though, he was more interested in vesting Congress with greater enforcement (executive) powers than in expanding the scope of its legislative powers.

Structural reforms would fail, though, if they were not presented as part of a broader appeal for national unity. Washington still believed that republican governments, regardless of form, could survive only if they were virtuous. Congress was much to blame for the army's difficulties, but Washington became less inclined to criticize that body as the war lengthened. Many of its members had at least *tried* to supply the army and support the great national patriotic cause. But the states, in Washington's eyes, had lost their nerve. Increasingly protective of localist, parochial notions of the public good, they undermined the common interest of all Americans in winning the war. Part of Washington's despair was grounded in a creeping fear that virtue was fighting a losing battle against self-interest and that republican government was impossible after all. Therefore, Washington spoke about arousing the talented, honorable men of America—men of acknowledged virtue—to save the republican spirit from the hydra of parochial factionalism. Congress needed more comprehensive powers, but without virtuous men at every level of government the great experiment was doomed to failure.

The second plank of Washington's constitutional reform program called for sharp constraints on the powers of the state governments. He did not propose to abolish the states (a position that only a few extreme nationalists were prepared to consider) and conceded their primacy in managing local affairs and maintaining public order. Moreover, part of his rationale for increasing the powers of the national government was that without more comprehensive central direction to the country's affairs each of the thirteen states, and the liberties they so jealously championed, would succumb separately to British military and economic pressure.[62] Only a national government with supremacy over the states in all areas of general interest could hope to bring the war to a successful conclusion. Congress, "after hearing the interests and views of the several States fairly discussed and explained by their respective representatives, must dictate, not merely recommend, and leave it to the states afterwards to do as they please, which . . . is in many cases, to do nothing at all."[63] Washington's federal model allowed for state interests to be represented only in Congress. Once Congress, composed as it was of delegations from each state, had determined the common national interest, further opposition or noncompliance by any state would be impermissible. The principle of democratic centralism would forbid any additional checks upon national authority from thence forward. State power would have to give way entirely in such matters.

Finally, Washington insisted that any expanded congressional powers could only be made effective by vigorous, responsible executive leadership. The antimonarchist, anticentralist, anticorruption sentiments held by many revolutionary legislators were slow to yield to Washington's claims. The history of Congress's efforts to manage the business of war demonstrates that the idea of a plural executive operating under the close supervision of a jealous legislature died especially hard. Congress initially supervised the army and its provisioning as a committee of the whole. When that proved unwieldy Congress established a committee of five of its members, the Board of War. Later still, the board was recast to allow members from outside Congress—men presumably with administrative skills. None of these arrangements met with much success or the commander-in-chief's approval. Even when Congress was able to raise the necessary supplies the distribution system was so disorganized that the provisions rarely reached the army expeditiously.

Washington campaigned for single executives—men vested with the kind of responsibility and authority to "act with dispatch and energy."[64] As early as 1775 Washington had lobbied for a clearer line of executive responsibility. Notes for a letter to Congress reveal that he had planned to "express gratitude for the readiness which the Congress and different committees have shown to make every thing as convenient and agreeable as possible, but point out the inconvenience of depending upon a number of men and different channels through which these supplies are to be furnished and the necessity of appointing a Commissary General for these purposes."[65] When his nationalist allies in Congress finally adopted a plan to allocate executive power to individual ministers Washington was ecstatic—an enthusiasm that was tempered somewhat by Congress's subsequent wrangling over the selection of the ministers. In his own mind, the value of energy in the executive branch was proven by the military campaign of 1781 when British military confidence was mortally wounded at Yorktown. Washington attributed much of the success of that campaign to Robert Morris, Congress's superintendent of finance. By raising the money necessary to supply the army and by taking personal responsibility for its effective distribution Morris confirmed Washington's confidence in a strong executive.

The Political Experience of War

The war did not create the political character of George Washington. Much of Washington the Virginia rebel of 1774 was still recognizable in Washington the triumphant commander-in-chief of 1783. But the war did compel him to rethink many of his assumptions about the prospects of republican government. While his optimism about an American empire of virtue and justice had been unreserved in 1774, his experiences in the war made him increasingly skeptical that such an empire was natural or inevitable. Believing in republicanism was one thing; raising it up in an increasingly chaotic, even revolutionary, America was quite another matter.

Several themes emerge from a close reading of Washington's wartime correspondence. First, he came to believe that no community could long rely solely on the virtue and public spiritedness of its ordinary citizens. Self-interest and factionalism would corrode public virtue if it was not invigorated by the leadership and public example of the better sort of men. In addition, a system of laws based on sound republican principles had to be vigorously enforced at all levels of government. Otherwise, citizens would come to see a real advantage in pursuing their own self-interest. Second, there were common interests (e.g., independence, economic prosperity, security against foreign intrigues) shared by all Americans that transcended the interests of smaller communities and states. Because these common interests benefitted the whole, they had a higher claim to authority than other, more local, public interests. Third, powers sufficient for attaining the general interests of all Americans had to be attached to a national government. Such a government (and Washington was still unsure of its precise form and structure) not only had to have plenary powers to deal with those common national interests, but its executive had to have enough authority to guarantee compliance with its measures. National supremacy thus had to be the rule in all areas affecting the common interest. Fourth, agencies of the national government had to be made permanent. The army surely would be one of those permanent institutions, but Washington anticipated that other national agencies would require the same continuity. Ministries for foreign affairs, finance, and war were essential, and he hinted at the possibility of a national bank, an agency for managing the western lands, and even a national university.

The war also reinforced a lesson learned in his Virginia years. Successful generals must immerse themselves in politics as much as in battlefield tactics. He had tried to remain aloof from American partisan politics early in the war, often seeking to project an image of the republican hero standing above the fray, motivated only by a sense of personal honor and public virtue. He feared, because of the ideological predisposition of most Americans against standing armies and placemen, that any political influence he might attempt to exercise could well backfire, undermining the war effort and destroying his own carefully constructed public persona. But to raise his army, keep it supplied, and earn the cooperation of Congress and the states Washington came to recognize that such a posture was untenable. Washington thus became an increasingly active and influential political player. He wrote candid, behind-the-scenes letters to Congressmen and state leaders (a practice he had avoided the first year or two of the war when he was playing the nonpartisan) whom he believed might influence political events. Political allies communicated with him regularly, keeping him informed of the political scene and soliciting his views on various plans and proposals. He surrounded himself with aides such as Alexander Hamilton, John Laurens, and Joseph Reed who were chosen deliberately for their political skills rather than their military experience.

After 1781, with military victory imminent, Washington turned his attention more and more to the political problems of an independent United States. He was full of political ideas—ideas he deemed vital to the success of the constitutional order. But the overwhelming demands of commander-in-chief had prevented him from embarking on the sort of careful reflection that would enable him to place these ideas within the sort of "system" that he so much admired. Sentiments, no matter how deeply felt, did not make a coherent political theory. Ironically, his impending retirement, which he often envisioned as a return to the simple life of a farmer, would immerse him ever more deeply in American political life and provide him the time to more fully contemplate his vision for an American empire.

Notes

1. GW perceived the military struggle as a war for independence rather than a revolution. Only toward the very end of the war does the word *revolution* appear in his letters, and only then because the term was being used widely (though subject to ambiguous and idiosyncratic meanings) by many of his correspondents—state political leaders, members of Congress, fellow officers—as part of the regular discourse of the day.

2. Several recent works have made much of GW's admiration of the hero of Joseph Addison's eighteenth-century play *The Tragedy of Cato*: Paul K. Longmore, *The Invention of George Washington* (Berkeley, Los Angeles, and London, 1988), 171–83; and Garry Wills, *Cincinnatus: George Washington and the Enlightenment* (Garden City, N.Y., 1984), in particular, have argued that much of GW's public behavior was patterned on the classical republican hero of the play.

3. British generals, of course, had their own reputations to protect and thus tended to inflate GW's prowess as a military strategist (Sir Henry Clinton, *The American Rebellion,* ed. William B. Wilcox [New Haven, 1954]; Charles, Earl Cornwallis, *An Answer to That Part of the Narrative of Lieutenant-General Sir Henry Clinton . . .* [London, 1783]; Sir William Howe, *The Narrative of Lieut. Gen. Sir William Howe* [London, 1780]).

4. Gordon S. Wood, *The Creation of the American Republic, 1776–1787* (Chapel Hill, N.C., 1969), 46–124.

5. Interestingly, one of the revolutionary transformations of the war was the dramatic change in the public's perception of the term *republican*. Before 1776 most Americans, including most Revolutionaries, avoided using the terms *republican* or *republicanism*. Classical taxonomies of government usually characterized republics as "democracies." Because democracy was generally thought of as a depraved or corrupted form of government, no public figure seeking legitimacy for his ideas would refer to them as republican. After 1776 republicanism became de rigueur. No one knows exactly why, but the best speculation seems to be that Americans had long endorsed the substance of republican ideology even as they distanced themselves from republican rhetoric. Once independence separated the states from the old constitution (as well as the old language and old forms that went with it), Americans were free to call themselves republicans unapologetically (Willi Paul Adams, "Republicanism in Political Rhetoric before 1776," *Political Science Quarterly* 85 [1970]: 397–421; Adams, *The First American Constitutions: Republican Ideology and the Making of the State Constitutions in the Revolutionary Era* [Chapel Hill, N.C., 1980], 6–26, 99–117; Cecelia Kenyon, "Republicanism and Radicalism in the American Revolution: An Old-Fashioned Interpretation," *WMQ* 19 [1962]: 166).

6. GW to Congress, Sept. 24, 1776, *GW: Writings* 6:107.

7. Ibid., 6:3.

8. GW to Lund Washington, Aug. 20, 1775, *PGW: Rev. Ser.* 1:336.

9. GW to Richard Henry Lee, Aug. 29, 1775, ibid., 1:372.

10. GW to John Hancock, Sept. 21, 1775, ibid., 2:24–30; GW to John Parke Custis, Jan. 22, 1777, *GW: Writings* 7:53–54; GW to Richard Henry Lee, Aug. 29, 1775, *PGW: Rev. Ser.* 1:372–75.

11. Ironically, the social character of the Continental army was probably "better" in 1775–76 than later in the war. The initial fever of patriotism in the first year of the war attracted volunteers from a cross section of colonial society: merchants, farmers, artisans, clergymen, in short, men of "respectability." But the productive middle class could not be expected to enlist for the duration of the conflict, so the army more and more came to represent the underclass of America: the unemployed, convicts, indentured men, recruits who had been paid by "respectable" men to take their place. . . . [Note shortened—Ed.]

12. GW to Jonathan Trumbull, Sept. 9, 1776, to Congress, Sept. 24, 1776, *GW: Writings* 6:39, 110–11.

13. GW to Massachusetts Provincial Congress, July 4, 1775, *PGW: Rev. Ser.* 1:60.

14. GW to Congress, Sept. 24, 1776, *GW: Writings* 6:108.

15. GW to Lund Washington, Aug. 20, 1775, *PGW: Rev. Ser.* 1:335.

16. GW to William Livingston, July 12, 1777, *GW Writings* 8:442.

17. GW to Henry Laurens, July 24, 1778, ibid., 12:224.

18. GW to Board of War, Jan. 9, 1779, ibid., 13:498.

19. GW to Committee of Conference, Jan. 20, 1779, ibid., 14:27.

20. GW to Congress, April 10, 1778, ibid., 11:237–38.

21. GW to William Maxwell, May 10, 1779, ibid., 15:33.

22. Military historians have generated a rich literature on the strategic character of the Revolutionary War. A particularly useful debate on the question of whether the war was a traditional conflict or an irregular one can be found in Ronald Hoffman and Peter J. Albert, eds., *Arms and Independence: The Military Character of the American Revolution* (Charlottesville, Va., 1984), esp. Don Higginbotham, "Reflections on the War of Independence, Modern Guerrilla Warfare, and the War in Vietnam," 1–24.

23. GW to Joseph Reed, May 28, 1780, *GW: Writings* 18:436.

24. See Bernard Bailyn, *The Ideological Origins of the American Revolution*, rev. ed. (Cambridge, Mass., 1992), 112–20.

25. Charles Royster, *A Revolutionary People at War: The Continental Army and American Character, 1775–1783* (Chapel Hill, N.C., 1979).

26. These fears, it seems, were not entirely unfounded (Richard H. Kohn, "The Inside Story of the Newburgh Conspiracy: America and the Coup d'Etat," *WMQ* 27 [1970]: 187–220; Kenneth Bowling, "New Light on the Philadelphia Mutiny of 1783: Federal-State Confrontation at the Close of the War of Independence," *PMHB* 101 [1977]: 419–50). [Note shortened—Ed.]

27. General Orders, Oct. 21, March 1, 1778, March 30, 1781, *GW: Writings* 13:118–19, 11:8–10, 21:159.

28. GW to Patrick Henry, March 28, 1778, ibid., 11:164.

29. Worthington C. Ford et al., eds., *Journals of the Continental Congress, 1774–1789*, 34 vols. (Washington, D.C., 1904–37), 2:96–97.

30. Royster, *A Revolutionary People at War*, 255–30.

31. GW to Congress, May 27, 1780, *GW: Writings* 18: 416–19.

32. Circular to the New England States, Jan. 5, 1781, GW to Congress, Jan. 6, 1781, ibid., 21:61–62, 64–66.

33. GW to Robert Howe, Jan. 22, 1781, ibid., 128–29.

34. GW to Lewis Nicola, May 22, 1782, ibid., 24:272–73.

35. The best account by far of the Newburgh Conspiracy is Kohn, "The Inside History of the Newburgh Conspiracy."

36. The Newburgh Address, March 11, 1783, in *Basic Documents on the Confederation and Constitution*, ed. Richard B. Morris (New York, 1970), 43–46.

37. General Orders, March 11, 1783, *GW: Writings* 26:208.

38. GW to the Officers of the Army, March 15, 1783, ibid., 224–25.

39. Ibid., 226–27.

40. There is some dispute about whether these words were spoken before or after GW's main address. Most accounts place the remark after the speech. In addition, the precise wording of GW's extemporaneous comment varies slightly among the witnesses. This particular version seems to be the most widely accepted one. It appears in *GW: Writings* 26:222n.

41. Wood, *Creation of the American Republic*, 499–506.

42. Ironically, GW's idea was adopted but without giving him the command he wanted. In fact, in this new joint colonial command he was made a subordinate to the governor of Maryland—hardly what GW had had in mind! For a fuller accounting, see Freeman, *Washington* 2:125–68.

43. Marc Egnal, "The Origins of the Revolution in Virginia: A Reinterpretation," *WMQ* 37 (1980): 401–28.

44. Most patriots accepted the notion that military victory over the British was essential. But patriots divided . . . over other goals of the Revolution. . . . the Revolution was not just to establish home rule; it was to determine who should rule at home (Carl Becker, *History of Political Parties in the Province of New York, 1760–1770* [Madison, Wis., 1909]). [Note shortened—Ed.]

45. GW to Benjamin Harrison, Dec. 18, 1778, *GW: Writings* 13:464.

46. Ibid., Dec. 30, 1778, 466.

47. Ibid., 467.

48. E. Wayne Carp, *To Starve the Army at Pleasure: Continental Army Administration and American Political Culture, 1775–1783* (Chapel Hill, N.C., 1984).

49. GW to Benjamin Harrison, March 21, 1781, *GW: Writings* 21:342.

50. GW to William Duer, Jan. 14, 1777, ibid., 7:13.

51. Behavior such as this was not unique to revolutionary state governments. This phenomenon, the "free rider" problem, characterizes many social

interactions . . . . See Mancur Olson, *The Logic of Collective Action* (Cambridge, Mass., 1965), 9–36. [Note shortened—Ed.]

52. "The States are not behind hand in making application for assistance notwithstanding scarcely any one of them . . . is taking effectual measure to compleat its quota of Continental Troops, or have even power or energy enough to draw forth their Militia" (GW to John Armstrong, May 18, 1779, *GW: Writings* 15:97). [Note shortened—Ed.]

53. On May 4, 1779, GW informed Governor William Livingston of New Jersey that "very disagreeable consequences" would occur if the militia's pay were increased, for regular soldiers would see it as giving greater rewards to temporary forces than to Continental rank and file (ibid., 14:489–90). [Note shortened—Ed.]

54. GW to John Armstrong, May 18, 1779, ibid., 15:97.

55. GW's troubles with Congress and the states over the appointment and promotion of officers is well documented elsewhere (Don Higginbotham, *George Washington and the American Military Tradition* [Athens, Ga., 1985]; Louis C. Hatch, *The Administration of the Revolutionary Army* [New York, 1904]; Jonathan Gregory Rossie, *The Politics of Command in the American Revolution* [Syracuse, N.Y., 1975]).

56. GW to James Varnum, Nov. 4, 1777, *GW: Writings* 10:5.

57. GW to John Bannister, April 21, 1778, ibid., 11:291–92.

58. An excellent summary of the dimensions of this debate from the perspectives of both the Revolutionary generation and contemporary historians can be found in Jack N. Rakove, *The Beginnings of National Politics: An Interpretive History of the Continental Congress* (New York, 1979), 163–91.

59. See E. Wayne Carp, "The Origins of the Nationalist Movement of 1780–1783: Congressional Administration and the Continental Army," *PMHB* 107 (1983): 363–92; E. James Ferguson, "The Nationalists of 1781–83 and the Economic Interpretation of the Constitution," *Journal of American History* 56 (1969): 241–61; Merrill Jensen, *The New Nation: A History of the United States during the Confederation, 1781–1789* (New York, 1950). For a significant modification of the thesis that there was a cohesive nationalist movement in this period, see Lance Banning, "James Madison and the Nationalists, 1780–1783," *WMQ* 40 (1983): 227–55; Rakove, *Beginnings of National Politics*, 307–24.

60. GW to Francis Lewis, July 6, 1780, *GW: Writings* 19:130–32.

61. Ibid.

62. See GW to Joseph Jones, March 24, 1781, to William Fitzhugh, March 25, 1781, to John Armstrong, March 26, 1781, ibid., 21:374, 375–76, 379–80.

63. GW to John Parke Custis, Feb. 28, 1781, ibid., 320–21.

64. GW to Joseph Jones, May 14, 1780, ibid., 18:356–57.

65. *PGW: Rev. Ser.* 1:84.

8. George Washington, the West, and the Union

W. W. Abbot

Land, western land, stretching endlessly toward the Mississippi River brought out the worst and the best in Washington and other Virginians of his generation. From his days as a sixteen-year-old surveyor in the Shenandoah Valley to the time of his death, Washington sought new realms in the continental interior. Though real estate anchored the British gentry both socially and economically, their opportunities, in the parent kingdom at least, faced geographic confines. Not so for Virginians, whose treatment of land as a commodity for profitable turnover lacked precedent in the mother country. The vast interior tracts that Virginia claimed on the basis of ancient charters loomed as valuable for investment purposes, for social status, for endowing heirs, and for replacing depleted tobacco rows. Few sons of the Old Dominion equaled Washington's zeal in playing the land game, for himself and for Virginia. His temperamental outburst against General James Forbes for building a road to the forks of the Ohio through Pennsylvania rather than through Virginia showed his partisanship at its worst. Historians have also raised legal and ethical questions about how Washington obtained choice lands for himself under royal government proclamations for awarding grants to French and Indian War veterans.

At the same time, the West, as W. W. Abbot's essay shows, stretched Washington's mind during the Revolution and the 1780s. He saw a larger picture, although he was honest enough to admit that he, like other men, often combined personal interest with public service. The West was a great national resource, one to be shared by all the states, one that would strengthen the ties of union. But as president, Washington saw that there *was still much to be done, owing partly to British intrigues in the North-west and Spanish machinations in the Southwest. Washington, in signing the Jay Treaty with England and the Pinckney Treaty with Spain, removed foreign threats, for the time being at least, and furthered the westward move-ment and the creation of new states. The West, America's colonial empire, would never fear a status of permanent subordination. The thirteen colonies had predicted such a grim future for themselves before they finally declared their independence from Britain in 1776. Washington's generation had learned an important lesson about relations between peripheries and cen-ter. History would not repeat itself.*

W. W. Abbot is James Madison Professor of History Emeritus at the Uni-versity of Virginia. He is former editor-in-chief of the Papers of George Washington. *His essay originally appeared in the* Indiana Magazine of His-tory 84 (1988): 3–14 *and is reprinted by permission of the journal and the author.*

GEORGE WASHINGTON'S involvement with the American West was life-long, beginning when he was sixteen years old and ending only with his death. From start to finish Washington's interest in his country's advanc-ing frontier was both personal and political. Private interest and public ad-vantage were for him seldom at odds as he extended or developed his hold-ings in the West and at the same time promoted public measures that made for the greater security and accessibility—and value—of such lands. A full review of Washington's enduring, complex, and deep involvement with the West and its land might indicate something heretofore missed about how George Washington and his times joined forces to make a great man or, to paraphrase Thomas Jefferson on Washington, how nature and fortune com-bined to make a man great.[1]

On the day after he crossed the Blue Ridge Mountains for the first time—it was a fine Saturday in March, 1748—the sixteen-year-old Wash-ington reported that the men in the surveying party rode their horses along the Shenandoah River "through most beautiful Groves of Sugar Trees & spent the best part of the Day in admiring the Trees & richness of the Land."[2] Before he was twenty Washington had surveyed for himself, or had bought, a number of tracts of fertile land on the Virginia frontier totaling at least two thousand acres.[3] At his death nearly one-half century later, he owned more than forty-five thousand acres of carefully chosen western lands in what are now Kentucky, Ohio, West Virginia, and Pennsylvania, as well as in the Shenandoah Valley of Virginia.[4]

From his initial trip to the Shenandoah until his marriage early in 1759 shortly before his twenty-seventh birthday, Washington more often than not was on the frontier, first as a very young surveyor and then for five years as a scarcely less precocious colonel of a regiment of soldiers. It was as a military man that Washington became familiar with the trans-Allegheny West and began to dream of what the future held for its fertile land and navigable streams. In 1753 the governor of Virginia, Robert Dinwiddie, sent young Washington over the mountains to the Ohio country to deliver a warning to the commandant of the French forces there. The next year, when Washington became colonel of the Virginia troops, he was again out on the Pennsylvania frontier, on land he was in a few years to own, when he was attacked and forced to surrender to a party of French soldiers and Indians, setting in motion, as it happened, a great war for empire between Britain and France. He was back in the west in 1755 with General Edward Braddock on the day that Braddock's army was ambushed and routed as it approached Fort Duquesne, the fort that the French had recently built at the forks of the Ohio. Three years later he was once again marching through the Ohio country in the successful campaign against Fort Duquesne mounted by General John Forbes during the summer and fall of 1758. Washington was in command of one of the three brigades of Forbes's army when the army finally reached the abandoned and burned out fort in November. After returning to Williamsburg in December of 1758, he did not go back to the Ohio country until his journey there in 1770, then not again until his shorter visit of 1784; but Washington's view of the West, and of its importance, which he held even through his presidency and to his death, had by 1758 been firmly fixed.

In the early stages of the Forbes campaign Washington engaged in a bitter controversy that revealed how completely his experiences of the previous four years had convinced him of the crucial importance of the transmontane west to the future of his country, at that time Virginia, soon to be the United States. Upon learning in July that for his army's march to the Ohio Forbes proposed to cut a new road from Raystown (now Bedford) in Pennsylvania rather than to use the old Braddock road from Winchester in Virginia, Washington persuaded himself that the British general had been duped by men in Pennsylvania. The Pennsylvanians would, Washington foresaw, use the new road after the war to monopolize trade with a burgeoning West rather than allowing commerce to flow, in the way Washington believed it otherwise would and should, along Braddock's road into Virginia. For six weeks the young provincial officer fought, right up to the brink of insubordination, first to sway the British general and then to thwart him as Forbes moved to begin construction of a new road. Finally, on September 1, 1758, bemoaning "the luckless Fate of poor Virginia to fall a Victim to the views of her Crafty Neighbours," Washington hinted to John Robinson, speaker of the Virginia House of Burgesses, that he (Washington) should be sent to London to reveal to George III the wrongheadedness, if not the duplicity, of the man who was the king's general and Washington's commanding officer.[5]

Besides this strong sense that whatever the future held for the West would vitally affect the people in the East, Washington also gained from the war what was to be a very large personal stake in the region beyond the mountains. In 1754 Governor Dinwiddie issued a proclamation declaring that two hundred thousand acres in the West should be set aside for the men participating in Virginia's military expedition of that year, the one ending with Washington's surrender at Fort Necessity; and at the end of the war in 1763 a royal proclamation held out the promise of land in America for the army officers who had fought there in the war against France. Before any grants could be made under either of the proclamations, the British government in 1763 closed the land beyond the mountains to further settlement. Even with the frontier closed, Washington continued to look upon the West as holding out the best hope both of enrichment for enterprising Virginians, himself included, and of an eventual return to prosperity for Virginia's faltering economy.

In 1767 Washington urged a friend and neighbor who had fallen on bad times to pull up stakes and move out to lands soon to be available in western Pennsylvania, "where an enterprizing Man with very little Money may lay the foundation of a Noble Estate . . . for himself and posterity. . . . for proof of wch only look to Frederick [County], & see what Fortunes were made by the . . . first takers up of those Lands; Nay how the greatest Estates we have in this Colony were made; Was it not by taking up & purchasing at very low rates the rich back Lands which were thought nothing of in those days, but are now the most valuable Lands we possess?"[6] Showing himself willing to put his money where he was advising others to put theirs, three months later, on September 17, 1767, he wrote to his old comrade-in-arms William Crawford on the Pennsylvania frontier, asking him "to look me out a Tract of about 1500, 2000, or more acres somewhere in your Neighbourhood" and find "some method to secure it immediately from the attempts of any other" to lay claim to it. Crawford found a suitable tract and surveyed it for his friend, and the next year Washington secured title to it, his first land west of the Alleghenies, on the Youghiogheny River thirty five miles southeast of Fort Pitt.[7] Many more acres to the south and west were soon to be his.

In the same letter that he wrote to Crawford about land in Pennsylvania, Washington proposed that the two of them join forces "in attempting to secure some of the most valuable Lands in the Kings part" to the West. Washington pointed out that anyone "who neglects the present oppertunity of hunting out good Lands & in some measure Marking & distinguishing them for their own (in order to keep others from settling them)" would be left out in the cold, for the Proclamation of 1763 forbidding settlement was certain to "fall" within "a few years." Crawford was to "be at the trouble of seeking out the Lands" while Washington took upon himself the task of securing them as soon as there was a possibility of doing so. He would also "be at all the Cost & charges of Surveying Patenting &ca." Washington warned Crawford to "keep this whole matter a profound Secret" by "a silent management . . . snugly carried on by you under the pretence of hunting other Game." As soon as there was the "bear possibility" of the Ohio country's being opened up, Washington would "have the lands immediately Surveyed to keep others off."

In the end it was Washington himself, though accompanied by Crawford, who went down the Ohio in search of good land. The tracts that he selected were to be surveyed not for himself and Crawford alone, however. On December 15, 1769, Washington petitioned the Virginia governor and council for two hundred thousand acres of land for the former Virginia officers and soldiers entitled to grants under the terms of Dinwiddie's Proclamation of 1754.[8] The council agreed that Washington and his associates could, in no more than twenty surveys, claim two hundred thousand acres of vacant land to the south and east of the Ohio River in an area recently made available for settlement as a consequence of two Indian treaties. The next fall Washington and Crawford spent a month on the Ohio and Great Kanawha rivers identifying approximately two hundred thousand acres that Crawford was later to survey in twenty-five surveys. From 1771 through 1773 Washington oversaw Crawford's activities and the collecting of money to defray the cost of Crawford's surveys, and he personally managed the distribution of the surveyed land to the old officers and soldiers or to their heirs. His own share of the two hundred thousand acres and the shares he acquired from others added up to more than twenty-three thousand acres stretching for forty unbroken miles along the Great Kanawha River and nearly ten thousand acres on the banks of the Ohio.[9]

Aside from strictly personal affairs and perhaps his involvement in Virginia's resistance to British policy between 1773 and 1775, Washington devoted more time and attention to managing the acquisition and distribution of western land for himself and his old comrades than to anything else between the French and Indian War and the Revolution. While with one hand in the early 1770s he was getting western land into private hands and amassing great holdings for himself, with the other he was doing what he could to promote the future development of these western lands by involving himself in a public project that was to become of consuming interest to him after the Revolution. In 1770 Washington wrote about the great advantage to Virginians and Marylanders of "making Potomack the Channel of commerce between Great Britain and that immense territory, which is unfolding to our view."[10] To hasten the day when the Potomac would become "the Channel of conveyance of the extensive & valuable Trade of a rising Empire,"[11] Washington in 1772 helped push through the Virginia General Assembly a bill to raise money "for opening and extending the Navigation of the River *Potowmack* from Fort *Cumberland* to Tide Water."[12] Opposition from Baltimore merchants and the war halted the project for the time being, and Indian unrest defeated Washington's two costly efforts before the Revolution to place people on his Ohio land, which he had been determined to do in order to secure his claim to the land and hasten the day when it would become profitable.

During the war years Washington was, of course, not able to devote much attention to his western lands, but immediately after the war his western claims became a main concern. In the first six months of 1784 after his return to Mount Vernon, he took steps to have legal title to the various parcels of his western lands confirmed by the state of Virginia, and he began to search for ways to make his holdings productive and profitable. He wrote and talked to people about what could be done with these lands; he ran notices in newspapers and distributed handbills, in Maryland and in Pennsylvania as well as in Virginia, inviting settlers to take up and improve small parcels under long-term leases; and he tried to identify and make contact with people abroad who might be induced to come to America and become his tenants.[13] A trip he made in September, 1784, to inspect his western holdings was cut short by reports of Indian violence, and he was not able to go down the Ohio to the Great Kanawha as he had done in 1770. On his return from the frontier, however, he single-mindedly and almost single-handedly mounted a campaign to have a company formed for developing a water passage up the Potomac, over to the Ohio, and from there to Lake Erie beyond. Here in 1784, as in 1773, personal profit and local advantage were very much at work; but changes wrought by independence, both in the relationship of the union of states to the West and in Washington's own perceptions, also were at work, fundamentally altering Washington's view of the potential dangers and advantages posed by the West for the thirteen confederated states. His activities in the fall and early winter of 1784–1785 merit examination in some detail.

A year earlier, in 1783, after touring upstate New York with Governor George Clinton shortly before he left the army, Washington wrote the French philosophe François Jean Chastellux on October 12, 1783, about his trip: "Prompted by these actual observations," he concluded in his letter, "I could not help taking a more contemplative & extensive view of the vast inland navigation of these United States . . . & could not but be struck with the immense diffusion & importance of it . . . . I shall not rest contented 'till I have explored the Western Country, & traversed those Lines . . . which have given bounds to a new Empire." A few months later, back at Mount Vernon, Washington received a letter from Thomas Jefferson dated March 15 urging him to give up "the sweets of retirement & repose" for a time in order to assume "the superintendance" of a project to open up the navigation of the upper James and Potomac rivers and to connect them with streams flowing into the Ohio. After expressing his strong support for the project and his equally strong doubts that sufficient public funds could be got for it, Washington on March 29 conceded that "the immense advantages which this Country would derive from the measure would be no small stimulus [for me] to the undertaking; if that undertaking could be made to comport with those ideas, & that line of conduct with which I meant to glide gently down the stream of life."

Jefferson knew that more than the "sweets of retirement" were at stake for Washington, and neither he nor anyone else would have had trouble understanding what Washington meant by "those ideas, & that line of Conduct" by which he was bound. When the hero of the Revolution laid down his arms in December, 1783, and returned to his farm, the world discovered a new Cincinnatus and began to bestow on Washington the *fame* that was to place him among the great men of history.[14] Washington well understood, and said as much often enough, that the fame being bestowed on him by the world, and yet to be ratified by posterity, required that he act the part until the end, lest it be diminished or ultimately lost. This is what Washington was referring to when he spoke of the "line of Conduct" that he had set for himself. His heightened, seemingly excessive concern for his reputation, especially apparent in his correspondence in the 1780s, was not entirely, or perhaps even primarily, for its own sake. His fame, though to be cherished for its own particular worth, had, as he and Jefferson and the rest knew, its great symbolic value for a newly independent people. If the need arose, its weight could be thrown into the balance to preserve the union of states and save the Revolution. The question in Washington's mind in the spring of 1787, for instance, and in the minds of his advisers, as the record shows,[15] was whether his hard-won reputation must be put on the line to give the constitutional convention its best chances of succeeding or whether it should be held in reserve as a rallying point in the crisis that would ensue if the convention failed. It was not as easy a decision as one might now suppose.

Despite the strength of the forces that pushed and pulled him into retirement in 1784, Washington did not, of course, wait until duty called in 1787 to put what he had learned and what he had become to the public use. He was hardly settled under his fig tree and vine at Mount Vernon before he began to persuade himself that Jefferson was right, that he might properly perform one last service for his country. To assure Washington that his efforts to enlist the great man in this important public project did not arise from selfish or unworthy motives, Jefferson had written that he himself was someone "not owning, nor ever having a prospect of owning one inch of land on any water either the Patowmac or Ohio." In his reply Washington wrote: "I am not so disinterested in this matter as you are; but I am made very happy to find a man of discernment and liberality (who has no particular interest in the plan) thinks as I do, who have Lands in the Country the value of which would be enhanced by the adoption of such a scheme." Although Washington recognized that both public and private interests were involved and was aware of the connections as well as the distinctions between the two, his initial hesitation about taking the lead in the Potomac River project probably had less to do with any fears that his motives would be misunderstood than with how his early emergence from his much vaunted retirement would be perceived. In any case, by the end of the summer of 1784 his mind seems to have been made up.

When he set out in September to inspect his western lands, Washington confided to his diary that "one object of my journey" was "to obtain information of the nearest and best communication between the Eastern & Western Waters; & to facilitate as much as in me lay the Inland Navigation of the Potomack." Because of the "discontented temper of the Indians," he decided not to go down the Ohio, but he quizzed the frontiersmen about navigable streams and about land portages between the Potomac and the Ohio and between the Ohio and the Great Lakes. After a month on horseback he arrived back at Mount Vernon in October, 1784, with misplaced confidence that convenient passage from the great falls of the Potomac all the way to Detroit on Lake Erie could be achieved with relative ease. Early in the journey prospects for success had been brightened for him when he watched a model of James Rumsey's boat mechanically propelling itself upstream.[16]

After his return to Mount Vernon Washington waited less than a week to write Virginia Governor Benjamin Harrison a remarkable letter in which he effectively put himself at the head of a public campaign to use the Potomac to develop better access to the West and tie it to the East. He urged Harrison to mark his administration "as an important œra in the Annals of this Country" by taking two specific steps to promote inland navigation: first, Harrison should arrange for the state to have the James and Potomac rivers surveyed "to their respective sources" and to have the same done for those "Waters East & West of the Ohio, which invite our notice by their proximity, & the ease with which Land transportation may be had between them & the Lakes on one side, & the rivers Potomac & James on the other"; and, second, if the Virginia assembly could not be persuaded to provide the funds—and Washington expected this to be the case—he should induce it to pass a bill empowering private citizens to set up a company for "extending the navigation of Potomac or James river."[17]

In this letter to Harrison written on October 10, and in those he wrote to others later in the fall of 1784 regarding the navigation of the Potomac, Washington set out his enlarged views of the West. It becomes clear why inland navigation was the one thing that could draw the hero of the Revolution back into the public arena so quickly and unequivocally. He was convinced, as he wrote Harrison, that the Ohio country would "settle faster than any other ever did, or any one would imagine." The hordes of new settlers inevitably would demand outlets for their products. Whoever provided the outlets—the Spanish to the south, the British to the north, or the Americans to the east—would win their allegiance. It is a matter "of great political importance," Washington wrote Jacob Read in Congress on November 3, "to prevent the trade of the Western territory from settling in the hands, either of the Spanish or British," for if "the trade of that Country should flow through the Mississipi or St Lawrence . . . they would in a few years be as unconnected with us, indeed more so, than we are with South America." Washington saw "a separation or a war" as a "consequence" if Britain and Spain, "instead of *throwing stumbling blocks* in their way as they now do, should hold out lures for [the settlers'] trade and alliance." When writing to Henry Knox a month later, on December 5, about his endeavors "to stimulate my Countrymen to the extension of the inland navigation of the rivers Potomac and James," he made his point unmistakably clear, declaring that "if this Country . . . cannot, by any easy communication be drawn this way . . . they will become a distinct people from us—have different views—different interests, & instead of adding strength to the Union, may in case of a rupture with either of those powers [Spain or Britain], be a formidable & dangerous neighbour."

Washington's solution was to provide westerners easy access to eastern markets. "The more communications are opened" between East and West, Washington wrote George Plater of Maryland on October 25, "the closer we bind that rising world (for indeed it may be so called) to our interests; and the greater strength shall we acquire by it. . . . These when viewed upon a Commercial scale, are alone sufficient to excite our endeavors; but the political object is, in my estimation, immense." He pointed to the advantages that would accrue to the states of Maryland and Virginia and to particular individuals in them as well from an active trade with the West along the Potomac. "But," he wrote Plater, "I consider this business in a far more extensive point of view—and the more I have revolved it, the more important it appears to me; not only as it respects our commerce, but our political interests, and the well being, & strength of the Union also." It was to advance national goals that Washington came out of retirement to create the Potomac River Company;[18] the enrichment of Virginia and of some Virginians was now, at best, a secondary consideration for him.

While Washington himself never lost sight of the larger implications—the "political object"—of inland navigation, in order to gain support for his Potomac project in the Virginia and Maryland legislatures he emphasized the wealth that would flow into the region from increased trade with the West—trade, he warned, that would be lost to the more commercial-minded Pennsylvanians and New Yorkers if the people did not act promptly. When calling upon the legislatures of Virginia and Maryland to create a private company for opening the upper Potomac to navigation, he reminded them that the company must be given the power "to hold out sufficient inducements to engage men to hazard their fortunes in an arduous undertaking."[19] Later when he was seeking funds for the company from men such as the Marquis de Lafayette and Robert Morris, he was careful to hold out for investors the prospect of great gains from fees collected on the waterways.[20] As he reminded James Madison on December 3, when

Madison was preparing to shepherd the bill creating the Potomac River Company through the Virginia legislature, "the motives which predominate most in human affairs is self-love and self-interest." To get his company and to get it going Washington talked as of old about sectional advantage and private gain, but he also spoke to investor and politician about his basic concern: how links to the West could well determine the future safety and prosperity of the Union.

Washington did more than talk and write. Nor was he content only to lend the prestige of his name, though even that in any other connection he consistently refused to do. He instead intervened, directly and decisively, to secure prompt interstate cooperation in forming a company to his liking for opening up communication to the West by way of the Potomac River. Convinced of the feasibility of the project by what he had learned on his recent journey to the West, Washington in October set to work, marshaling support for it among his friends and neighbors on both sides of the Potomac. A large number of these met in Alexandria, Virginia, on November 14 and drafted a bill for creating a company to finance and oversee the opening of the upper Potomac for navigation. In the meantime Washington was in touch with the governor and with friends in the Virginia legislature in Richmond, and on November 13 or 14 he arrived at the state capital for ten days to talk, particularly to James Madison and Joseph Jones in the House of Delegates, about creating a Potomac River Company.[21] Within a week of leaving Richmond he was in Annapolis where, as he reported to Madison on December 3 after his return to Mount Vernon, he found "opportunities of conversing with some of the leading characters in the different branches of the Legislature of Maryland, on the subject of inland navigation, and the benefits which might arise from a commercial intercourse with the Western Territory." He suggested to Madison that to save time and to "prevent dissimilar proceedings," which would be "as unproductive as no bill" at all, the two legislatures should "depute one or more members to meet at some intermediate place, and agree . . . upon an adequate bill to be adopted by both States." The two legislatures were agreeable, and Washington was named one of three Virginia commissioners to meet with the Marylanders.[22] By December 3 he was back in Annapolis where he acted as the sole Virginia commissioner. Working with a joint committee of the Maryland legislature, he secured a draft of a Potomac River bill that met his wishes. The Maryland legislature passed the bill on December 28 with only nine dissenting votes.[23] Washington immediately sent it to Madison with the admonishment that "to alter the Act now . . . will not do." At Washington's urging and under Madison's management, the Virginia legislature ten days later adopted the Maryland act unaltered.[24] Washington had his Potomac River Company, and on May 17, 1785, he became its first president, a position he held until he became president of the United States. Before he was done with that job, he had put to use all he had learned about the West since 1748.

No attempt has been made in this discussion of George Washington, the West, and the Union to define where Washington's activities in the fall of 1784 fit into the genealogy of the federal union formed in 1789, though clearly they do fit. Even less has the impact of Washington's ideas and deeds on the Old Northwest been measured, though, again, they were not without influence. The evidence presented does suggest, however, that Washington's long experience with the West and his strongly held views about its importance, leading in 1784 to his active participation in measures to bind it to the newly confederated states, more than anything else, except the war itself, served to prepare him for the role of nation builder. The West made the Virginia farmer lift his eyes to prospects beyond his own fields and his native Virginia. In his brief years of retirement after the war, it stretched his mind, stirred his imagination, enlisted his energies, and nourished his hopes for the future. It kept the old hero in trim for the demands of 1787 and 1789. As Madison put it when giving Jefferson an account of Washington's role in the establishment of the Potomac River Company, "The earnestness with which he espouses the undertaking is hardly to be described, and shews that a mind like his, capable of great views & which has long been occupied with them, cannot bear a vacancy; and surely he could not have chosen an occupation more worthy of succeeding to that of establishing the political rights of his Country."[25]

Notes

1. Jefferson's famous appraisal of GW's character appears in a letter to Dr. Walter Jones, Jan. 2, 1814, in Paul Leicester Ford, ed., *The Writings of Thomas Jefferson*, 10 vols. (New York, 1892–99), 9:446–51.

2. *PGW: Diaries* 1:7.

3. For GW's surveys and his landholding in Frederick County, Virginia, see "George Washington's Professional Surveys, July 22, 1749–October 25, 1752," *PGW: Col. Ser.* 1:8–37, esp. 35n.

4. Roy Bird Cook pulled together a great deal of information on GW's landholdings in his *Washington's Western Lands* (Strasburg, Va., 1930). A great deal more may be gained from the texts and annotation in the *PGW: Diaries* and the

various chronological series of *The Papers of George Washington*. See particularly GW's Advertisement of March 1784, *PGW: Conf. Ser.* 1:201–4.

5. GW to John Robinson, Sept. 1, 1758, *PGW: Col. Ser.* 5:432–33.

6. GW to John Posey, June 24, 1767, ibid., 8:1–4.

7. GW to William Crawford, Sept. 17, 1767, William Crawford to GW, Jan. 7, 1769, ibid., 26–32, 156–59.

8. H. R. McIlwaine et al., eds., *Executive Journals of the Council of Colonial Virginia*, 6 vols. (Richmond, 1925–66), 6:337–38.

9. See Cook, *Washington's Western Lands,* esp. chaps. 1–4; *PGW: Diaries* 2:277–328; and correspondence between GW and Crawford, 1767–73, in *PGW: Col. Ser.,* vols. 8–9. Some of this land was a part of the 5,000 acres GW obtained under the terms of the royal proclamation of 1763 and some of it was what others had received under its terms and conveyed to GW.

10. GW to Thomas Johnson, July 20, 1770, *PGW: Col. Ser.* 8:357–60. See also GW to Thomas Jefferson, March 29, 1784, *PGW: Conf. Ser.* 1:237–41.

11. GW to Thomas Johnson, July 20, 1770, *PGW: Col. Ser.* 8:357–60.

12. H. R. McIlwaine and John P. Kennedy, eds., *Journals of the House of Burgesses of Virginia,* 13 vols. (Richmond, 1905–15), 1770–72: 292, 312. See also GW to Jonathan Boucher, May 4, 1772, *PGW: Col. Ser.* 9:38–39; GW to Jefferson, March 29, 1784, *PGW: Conf. Ser.* 1:237–41. See also Corra Bacon-Foster, *Potomac Route to the West* (Washington, D.C., 1912), 17–21.

13. Much of his correspondence at this time deals with one or another of these matters, but see particularly his letters to Samuel Lewis, Feb. 1, to Thomas Lewis, Feb. 1, to John Harvie, Feb. 10, to Gilbert Simpson, Feb. 13, to John Witherspoon, March 10, and his Advertisement, March 10, all in 1784, *PGW: Conf. Ser.* 1:91–100, 107–9, 117–18, 197–204.

14. For the meaning of *fame* to GW and his contemporaries, see Douglass Adair, *Fame and the Founding Fathers: Essays,* ed. Trevor Colbourn (New York, 1974). A passage from an address to GW from the Virginia legislature, dated June 24, 1784, conveys something of what fame meant to this generation of Americans: "Nor shall we ever forget the exemplary respect which in every instances you have shewn to the rights of civil authority: or the exalted virtue, which on many occasions led you to commit to danger your fame itself, rather than hazard for a moment the true interest of your country" (*Journal of the House of Delegates of the Commonwealth of Virginia* [Richmond, 1828], 1781–85, June 22, 1784).

15. See in particular GW to David Humphreys, Dec. 26, 1786, Humphreys to GW, Jan. 20, 1787, GW to Edmund Randolph, April 9, 1787, *PGW: Conf. Ser.* 4:477–81, 526–30, 5:135–36.

16. GW's journal of his trip to the frontier is in *PGW: Diaries* 4:1–71 (quotations on 4, 21).

17. GW to Benjamin Harrison, Oct. 10, 1784, *PGW: Conf. Ser.* 2:86–98.

18. For GW's attempts to draw the Confederation Congress into his scheme

for opening up communications to the West, see particularly his letter to Richard Henry Lee, Dec. 14, 1784, ibid., 181–83.

19. GW to Joseph Jones and James Madison, Dec. 3, 1784, ibid., 165–68.

20. See GW to Robert Morris, Feb. 1, 1785, to the marquis de Lafayette, Feb. 15, 1785, ibid., 309–15, 363–67.

21. On Nov. 18, 1784, Henry Lee wrote from Alexandria to GW in Richmond reporting that the Alexandria meeting had completed its business and that he had enclosed a copy of the bill it had drafted for GW to peruse and then place "in proper hands" (ibid., 139–41). GW had left Richmond before the bill could get to him, and it did not reach him at Mount Vernon until Nov. 28, when he immediately forwarded it to Madison (GW to Henry Lee, Nov. 24, 1784, to Madison, Nov. 28, 1784, ibid., 144–45, 155–57). No GW diaries exist for this period, but GW's movements may be pieced together from his correspondence.

22. Beverley Randolph to GW, Dec. 15, 1784, GW to Randolph, Dec. 20, 1784, ibid., 185–87, 223.

23. See GW to Thomas Blackburn, to William Paca, both dated Dec. 19, 1784, Blackburn to GW, Dec. 20, 1784, Horatio Gates to GW, Dec. 24, 1784, GW to Madison, Dec. 28, 1784, GW and Horatio Gates to Virginia Legislature, Dec. 28, 1784, ibid., 195–96, 229–36. See also GW to Henry Knox, Jan. 5, 1785, and the journals of the legislatures of both states, ibid., 253–56.

24. See particularly Madison to GW, Jan. 9, 1785, ibid., 260–61.

25. Madison to Jefferson, Jan. 9, 1785, in William T. Hutchinson et al., eds., *The Papers of James Madison: Congressional Series,* 17 vols. (Chicago and Charlottesville, Va., 1962–91), 8:222–34.

9. The Farewell

Washington's Wisdom at the End

JOSEPH J. ELLIS

Washington's presidency has received less attention than his career as a soldier. Perhaps the reason is that there is more glamour and excitement to the field of battle than there is to the routine, bureaucratic doings of the chief executive's office. Indeed, Washington himself preferred soldiering. There is abundant evidence for that, beginning as early as 1754 when he said he had heard the whir of nearby bullets and found something charming in the sound. Moreover, he protested, in response to appeals to accept the presidency, that war, not statecraft, claimed his fancy. In fact, he had had extensive experience in the political realm—as member of the House of Burgesses, delegate to the Continental Congress, persistent and penetrating critic of the Articles of Confederation, backstage mover behind the Annapolis Convention to strengthen interstate commercial ties, and president of the Constitutional Convention. No one had more hands-on experience with public life at both state and national levels than the first president, with the notable exception of Benjamin Franklin, who died in his eighties a year after Washington took office in 1790.

It is arguable, however, that there is a second reason why Washington's presidential years have often been neglected by so many of his biographers and other specialists. It is the specter of Alexander Hamilton. Would one find on thorough investigation that an aging president, seemingly in declining health, served as a front or prop for an aggressive, ambitious Hamilton, the secretary of the treasury from 1789 to 1795 and the real father of the emerging Federalist party? Joseph Charles, in The Origins of the Party System *(1956), made such a claim, one that resonated with countless read-*

ers who saw a parallel with their own president, Dwight D. Eisenhower, an elderly military hero, who, his critics alleged, suffered from captivity at the hands of staff members and other Republican stalwarts. Forrest Mc-Donald's The Presidency of George Washington *(1974) likewise minimizes Washington's own initiatives and accomplishments, seeing his role in the creation of the new federal government in symbolic terms. Ellis stands with numerous scholars of the last two decades who describe Washington's presidential performance in a much more positive light.*

Joseph J. Ellis is the Ford Foundation Professor of History at Mount Holyoke College. His books include Passionate Sage: The Character and Legacy of John Adams *and* American Sphinx: The Character of Thomas Jefferson, *which won the National Book Award in 1997. This chapter is from* Founding Brothers *by Joseph J. Ellis. Copyright © 2000 by Joseph J. Ellis. Reprinted (adapted) by permission of Alfred A. Knopf, a Division of Random House Inc.*

THROUGHOUT THE FIRST HALF of the 1790s, the closest approximation to a self-evident truth in American politics was George Washington. A legend in his own time, Washington had been described as "the Father of the Country" since 1776, which is to say before there was even a country. By the time he assumed the presidency in 1789—no other candidate was thinkable—the mythology surrounding Washington's reputation had grown like ivy over a statue, effectively covering the man with an aura of omnipotence, rendering the distinction between his human qualities and his heroic achievements impossible to delineate.[1]

If there was a Mount Olympus in the new American Republic, all the lesser gods were gathered farther down the slope. The only serious contender for primacy was Benjamin Franklin, but just before his death in 1790 Franklin himself acknowledged Washington's supremacy. In a characteristically Franklinesque gesture, he bequeathed to Washington his crabtree walking stick, presumably to assist the general in his stroll toward immortality. "If it were a sceptre," Franklin remarked, "he has merited it and would become it."[2]

In the America of the 1790s, Washington's image was everywhere: in paintings, prints, lockets; on coins, silverware, plates, and household bric-a-brac. And his familiarity seemed forever. His commanding presence had been the central feature in every major event of the Revolutionary era: the linchpin of the Continental army throughout eight long years of desperate fighting from 1775 to 1783; the presiding officer at the Constitutional Convention in 1787; the first and only chief executive of the fledging federal government since 1789. He was the palpable reality that clothed the Revolutionary rhapsodies in flesh and blood, America's one and only indispensable character.

Although Thomas Jefferson was predisposed to regard the American Revolution as a product of principles rather than personalities—and in fact was just being recognized in the 1790s as the author of those lyrical words in the Declaration of Independence—even Jefferson described Washington as the embodiment of American providence: "There is sometimes an eminence of character on which society have such peculiar claims," Jefferson wrote to Washington in 1792. "This seems to be your condition." Washington was the core of gravity that prevented the American Revolution from flying off into random orbits. As one popular toast of the day put it, he was "the man who unites all hearts." He was the American Zeus, Moses, and Cincinnatus all rolled into one.[3]

Then, all of a sudden, on September 19, 1796, an article addressed to "the PEOPLE of the United States" appeared on the inside pages of the *American Daily Advertiser,* Philadelphia's major newspaper. The conspicuous austerity of the announcement was matched by its calculated simplicity. It began: "Friends, and Fellow Citizens: The period for a new election of a Citizen, to Administer the Executive government of the United States, being not far distant . . . , it appears to me proper, especially as it may conduce to a more distinct expression of the public voice, that I should now apprise you of the resolutions I have formed, to decline being considered among the number of those, out of whom a choice is to be made." It ended with the unadorned signature, "G. Washington, United States."[4]

Every major newspaper in the country reprinted the article over the ensuing weeks, though only one, the *Courier of New Hampshire,* gave it the title that would echo through the ages: "Washington's Farewell Address." Contemporaries began to debate its contents almost immediately, and a lively argument soon ensued about whether Washington or Hamilton actually wrote it. Over a longer stretch of time the Farewell Address achieved transcendental status, ranking alongside the Declaration of Independence and the Gettysburg Address as a seminal statement of America's abiding principles. Its Olympian tone made it a perennial touchstone at those political occasions requiring platitudinous wisdom. And in the late nineteenth century, the Congress made its reading a mandatory ritual on Washington's birthday. Meanwhile, several generations of historians, led by students of American diplomacy, have made the interpretation of the Farewell Address into a cottage industry of its own, building up a veritable mountain of commentary around its implications for an isolationist foreign policy and a bipartisan brand of American statecraft.[5]

But in the crucible of the moment none of these subsequent affectations or interpretations mattered. What did matter, what struck most readers as the only thing that truly mattered, was that George Washington was retiring. The constitutional significance of the decision, of course, struck home immediately, signaling as it did Washington's voluntary surrender of the presidency after two terms, thereby setting the precedent that held firm until 1940, when Franklin Delano Roosevelt broke it. (It was reaffirmed in 1951 with passage of the Twenty-second Amendment.) But that landmark precedent, so crucial in establishing the republican principle of rotation in office, paled in comparison to an even more elemental political and psychological realization.

For twenty years, over the entire life span of the Revolutionary War and experiment with republican government, Washington had stood at the helm of the ship of state. Now he was sailing off into the sunset. The precedent he was setting may have seemed uplifting in retrospect, but at the time the glaring and painful reality was that the United States without Washington was itself unprecedented. The Farewell Address was an oddity in that it was not really an address; it was never delivered as a speech. It should, by all rights, be called the Farewell Letter, for it was in form and tone an open letter to the American people, telling them they were now on their own.

Insiders had suspected that this was coming for about six months. In February 1796 Washington had first approached Alexander Hamilton about drafting some kind of valedictory statement. Shortly thereafter the gossip network inside the government had picked up the scent. By the end of the month, James Madison was writing James Monroe in Paris, "It is pretty certain that the President will not serve beyond his present term." On the eve of the Farewell Address, the Federalist leader from Massachusetts, Fisher Ames, predicted that Washington's looming announcement would constitute "a signal, like dropping a hat, for the party races to start," but in fact they had been going on unofficially throughout the preceding spring and summer. In May, for example, Madison had speculated—correctly it turned out—that in the first contested election for president in American history, "Jefferson would probably be the object on one side [and] Adams apparently on the other." By midsummer Washington himself was apprising friends of his desire to leave the government when his term was up, "after which no consideration under heaven that I can foresee shall again withdraw me from the walks of private life." He had been dropping hints throughout his second term, describing himself as "on the advanced side of the grand climacteric" and too old for the rigors of the job, repeating his familiar refrain about the welcome solace of splendid isolation beneath his "vine and fig tree" at Mount Vernon.[6]

But did he mean it? Protestations about the tribulations of public life, followed by incantations about the bucolic splendor of retirement to rural solitude, had become a familiar, even formulaic, posture within the leadership class of the Revolutionary generation, especially within the Virginia dynasty. Everyone knew the classical models of latter-day seclusion represented by Cincinnatus and described by Cicero and Virgil. Declarations of principled withdrawal from the hurly-burly of politics to the natural rhythms of one's fields or farms had become rhetorical rituals. If Washington's retirement featured the "vine and fig tree," Jefferson's idolized "my family, my farm, and my books." The motif had become so commonplace that John Adams, an aspiring Cicero himself, claimed that the Virginians had worn out the entire Ciceronian syndrome. "It seems the Mode of becoming great is to retire," he wrote Abigail in 1796. "It is marvellous how political Plants grow in the shade." Washington had been threatening to retire even before he was inaugurated as president in 1789 and had repeated the threat in 1792 before his reelection. Although sincere on all occasions, his preference for a virtuous retirement had always been trumped by a more public version of virtue, itself reinforced by the unanimous judgment of his political advisers that he and he alone was indispensable. Why expect a different conclusion in 1796?[7]

The short answer was age. Throughout most of his life, Washington's physical vigor had been one of his most priceless assets. A notch below 6 feet 2 inches and slightly above 200 pounds, he was nearly a head taller than most of his male contemporaries. (John Adams claimed that the reason Washington was invariably selected to lead every national effort was that he was always the tallest man in the room.) A detached description of his physical features would have made him sound like an ugly, misshapen oaf: pockmarked face, decayed teeth, oversized eye sockets, massive nose, heavy in the hips, gargantuan hands and feet. But somehow, when put together and set in motion, the full package conveyed sheer majesty. As one of his biographers put it, his body did not just occupy space; it seemed to organize the space around it. "He had so much martial dignity in his deportment," observed Benjamin Rush, "that there is not a king in Europe but would look like a valet de chambre by his side."[8] The inevitable chinks in his cast-iron constitution began to appear in 1790. In that year he came down with influenza, then raging in New York, and nearly died from pulmonary complications. Jefferson's statements about Washington were notoriously contradictory and unreliable, but he dated Washington's physical decline from this moment: "The firm tone of his mind, for which he had been remarkable, was beginning to relax; a listlessness of labor, a desire for tranquility had crept on him, and a willingness to let others act, or even think, for him." In 1794, while on a tour of the terrain around the new national capital that would bear his name, the president badly wrenched his back. After a career of galloping to hounds and earning a historic reputation as America's premier man on horseback, he was never able to hold his seat in the saddle with the same confidence. As he moved into his mid-sixties, the muscular padding around his torso softened and sagged, his erect bearing started to tilt forward, as if he were always leaning into the wind, and his energy flagged by the end of each long day. Hostile newspaper editorials spoke elliptically of encroaching senility. Even his own vice president, John Adams, conceded that Washington seemed dazed and wholly scripted at certain public ceremonies, like an actor reading his lines or an aging athlete going through the motions.[9]

Perhaps age alone would have been sufficient to propel Washington down the road from Philadelphia to Mount Vernon one last time. Surely if anyone deserved to spend his few remaining years reclining under his "vine and fig tree," it was Washington. Perhaps, in the eerily instinctive way that he always grasped the difference between the essential and the peripheral, he literally felt in his bones that another term as president meant that he would die in office. By retiring now he avoided that fate, which would have established a precedent that smacked of monarchical longevity by permitting biology to set the terminus of his tenure. Our obsession with the two-term precedent obscures the more elemental principle established by Washington's voluntary retirement; namely that the office would routinely outlive the occupant, that the American presidency was fundamentally different from a European monarchy, that presidents, no matter how indispensable, were inherently disposable.

But advancing age and sheer physical fatigue were only part of the answer. Washington was leaving office not just because he was hearing whispers of mortality, but also because he was wounded. What no British bullet could do in the Revolutionary War, the opposition press had managed to do in the political battles during his second term. In the wake of his Farewell Address, for example, an open letter appeared in Benjamin Franklin Bache's *Aurora,* in which the old firebrand Tom Paine celebrated Washington's departure, actually prayed for his imminent death, then predicted that "the world will be puzzled to decide whether you are an apostate or an impostor, whether you have abandoned good principles, or whether you ever had any."[10]

Some of the articles were utterly preposterous, like the charge, also made in the *Aurora,* that recently obtained British documents from the wartime years revealed that Washington was secretly a traitor who had fully intended to sell out the American cause until Benedict Arnold beat him to the punch. His critics, it should also be noted, were a decided minority, vastly outnumbered by his countless legions of supporters. The rebuttals to Paine's open letter, for example, appeared immediately, describing Paine as "that noted sot and infidel" whose efforts to despoil Washington's reputation "resembled the futile efforts of a reptile infusing its venom into the Atlantic or ejecting its filthy saliva towards the Sun." Paine's already questionable reputation, in fact, never recovered from this episode. Taking on Washington was the fastest way to commit political suicide in the Revolutionary era.[11]

Nevertheless, the attacks had been a persistent feature of his second term, and despite his customarily impenetrable front, Washington was deeply hurt by them. "But these attacks, unjust and unpleasant as they are, will occasion no change in my conduct; nor will they work any other effect in my mind," he postured. (Although Washington was not, like Adams or Jefferson, a prodigious reader of books, he was an obsessive consumer of newspapers, subscribing at one point to ten gazettes.) His pose of utter disregard was just that, a pose. "Maligning therefore may dart her shafts," he explained, "but no earthly power can deprive me of the consolation of knowing that I have not . . . been guilty of willful error, however numerous they may have been from other causes." This outwardly aloof but blatantly defensive tone seemed to acknowledge, in its backhanded way, that his critics had struck a nerve.[12]

The main charge levied against Washington was that he had made himself into a quasi-king. "We have given him the powers and prerogatives of a King," claimed one New York editorial. "He holds levees like a King, receives congratulations on his birthday like a King, employs his old enemies like a King, shuts himself up like a King, shuts up other people like a King, takes advice of his counsellors or follows his own opinions like a King."

Several of these charges were patently false. The grain of truth in them involved Washington's quite conspicuous embodiment of authority. He had no compunction about driving around Philadelphia in an ornate carriage drawn by six cream-colored horses; or, when on horseback, riding a white stallion with a leopard cloth and gold-trimmed saddle; or accepting laurel crowns at public celebrations that resembled coronations. It also did not help that when searching for a substitute for the toppled statue of George III in New York City, authorities chose a wooden replica of Washington, encouraging some critics to refer to him as George IV.[13]

The requirements of the American Revolution, in effect, cut both ways at once. To secure the Revolution and stabilize its legacy on a national level required a dominant leader who focused the energies of the national government in one "singular character." Washington had committed himself to that cause and in so doing had become the beneficiary of its political imperatives, effectively being cast in the role of a "republican king" who embodied national authority more potently and more visibly than any collective body like Congress could possibly convey.[14]

At the very core of the Revolutionary legacy, however, was a virulent hatred of monarchy and an inveterate suspicion of any consolidated political authority. A major tenet of the American Revolution—Jefferson had given it lyrical expression in the Declaration of Independence—was that all kings, and not just George III, were inherently evil. The very notion of a "republican king" was a repudiation of "the Spirit of '76" and a contradiction in terms. Washington's presidency had become trapped within that contradiction. He was living the great paradox of the early American Republic: what was politically essential for the survival of the infant nation was ideologically at odds with what it claimed to stand for. He fulfilled his obligations as a "singular character" so capably that he seemed to defy the republican tradition itself. He had come to embody national authority so successfully that every attack on the government's policies seemed to be an attack on him.

This is the essential context for grasping Washington's motives for leaving public office in 1796. By resigning voluntarily, he was declaring that his deepest allegiances, like those of his critics, were thoroughly republican. He was answering his detractors not with words but with one decisive, unanswerable action. And this is also the proper starting point for understanding the words he left as his final valedictory, the Farewell Address. Washington was making his ultimate statement as America's first and last benevolent monarch. Whatever the Farewell Address has meant over the subsequent two centuries of its interpretive history, Washington intended it as advice to his countrymen about how to sustain national unity and purpose, not just without him but without a king.

The main themes of the Farewell Address are just as easy to state succinctly as they are difficult to appreciate fully. After declaring his irreversible intention to retire, Washington devoted several paragraphs to national unity. He denounced excessive partisanship, most especially when it took the form of political parties pursuing vested ideological agendas or sectional interest groups oblivious to the advantages of cooperation. The rest of the Farewell Address was then devoted to foreign policy, calling for strict American neutrality and diplomatic independence from the tangled affairs of Europe. He did not use the term "entangling alliances" so often attributed to him—Jefferson actually coined the phrase in his First Inaugural (1801)—but Washington's message of diplomatic independence from Europe preceded Jefferson's words to the same effect. Taken together, his overlapping themes lend themselves to easy summary: unity at home and independence abroad.

The disarming simplicity of the statement, combined with its quasi-Delphic character, has made the Farewell Address a perennial candidate for historical commentary. Throughout the nineteenth and most of the twentieth century, the bulk of attention has focused on the foreign policy section, with advocates of American isolationism citing it as the classic statement of their cause and others arguing that strict isolation was never Washington's intention, or that America's emergence as a world power has rendered Washington's wisdom irrelevant. More recently the early section of the Farewell Address has been rediscovered, its plea for a politics of consensus serving as a warning against single-issue political movements or the separation of America into racial, ethnic, or gender-based constituencies. Like the classic it has become, the Farewell Address has demonstrated the capacity to assume different shapes in different eras, to change color in different shades of light.[15]

Although Washington's own eyes never changed color and were set very much on the future, he had no way of knowing (much less influencing) the multiple meanings that future generations would discover in his words. The beginning of all true wisdom concerning the Farewell Address is that Washington's core insights were firmly grounded in the lessons he had learned as America's premier military and civilian leader during the Revolutionary era. Unless one believes that ideas are like migratory birds that can fly unchanged from one century to the next, the only way to grasp the authentic meaning of his message is to recover the context out of which it emerged. Washington was not claiming to offer novel prescriptions based on his original reading of philosophical treatises or books; quite the opposite, he was reminding his countrymen of the venerable principles he had acquired from personal experience, principles so obvious and elemental that they were at risk of being overlooked by his contemporaries and so thoroughly grounded in the American Revolution that they are virtually invisible to a more distant posterity.

First, Washington's extraordinary reputation rested less on his prudent exercise of power than on his dramatic flair at surrendering it. He was, in fact, a veritable virtuoso of exits. Almost everyone regarded his retirement of 1796 as a repeat performance of his resignation as commander of the Continental army in 1783. Back then, faced with a restive and unpaid remnant of the victorious American army quartered near Newburgh, New York, he had appeared unannounced at a meeting of officers who were contemplating insurrection. After denouncing their activities, he made a melodramatic gesture that immediately became famous, pulling a pair of glasses out of his pocket. "Gentlemen, you WILL permit me to put on my spectacles," he asked rhetorically, "for I have not only grown gray but almost blind in service to my country." Upon learning that Washington intended to retire voluntarily, no less an authority than George III allegedly observed, "If he does that, he will be the greatest man in the world." True to his word, on December 22, 1783, Washington surrendered his commission to the Congress, then meeting in Annapolis. "Having now finished the work assigned me," he announced, "I now retire from the great theater of action." In so doing, he became the supreme example of the leader who could be trusted with power because he was so ready to give it up.[16]

Second, when Washington spoke about the need for national unity in 1796, his message resonated with the memories of his conduct during the Revolutionary War. Although he actually lost more battles than he won and spent the first two years of the war making costly tactical mistakes that nearly lost the American Revolution at its very start, by 1778 he had reached an elemental understanding of his military strategy: namely, that captured ground—what he termed "a war of posts"—was virtually meaningless. The strategic key was the Continental army. If it remained intact as an effective fighting force, the American Revolution remained alive. The British army could occupy Boston, New York, and Philadelphia, and it did. The British navy could blockade and bombard American seaports with impunity, and it did. The Continental Congress could be driven from one location to another like a traveling circus, and it was. But as long as Washington held the Continental army together, the British could not win the war, which meant that they would eventually lose it. And that is precisely what happened.[17]

Third, when Washington talked about independence from foreign nations, his understanding of what American independence entailed cut much deeper than the patriotic veneer customarily suggested by the term. Once again, the war years shaped and hardened his convictions on this score, though the basic attitudes on which they rested were in place long before he assumed command of the Continental army. Simply put, Washington had developed a view of both personal and national independence that was completely immune to sentimental attachments or fleeting ideological enthusiasms. He was a rock-ribbed realist, who instinctively mistrusted all visionary schemes dependent on seductive ideals that floated dreamily in men's minds, unmoored to the more prosaic but palpable realities that invariably spelled the difference between victory and defeat. At its psychological nub Washington's inveterate realism was rooted in his commitment to control, over himself and all events with the power to determine his fate. At its intellectual core it meant he was the mirror image of Jefferson, for whom ideals were the supreme reality and whose inspirational prowess derived from his confidence that the world eventually would come around to fit the pictures he had in his head. Washington regarded such pictures as dangerous dreams.

In 1778, for example, at a time when patriotic propagandists were churning out tributes to the superior virtue of the American cause, Washington confided to a friend that though virtue was both a wonderful and a necessary item, it was hardly sufficient to win the war. "Men may speculate as they will," he wrote, "they may draw examples from ancient story, of great achievements performed by its influence; but whoever builds upon it, as a sufficient basis for conducting a long and bloody War, will find themselves deceived in the end. . . . For a time it may, of itself, be enough to push Men to Action; to bear much, to encounter difficulties; but it will not endure unassisted by Interest."[18]

Or, another example, shortly after the French entry into the war in 1778, several members of the Continental Congress began to lobby for a French invasion of Canada, arguing that the likelihood of French military success was greater because Canada was populated by Frenchmen. Washington opposed the scheme on several grounds but confided his deepest reasons to Henry Laurens, president of Congress. He feared "the introduction of a large body of French troops into Canada, and putting them in possession of the capital of that Province, attached to them by all the ties of blood, habits, manners, religion and former connexions of government." The French were America's providential allies, to be sure, but once they were ensconced in Canada, it would be foolish to expect them to withdraw: "I fear this would be too great a temptation to be resisted by any power actuated by the common maxims of national policy." He went on to offer his advice to the Congress in one of his clearest statements about the motives governing nations. "Men are very apt to run into extremes," he explained; "hatred to England may carry some into an excess of Confidence in France. . . . I am heartily disposed to entertain the most favourable sentiments of our new ally and to cherish them in others to a reasonable degree; but it is a maxim founded on the universal experience of mankind, that no nation is to be trusted farther than it is bound by its interest; and no prudent statesman or politician will venture to depart from it." There was no such thing as a permanent international alliance, only permanent national interests.[19]

The clearest statement Washington made on America's national interest came in his Circular Letter of 1783, the last of his letters to the state governments as commander in chief. He projected a panoramic and fully continental vision of an American empire, and he expressed his vision in language that at least for one moment soared beyond the usually prosaic boundaries of his subdued style: "The Citizens of America, placed in the most enviable condition, as the sole Lords and Proprietors of a vast Tract of Continent, comprehending all the various soils and climates of the World, and abounding with all the necessaries and conveniences of life, are now by the late satisfactory pacification, acknowledged to be possessed of absolute freedom and Independence; They are, from this period, to be considered as Actors on a most conspicuous Theatre, which seems to be peculiarly designated by Providence for the display of human greatness and felicity."[20]

The breathtaking vision is remarkable. Washington had spent his young manhood fighting with the British to expel the French from North America. With American victory in the War of Independence, the English had then been expelled. The entire continent was now a vast American manor within which the American people could expand unrestricted by foreign opposition. (Presumably the Native Americans would be assimilated or conquered; and the Spanish west of the Mississippi, Spain being Spain, would serve as a mere holding company until the American population swept over them.) Within the leadership of the Revolutionary generation, Washington was, if not unique, at least unusual for never having traveled or lived in Europe. (His only foreign excursion was to Barbados as a young man.) His angle of vision for the new American nation was decidedly western.

The chief task facing the next several generations was to consolidate control of the North American continent. Anything that impaired or deflected that central mission must be avoided at all cost.

In the same Circular Letter he laid down the obligations and opportunities implicit in his national vision, again in some of his most poetic language: "The foundation of our Empire was not laid in the gloomy age of Ignorance and Suspicion, but at an Epoch when the rights of mankind were better understood and more clearly defined, than at any former period." He then went on to specify the treasure trove of human knowledge that had accumulated over the past two centuries—it was about to be called the Enlightenment—and which constituted a kind of intellectual or philosophical equivalent of the nearly boundless natural resources waiting to be developed in the West. It was the fortuitous conjunction of these two vast reservoirs of philosophical and physical wealth that defined America's national interest and made it so special. "At this auspicious period," he wrote, "the United States came into existence as a Nation, and if their Citizens should not be completely free and happy, the fault will be entirely their own."[21]

The modern British philosopher Isaiah Berlin described the different perspectives that political leaders bring to the management of world affairs as the difference between the hedgehog and the fox: the hedgehog knows one big thing, and the fox knows many little things. Washington was an archetypal hedgehog. And the one big thing he knew was that America's future as a nation lay to the West, in its development over the next century of a continental empire. One of the reasons he devoted so much time and energy planning the construction of canals and shared in the misguided belief of his fellow Virginians that the Potomac constituted a direct link to the river system of the interior was that he knew in his bones that the energy of the American people must flow in that direction. Europe might contain all the cultural capitals and current world powers, but in terms of America's national interest it was a mere sideshow and distraction. The future lay in those forests he had explored as a young man. All this he understood intuitively and unreservedly by the time of his first retirement in 1783.[22]

Grand visions, even ones that prove as prescient as Washington's, must nevertheless negotiate the damnable particularities that history-in-the-short-run toss up before history-in-the-long-run arrives to validate the vision. In Washington's case the most obvious corollary to his view of American national interest was the avoidance of a major war during the gestative phase of America's national development. It so happened, however, that England and France were engaged in a century-old struggle for dominance of Europe and international supremacy, a struggle in which both the French and Indian War and the American Revolution were merely peripheral episodes, and which would end only with Napoleon's defeat at Waterloo in 1815. Washington's understanding of the proper American response to this global conflict was clear. "I trust that we shall have too just a sense of our own interest to originate any cause that may involve us in it," he wrote in 1794, "and I ardently wish we may not be forced into it by the conduct of other nations. If we are permitted to improve without interruption, the great advantages which nature and circumstances have placed within our reach, many years will not revolve before we may be ranked not only among the most respectable, but among the happiest people on earth."[23]

The linchpin of his foreign policy as president, it followed naturally, was the Proclamation of Neutrality (1793), which declared America an impartial witness to the European conflict. His constant refrain throughout his presidency emphasized the same point, even offering an estimate of the likely duration of America's self-imposed alienation from global politics. "Every true friend to this Country must see and feel that the policy of it is not to embroil ourselves with any nation whatsoever, but to avoid their disputes and politics; and if they will harass one another, to avail ourselves of the neutral conduct we have adopted. Twenty years peace with such an increase of population and resources as we have a right to expect; added to our remote situation from the jarring powers, will in all probability enable us in a just cause to bid defiance to any power on earth." In a sense it was a fresh application of the same strategic lesson he had learned as head of the Continental army, namely, to avoid engagement with a superior force until the passage of time made victory possible, what we might call the strategy of enlightened procrastination. In retrospect and with all the advantages of hindsight, Washington's strategic insights as president were every bit as prescient as his strategic insights as commander in chief during the American Revolution, right down to his timing estimate of twenty years, which pretty much predicted the outbreak of the War of 1812.[24]

Because Washington's seminal insight was also the core piece of foreign policy wisdom offered in the Farewell Address, and because every major American statesman of the era also embraced the principle of neutrality as an obvious maxim, the meaning of the Farewell Address would seem to be incontrovertible. But that was not at all how the message was heard at the time, in part because there was a deep division within the Revolutionary generation that Washington was trying to straddle over just what a policy of American neutrality should look like and in part because there was an alternative vision of the national interest circulating in the higher reaches of America's political leadership. All this came to a head in Washington's second term in the debate over the Jay Treaty, creating the greatest crisis of Washington's presidency, the most virulent criticism of his monarchical tendencies, and the immediate context for every word he wrote in the Farewell Address.[25]

The Jay Treaty was a landmark in the shaping of American foreign policy. In 1794 Washington had sent Chief Justice John Jay to London to negotiate a realistic bargain that avoided a war with England at a time when the United States was ill prepared to fight one. Jay returned in 1795 with a treaty that accepted the fact of English naval and commercial supremacy and implicitly endorsed a pro-English version of American neutrality. It accepted England's right to retain tariffs on American exports while granting English imports most-favored status in the United States; it implicitly accepted English impressment of American sailors. It also committed the United States to compensate English creditors for outstanding pre-Revolutionary debts, most of which were owed by Virginia's planters. In return for these concessions, the English agreed to submit claims by American merchants for confiscated cargoes to arbitration and to abide by the promise made in the Treaty of Paris (1783) to evacuate its troops from their posts on the western frontiers. In effect, the Jay Treaty was a repudiation of the Franco-American alliance of 1778, which had been so instrumental in gaining French military assistance in winning the American Revolutionary War.[26]

Although the terms of the treaty were one-sided in England's favor, most careful students of the subject believe that the Jay Treaty was a shrewd bargain for the United States. It bet, in effect, on England rather than France as the hegemonic European power of the future, which proved prophetic. It recognized the massive dependence of the American economy on trade with England. In a sense it was a precocious preview of the Monroe Doctrine (1823), for it linked American security and economic development to the British fleet, which provided a protective shield of incalculable value throughout the nineteenth century. Mostly, it postponed war with England until America was economically and politically more stable.

The long-term advantages of the Jay Treaty, however, were temporarily invisible to most Americans. Sensing the unpopularity of the treaty, Washington attempted to keep its terms secret until the Senate had voted. But word leaked out in the summer of 1795 and then spread, as Madison put it, "like an electric velocity to every part of the Union." Jay later claimed that the entire eastern seaboard was illuminated each evening by protesters burning him in effigy. In New York, Hamilton was struck in the head by a rock while attempting to defend the treaty to a crowd. John Adams recalled that Washington's house in Philadelphia was "surrounded by an innumerable multitude, from day to day buzzing, demanding war against England, cursing Washington, and crying success to the French patriots and virtuous Republicans." Any concession to British economic and military power, no matter how strategically astute, seemed a betrayal of the independence won in the American Revolution. Washington predicted that after a few months of contemplation "when passion shall have yielded to sober reason, the current may possibly turn," but in the meantime "this government, in relation to France and England, may be compared to a ship between the rocks of Sylla and Charybalis."27

To make matters worse, the debate over the treaty prompted a constitutional crisis. Perhaps the most graphic illustration of the singular status that Washington enjoyed was the decision of the Constitutional Convention to deposit the minutes of its secret deliberations with him for safekeeping. Washington therefore had exclusive access to the official record of the convention and used it to argue that the clear intent of the Framers was to vest the treaty-making power with the executive branch, subject to the advice and consent of two-thirds of the Senate. Madison, however, had kept his own extensive "Notes on the Debates at the Constitutional Convention" and shared them with Jefferson, then in retirement at Monticello.

Although a careful reading of Madison's notes revealed that Washington was correct, and indeed that Madison himself had been one of the staunchest opponents of infringements on executive power over foreign policy at the convention, Jefferson managed to conclude that the House was intended to be an equal partner in approving all treaties, going so far as to claim that the House was the sovereign branch of the government empowered to veto any treaty it wished, thereby "annihilating the whole treaty making power" of the executive branch. "I trust the popular branch of our legislature will disapprove of it," Jefferson wrote from Monticello, "and thus rid us of this infamous act, which is really nothing more than a treaty of alliance between England and the Anglomen of this country against the legislatures and people of the United States."28

The actual debate in the House in the fall and winter of 1795 proceeded under Madison's more cautious leadership and narrower interpretation of the Constitution (Jefferson's position would have re-created the hapless and hamstrung conditions that he himself had decried while serving as minister to France under the Articles of Confederation, essentially holding

American foreign policy hostage to congressional gridlock and the divisive forces of domestic politics). Madison instead argued that the implementation of the Jay Treaty required the approval of the House for all provisions dependent on funding. This achieved the desired result, blocking the treaty while avoiding a frontal assault on executive power.[29]

Madison served as the floor leader of the opposition in the House during the debate that raged throughout the winter and spring of 1796. At the start he enjoyed an overwhelming majority and regarded his position as impregnable. But as the weeks rolled on, he experienced firsthand the cardinal principle of American politics in the 1790s: whoever went face-to-face against Washington was destined to lose. The majority started to melt away in March. John Adams observed bemusedly that "Mr. Madison looks worried to death. Pale, withered, haggard." When the decisive vote came in April, Madison attributed his defeat to "the exertions and influence of Aristocracy, Anglicism, and mercantilism" led by "the Banks, the British Merchts., the insurance Comps." Jefferson was more candid. The Jay Treaty had passed, he concluded, because of the gigantic prestige of Washington, "the one man who outweighs them all in influence over the people." Jefferson's sense of frustration had reached its breaking point a few weeks earlier when, writing to Madison, he quoted a famous line from Washington's favorite play, Joseph Addison's *Cato,* and applied it to Washington himself: "A curse on his virtues, they've undone his country."[30]

What could Jefferson's extreme reaction possibly mean? After all, from our modern perspective Washington's executive leadership throughout the debate over the Jay Treaty was nothing less than we would expect from a strong president, whose authority to shape foreign policy is taken for granted. But in this instance hindsight does not make us clairvoyant so much as blind to the ghosts and goblins that floated above the political landscape in the 1780s. What we might describe as admirably strong executive leadership struck Jefferson and his Republican followers as the arbitrary maneuverings of a king. And what appears in retrospect like a prudent and farsighted vision of the national interest looked to Jefferson like a betrayal of the American Revolution.

For Jefferson also had a national vision and a firm conviction about where American history was headed, or at least where it ought to be headed. The future he felt in his bones told him that the true "Spirit of '76," most eloquently expressed in the language he had drafted for the Declaration of Independence, was a radical break with the past and with all previous versions of political authority. Like Voltaire, Jefferson longed for the day when the last king would be strangled with the entrails of the last priest. The political landscape he saw in his mind's eye was littered with the dead bodies of despots and corrupt courtiers, a horizon swept clean of all institutions capable of coercing American citizens from pursuing their happiness as they saw fit. Thomas Paine's *The Rights of Man* (1791) captured the essence of his vision more fully than any other book of the age, depicting as it did a radical transformation of society once the last vestiges of feudalism were destroyed and the emergence of a utopian world in which the essential discipline of government was internalized within the citizenry. The only legitimate form of government, in the end, was self-government.[31]

Shortly after his return to the United States in 1790, Jefferson began to harbor the foreboding sense that the American Revolution, as he understood it, had been captured by alien forces. The chief villain and core counterrevolutionary character in the Jeffersonian drama was Alexander Hamilton, and the most worrisome feature on the political landscape was Hamilton's financial scheme, with its presumption of a consolidated federal government possessing powers over the states that Parliament had exercised over the colonies. Under Hamilton's diabolical leadership the United States seemed to be re-creating the very political and economic institutions—the national bank became the most visible symbol of the accumulating corruption—that the American Revolution sought to destroy. Jefferson developed a full-blooded conspiracy theory in which bankers, speculators, federal officeholders, and a small but powerful congregation of closet tories permanently alienated from the agrarian majority ("They all live in cities") had captured the meaning of the American Revolution and were now strangling it to death behind the closed doors of investment houses and within the faraway corridors of the Federalist government in New York and Philadelphia.[32]

Exactly where Washington fit in this horrific picture is difficult to determine. Washington presumably knew something about the meaning and purpose of the American Revolution, having done more than any man to assure its success. (As Jefferson's critics observed, the man ensconced at Monticello had never fired a shot in anger throughout the war.) Initially Jefferson refused to assign Washington any culpability for the Federalist conspiracy, somehow suggesting that the person at the very center of the government was wholly oblivious to the schemes swirling around him. At some unspoken level of understanding, Jefferson recognized that any effort to include Washington in the indictment placed his entire case against the Federalists permanently on the defensive.

Jefferson's posture toward Washington shifted perceptibly in 1794 with the Whiskey Rebellion, a popular insurgency in western Pennsylvania protesting an excise tax on whiskey. Washington viewed the uprising as a direct threat to the authority of the federal government and called out the militia from the immediate states, a massive 13,000-man army, to squelch the uprising. Jefferson regarded the entire affair as a shameful repetition of the Shays's Rebellion fiasco nearly a decade earlier, in which a healthy and harmless expression of popular discontent by American farmers, so he thought, had prompted an unnecessary military response. Although his first instinct was to blame Hamilton for the whole sorry mess, Washington's speech justifying the action could not be so easily dismissed.[33]

Jefferson denounced Washington's speech as "shreds of stuff from Aesop's fables and Tom Thumb." In Jefferson's new version of the Federalist conspiracy, Washington was an unknowing and somewhat pathetic accomplice, like an overaged "captain in his cabin" who was sound asleep while "a rogue of a pilot [presumably Hamilton] has run them into an enemy's port." Washington was certainly the grand old man of the American Revolution, but his grandeur had now been eclipsed by his age, providing the Hamiltonians with "the sanction of a name which has done too much good not to be sufficient to cover harm also." Washington simply did not have control of the government and was inadvertently lending credibility to the treacheries being hatched all around him. Washington, in effect, was senile.[34]

While hardly true, this explanation had the demonstrable advantage of permitting Jefferson's vision of a Federalist conspiracy to congeal in a plausible pattern that formed around Washington without touching him directly. Jefferson was also careful never to utter any of his criticisms of Washington in public. But in his private correspondence with trusted Republicans, he developed the image of an old soldier past his prime, reading speeches he did not write and could not comprehend, lingering precariously in the misty edges of incompetence, a hollow hulk of his former greatness. The most famous letter in this mode—famous because it eventually found its way into the newspapers against Jefferson's wishes—was prompted by the passage of the Jay Treaty. "It would give you a fever," Jefferson wrote to his Italian friend Philip Mazzei, "were I to name to you the apostates who have gone over to these heresies, men who were Samsons in the field and Solomons in the Council, but who have had their heads shorn by the harlot of England." Because there was only one person who could possibly merit the mantle of America's Samson and Solomon, Jefferson's customary sense of discretion allowed him to make his point without mentioning the name. But everybody knew.[35]

For the next year Jefferson attempted to sustain at least the veneer of a friendship with Washington by writing him letters in the Virginia gentleman mode, avoiding politics and foreign policy altogether, focusing on his crop rotation scheme at Monticello, the weather, his vetch and wheat crop, and—a rather potent metaphor—the best way to spread manure. Washington responded in kind, that is until the newspapers printed Jefferson's letter to Mazzei. Then communication from Mount Vernon to Monticello ceased forever.[36]

Beyond the purely personal dimensions of their estrangement, beyond Washington's sense of betrayal and Jefferson's artful minuet with duplicity, this episode provides an invaluable clue to the larger and more impersonal political concerns on Washington's mind when he sat down to compose the Farewell Address. They went far past the loss of Jefferson's friendship, important though it was, because Jefferson's behavior was symptomatic of more than a betrayal of trust; it reflected a fundamental division within the Revolutionary generation over the meaning of the American Revolution and the different versions of American national interest that followed naturally from that disagreement. The words that were used at the time or the words employed by historians later to capture the argument are mere labels: Federalists versus Republicans; pro-English versus pro-French versions of American neutrality. Underlying the debate that surfaced in full-blown fashion over the Jay Treaty lurked a classic confrontation between those who wished America's Revolutionary energies to be harnessed and those who interpreted that very process as a betrayal of the Revolution itself.

From Washington's perspective the American Republic established by the Constitution created a government of laws that must be obeyed once the duly elected representatives had reached a decision. That was why he had acted decisively to put down the Whiskey Rebellion and why he expected compliance with the Jay Treaty once the Congress approved its terms. From Jefferson's perspective, on the other hand, all laws and treaties that reined in the liberating impulses of the American Revolution were illegitimate. That was why he regarded the suppression of the Whiskey Rebellion as reprehensible. Were not these Pennsylvania farmers protesting taxes to which they did not consent? As for the Jay Treaty, who in his right mind would countenance the acceptance of neocolonial status within the hated British Empire? Not obeying but rather violating such unjust laws and treaties was the obligation of every citizen. Was this not precisely the practice followed by American patriots in the glory days of the American Revolution? Was this not the higher law that Americans should follow, arm-in-arm again with our trusted French brethren? In this formulation political behavior that was, strictly speaking, traitorous and treasonable was the only course consistent with America's most hallowed principles.

Perhaps the most extreme example of this Republican mentality was James Monroe, a zealous Jefferson protégé currently serving as the American minister to France. Though not in Jefferson's league as a thinker or political strategist, Monroe more than made up for these deficiencies by embracing the core articles of the Republican faith with near abandon. He assured his French hosts that the Jay Treaty would never be approved by the American Congress, that the vast majority of the American people were eager to join France in war with England, that the American government stood ready to advance France a $5 million loan to subsidize its military expenses, and when none of these wild predictions materialized, that the French government should patiently but firmly disregard all messages from the American president, because he obviously spoke for the aristocratic Anglomen and would soon be hurled from office by the American people. In the meantime, the French should feel free to retaliate against American ships on the high seas. When they began to do so in the spring of 1796 and the first prize confiscated was an American ship named the *Mount Vernon,* Monroe saw a providential version of poetic justice. All this from America's official emissary to the French government.[37]

A slightly less extreme but more befuddled example of the same mentality had surfaced inside Washington's cabinet at the moment he was making the decision to send the Jay Treaty to the Senate in August 1795. The successor to Jefferson as secretary of state was Edmund Randolph, like Monroe a second-tier member of the Virginia dynasty, whose principal recommendation for the job was an unblinking loyalty to Washington, but whose chief political habit was to blink incessantly at any decision that demanded clear convictions of his own. Poor Randolph, a decent man who was in over his head, had granted an interview with the outgoing French minister to the United States, Joseph Fauchet, who had then transcribed the high points of the conversation in a dispatch subsequently intercepted at sea by a British cruiser. The British were only too willing to forward the dispatch to the American government. The day after Washington read it out loud to the full cabinet, Randolph submitted his resignation.[38]

What the Fauchet dispatch claimed and what we know on the basis of subsequent scholarship are not synonymous. According to Fauchet, Randolph requested a bribe as part of some mysterious scheme in support of the Whiskey Rebellion. Although Randolph was almost certainly innocent of this charge, the whole tenor and tone of Fauchet's account revealed that

Randolph had confided his personal opposition to the entire domestic and foreign policy of the Washington administration, lamented the ascendance of a "financiering class" aimed at the restitution of monarchy, and decried the enslavement of American trade to "the audacity of England." Randolph had depicted himself as the sole voice of "the patriotic party" within the government and the last hope for bringing a dazed and confused President Washington to his senses. Randolph's unfortunate utterances were not treasonable, as he spent the remainder of his life trying vainly in his foggy style to explain. Randolph had simply allowed himself to get caught talking the same conspiratorial talk that Jefferson was conveying to private confidants and Monroe was sputtering in Paris. The notion that a conspiracy of moneymen and monarchists had seized control of the federal government under Washington's nose was so widespread within Virginia's political elite that they had lost all perspective on how conspiratorial their own words sounded to those denied their vision.[39]

And so when Washington drafted his Farewell Address, three salient features rose up out of the immediate political terrain to command his attention: first, he needed to demonstrate that although poised for retirement, he was still in charge, that those rumors of creeping senility and routinized ineptitude were wrong; second, he wanted to carve out a middle course, and do so in a moderate tone, that together pushed his most ardent critics to the fringes of the ongoing debate, where their shrill accusations and throbbing moral certainty could languish in deserved obscurity; third, the all-time master of exits wanted to make his final exit the occasion for his own version of what the American Revolution meant. Above all, it meant hanging together as a united people, much as the Continental army had hung together once before. Those who were making foreign policy into a divisive device in domestic politics, all in the name of America's Revolutionary principles, were themselves subverting the very cause they claimed to champion. He was stepping forward into the battle one final time, planting his standard squarely in the center of the field, inviting the troops to rally around him rather than wander off in romantic cavalry charges at the periphery, assuring them by his example that if they could only hold the position he defined, they would again prevail.

The manner in which the Farewell Address was actually composed, as it turned out, served as a nearly perfect illustration of its central message: the need to subordinate narrow interests to the larger cause. Much ink has been spilled by scholars in an effort to determine who wrote the bulk of the words that eventually found their way into print and then into the history books. Like a false scent, the authorship question has propelled hordes of baying historians down labyrinthine trails of evidence in quest of the true author. Meanwhile, the object of the hunt sits squarely in the middle of the evidentiary trail, so obvious that it is ignored. Namely, the creation of the Farewell Address was an inherently collaborative process. Some of the words were Madison's; most of the words were Hamilton's; all the ideas were Washington's. The drafting and editing of the Farewell Address in effect became a metaphor for the kind of collective effort Washington was urging on the American people as a whole.[40]

The story had its start four years earlier, in May 1792, when Washington approached Madison to help him compose a valedictory address. Convinced that he would step down after one term, Washington chose Madison because his two most trusted cabinet members, Hamilton and Jefferson, were closely associated with the party disputes he wanted to condemn. Madison made extensive notes on the basis of three conversations with Washington, then drafted a document that employed Washington's own language for many key passages: "a spirit of party in the Government was becoming a fresh source of difficulty"; "we are all Children of the same Country"; the nation's "essential interests are the same . . . its diversities arising from climate and from soil will naturally form a mutual relation of parts" and serve as the formulation for "an affectionate and permanent Union." It was then Madison who first proposed that the Farewell Address not be delivered as a speech to Congress but printed in the newspapers as "a direct address to the people who are your only constituents." After Washington listened to the unanimous advice of all his cabinet officers and reluctantly agreed to a second term, he saved Madison's draft for another day.[41]

That day arrived exactly four years later. On May 15, 1796, Washington sent Hamilton the "first draft" of a retirement address—no amount of persuasion could change his mind this time—that would announce his departure from public life. The first section of this document reproduced Madison's draft of 1792, which was highly ironic because Madison had become the primary leader of the Republican opposition to Washington's policies in the Congress and was therefore a rather dramatic example of the party spirit that his prior words had warned against. (The Federalists referred to Madison as "the general" of the opposition, calling Jefferson, his mentor secluded at Monticello, "the generalissimo.") Washington included the earlier Madison draft for two reasons: first, it expressed in clear and forceful language a major point he still wanted to make about subordinating sectional and ideological differences to larger national purposes, all the more resonant coming from someone who seemed to have forgotten the lesson; and second, its inclusion publicized the fact that he had wanted to retire four years ago, so his current decision was really the culmination of a long-standing preference.[42]

This latter point was extremely important to Washington because his most virulent critics were claiming that his support for the unpopular Jay Treaty made him unelectable in 1796, so his decision to retire was not a voluntary act but a forced recognition of political realities. Hamilton tried to reassure him that his sensitivities on this score were excessive, that if he did choose to run for a third term he would win in a walk. (And Hamilton was surely correct.) But Washington wanted not a shred of doubt to remain that his decision to step aside was voluntary. This was both a matter of personal pride and a crucial political precedent. By including the Madison draft of 1792, he advertised his reluctance to serve even his second term, thereby enhancing the credibility of his voluntary rejection of a third. As Washington put it, "it may contribute to blunt, if it does not turn aside, some of the shafts . . . , among which—conviction of fallen popularity, and despair of being re-elected, will be levelled at me with dexterity & keenness."[43]

The second section of the "first draft" that Washington sent to Hamilton focused on the foreign policy issues that had dominated his second term. He was fully aware that Hamilton had supported the Jay Treaty. He even recommended that Hamilton consult Jay before putting pen to paper. But he also wanted Hamilton to know that none of his or Jay's pro-English prejudices should seep into his draft of the document; it should emphasize American neutrality and "promote the true and permanent interests of the country." Washington's views, not Hamilton's, must prevail. Hamilton would be the draftsman, but Washington must be the author. "I am anxious, always, to compare the opinions of those in whom I confide with one another," Washington explained, "and these again (without being bound by them) with my own, that I may extract all the good I can." Hamilton required no elaborate instructions on the procedure. It was the same process Washington had developed with his staff as commander in chief of the Continental army, then implemented with his cabinet as president. Hamilton had played the same role in both contexts. All major decisions were collective occasions in which advisers, like spokes on a wheel, made contributions, usually in written form. But in the end the final decision, to include the final choice of words, came together at the center, which was Washington.[44]

Hamilton also realized that he was being asked to write for posterity as much as for the present. "It has been my object to render this act importantly and lastingly useful," he confided to Washington, "and avoid all just cause of present exception, to embrace such reflections and sentiments as will wear well, progress in approbation with time & redound to future reputation." He devoted a full two months to revising Washington's "first draft," amplifying Madison's earlier account of the need to rise above sectional and party differences and come together on common ground as Americans behind the freely elected representatives of the national government, then elaborating Washington's sketch of foreign policy so as to make the Proclamation of Neutrality, not the Jay Treaty, the centerpiece of Washington's legacy.[45]

On July 30 he sent the fruits of his labors to Washington, who found the Hamilton draft "exceedingly just, & just such as ought to be inculcated." His only reservation related to length. "All the columns of a large Gazette would scarcely, I conceive, contain the present draft," Washington noted, adding at the end, "I may be mistaken." (He was.) Hamilton was less sure he had done the best job possible and immediately began work on a wholly new draft, which he submitted to Washington two weeks later. But Washington liked the earlier draft better.[46]

Over the next month edited versions of that draft passed back and forth several times, with Washington pressing Hamilton for clarifications, deleting certain passages; adding others. "I shall expunge all that is marked in the paper as unimportant," the president wrote on August 25, "and as you perceive some marginal notes, written with a pencil, I pray you to give the sentiments mature consideration." If Hamilton saw fit to make additional revisions on his own, he should "let them be so clearly interlined—erased—or referred to in the margins that no mistake may happen." Washington wanted no last-minute changes smuggled in without his approval. Even when the final draft was ready for the printer in September, Washington made changes in 174 out of 1,086 lines in his own hand and reviewed the punctuation throughout—a final scan, so the printer observed firsthand, "in which he was very minute." It seems fair to conclude that what we call "Washington's Farewell Address" is not misnamed.[47]

What was Hamilton's contribution? Chiefly to assure that the elaboration of Washington's ideas occurred within a rhetorical framework that maintained a stately and dignified tone throughout and to sustain a palpable cogency and sense of proportion in developing Washington's argument, which itself embodied the self-assurance so central to his major theme about the nation itself. Hamilton had nearly perfect pitch for Washington's language, having begun his public career drafting letters and memoranda for Washington's signature as a staff officer during the war. He was therefore well practiced in subordinating his own inclinations and style to Washington's larger purposes. In the Farewell Address the result is nearly seamless. When combined with the collaborative character of the drafting process, it becomes virtually impossible to tell where one voice ends and another begins.

But Hamilton was also such a virtuoso performer in his own right, unmatched within the Revolutionary generation for his capacity to deliver powerful prose on a tight deadline, that there are moments in the Farewell Address when his own distinctive voice breaks through. For example, while Washington agreed with Hamilton's version of what the constitutional settlement of 1787–88 meant, only Hamilton could have put it this way: "This government, the offspring of our own choice uninfluenced and unawed, adopted upon full investigation and mature deliberation, completely free in its principles, in the distribution of its powers, uniting security with energy, and containing within itself a provision for its own amendment, has a just claim to your confidence and support. . . . The very idea of the power and right of the People to establish Government presupposes the duty of every Individual to obey the established Government."[48]

Or on the question of America's national interest and the foreign policy it dictated, again the idea is pure Washington, but expressed in language that flowed in Hamiltonian cadences:

> The Great role of conduct for us, in regard to foreign nations is in extending our commercial relations to have with them as little political connection as possible. . . . Europe has a set of primary interests, which to us have none, or a very remote relation. Hence she must be engaged in frequent controversies, the causes of which are essentially foreign to our concerns. . . . 'Tis our true policy to steer clear of permanent Alliances with any portion of the foreign world. . . . 'Tis folly for one Nation to look for disinterested favors from another. . . . There can be no greater error than to expect, or calculate upon real favours from Nation to Nation. 'Tis an illusion which experience must cure, which a just pride ought to discard.[49]

When Hamilton showed a later draft of this passage to John Jay for his commentary, Jay expressed admiration for the style but slight discomfort with the argument. "It occurs to me," he wrote to Washington, "that it may not be perfectly prudent to say that we can never expect Favors from a nation, for that assertion seems to imply that nations always are, or always ought to be moved only by interested motives." Jay's suggestion came

too late—the Farewell Address was already in the hands of the printer—
but would have made no difference. Washington meant exactly what
Hamilton had said. Jay's views of prospective English beneficence, like
Jefferson's views of French solidarity with America, were only seductive
pieces of sentimentality, juvenile illusions in the real world of international
relations.[50]

Beyond the tight cogency and felicitous cadences, Hamilton's major
contribution was to save Washington from his own personal sentiments.
In his "first draft" of May, Washington had included the following paragraph near the start:

> I did not seek the office with which you have honored me . . . [and now
> possess] the grey hairs of a man who has, excepting the interval between
> the close of the Revolutionary War, and the organization of the new
> government—either in a civil, or military character, spent five and forty
> years—All the prime of his life—in serving his country; [may he] be suf-
> fered to pass quietly to the grave—and that his errors, however numerous;
> if they are not criminal, may be consigned to the Tomb of oblivion, as he
> himself will soon be to the Mansion of Retirement.[51]

Hamilton eliminated the references to "grey hairs," "prime of his life"
and "errors, however numerous"; he also altered the wounded tone of the
passage by placing it at the end rather than the beginning of the Farewell
Address, where it seems less like a somewhat pathetic cri de coeur than a
personal testimonial of a great man's humanity at the close of an otherwise dignified presentation of the larger issues at stake. Washington recognized the improvement, congratulating Hamilton for rendering him
"with less egotism," meaning the Hamilton draft covered the wounds, or
at least prevented Washington from displaying them too conspicuously.[52]

Hamilton's exquisite sense of affinity for Washington's mentality only
failed him once, though the failure, and therefore what is in effect the missing section of the Farewell Address, opens a more expansive window into
the national vision that Washington was trying to project. During the drafting process in the summer of 1796, Washington kept urging Hamilton to
insert a separate section on the creation of a national university in the just-
being-constructed capital on the Potomac. Hamilton resisted the recommendation, arguing quite plausibly that such a specific proposal was in-
appropriate for an address designed to operate at a higher altitude. It was,
he suggested, the kind of recommendation better made in the final mes-

sage to Congress in the fall. But Washington kept insisting that he wanted the idea to be a featured element in the Farewell Address. "But to be candid," he explained, "I much question whether a recommendation of this measure to the Legislature will have a better effect now than formerly— It may skew indeed my sense of its importance, and that it is a sufficient inducement with me to bring the matter before the public in some shape or another, at the closing Scenes of my political exit . . . to set the People ruminating on the importance of the measure."53

Hamilton eventually relented, though grudgingly. At the last moment he inserted a brief two-sentence paragraph rather awkwardly near the middle of the Farewell Address, calling for "Institutions for the general diffusion of knowledge" and urging harmlessly that "public opinion should be enlightened." Washington was not satisfied with the result but decided to drop the matter. In so doing, however, he let Hamilton know that something was being lost, that his hopes for a national university linked up to something larger. "In the general Juvenal period of life, when friendships are formed, & habits established that will stick by one," he explained, "the Youth, or young men from different parts of the United States would be assembled together, & would by degrees discover that there was not just cause for those jealousies & prejudices which one part of the Union had imbibed against another part. . . . What, but the mixing of people from different parts of the United States during the War rubbed off these impressions? A Century in the ordinary intercourse, would not have accomplished what the Seven years association in Arms did."54

Here was a characteristically Washingtonian insight: rooted in his experience during the war years; simple but essential; projecting developments into the future on the basis of patterns that were still congealing and that only now, in retrospect, seem obvious. Like his misguided obsession with those Potomac canals, his campaign for a national university in the capital never bore fruit. But both failed projects were also visionary projections linked to larger expectations. In the case of the national university, it was the recognition that the United States was still a nation-in-the-making because its population was still a people-in-the-making. Time, indeed a considerable stretch of time, would be required to allow the bonding together of this large, widely dispersed, and diverse population. But institutions devoted to focusing our national purposes, again like the Continental army during the war, could accelerate time and move America past that vulnerable and problematic phase of its development when fragmentation, perhaps civil war, was a distinct possibility.

Throughout the Farewell Address, Washington had been exhorting

Americans to think of themselves as a collective unit with a common destiny. To our ears it sounds so obvious because we occupy the future location that Washington envisioned. But Washington's exhortations toward national unity were less descriptions than anticipations, less reminders of the way we were than predictions of what we could become. Indeed, the act of exhorting was designed to enhance the prospect by talking about it as if it were a foregone conclusion. In the end, the Farewell Address was primarily a great prophecy, accompanied by advice about how to make it come true.

It was also, at least implicitly, a justification for the strong executive leadership Washington had provided in the 1790s and that his critics had stigmatized as a monarchy. Without a republican king at the start, he was saying, the new quasi-nation called the United States would never have enjoyed the opportunity to achieve its long-run destiny; it would have expired in the short run. In a sense, Washington was defending his presidency as an essential exception to full-blooded republican principles. Down the road, when the common experience of conquering the continent and the sheer passage of time had bound the American people together into a more cohesive whole, the more voluntaristic habits at the core of republican mentality could express themselves fully. For now, however, the center needed to hold. That meant a vigorous federal government with sufficient powers to coerce the citizenry to pay taxes and obey the laws. Veterans of the Continental army like Hamilton and John Marshall understood this essential point. Intriguingly, the two chieftains of the Republican opposition, Jefferson and Madison, had never served in the army. They obviously did not understand.

How could this emerging nation manage its way through this first post-Washington phase of its development? In the Farewell Address, Washington offered his general answer: think of yourself as a single nation; subordinate your regional and political differences to your common identity as Americans; regard the federal government that represents your collective interest as an ally rather than an enemy.

In his eighth and final message to Congress, delivered the following December, Washington provided a more specific directive. Republican critics had described the Jay Treaty as a pact with the devil that would produce domestic and diplomatic catastrophe. Upon scanning the horizon for the last time, however, Washington saw serenity setting in: treaties were being negotiated with the hostile Indian tribes on the southern and western frontiers; the British were removing their troops from posts in the West in accord with the Jay Treaty; thanks primarily to the resumption of trade with Great Britain, the American economy was humming along nicely, with revenues from the increased trade reducing the national debt faster than had been anticipated. The only dark spot on the political horizon was France, whose cruisers were intercepting American shipping in the West Indies. Washington counseled patience with what would soon be called this "quasi-war" with the French republic, predicting (correctly, as it turned out) that "a spirit of justice, candour and friendship . . . will eventually insure success." Confidence, he seemed to be saying, is a self-fulfilling prophecy, all the more so when the confidence was justified.[55]

More specifically, Washington suggested that his departure from the national scene would require the enlargement, not the diminution, of the powers of the federal government in order to compensate for his absence. Washington recommended that Congress undertake a whole new wave of federal initiatives: another federal program to encourage domestic manufactures; a similar federal program to subsidize agricultural improvements; the creation of a national university (his old hobbyhorse) and a national military academy; the construction of an expanded navy to protect American shipping in the Mediterranean and the Caribbean; increased compensation for federal officials in order to ensure that public service was not dependent on private wealth. It was the most expansive presidential program for enlarged federal power until John Quincy Adams proposed a similar vision in his inaugural address of 1824, for which he was despised, decried, and cast from office. It was the tradition that the Whig party of Henry Clay and the Republican party of Abraham Lincoln sustained and that the Democratic party of Jefferson and Andrew Jackson rejected. In the immediate context of 1796, Washington seemed to be saying that the departure of America's only republican king necessitated the creation of centering forces institutionalized at the federal level to maintain the focusing functions he had performed personally.[56]

Finally, who were these American people being bonded together? If Washington wished the national government to be regarded as "us" rather than "them," how did he define the "us"? He addressed his remarks in the Farewell Address to his "Friends, and Fellow-Citizens." Although he undoubtedly thought this description cast a wide and inclusive net that pulled in residents from all the regions or sections of the United States, it did not include all inhabitants. The core of the audience he saw in his mind's eye consisted of those adult white males who owned sufficient property to qualify for the vote. Strictly speaking, such men were the only citizens. He told Hamilton that his Farewell Address was aimed especially at "the Yeomanry of the country," ordinary farmers working small plots of land and living in households. This brings women and children into the picture, not as full-blooded citizens, to be sure, but as part of the American people whose political identity was subsumed within the family and conveyed by the male heads of household. They were secondary citizens but unquestionably Americans. Landless rural residents and impoverished city dwellers lay outside the picture, though they, or more likely their descendants, could work their way into the American citizenry over time. If only potentially and prospectively, they were included.[57]

On the African-American population he was silent. The topic was too controversial to raise in a message designed to create a national consensus. But he could and did imagine the inclusion of Native Americans. Late in August 1796, at the same time he was making final revisions on his Farewell Address, Washington wrote his "Address to the Cherokee Nation." From a strictly legal point of view, each of the various Indian tribes east of the Mississippi was already a nation, or an indigenous quasi-nation within the expanding borders of the United States. Therein, of course, lay the chief problem and the makings for an apparently inevitable tragedy. For in Washington's projection the westward flow of the American population would prove relentless and unstoppable. "I also have thought much on this subject," Washington declared to the Cherokees, "and anxiously wished that the various Indian tribes, as well as their neighbours, the White people, might enjoy in abundance all the good things which make life comfortable and happy. I have considered how this could be done; and have discovered but one path that would lead them to that desirable solution. In this path I wish all the Indian nations to walk."[58]

The "one path" Washington identified required the Indians to recognize that contesting the expansion of the white population was suicidal. The only realistic solution required the Indians to accept the inevitable, abandon their hunting and gathering economies, which required huge tracts of land to work effectively, embrace farming as their preferred mode of life, and gradually over several generations allow themselves to be assimilated into the larger American nation. Washington acknowledged that he was asking a lot, that "this path may seem a little difficult to enter" because it meant subduing their understandable urge to resist and sacrificing many of their most distinctive and cherished tribal values. As he prepared for his own retirement, in effect he was encouraging the Indian tribes to retire from their way of life as Indians. "What I have recommended to you," he wrote somewhat plaintively, "I am myself going to do. After a few moons are passed I shall leave the great town and retire to my farm. There I shall attend to the means of increasing my cattle, sheep and other useful animals." If the Indians would follow his example, the peaceful co-existence of Indians and whites could follow naturally, and their gradual merger into a single American people would occur within the arc of the next century. Whatever moral deficiencies and cultural condescensions a modern-day American audience might find in Washington's advice, two salient points are clear: first, it was in keeping with his relentless realism; and second, it projected Indians into the mix of peoples called Americans.[59]

Reactions to the Farewell Address fell into the familiar grooves. The overwhelming public response was tearfully exuberant, regretting the departure of America's political centerpiece for the last quarter century but embracing his message, as one member of the Cabinet put it, "as a transcript of the general expression of the people of the United States." Meanwhile, the Republican press denounced his warnings against political divisions at home and diplomatic involvement abroad as "the loathings of a sick mind." In the *Aurora,* Benjamin Franklin Bache reprinted the old charge that Washington had been a traitor who conspired with the English government during the war. "This man has a celebrity in a certain way," Washington remarked concerning Bache, "for his calumnies are to be exceeded only by his impudence, and both stand unrivaled." One of his last acts as president was to place on file in the State Department his rejoinder to Bache's accusations, which historians have long since discovered were based on forged English documents. He left office in March 1797 with the resounding cheers of his huge army of supporters and the howls of that much smaller pack of houndish critics echoing in his ears.[60]

Passing through Alexandria on his way to Mount Vernon, he stopped to deliver a speech in which he reiterated his allegiance to the principles articulated in the Farewell Address. "Clouds may and doubtless often will in the vicissitudes of events, hover over our political concerns," he announced, "but a steady adherence to these principles will not only dispel but render our prospects the brighter by such temporary obscurities." He remained supremely confident to the end that he was right, though the "temporary obscurities" being ladled out by the Republican press—France was America's international ally and the national government its domestic enemy—produced fits of private despair and periodic flare-ups of the famous Washington temper. (Even ensconced under his vine and fig tree in retirement, he continued to subscribe to ten newspapers.) More than any great leader in American history before or since, he was accustomed to getting his way, and equally accustomed to having history prove him right. But his final two-and-a-half years at Mount Vernon were beclouded by the incessant apprehension that his final advice to the country would be ignored and his legacy, and with it his own place in history, corrupted.[61]

Part of his problem was a function of location. Mount Vernon, of course, lay within the borders of Virginia, now homeland of the Republican opposition, which was dedicated to overturning the foreign policy and the entire edifice of national sovereignty that Washington stood for. In effect, Mount Vernon became an enclave within enemy territory, surrounded by neighbors committed to a Virginia-writ-large version of the American Republic. Washington, once the supreme Virginian, had in their eyes gone over to the other side. Once the all-purpose solution, Washington was now the still-potent problem, a kind of Trojan horse planted squarely in the Virginian fortress. The fact that he devoted so much of his remaining time and energy to overseeing the construction of the new capital on the Potomac—it was a foregone conclusion that it would be named after him—only confirmed their worst fears. For that city, and the name it was destined to carry, symbolized the conspiracy that threatened, so Jefferson and his followers thought, all that Virginia stood for. Washington, for his part, obliged his Virginia critics by urging his grandson to attend Harvard in order to escape the provincial versions of learning currently ascendant in the Old Dominion. Increasingly, Washington seemed to think of his home state in the same vein as the Indian tribes in his letter to the Cherokees. The destiny of the American nation was pointing one way, and if the tribal chieftains of Virginia chose to oppose that direction, so be it; but they were aligning themselves with a cause destined to lose. On this score history proved him right once again.[62]

Notes

1. On the GW mythology, three books provide excellent surveys: Marcus Cunliffe, *George Washington: Man and Monument* (Boston, 1958); Paul K. Longmore, *The Invention of George Washington* (Berkeley, Los Angeles, and London, 1988); Barry Schwartz, *George Washington: The Making of an American Symbol* (New York, 1987).

2. Albert H. Smyth, ed., *The Writings of Benjamin Franklin,* 10 vols. (New York, 1905–7), 10:111–12.

3. Jefferson to GW, May 23, 1792, in Julian P. Boyd et al., eds., *The Papers of Thomas Jefferson,* 27 vols. to date (Princeton, N.J., 1950—), 23:123; Schwartz, *George Washington,* 38–39; Garry Wills, *Cincinnatus: George Washington and the Enlightenment* (New York, 1984).

4. Matthew Spalding and Patrick J. Garrity, *A Sacred Union of Citizens:*

George Washington's Farewell Address and the American Character (Lantham, Md., 1996), is the most recent and comprehensive scholarly study. The authoritative collection of primary sources on the Farewell Address is Victor H. Palitsits, ed., *Washington's Farewell Address* (New York, 1935), which contains a bibliography of all newspaper and pamphlet editions of the address. On the historiography, see Burton J. Kaufman, *Washington's Farewell Address: The View from the Twentieth Century* (Chicago, 1969). The account in Stanley Elkins and Eric McKitrick, *The Age of Federalism: The Early American Republic, 1788–1800* (New York and Oxford, 1993), 489–528, provides the best incisive summary of the larger implications of GW's retirement within the political culture of the 1790s.

5. Spalding and Garrity, *Sacred Union,* 45–48; Palitsits, *Address,* 308–88.

6. Harold Syrett et al., eds., *The Papers of Alexander Hamilton,* 27 vols. (New York, 1961–87), 20:169–73, for an excellent editorial note on Hamilton's role; Palitsits, *Address,* 30–31; James Morton Smith, ed., *The Republic of Letters: The Correspondence between Thomas Jefferson and James Madison, 1776–1826,* 3 vols. (New York, 1995), 2:940, for the Ames quotation; Madison to Monroe, May 14, 1796, ibid., 941; Flexner, *Washington* 4:292–307.

7. John Adams to Abigail Adams, Jan. 14, 1797, quoted in Smith, *Republic of Letters* 2:895. For Jefferson's version of the Ciceronian posture, see Joseph E. Ellis, *American Sphinx: The Character of Thomas Jefferson* (New York, 1997), 139–41.

8. Schwartz, *George Washington,* 18–19, for an excellent physical description of GW, which also includes the quotation from Rush; Richard Brookhiser, *Founding Father: Rediscovering George Washington* (New York, 1996), 114–15, is also fine on GW's physical presence. Mantle Fielding, *Gilbert Stuart's Portraits of Washington* (Philadelphia, 1933), 77–80, offers the best contemporary description of GW's physical features as rendered by an artist whose eye was trained to notice such things. GW to Robert Lewis, June 26, 1796, *GW: Writings* 35:99, provides GW's own testimony on aging.

9. The Jefferson quotation is from his "Anas" in Paul Leicester Ford, ed., *The Writings of Thomas Jefferson,* 10 vols. (New York, 1892–99), 1:168. In the same vein, see Jefferson to Madison, June 9, 1793, in Smith, *Republic of Letters* 2:780–82. For manifestations of physical decline, see Flexner, *Washington* 4:156–57.

10. *Aurora,* Oct. 17, 1796.

11. Ibid., March 6, 1796; Schwartz, *George Washington,* 68, 99; John Keane, *Tom Paine: A Political Life* (Boston, 1995), 430–52.

12. GW to David Humphreys, June 12, 1796, *GW: Writings* 35:91–92.

13. The newspaper quotation is from Freeman, *Washington* 7:321. On GW's royal style, see esp. Schwartz, *George Washington,* 48–61.

14. The most insightful contemporary commentator on GW's unique and highly paradoxical status was John Adams, who recognized the necessity of a singular leader and simultaneously recognized the dangers inherent in making GW superhuman. The most explicit discussion of this dilemma occurs in John A. Schutz

and Douglass Adair, eds., *The Spur of Fame: Dialogues of John Adams and Benjamin Rush, 1805–1813* (San Marino, Calif., 1966), 185–86.

15. The best synthesis of the different scholarly interpretations of the Farewell Address is Arthur A. Markowitz, "Washington's Farewell and the Historians," *PMHB* 94 (1970): 173–91. See also Felix Gilbert, *To the Farewell Address: Ideas of Early American Foreign Policy* (Princeton, N.J., 1961).

16. For his response to the army, then his address to Congress upon resigning, see *GW: Writings* 26:208, 211–12, 222–27, 27:284–85. For George III's remark, see Wills, *Cincinnatus*, 13.

17. The two outstanding scholarly books on the subject are Don Higginbotham, *George Washington and the American Military Tradition* (Athens, Ga., 1985), and Charles Royster, *A Revolutionary People at War: The Continental Army and American Character, 1775–1783* (Chapel Hill, N.C., 1979).

18. GW to John Barrister, April 21, 1778, *GW: Writings* 11:286.

19. GW to Henry Laurens, Nov. 14, 1778, ibid., 13:254–57. Edmund S. Morgan emphasized the significance of this observation in his biographical essay on GW in *The Meaning of Independence: John Adams, George Washington, Thomas Jefferson* (Charlottesville, Va., 1976), 47–48.

20. *GW: Writings* 26:484–85.

21. Ibid., 485.

22. Isaiah Berlin, *The Hedgehog and the Fox: An Essay on Tolstoy's View of History* (London, 1954).

23. GW to David Humphreys, March 3, 1794, *GW: Writings* 32:398–99.

24. GW to Charles Carroll, May 1, 1796, ibid., 35:30–31.

25. Lawrence Kaplan, *Entangling Alliances with None: American Foreign Policy in the Age of Jefferson* (Kent, Ohio, 1987), emphasizes the consensus among American political leaders; Elkins and McKitrick, *Age of Federalism,* 375–450, takes the party divisions as more serious expressions of deep division. The latter is closer to the truth.

26. Three scholarly accounts are seminal: Samuel Flagg Bemis, *Jay's Treaty: A Study in Commerce and Diplomacy* (New Haven, 1962); Jerald A. Combs, *The Jay Treaty: Political Background of the Founding Fathers* (Berkeley, Los Angeles, and London, 1970); Elkins and McKitrick, *Age of Federalism,* 375–450.

27. Smith, *Republic of Letters* 2:882–83; Adams to William Cunningham, Oct. 15, 1808, *Correspondence between the Honorable John Adams . . . and William Cunningham, Esq.* (Boston, 1823), 34; GW to Edmund Randolph, July 31, 1795, *GW: Writings* 34:266.

28. Madison to Jefferson, April 4, 1796, in Smith, *Republic of Letters* 2:929–30; Jefferson to Edward Rutledge, Nov. 30, 1795, in Ford, *Writings of Jefferson* 7:67–68.

29. Smith, *Republic of Letters* 2:887–88; Jefferson to James Monroe, March 21, 1796, in Ford, *Writings of Jefferson* 7:80.

30. Jefferson to Madison, March 27, 1796, Madison to Jefferson, May 9, 1796, in Smith, *Republic of Letters* 2:928, 937; Jefferson to James Monroe, June 12, 1796, in Ford, *Writings of Jefferson* 7:80. Jefferson's political assessment of the reasons for passage of the Jay Treaty were shrewd, but GW's influence, while crucial, was aided immeasurably by a shift among voters primarily concerned with access to lands in the West. The English promise to withdraw from forts, in effect to implement commitments made in the Treaty of Paris (1783), was itself important in producing the shift. But equally important was the news of Pinckney's Treaty, in which Spain granted access to the Mississippi River and thereby enhanced the prospects for settlements and commerce in the vast interior.

31. For a fuller version of this side of Jefferson's mentality, see Ellis, *American Sphinx*, esp. 151–52.

32. This is the conspiratorial perspective Jefferson embraced in his "Anas," the collection of anecdotes and gossip he gathered for eventual publication during his retirement years. For the anecdotes themselves, see Ford, *Writings of Jefferson* 1:168–78. The best analysis of the "Anas" is Joanne Freeman, "Slander, Poison, Whispers, and Fame: Jefferson 'Anas' and Political Gossip in the Early Republic," *Journal of the Early Republic* 15 (1995): 25–58. The most revealing statement by Jefferson, which includes the "they all live in cities" remark, is "Notes on Professor Ebeling's Letter of July 30, 1785," in Ford, *Writings of Jefferson* 7:44–49.

33. See Thomas P. Slaughter, *The Whiskey Rebellion* (New York, 1986); Richard H. Kohn, "The Washington Administration's Decision to Crush the Whiskey Rebellion," *Journal of American History* 59 (1972): 567–74.

34. Jefferson to Mann Page, Aug. 30, 1795, in Ford, *Writings of Jefferson* 7:24–25. See also Jefferson to James Monroe, May 26, 1795, ibid., 16–17; Jefferson to Madison, Oct. 30, 1794, in Smith, *Republic of Letters* 2:858. The standard assessment of Jefferson's conspiratorial perspective is Lance Banning, *The Jeffersonian Persuasion: Evolution of a Party Ideology* (Ithaca, N.Y., 1978).

35. Jefferson to Philip Mazzei, April 24, 1796, in Ford, *Writings of Jefferson* 7:72–78. The letter was eventually published in a New York newspaper, the *Minerva*, on March 14, 1797.

36. GW to Jefferson, July 6, 1796, *GW: Writings* 35:118–20. For a pro-Jefferson version of this episode, see Dumas Malone, *Jefferson and His Time*, 6 vols. (New York, 1948–81), 3:307–11.

37. The best analysis of Monroe's behavior as minister to France is Elkins and McKitrick, *Age of Federalism*, 497–504. The correspondence in which GW tried to fathom Monroe's statements includes: GW to Hamilton, June 26, 1796, in Syrett, *Hamilton Papers* 20:239; GW to Secretary of State, July 25, 27, 1796, to James Monroe, Aug. 26, 1796, *GW: Writings* 35:155, 157, 187–90. See also the note on Monroe's support for French seizures of American shipping in Syrett, *Hamilton Papers* 20:227.

38. The most succinct summary of Randolph's fiasco in the scholarly litera-
ture is Elkins and McKitrick, *Age of Federalism,* 424–31. A recent account sym-
pathetic to Randolph is Mary K. Bonsteel Tachau, "George Washington and the
Reputation of Edmund Randolph," *Journal of American History* 73 (1986): 15–34.
See also two old but helpful accounts: W. C. Ford, "Edmund Randolph on the
British Treaty, 1795," *American Historical Review* 12 (1907): 587–99; Moncure
D. Conway, *Omitted Chapters in the History Disclosed in the Life and Papers of
Edmund Randolph* (New York, 1888).

39. The correspondence on the episode includes: Randolph to GW, July 20,
29, 31, 1795, GW to Randolph, July 22, Aug. 3, 1795, *GW: Writings* 35:244–55;
also GW to Hamilton, July 29, 1795, in Syrett, *Hamilton Papers* 18:525. Randolph's reputation is defended in excessive fashion in Irving Brant, "Edmund Randolph: Not Guilty!" *WMQ* 7 (1950): 179–98.

40. For a convenient summary of the authorship debate, see Spalding and
Garrity, *Sacred Union,* 55–58.

41. Palitsits, *Address,* 160–63, 212–17, 227.

42. Ibid., 14–15, 241–43. The story is nicely summarized in Spalding and Garrity, *Sacred Union,* 46–49.

43. Palitsits, *Address,* 242.

44. Ibid., 246–47; the "first draft" GW sent to Hamilton is in ibid., 164–73.

45. Ibid., 249–50.

46. Ibid., 250–53, 257. See also Syrett, *Hamilton Papers* 20:265–68, 292–93.

47. GW to Hamilton, Aug. 25, 1796, in Syrett, *Hamilton Papers* 20:307–9.
The "incorporating draft" that GW did not like as well is reproduced in ibid.,
294–303. On the editorial process and changes GW made, see Spalding and Garrity, *Sacred Union,* 53–54.

48. John C. Rhodehamel, ed., *George Washington: Writings* (New York,
1997), 968.

49. Ibid., 974–75.

50. Palitsits, *Address,* 260.

51. Ibid., 172.

52. Ibid., 252–53.

53. Ibid., 258–59.

54. Ibid., 254–57; Rhodehamel, *Writings,* 972.

55. For GW's Eighth Annual Address, see Rhodehamel, *Writings,* 978–85.
Hamilton's draft is in Syrett, *Hamilton Papers* 20:382–88.

56. Flexner, *Washington* 4:324–27, and Elkins and McKitrick, *Age of Federalism,* 495–96, call attention to the strongly nationalistic message GW delivered.
He required no instruction from Hamilton on these issues and retained his own
reasons for regarding the enhanced powers of the federal government as indispensable instruments, the chief reason being that his own departure created a vac-
uum that would need to be filled by federal institutions. Even Jefferson, who as-
cended to the presidency in 1800 intending to dismantle rather than buttress those

institutions and policies, discovered in his first term that GW's projection, though the great man was now in the grave, still haunted the political landscape. Even with Jefferson's triumph in the early years of the nineteenth century and the parallel defeat of the Federalist party as a national force, the core of GW's vision remained alive, because without it the American nation itself would have ceased to exist. A reincarnated GW, I am suggesting, would have gone with Lincoln and the Union in 1861.

57. Palitsits, *Address*, 252–53.

58. Rhodehamel, *Writings*, 956–57.

59. Ibid., 957–60.

60. Palitsits, *Address*, 261–62; William Duane, *A Letter to George Washington . . . Containing Strictures of His Address* (Philadelphia, 1796), 11–12; *Aurora*, Oct. 17, 1796; GW to Benjamin Walker, Jan. 12, 1797, *GW: Writings* 35:363–65.

61. GW to Citizens of Alexandria, March 23, 1797, *GW: Writings* 35:423.

62. GW's opinion concerning the state of Virginia politics is best expressed in GW to Patrick Henry, Oct. 9, 1795, ibid., 335. His views of the Republican party in the state after his retirement are illustrated in GW to Henry Knox, March 2, 1797, in Rhodehamel, *Writings*, 986–87, and to Lafayette, Dec. 25, 1798, *GW: Writings* 37:66. Jefferson's immediate opinion of GW was equally critical: "The President is fortunate to get off just as the bubble is bursting, leaving others to hold the bag. . . . He will have his usual good fortune of reaping credit from the good arts of others, and leaving to them that of his errors" (Jefferson to Madison, Jan. 8, 1797, in *Republic of Letters* 2:955, and Malone, *Jefferson* 3:307–11, who tries to paper over the rift).

10. The Final Struggle between George Washington and the Grim King

Washington's Attitude toward Death and an Afterlife

PETER R. HENRIQUES

Historians generally agree that six men of the Revolutionary era deserve the designation of great: Washington, Franklin, Hamilton, John Adams, Jefferson, and Madison. A distinguished Columbia University historian, Richard B. Morris, in Seven Who Shaped Our Destiny *(1973), made a fairly plausible case for a seventh worthy, adding to the list John Jay, the New Yorker, president of Congress, secretary of foreign affairs under the Confederation, twice a diplomat in Europe, and first chief justice of the United States. But Morris's case is still out, to say the least. Of the six, Franklin died first, in 1790, willing his favorite walking stick to Washington. Washington expired in 1799. Hamilton, fatally wounded in a duel with Aaron Burr, met death in 1804. Both Jefferson and Adams died on July 4, 1826, fifty years to the day from the adoption of the Declaration of Independence. Madison, the youngest of the fathers, was also "the last of the fathers," as Drew McCoy entitles a book on Madison's nineteen postpresidential years, dying in 1836. If any of the six had a great fear of death, their biographers do not record it. Washington, Jefferson, Madison, and Franklin were deists or freethinkers of varying degrees. Adams waffled, expressing at various times both modest skepticism and general orthodoxy but not Calvinist dogma. Hamilton too resists easy categorization. A onetime freethinker, he died professing customary Christian tenets.*

All of the six abhorred narrow sectarianism and staunchly advocated religious toleration, although there were shades of difference among them. Certainly none matched Jefferson and Madison, fathers of the Virginia Act for Establishing Religious Freedom (1786), in their eloquence or in their efforts to bring about complete separation of church and state. Adams, at the time he wrote the Massachusetts Constitution of 1780, had no problem with assessment by towns for the support of religion, a stipulation similar to what Patrick Henry and other religious conservatives tried to enact in the Old Dominion. None outdid Washington in his commitment to religious pluralism, frequently attending churches of various denominations, including Roman Catholic, and maintaining that he would as readily employ a Muhammadan, a Jew, or an atheist as he would a Christian.

Peter R. Henriques is associate professor of history at George Mason University and the author of several important articles on Washington. His essay originally appeared in the Virginia Magazine of History and Biography *107 (1999): 73–97 and is reprinted by permission of the Virginia Historical Society.*

THE FINAL YEAR of the eighteenth century witnessed the deaths of Virginia's two most popular and beloved heroes—Patrick Henry and George Washington. Patrick Henry, suffering from severe intestinal blockage, met his death in June with the courage of a convinced Christian. More than a decade earlier he had consoled his sister on the death of her husband: "This is one of the trying scenes, in which the Christian is eminently superior to all others and finds a refuge that no misfortunes can take away." Confronting his own imminent demise, Henry used his confidence in boldly facing death as a means of testifying to his skeptical physician about the truth of the Christian religion. He believed he would go to a place where "sorrow never enters." According to his second wife's account of his final scene, "He met death with firmness and in full confidence that through the merits of a bleeding saviour that his sins would be pardoned."[1]

Six months later George Washington died an even more painful death and faced his ordeal with a courage every bit equal to that demonstrated by Patrick Henry. Yet, unlike Henry, Washington did not draw his courage from a Christian concept of redemption and the hope of eternal bliss through the sacrifice of Christ. A thorough examination of Washington's religious views, which have been hotly debated,[2] is beyond the scope of this essay, but a careful examination of the way he faced death and what he wrote to others at times of their great personal grief sheds light on Washington's attitude toward death and an afterlife and gives insight into his character.

George Washington's brief fatal illness in December of 1799 came suddenly and with little warning, but it was not unexpected. Although it would be incorrect to aver, as one historian has, that Washington was "haunted by premonitions of death,"[3] there is no question that it was often on his mind, especially in the last years of his life and when he was not involved in important activities. He was acutely aware that he was from a short-lived family, that he was approaching the biblical life span of three score and ten, that he was worn out from a lifetime of service, that his remaining days could "not be many," and that his "glass was almost run."[4] A constant image in his later correspondence is that of gently drifting down the stream of life.[5] When his sole surviving brother, Charles, died earlier in 1799, Washington wrote, "I was the *first*, and am now the *last*, of my fathers Children by the second marriage who remain, when I shall be called upon to follow them, is known only to the giver of life. When the summons comes I shall endeavour to obey it with a good grace."[6]

It was extremely important to Washington to meet death with "good grace." For much of Washington's adult life, he was in one sense or another playing a role—the classical republican general, the patriot king, the father of his country. The desire for the approbation of the people—properly earned through disinterested service for the common good—lay very close to the core of Washington's being. He hoped that in facing death he would do nothing to sully the reputation he had spent a lifetime building.[7]

Certainly, Washington's courage in the face of the prospect of death, stoical in nature from whatever source it was drawn, was one of the trademarks of his life. At the age of seventeen, young Washington owned an outline in English of the principal *Dialogues of Seneca the Younger.* One of the chapter headings was, "The Contempt of Death makes all the Miseries of Life Easy to Us." Seneca also wrote, "He is the brave man . . . that can look death in the face without trouble or surprise."[8] In classical stoicism, the true stoic may fall victim to circumstances beyond his control, suffer and perhaps die, but his superior control over his passions calls forth admiration and leads to a reaffirmation of the dignity of man.

Washington displayed a stoic's contempt for death, an attitude that awed his contemporaries. His response to his baptism by fire, which triggered the start of the French and Indian War in 1754, was, "I heard Bulletts whistle and believe me there was something charming in the sound." Published in England, it reportedly drew a reaction even from King George II.[9] During the French and Indian War, Washington ignored threats from angry frontiersmen "to blow out my brains," put his life at extreme risk by going between his soldiers and knocking up their guns with his sword after they accidentally opened fire on each other, and offered to "die by inches" a horrible death if it would stop the suffering in the backcountry he was sworn to protect. He wrote truthfully, if with a touch of arrogance, "I have . . . [the] resolution to Face what any Man durst."[10]

His legendary courage as commander in chief of the Continental Army might have worried his aides, but it inspired his men. His actions at Princeton and Monmouth, and his response to the falling shells at Yorktown, demonstrated a character seemingly immune from normal fear in the presence of death. So great was his courage that even his harshest critics never brought it into question.[11] So extreme was it that one biographer observed, "There is a streak of something close to a mad nature in a man whose instinctive reaction to near death is sheer exhilaration, who finds the whine of bullets 'charming,' and to whom the swirl of violence is a fine tonic that calms his nerves remarkably and serves to clear his head."[12]

Washington's courage was sorely tested one last time in his final struggle with what he once referred to as "the grim King."[13] Thanks primarily to the invaluable accounts left by Washington's personal secretary, friend, and avid admirer, Tobias Lear, and augmented by a letter from his physicians, Dr. James Craik and Dr. Elisha Cullen Dick, published within days of his death, we have a good general sense of what happened during Washington's final illness, even though some details remain in dispute.[14] It is a story that has been repeated many times, though often the telling has concentrated on the calmness with which Washington faced his demise and in so doing has downplayed the horrific nature of Washington's last day on earth.

Death was not likely to have been on Washington's mind as he went out to check on his farms on Thursday, 12 December 1799. His recent health had never been better, he was making various plans for the future, and he had even signed a jocular pact not to die until the dawn of the new century. Washington remained outside for approximately five hours despite the fact that "the weather was very disagreeable, a constant fall of rain, snow and hail with a high wind."[15]

Apparently, at some time during his rounds, Washington was stricken with the virulent infection that quickly claimed his life. His remarkably hardy constitution in this case may have actually worked to his detriment. "Alas! He relied upon it too much and exposed himself without common caution to the heat in summer and cold in winter," lamented Thomas Law, the husband of Martha Washington's eldest granddaughter.[16] Despite getting soaked by the snow and rain, Washington did not change clothes before dinner. Already beginning to show signs of a cold and a sore throat Friday morning, and despite continued bad weather, he went out briefly in the afternoon to mark some trees he wanted to have cut down. By evening he was very hoarse but still in good spirits. He insisted on reading sections of the paper out loud to his wife, Martha, and secretary, Tobias Lear. Rejecting advice to take medication, he said of his cold, "Let it go as it came."[17] In retrospect, these actions exacerbated his condition.

Over the years there has been considerable debate on the nature of Washington's final illness. The latest and most convincing medical studies indicate that George Washington died from acute epiglottitis caused by a virulent bacteria, possibly *Hemophilus* influenza type b. The epiglottis is a cartilaginous plate located at the base of the tongue and at the entrance to the larynx, or voice box. It is at the entrance to the airway that goes through the larynx to the lungs. If it swells up, it can block the airway, and in extreme cases, in which the epiglottis is enlarged to ten times its normal size, a ball-valve mechanism develops when trying to draw in sufficient air. The symptoms exhibited during Washington's final illness—rapid onset, a severely sore throat, difficulty in swallowing, difficulty in speaking, increased airway obstruction, especially when leaning backward, a desire to assume a sitting position in spite of weakness, persistent restlessness, and finally an apparent improvement shortly before death—dovetail exactly with acute epiglottitis.[18]

By the early hours of Saturday morning, the disease had progressed so rapidly that Washington was very uncomfortable and had difficulty breathing. During the rest of the day—nearly twenty hours—George Washington slowly and painfully choked to death. In Lear's words, "He suffered extremely." "His distress, through the day, was extreme." "He appeared to be in great pain and distress, from the difficulty of breathing, and frequently changed his position in the bed" and tried to sit up.[19] (Sitting up and leaning forward minimizes the ball-valve effect from the enlarged epiglottis.) Sadly, the pain of constantly struggling for breath was significantly aggravated by the medical treatment given him.

Dr. James Craik, Washington's longtime personal physician and dear friend, arriving later on the morning of 14 December, immediately recognized the gravity of the situation and urged that another physician, Dr. Elisha Cullen Dick, be called in as a consultant. Martha Washington had earlier sent word to Dr. Gustavus Brown of Port Tobacco about the general's condition. Dick arrived about 3 P.M. and Brown shortly after. Although Washington received excellent care from the three attending physicians according to the accepted medical practice of the time, much of their treatment was in fact detrimental.[20]

During the course of less than twelve hours, George Washington was bled four different times and lost approximately five pints of blood. (Several accounts put the figure even higher.)[21] The first bleeding was ordered by the general himself, who was a firm believer in the efficacy of the procedure. Of course, the theory behind bleeding was to remove the diseased matter from the body. In fact, such excessive bloodletting severely weakened Washington. In addition, the aggressive treatment compromised his circulation. In acute epiglottitis, it is not difficult to expel air, but it is hard to inhale it and receive sufficient oxygen. As a result, the patient suffers from hypoxemia, deficient oxygenation of the blood. The significant loss of blood, at least one-half of Washington's total, further reduced his oxygen supply because the hemoglobin in the blood carries oxygen. The use of purgatives, by significantly reducing his body fluids, compounded the situation.[22]

Not only did the purgatives compromise circulation, but they also inflicted significant additional suffering. Two moderate doses of calomel, a white, tasteless medicine used as a purgative, were given, and an injection was administered. Later, ten more grains of calomel were prescribed, followed by repeated doses of emetic tartar totaling five or six grains. The result was a "copious discharge from the bowels." How much discomfort this would have inflicted on a man struggling for each breath is easier to imagine than to describe. Blistering added to the distress but did nothing to alleviate the situation. It is not surprising that Washington, who appeared to realize early on in the day that the disease would prove fatal, struggled valiantly to make his physicians aware that although he appreciated their efforts, he desired them to stop their ministrations. "[L]et me go off quietly," he asked.[23]

Throughout the entire ordeal the general displayed remarkable fortitude and patience. According to Lear, "not a complaint escaped him."[24] Clearly, the symptoms surrounding his fatal illness were excruciating, and they were beyond Washington's power to change. Somehow, Washington kept his dignity despite the circumstances, which were anything but dignified.

While his courage, which was so much a part of his identity, shone brightly, other aspects of his character were highlighted during the ordeal as well. Lear wrote the following day, "He died as he lived." In the midst of his own personal agony, Washington's concern for others stands out.

He refused to allow his wife to seek help in the middle of the night for fear she would take cold. He calmed the fears of the overseer, George Rawlins, who took the first blood. He apologized to Tobias Lear, who was helping move him to different positions in the general's endless quest for oxygen, and worried that the effort would fatigue Lear. He thanked his physicians for their heroic efforts. He urged his personal body servant, Christopher Scheels, who had been standing by the bed throughout the day, to sit down. These actions speak volumes about Washington's character.[25]

The authors of a major biography of Washington emphasized another aspect of his character. "The same self-discipline served George Washington as patient that had served him as a planter, as Commander-in-Chief, as President," wrote John Alexander Carroll and Mary Wells Ashworth. "Duty . . . was his governing principle. . . . Today, this 14th of December, 1799, he had responded as if clearly it was his duty not to deny the doctors and others their valiant efforts to restore him, unavailing though he believed them to be."[26]

George Washington was a man who liked to be in control, and, as death approached, he did what he could to ensure that what was important to him would be carried out after he was gone. He had his wife bring him two wills and made sure the old one was burned. His final testament was a massive document expressing his wishes on a great number of things. One of his very last requests, when speaking was done only with great pain and effort, involved his public and personal papers. As W. W. Abbot has demonstrated, these were of the utmost importance to him and to his perceived place in history.[27] His very last request to Lear was for Lear not to have him buried until he had been dead for at least two days.[28] The idea of being buried alive was a more realistic concern then than it would be today, and apparently this thought, for a man always desiring control, was a very disquieting one. For whatever reason, his wish was clearly important to Washington because he wanted to make absolutely sure Lear understood him.

As the lack of oxygen becomes extreme in acute epiglottitis, a euphoric state develops that may be interpreted as improvement. Lear noted, "About ten minutes before he expired . . . his breathing became easier; he lay quietly;—he withdrew his hand from mine, and felt his own pulse." Then the patient's expression changed, his hand fell, and sometime late in the evening of 14 December George Washington's life on earth was over.[29]

Did Washington see this physical death as the end of his life? How did Washington view death? Did he believe death the entryway to a better world? How did he think one should face death—one's own and those of friends and loved ones? Washington's answers to these questions may help us better understand his philosophy and what motivated his actions. Efforts to comprehend Washington's attitude toward death and an afterlife are complicated by the fact that he was reticent to discuss such issues and, as far as the record shows, never formulated a comprehensive view about them. The confusion is compounded because almost from the very moment of his death apologists sought to make Washington's position conform to their own. Despite these obstacles, a careful reading of Washington's correspondence and attention to what he said—and, equally important, to what he did not say—can help clarify these issues.

During his sixty-seven years of life, George Washington often had to face the death of relatives and friends close to him. Although no extant material records his reaction to the deaths of some people important to him, such as his father, Augustine, who died when Washington was only eleven, or his half brother, Lawrence, who died nine years later, there still is a significant corpus of evidence on this subject. Relevant correspondence preserves Washington's reactions to the deaths of such family members as his mother, Mary Ball Washington; his stepchildren, Patsy and Jacky Custis; his brothers, John Augustine Washington and Charles Washington; his sister, Betty Lewis; his nephew, George Augustine Washington; and his niece, Fanny Bassett Washington Lear; and such friends as Burwell Bassett's daughter and Bassett himself; General Nathanael Greene; Colonel Tench Tilghman; Patrick Henry; Henry Lee's first wife and daughter; Benjamin Lincoln's son; Henry Knox's son; William Pearce's daughter; and Archibald Cary's wife.[30]

Daniel Blake Smith has written, "A controlled style of bereavement—submission to God's authority with no 'affectation of overflowing grief'—remained the *ideal* way to confront family death throughout the eighteenth century." Kathleen M. Brown has concluded, "Elite men interpreted control over emotions such as . . . sadness . . . as the triumph of reason over passion."[31] George Washington tried—with considerable but not total success—to live up to those ideals.[32]

Washington's views on the proper way to face death and loss were remarkably consistent throughout his adult life and encompassed several aspects. At the center of his thought was the concept of God or Providence. (Washington used a remarkable number of names for this force, such as "the supreme disposer of all events," the "Grand Architect," "the Almighty ruler of the universe," the "great governor of the Universe," and dozens of others.) Washington understood this supernatural force as the giver of life and as actively intervening in human affairs. The first president has often been described as a deist, but if he was, he best fits into the category of what Edwin S. Gaustad has called a "warm deist."[33] Deism in the eighteenth century denied the interference of the Creator with the laws of the universe, but the image of the great "watchmaker" who created the world but does not intervene in it does not comport with Washington's ideas. By contrast, a "warm deist" sees Providence regularly shaping and molding history. In writing to people in times of personal bereavement, Washington consistently stressed three aspects of this supernatural force: It is wise, it is inscrutable, and it is irresistible.[34] Washington often emphasized the inscrutable nature of Providence. Its actions could not be understood from man's perspective. Man "can only form conjectures agreable to the small extent of our knowledge—and ignorant of the comprehensive Schemes intended." It was best to trust Providence "without perplexing ourselves to seek for that, which is beyond human ken."[35]

Washington recognized that it is often impossible for man to understand why tragedy occurs. He described death with emotive words such as a "stroke," "a severe stroke," a "blow," a "test," a "trial," "an afflictive trial," a "debt" we must all pay.[36] And although we may not understand why it occurs, we cannot prevent it from happening. As a young man Washington wrote to Sally Cary Fairfax, "[T]here is a Destiny, which has the Sovereign controul of our Actions—not to be resisted by the strongest efforts of Human Nature."[37] He never changed his mind.

Ultimately, Washington fell back on the position that "He that gave has a right to take away." Writing to his dying nephew, George Augustine Washington, he declared, "The will of Heaven is not to be controverted or scrutinized by the children of this world. It therefore becomes the Creatures of it to submit with patience and resignation to the will of the Creator whether it be to prolong, or to shorten the number of our days. To bless them with health, or afflict them with pain."[38] Over and over again, Washington urged those in grief to seek the "comforts of religion and philosophy" but primarily to submit with resignation.[39] He reported to Bryan Fairfax almost with pride how he responded to his nephew's death: "It is a loss I sincerely regret, but as it is the will of Heaven, whose decrees are always just and wise, I submit to it without a murmur."[40]

Yet even as Washington set this up as the ideal response, he realized the impossibility of achieving it in cases of great loss. Instead, he qualified his call for resignation and acceptance with the proviso, "as far as feelings of humanity will allow." Whatever the ideal, he was acutely aware that human beings must grieve for their loved ones. "It is the nature of humanity to mourn for the loss of our friends," he wrote, "and the more we loved

them, the more poignant is our grief."⁴¹ Consoling his good friend, Henry
Knox, on the loss of his son, Washington recognized that "parental feelings are too much alive in the moment of these misfortunes to admit the
consolations of religion or philosophy." He expressed similar sentiments
to his nephew, George Lewis: "[T]ime alone can ameliorate, & soften the
pangs we experience at parting."⁴²

George Washington certainly grieved intensely for the loss of people
close to him, although he did so privately. Adopting the view that controlling sadness was a sign of the triumph of reason over passion and that
it was generally unmanly to weep, Washington shunned public displays of
grief. Reflecting the mores of the time, Jacky Custis apologized to his stepfather for acting "Like a woman" upon hearing of his sister's death and
giving himself "up entirely to melancholy for several Days."⁴³ When Custis
himself died eight years later following the American victory at Yorktown,
an associate noted that Washington was "uncommonly affected," and he
stopped his diary in mid-sentence.⁴⁴ Washington so regretted Nathanael
Greene's death that he could "scarce persuade myself to touch upon it."⁴⁵

The absence of specific references to grieving for his father or half
brother, Lawrence, does not mean Washington did not do so. On other occasions, Washington noted that "[d]eath of near relations always produces
awful and affecting emotions." "The death of a Parent is . . . Awful, and
affecting." "Separation from our nearest relatives is a heart rending circumstance."⁴⁶ Several extant letters further help us understand why we have
so few examples of an openly grieving Washington. Writing to Bushrod
Washington, son of his favorite brother, John Augustine, who had just died,
Washington declared, "[T]o attempt an expression of my sorrow on this
occasion would be as feebly described, as it would be unavailing when related." Later, in a letter to Fanny Bassett Washington on the death of her
husband (his nephew), Washington asserted, "To express this sorrow with
the force I feel it, would answer no other purpose than to revive, in your
breast, that poignancy of anguish, which, by this time, I hope is abated."
Time and time again, Washington wrote that he felt "most sensibly" the
loss of a loved one or friend that death had "snatched from us."⁴⁷

Did Washington expect to be reunited with those who were snatched
from him by death? Although the evidence is admittedly fragmentary and
inconsistent, a careful reading of what Washington said—and did not
say—indicates that he was skeptical about a reunion with loved ones in
another life.

The most striking aspect of Washington's view of life after death centers on what he did not say. Not once in all of his authentic, extant corre-

spondence did he explicitly indicate his belief in the reunion of loved ones in Heaven. Certainly the greatest comfort of religion in general and of Christianity in particular is this hope. Washington may have urged those in grief to find consolation in religion, but in all the letters of condolence he wrote, he never gave his recipients the comfort of his assurance that he believed they would meet again with their loved ones. In contrast, William Fairfax, following the death of his wife and Lawrence Washington's baby in 1747, wrote to Lawrence, "As it has been the Will of God lately to take to his mercy the spirits of my late Wife and your child we submit to his Divine Pleasure." When George Mason's daughter lost a child in 1785, Mason attempted to console her with the words, "Your dear baby has died innocent and blameless, and has been called away by an all wise and merciful Creator, most probably from a life of misery and misfortune, and most certainly to one of happiness and bliss."[48] Thomas Jefferson comforted John Adams following the death of his beloved Abigail with the thought that Adams should look forward to that "ecstatic meeting with friends we have loved and lost and whom we shall still love and never lose again."[49] Patrick Henry encouraged his sister with the hope that "we [shall] meet in that heaven to which the merits of Jesus will carry those who love and serve him."[50] Washington did not use such language. As Paul F. Boller, Jr., has written in another context, there is a "rugged honesty" in Washington's refusal to assume religious postures that he did not feel privately.[51]

Neither did Washington comfort himself with such a vision. Indeed, to the degree that he wrote about death, the emphasis was on separation. After his brother Jack's death, he lamented that he had "just bid an eternal farewell to a much loved Brother who was the intimate companion of my youth and the most affectionate friend of my ripened age." Shortly before his mother died, Washington visited her in Fredericksburg. "I took a final leave of my Mother, never expecting to see her more," he confided to his sister. Parting from his beloved friend, the marquis de Lafayette, following the end of the war, Washington pined, "I often asked myself, as our Carriages distended, whether that was the last sight, I ever should have of you? And tho' I wished to say no—my fears answered yes."[52] These assertions were not moderated with such words as "in this world" or the like.

Although no one can know what Washington was thinking on this subject on 14 December, the complete lack of religious context is striking. In Washington's final hours, as faithfully recounted by Lear, there is no reference to any religious words or prayers, no request for forgiveness, no fear of divine judgment, no call for a minister (although ample time existed to summon one if desired), no deathbed farewell, no promise or hope of meeting again in Heaven.[53] It is significant that Tobias Lear ended his personal account with the explicit hope that he would meet Washington in Heaven, but his sense of fidelity to a true record kept him from putting such words in Washington's mouth. (Of course, others were not so scrupulous, and accounts quickly emerged of Washington's having died a "Christian" death.)[54] Martha Washington, a devout Episcopalian, indicated soon afterward that she hoped to meet her husband in Heaven. Perhaps Washington did not take special leave of his wife because, as Thomas Law wrote, "he had frequently disapproved of the afflicting farewells which aggravated sorrows on those melancholy occasions," but words of hope of a future reunion—if honestly voiced—would surely have given comfort to those left behind.[55]

The argument that George and Martha Washington viewed the concept of an afterlife differently is further supported by examining the letters written to each by Jacky Custis on learning of the sudden death of his sister, Patsy, from seizures in 1773. In his letter to his mother, Jacky urged her to "remember you are a Christian." Patsy's "case is more to be envied than pitied, for if we mortals can distinguish between those who are deserveing of grace & who are not, I am confident she enjoys that Bliss prepar'd only for the good & virtuous, let these considerations, My dear Mother have their due weight with you and comfort yourself with reflecting that she now enjoys in substance what we in this world enjoy in imagination & that there is no real Happiness on this side of the grave." His letter to his stepfather was completely void of such sentiments, as if they would not have given solace to Washington.[56]

Although Washington's view of the afterlife does not seem to be Christian, the record is clear that he did believe in some type of life after death, although it may be tempting to read more into his offhand comments than might be merited. For example, Washington at least twice made reference to going to "the World of Spirits." He wrote Lafayette about searching for Elysium, the happy otherworld for heroes favored by the gods. When Patsy Custis died of epilepsy, he believed she had gone "into a more happy, & peaceful abode." Following his mother's death, he reflected the hope that she was in a "happier place."[57] Washington hoped that God would bless a group of ministers "here and hereafter." He referred to nurturing the plants of friendship "before they are transplanted to a happier clime." In a draft written by Timothy Pickering to two Philadelphia churches, Washington looked forward to retirement, "which can only be exceeded by the hope of future happiness." While he was dying, he declared several times, "I am going. . . . I die hard but am not afraid to go." According to Lear's letter to his mother on 16 December, Washington told his secretary, "I am just going to change my scene."[58] The image of "going" implies some kind of continuation of existence. It is apparent that Washington had difficulty accepting or conceiving of the idea of nothingness. He did not believe that a person simply ceases to exist upon his or her death.

Although life goes on—in some fashion—the picture Washington painted of it was generally a gloomy one. "The World of Spirits" may or may not be a happy place. When Washington wrote of Patsy Custis going to a happier place, he specifically contrasted it with "the afflicted Path she hitherto has trod." A relative had written Washington that his mother was in fact in a happier place. Significantly, Washington added his hope that this was true rather than simply agreeing with the statement.[59] The passing reference to Elysium may well have been made tongue in cheek. Although there are clear references to an afterlife, and some of them are quite positive, Washington's references to death and what follows were more often gloomy and pessimistic.

Death was "the grim King" whom Washington, not yet thirty and very near his "last gasp," feared would master his "utmost efforts" and cause him to "sink in spite of a noble struggle."[60] Much later, to demonstrate how much he did not want to take on yet another new responsibility, Washington told Alexander Hamilton that he would leave his peaceful abode (Mount Vernon) with as much reluctance as he would go to the tomb of his ancestors.[61] When people died, he spoke of them as "poor Greene" or "poor Laurens" or "poor Colo. Harrison" or "poor Mr. Custis." Referring to death, Washington wrote about his "approaching decay," the "hour of my dissolution," of going "to the shades of darkness," "to sleep with my Fathers," to "the shades below," "to the tomb of my ancestors," "to the dreary mansions of my Fathers." Death was "that country from whence no Traveller returns."[62] The overall image is not a bright one, certainly not a Christian one.

The Christian images of judgment, redemption through the sacrifice of Christ, and eternal life for the faithful find no resonance in any of Washington's surviving writings. Indeed, in his personal correspondence he never referred to Jesus or the Christ or the Savior at all. In a revealing letter to Lafayette, to whom he wrote with a frankness shared with few if any other correspondents, Washington described Christianity as if he were an outsider. "Being no bigot myself to any mode of worship," he confided, "I am disposed to indulge professors of Christianity . . . that road to Heaven, which to them shall seem the most direct plainest easiest and least liable to exception." Douglas Southall Freeman concluded that at age twenty-seven, Washington found "no rock of refuge in religion."[63] Forty years later, he still had not found it.

Washington appeared to be more interested in acquiring a different type of immortality, a secular immortality achieved by attaining fame across the ages.[64] In another letter to Lafayette, Washington mentioned the "Bards," those poets "who hold the keys of the gate by which Patriots, Sages and Heroes are admitted to immortality." He considered the "Antient Bards" "both the preist and door-keepers to the temple of fame." David Humphreys understood Washington's desires. In connection with Jean-Antoine Houdon's visit to Mount Vernon to take likenesses for a statue of Washington, Humphreys observed, "[I]ndeed, my dear General, it must be a pleasing reflection to you amid the tranquil walks of private life to find that history, poetry, painting, & sculpture will vye with each other in consigning your name to immortality."[65] One can sense Washington strongly shared the sentiments his aide expressed when the general wrote to James Tilghman following the death of his son, Tench: "[T]here is this consolation to be drawn, that while living, no man could be more esteemed—and since dead, none more lamented than Colo. Tilghman."[66]

To be revered in life, to be lamented in death, to be remembered with honor in history were concrete things that could give real consolation in a time of grief. Writing to Sally Cary Fairfax at age twenty-six, Washington mused about the fall of a British officer and declared, "[W]ho is there that does not rather Envy, than regret a Death that gives birth to Honour & Glorious memory."[67] This glorious memory was something to envy and desire and strive to achieve.

For Washington, exactly what happens after death is beyond man's ability either to know or to control. In the face of this fact, what can man do beyond trusting in the goodness of Providence? A hint of Washington's view can be found in one of his favorite passages from his favorite play, Joseph Addison's *Cato:* "It is beyond the power of mortals to command success. We'll do more, Sempronius. We will deserve it."[68] On the death of a beloved niece, Washington rather paradoxically wrote, "She is now no more! But she must be happy, because her virtue has a claim to it."[69]

Not only personal courage allowed Washington to face his final struggle with the Grim King with perfect resignation and equanimity. Also fortifying him was the conviction that he had lived his life with honor and that he had "always walked on a straight line, and endeavoured as far as human frailties, and perhaps strong passions, would enable him, to discharge the relative duties to his Maker and fellow-men, without seeking any indirect or left-handed attempts to acquire popularity."[70] Thus armed with virtue, he ventured out prepared and unafraid to meet whatever the future might hold.

Whatever future tests might or might not lie ahead, George Washington met his final test on earth—as he had lived his life—with the type of grace and courage and character that affirms the dignity of man and commands respect and admiration. If ever a man deserved the secular immortality he so avidly sought, that man was George Washington.

Notes

1. Patrick Henry to Anne Henry Christian, May 15, 1786, to Bartholomew Dandridge, Jan. 21, 1785, in William Wirt Henry, *Patrick Henry: Life, Correspondence, and Speeches,* 3 vols. (1891; New York, 1969), 2:286–87 (first quotation), 252 (second quotation); Dorothea Dandridge Henry to Elizabeth Henry Aylett, n.d. (but probably written from Red Hill shortly after Patrick Henry's death), Patrick Henry Memorial Association, Brookneal, Va. James M. Elson, "The Death of Patrick Henry," summarizes these events (Patrick Henry Essay no. 2–98, *Newsletter of the Red Hill Patrick Henry National Memorial* [May 1996]).

2. Because of GW's centrality to American history, people with diametrically opposed views on religion have claimed him as one of their own. Within the Christian right, GW is sometimes portrayed as a born-again fundamentalist. This is accomplished by accepting as authentic a spurious collection of "Washington Prayers," supposedly copied by GW as a young man and then using those sentiments to express GW's mature faith. On the other hand, and with no more validity, freethinkers argue that GW should rightly be viewed as one of them. Good examples of this position are Franklin Steiner, *The Religious Beliefs of Our Presidents* (Amherst, N.Y., 1995), and John E. Remsburg, *Six Historic Americans: Paine, Jefferson, Washington, Franklin, Lincoln, Grant, the Fathers and Saviors of Our Republic, Freethinkers* (New York, 1906). Still the best overview of the subject is Paul F. Boller Jr.'s *George Washington and Religion* (Dallas, 1963). Although not a communicant, GW was a lifelong member of the Anglican-Episcopal church and for a time a vestryman. Still, as Dorothy Twohig has noted, GW's "interest in religion always appears to have been perfunctory" ("The Making of George Washington," in *George Washington and the Virginia Backcountry,* ed. Warren R. Hofstra [Madison, Wis., 1998], 19). GW once wrote, "In religion my tenets are few and simple" (GW to James Anderson, Dec. 24, 1795, *GW: Writings* 34:107). Any attempt to connect GW closely to orthodox Christian thinking must take into account the complete lack of reference to Jesus (or Christ) in his private correspondence.

3. Flexner, *Washington* 3:341. Flexner implies this concern was characteristic of GW throughout his adult life (James Thomas Flexner, *Washington: The Indispensable Man* [Boston and Toronto, 1974], 47).

4. GW to Lafayette, Dec. 8, 1784, Oct. 8, 1797, *GW: Writings* 28:7, 36:41, 263; Freeman, *Washington* 7:582. The final quotation is in Willard Sterne Randall, *George Washington: A Life* (New York, 1997), 499.

5. Among many examples, *GW: Writings* 27:318, 28:371, 29:170, 211.

6. GW to Burgess Ball, Sept. 22, 1799, ibid., 37:372.

7. The idea of GW playing a role is well developed in Paul K. Longmore, *The Invention of George Washington* (Berkeley, Los Angeles, and London, 1988), esp. 52, 202–11. See also Gordon S. Wood, *The Radicalism of the American Revolution* (New York, 1992), 205–10.

8. Sir Roger L'Estrange, ed., *Seneca's Morals: By Way of Abstract . . .* (1682; New York, 1930), 10 (quotation); Samuel Eliot Morison, "The Young Man Washington," in *George Washington: A Profile,* ed. James Morton Smith (New York, 1969), 46. Morison credits the Fairfax family as the key influence on GW and declares they fell in the tradition of eighteenth-century whig gentry who conformed outwardly to Christianity but derived their real inspiration from the Stoic philosophers. Although this characterization may be true, it is worth noting that William Fairfax once considered becoming an Anglican clergyman and that his son Bryan did take holy orders.

9. GW to John Augustine Washington, May 31, 1754, *PGW: Col. Ser.* 1:118. The king commented that GW would not say so if he had heard many (ibid., 1:119n).

10. GW to Robert Dinwiddie, Oct. 11, 1755, ibid., 2:102 (first quotation); Rosemarie Zagarri, ed., *David Humphreys' "Life of General Washington" with George Washington's "Remarks"* (Athens, Ga., and London, 1991), 22; GW to Robert Dinwiddie, April 22, 1756, May 29, 1754, *PGW: Col. Ser.* 3:33 (second quotation), 1:107 (third quotation).

11. Freeman, *Washington* 5:489. The description of GW —"cool like a Bishop at his prayers"—by Roger Atkinson in 1774 seems particularly appropriate for his actions under fire (quoted ibid., 3:370n).

12. Noemie Emery, *Washington: A Biography* (New York, 1976), 378–79. GW was aware of and impressed by the idea of heroic death. Several paintings that hung in Mount Vernon's two dining rooms dealt with this theme: the death of Richard Montgomery, Bunker Hill, the death of James Wolfe, and the death of the earl of Chatham. See Garry Wills, *Cincinnatus: George Washington and the Enlightenment* (Garden City, N.Y., 1984), 174–75. I thank one of the outside readers for bringing this point to my attention.

13. GW to Richard Washington, Oct. 20, 1761, *PGW: Col. Ser.* 7:80. Although GW used this phrase only once, it fit with his later reference to death "snatching" people. The "Grim King" was a popular ballad. Air 8 in *The Beggar's Opera* (1728) is entitled "Grim King of the Ghosts."

14. On Tobias Lear, see Jon Knowlton, "Tobias Lear and George Washington: In Support of Greatness" (M.A. thesis, University of Maine, 1967). A rather unsympathetic account may be found in Ray Brighton, *The Checkered Career of*

Tobias Lear (Portsmouth, N.H., 1985). Lear left two accounts, a "journal" entry written on Dec. 15 and a longer "diary" account compiled later in the month. Dr. James Craik later endorsed the larger "diary" account as accurate "so far as I can recollect." Although there are slight differences and discrepancies between the two versions, the second, longer narrative appears to have been an effort to expand and augment the one set down very shortly after GW's death so as to include more information while it was fresh in Lear's memory. How much credence to give Lear's account is, of course, a major consideration. Clearly, he sanitized GW's death and downplayed the agonizing aspects of it. Although Lear had several purposes in writing his accounts, they have the ring of truth about them, even if they may be incomplete and incorrect in some details. There is a tremendous vividness to a deathbed scene such as Lear witnessed. He wrote about it immediately, including in a private letter to his mother, which he told her not to make public. His account was supported by Craik. GW had demonstrated remarkable courage throughout his life, was very much aware of the concept of heroic death, knew this was his final act, and would have done everything he could, consistent with human reaction to pain and difficult breathing, to end his life in a praiseworthy way. Such a death would be in keeping with Seneca's description of a Stoic as a man "who, if his body were to be broken upon the wheel or melted lead poured down his throat, would be less concerned for the pain itself than for the dignity of bearing it" (L'Estrange, *Seneca's Morals,* 10). Lear's original "journal" account is in the William L. Clements Library at the University of Michigan, Ann Arbor. His original "diary" account is in the Historical Society of Pennsylvania. Both documents are available on the Web at <http//www.virginia.edu/gwpapers/exhibits/mourning/lear.html>.

15. Tobias Lear to Mary Stillson Lear, Dec. 16, 1799, copy in file on GW's death, MTVL (quotation); Martha Washington to Elizabeth Willing Powel, Dec. 18, 1797, in Joseph E. Fields, ed., *"Worthy Partner": The Papers of Martha Washington* (Westport, Conn., and London, 1994), 310.

16. Thomas Law to Edward Law, Dec. 15, 1799, *Papers of George Washington* project, University of Virginia.

17. Tobias Lear, "journal" account, MTVL.

18. White McKenzie Wallenborn, "George Washington's Terminal Illness," *Papers of George Washington* project, University of Virginia, available on-line at <http://www.virginia.edu/gwpapers/exhibits/mourning/wallenborn>; Heinz H. E. Scheidemandel, "Did George Washington Die of Quinsy?" *Archives of Otolaryngology* 102 (1976): 519–21. The traditional diagnosis is quinsy, but Scheidemandel argues that in the short space of roughly twenty-one hours a peritonsillar abscess would not have produced total obstruction of the airway. Furthermore, there was no indication of swelling caused by an abcess. And although GW had trouble speaking, he was not hoarse from a raspy throat. The symptoms simply fit together better for a diagnosis of acute epiglottitis rather than quinsy.

19. Tobias Lear to Lawrence Lewis, Dec. 15, 1799, to George Washington

Parke Custis, Dec. 15, 1799, to Mary Stillson Lear, Dec. 16, 1799, copy in file on GW's death, MTVL; Tobias Lear, "journal" account, ibid.

20. Paul Leicester Ford, *The True George Washington* (1896; Philadelphia, 1911), asserted that "[t]here can be scarcely a doubt that the treatment of his last illness by the doctors was little short of murder" (58). Certainly such a charge is unfair, given the state of medical knowledge at the time.

21. It is difficult to estimate the amount of blood actually drawn. J. Worth Estes computes the amount at ninety-six ounces ("Treating America's First Superhero," *Medical Heritage* 1 [1985]: 54, copy in file on GW's death, MTVL).

22. Wallenborn, "Washington's Terminal Illness"; Scheidemandel, "Did Washington Die of Quinsy?" It is unclear whether the interior of GW's throat was ever examined by his physicians. Although most scholars conclude it was not, use of the word *inflammatory* to describe GW's throat suggests that one or more of the doctors did examine it. I want to acknowledge the outside reader who brought this point to my attention.

23. James Craik and Elisha C. Dick, account published in the *Times and Alexandria Advertiser,* Dec. 19, 1799 (copy in file on GW's death, MTVL; available on line at <http//www.virginia.edu/gwpapers/exhibits/mourning/craik.html>); Tobias Lear, "journal" account, MTVL.

24. Tobias Lear to Mary Stillson Lear, Dec. 16, 1799, MTVL.

25. Tobias Lear to William Augustine Washington, Dec. 15, 1799, in Worthington Chauncey Ford, ed., *The Writings of George Washington,* 14 vols. (New York and London, 1889–93), 14:257 (quotation); Tobias Lear, "journal" account, MTVL.

26. Freeman, *Washington* 7:624.

27. W. W. Abbot, "An Uncommon Awareness of Self: The Papers of George Washington," *Prologue* 21 (1989): 7–19 (see chap. 11 below).

28. Tobias Lear, "journal" account, MTVL. Lear's later "diary" account records "three days," which was more customary. GW most likely said "two days," for that is what Lear wrote the day following the president's death and repeated in his letter to his mother on December 16. Thomas Law, writing on the day after GW died, quoted "two days" as well, either repeating what Lear told him or relying on Lear's account.

29. Tobias Lear, "journal" account, MTVL. A fourth physician, Dr. William Thornton, arrived shortly after GW's demise and wanted to try to resuscitate him. "First . . . thaw him in cold water," he instructed, "then . . . lay him in blankets, and by degrees and by friction . . . give him warmth, . . . open a passage to the lungs by the trachea, and . . . inflate them with air, to produce an artificial respiration, and . . . transfuse blood into him from a lamb." Fortunately, this desecration of GW's remains was not carried out (William Thornton, draft appended to essay "On Sleep," ca. 1822–25, in C. M. Harris and Daniel Preston, eds., *Papers of William Thornton,* 1 vol. to date [Charlottesville and London, 1995—], 528, copy in file on GW's death, *Papers of George Washington* project, Univer-

sity of Virginia; available on-line at <http//www.virginia.edu/gwpapers/exhibits/mourning/thornton.html>).

30. For Mary Ball Washington, see *PGW: Pres. Ser.* 4:32; for Martha Parke Custis, see *PGW: Col. Ser.* 9:243; for John Parke Custis, see *GW: Writings* 23:340; for John Augustine Washington, see *PGW: Conf. Ser.* 4:509–10; for Charles Washington, see *GW: Writings* 37:372; for Betty Washington Lewis, see *PGW: Ret. Ser.* 1:90; for George Augustine Washington, see *GW: Writings* 32:315, 354; for Fanny Bassett Washington Lear, see ibid., 35:5–6, 26–27; for Burwell Bassett and his daughter, see *PGW: Col. Ser.* 9:219 and *GW: Writings* 32:310; for Nathanael Greene, see *PGW: Conf. Ser.* 4:171, 5:107; for Tench Tilghman, see ibid., 4:96; for Patrick Henry, see *GW: Writings* 37:244; for Henry Lee's wife and daughter, see *PGW: Pres. Ser.* 6:347; for Benjamin Lincoln's son, see *GW: Writings* 29:412–13; for Henry Knox's son, see ibid., 31:360; for William Pearce's daughter, see ibid., 33:429; for Archibald Cary's wife, see ibid., 24:346.

31. Daniel Blake Smith, *Inside the Great House: Planter Family Life in Eighteenth-Century Chesapeake Society* (Ithaca, N.Y., and London, 1980), 265; Kathleen M. Brown, *Good Wives, Nasty Wenches, and Anxious Patriarchs: Gender, Race, and Power in Colonial Virginia* (Chapel Hill, N.C., and London, 1996), 324.

32. Jan Lewis, *The Pursuit of Happiness: Family and Values in Jefferson's Virginia* (Cambridge, London, and New York, 1983), devotes a chapter to contrasting mourning styles and attitudes toward death in eighteenth- and nineteenth-century Virginia (69–105). The differences might not be as pronounced as indicated. Thomas Jefferson's extremely emotional reaction to his wife's death may not have been that unusual.

33. Edwin S. Gaustad, *Sworn on the Altar of God: A Religious Biography of Thomas Jefferson* (Grand Rapids, Mich., and Cambridge, 1996), 143. For the variety of terms GW used for this supernatural force, see the sources cited in note 30.

34. GW to Henry Knox, Sept. 8, 1791, *GW: Writings* 31:360.

35. GW to David Humphreys, March 23, 1793, ibid., 32:398.

36. Ibid., 36:171, 37:109, 23:392.

37. GW to Sarah Cary Fairfax, Sept. 12, 1758, *PGW: Col. Ser.* 6:11. Although GW was only twenty-six at the time of the letter, he said he had "long entertained" this view of Providence.

38. GW to Archibald Cary, June 15, 1782, to George Augustine Washington, Jan. 27, 1793, *GW: Writings* 24:346 (first quotation), 32:315–16 (second quotation).

39. This advice appears at least a dozen times in his writings cited in note 30. It is a constant refrain in GW's correspondence, and it was something that he practiced as well as preached. Twice, as president, he was gravely ill, once in 1789 and again in 1790. In the first instance, GW told his physician, Dr. Samuel Bard, "Do not flatter me with vain hopes; I am not afraid to die, and therefore can bear the worst!" Bard's answer admitted the danger, and the president replied, "Whether

to-night or twenty years hence, makes no difference" (quoted in Ford, *True Washington*, 53). During his even closer brush with death in 1790, his aide and later biographer, David Humphreys, wrote that GW spoke directly to him and said, "I know it is very doubtful whether ever I shall rise from this bed, & God knows it is perfectly indifferent to me whether I do or not" (Zagarri, *Humphreys' "Life of General Washington,"* 57). Martha Washington commented on the anxiety caused by her husband's illness and noted, "He seemed less concerned himself as to the event, than perhaps any other person in the United States" (Martha Washington to Mercy Otis Warren, June 12, 1790, *PGW: Pres. Ser.* 5:397).

40. GW to Bryan Fairfax, March 6, 1793, *GW: Writings* 32:376.

41. GW to Henry Lee, Aug. 27, 1790, *PGW: Pres. Ser.* 6:347 (first quotation); GW to Tobias Lear, March 30, 1796, *GW: Writings* 35:5 (second quotation). Seneca himself recognized this need to grieve and counseled, "To lament the death of a friend is both natural and just; a sigh or a tear I would allow to his memory: but no profuse or obstinate sorrow. . . . I would not advise insensibility and hardness; it were inhumanity, and not virtue, not to be moved at the separation of familiar friends and relations: now, in such cases, we cannot command ourselves, we cannot forbear weeping, and we ought not to forbear" (L'Estrange, *Seneca's Morals*, 212).

42. GW to Henry Knox, Sept. 8, 1791, *GW: Writings* 31:360 (first quotation); GW to George Lewis, April 9, 1797, *PGW: Ret. Ser.* 1:90 (second quotation).

43. John Parke Custis to GW, July 5, 1773, *PGW: Col. Ser.* 9:265.

44. John E. Ferling, *The First of Men: A Life of George Washington* (Knoxville, Tenn., 1988), 306.

45. GW to Lafayette, March 25, 1787, *PGW: Conf. Ser.* 5:107.

46. GW to Burgess Ball, Sept. 22, 1799, *GW: Writings* 37:372; GW to Betty Washington Lewis, Sept. 13, 1789, to George Lewis, April 9, 1797, *PGW: Pres. Ser.* 4:32, 1:190. Between his father's business ventures in various parts of Virginia and trips to England, GW had relatively little contact with him and, according to George Washington Parke Custis, only remembered that his father was a large man with a fair complexion. I thank one of the outside readers for this observation.

47. GW to Bushrod Washington, Jan. 10, 1787, *PGW: Conf. Ser.* 4:509–10 (first quotation); GW to Fanny Bassett Washington (later Lear), Feb. 24, 1793, to Henry Lee, Jan. 20, 1793, *GW: Writings* 32:354 (second quotation), 309 (third and fourth quotations).

48. William Fairfax to Lawrence Washington, Oct. 2, 1747, Moncure Daniel Conway, *Barons of the Potomack and the Rappahannock* (New York, 1892), 256; George Mason to Sarah Mason McCarty, Feb. 10, 1785, in Robert A. Rutland, ed., *The Papers of George Mason, 1725–1792*, 3 vols. (Chapel Hill, N.C., 1970), 2:810. Mason also spoke of his wife dying confident of "eternal Happiness" (Mason family Bible, ibid., 1:481).

49. Quoted in Gaustad, *Sworn on the Altar of God*, 142.

50. Patrick Henry to Anne Henry Christian, May 15, 1786, in Henry, *Patrick Henry* 2:287. Mechal Sobel devoted a chapter to the question of attitudes toward death and afterlife in Virginia (*The World They Made Together: Black and White Values in Eighteenth-Century Virginia* [Princeton, N.J., 1987], 214–25). She credited African influence for the growing belief in reunion of loved ones in Heaven. "By the late eighteenth century," she wrote, "heaven was being written of widely by whites. The dying spoke to their kin of the afterlife as a perfect world where 'we shall ere long be reunited never again to be separated from those we love.' 'We'll meet in heaven' became the acceptable parting for loved ones" (ibid., 223).

51. Boller, *Washington and Religion*, 114.

52. GW to Henry Knox, April 27, 1787, *PGW: Conf. Ser.* 5:157 (first quotation); GW to Betty Washington Lewis, Sept. 13, 1789, *PGW: Pres. Ser.* 4:32 (second quotation); GW to Lafayette, Dec. 8, 1784, *PGW: Conf. Ser.* 2:175 (third quotation).

53. According to the Reverend James Muir, minister of the Presbyterian church in Alexandria, GW's last words included the statement, "I die hard . . . will this Struggle last long?—I hope I have nothing to fear" (Mary Thompson, "George Washington and Religion," copy in the files on GW's death, MTVL). Although clearly this quotation implies concern about being judged, preference must be given to Lear's account, because he was there and Muir's account is secondhand at best. The query of the Reverend Samuel Miller of New York is pertinent: "How was it possible, he asked, for a true Christian, in the full exercise of his mental faculties, to die without one expression of distinctive belief, or Christian hope?" (Boller, *Washington and Religion*, 89).

54. Tobias Lear, "journal" account, MTVL. The efforts to make GW more of a Christian than the facts warrant began early and continue to this day. Among the early biographies the classic example is Parson Weems's, which had GW send everyone out of the room so that he could commune alone with God and then die with the final words, "Father of mercies! take me to thyself" (Mason Locke Weems, *The Life of Washington*, ed. Peter S. Onuf [Armonk, N.Y., and London, 1996], 134–35). Other early examples occur in David Ramsay, *The Life of George Washington: Commander in Chief of the Armies of the United States . . .* (New York, 1807), 319; John Marshall, *The Life of George Washington . . .* , 5 vols. (1804–7; New York, 1969), 5:375; Jared Sparks, *Life of Washington* (Boston, 1839), 525.

55. Martha Washington to Jonathan Trumbull, Jan. 15, 1800, in Fields, *"Worthy Partner,"* 339; Thomas Law to Edward Law, Dec. 15, 1799, *Papers of George Washington* project, University of Virginia.

56. John Parke Custis to Martha Washington, July 5, 1773, in Fields, *"Worthy Partner,"* 152–53; John Parke Custis to GW, July 5, 1773, *PGW: Col. Ser.* 9:265.

57. GW to Robert Morris, May 5, 1787, to Henry Knox, Jan. 10, 1788, Feb. 25, 1787, to Lafayette, March 25, 1787, *GW: Writings* 29:211, 378, 170, 184; GW to Burwell Bassett, June 20, 1773, *PGW: Col. Ser.* 9:243; GW to Betty Washington Lewis, Sept. 13, 1789, *PGW: Pres. Ser.* 4:32.

58. GW to clergy of the Protestant Episcopal Church, Aug. 19, 1789, *PGW: Pres. Ser.* 3:497; GW to Jonathan Trumbull Jr., Jan. 5, 1784, to the rector et al. of the United Episcopal Churches of Christ Church and St. Peter's, Philadelphia, [March 2, 1797], *GW: Writings* 27:294, 35:411; Tobias Lear to Mary Stillson Lear, Dec. 16, 1799, copy in file on GW's death, MTVL.

59. GW to Burwell Bassett, June 20, 1773, *PGW: Col. Ser.* 9:243 (quotation); Burgess Ball to GW, Aug. 25, 1789, GW to Betty Washington Lewis, Sept. 13, 1789, *PGW: Pres. Ser.* 3:536, 4:32.

60. GW to Richard Washington, Oct. 20, 1761, *PGW: Col. Ser.* 7:80.

61. GW to Alexander Hamilton, May 27, 1798, *PGW: Ret. Ser.* 2:298.

62. GW to George Augustine Washington, Oct. 25, 1786, *GW: Writings* 29:28; GW to Lafayette, Feb. 1, Dec. 8, 1784, to Adrienne, marquise de Lafayette, April 4, 1784, *PGW: Conf. Ser.* 1:88, 2:175–76, 1:258; GW to James Craik, Sept. 8, 1789, *PGW: Pres. Ser.* 4:1; GW to Alexander Hamilton, Dec. 17, 1797, *GW: Writings* 36:108.

63. GW to Lafayette, Aug. 15, 1787, *PGW: Conf. Ser.* 5:294–96; Freeman, *Washington* 2:387–88, 397.

64. Douglass Adair, *Fame and the Founding Fathers: Essays,* ed. Trevor Colbourn (New York, 1974).

65. GW to Lafayette, May 28, 1788, David Humphreys to GW, July 17, 1785, *PGW: Conf. Ser.* 6:297, 3:131.

66. GW to James Tilghman, June 5, 1786, ibid., 4:96.

67. GW to Sarah Cary Fairfax, Sept. 25, 1758, *PGW: Col. Ser.* 6:42.

68. Quoted in Morison, "Young Man Washington," 47.

69. GW to Tobias Lear, March 30, 1796, *GW: Writings* 35:6.

70. GW to Bryan Fairfax, Jan. 20, 1799, ibid., 37:94–95.

Images of the Man

11. An Uncommon Awareness of Self

The Papers of George Washington

W. W. Abbot

Among the so-called six great men of the Revolutionary era, Washington hardly stands unique in his belief that the preservation of his papers was important. All of them but Hamilton, who died at age forty-nine, lived to retirement and old age (the rest, save Washington, survived into their eighties or later) and recognized their literary offerings as historical treasures. But, as W. W. Abbot remarks in this essay, none, "perhaps even Jefferson," matched the Father of His Country in "appetite for paperwork." Preferring to leave history to the historians, Washington, unlike Franklin and John Adams, declined to write an autobiography, although he assisted some individuals who aspired to write histories of the period or his biography. David Humphreys, loyal friend and secretary, who assisted in the task of organizing Washington's writings and other records, received from his employer a brief account of his early life, focusing on his French and Indian War record. For some reason Humphreys never completed his ambitious biographical undertaking. Rosemarie Zagarri has published a book about his project, including Humphreys's early partial drafts: David Humphreys' "Life of General Washington" with George Washington's "Remarks" *(1991). Most recently, Abbot has returned to the subject in an address at the University of Virginia commemorating the bicentennial of Washington's death:* The Young George Washington and His Papers *(1999), published in a limited edition by the Papers of George Washington.*

The Founders' desire to preserve their literary remains is linked to something else they considered vitally important. They believed that the greatest rewards for public service were not wealth or power for the sake of

*power. Those rewards took the form of esteem and respect of their coun-
trymen and of their place in history. This explains in part why the word
posterity appears so repeatedly in their correspondence. And, in a nutshell,
what they wanted was what they called "fame."*

*Public figures in the twentieth century had a different approach to carv-
ing their historical niche. As Winston Churchill put it, historians would be
kind to him because he would write the history they drew on. American
leaders have almost unfailingly embraced his opinion—presidents, cabinet
members, congressmen, and diplomats. Henry Kissinger, who served under Presidents Nixon and Ford, has at last completed what emerged as the
"weightiest" memoir in years, exceeding 3,900 pages.*

*W. W. Abbot is James Madison Professor Emeritus at the University of Vir-
ginia and former editor-in-chief of* The Papers of George Washington. *His
essay originally appeared in* Prologue: Quarterly Journal of the National
Archives and Records Administration 29 (1989): 7–19, *from which it is
reprinted by permission of the author, who made some revisions for this
volume.*

WHEN WRITING TO GEORGE WASHINGTON on January 20, 1787, to advise him not to attend the convention at Philadelphia in May, David
Humphreys made this point: "I know your personal influence & character, is, justly considered, the last stake which America has to play. Should
you not reserve yourself for the united call of a Continent entire?"[1] Although Washington in the end rejected Humphreys' advice and went to
Philadelphia, no one knew better in 1787 than he that his "character," his
reputation, his hard-won *Fame*, could well become crucial in a "last dying essay" to avoid there being "an end put to Foederal Government" in
America. In a letter to Humphreys that he wrote on December 26, 1786,
before deciding to go to the convention and in another that he directed to
Edmund Randolph on April 9, 1787, after deciding to attend, Washington expressed his fears that the convention might fail, and then, in effect,
acknowledged the force of Humphreys' words, first to Humphreys: "This
would be a disagreeable predicament for any of them [the delegates] to be
in, but more particularly so for a person in my situation"; and then to Ran-

dolph: "under the peculiar circumstances of my case, [this] would place me in a more disagreeable Situation which no other member present would stand in."[2]

An attentive reader of the letters that George Washington wrote beginning with those to Governor Robert Dinwiddie in 1756 and continuing to, for instance, his letter to Dr. James Craik of October 25, 1784, has to be struck by the man's uncommon awareness of self: his strong sense that what he decided and what he did, and how others perceived his decisions and deeds, always mattered. These things mattered to Washington so intensely not because he had any grand sense of destiny as many have surmised, or that he had a nasty itch for power as others might suspect, but because he saw life as something a person must make something of. More than most, Washington's biography is the story of a man constructing himself. Even the increasing care with which he guarded his words after 1776 so as not to reveal more of the inner man than he intended shows Washington at work on Washington.

For a while in the 1750s the young Washington was determined to make his reputation in the British Army; he hoped to find honor and perhaps even glory as a military man. What reputation he earned as a colonel of the Virginia troops in Britain's war against the French and their Indian allies was not enough to secure for him a place in Britain's army, but it was enough fifteen years later to gain for him command of the forces fighting the British in a war for American independence. As commander in chief of the Continental Army for more than eight years, he won abundant honor and glory. Then, the war over, in December 1783 he gave up his command to become a private citizen at Mount Vernon, and in an instant also attained the immortality that fame bestows. And he knew it. He knew too that at any time an unworthy or ill-considered act of his could diminish his stature and tarnish his fame. The speed and decisiveness with which he as president of the Society of the Cincinnati moved in 1784 to eliminate the unpopular features of the society's constitution is only one of the earliest and most public occasions when Washington acted to protect his reputation as hero of the Revolution—and so to defend the Revolution for which the hero had fought.

That Washington ardently sought fame, "the spur that the clear spirit doth raise . . . To scorn delights, and live laborious dayes" (John Milton, "Lycidas")—and also that once it was his he was ever after at pains to preserve it—have often been noted and can be demonstrated over and over by his own words. At no time is he more explicit than in the fall of 1788 and in early 1789 when he writes to friends of the possibility, and then of the certainty, of his becoming President. In a letter to Henry Lee on September 22, 1788, in response to Lee's insistence upon the inevitability of his friend's election to the presidency, Washington wrote: "Should the contingency you suggest take place, and (for argument sake alone let me say) should my unfeigned reluctance to accept the Office be overcome by a deference for the reasons and opinions of my friends; might I not after the Declarations I have made (and Heaven knows they were made in the sincerity of my heart) in the judgment of the impartial World and of Posterity, be chargable with levity and inconsistency; if not with rashness & ambition?" After continuing in this vein for some space, he then wrote: "And certain I am, whensoever I shall be convinced the good of my Country requires my reputation to be put in risque, regard for my own fame will not come in competition with an object of so much magnitude."[3] To go beyond his words for confirmation that Washington valued and sought to safeguard his fame after 1783, we have only to look at the record of his willingness to sit for any artist who wished to paint his portrait, to correspond with any French, German, English, Dutch, Irish, Italian, Swedish, or American man or woman who wrote him a letter, and to open the doors of his house to any stranger, foreign or domestic, who came to pay homage or only to have a look.

But Washington reveals perhaps most clearly, if indirectly, the sense he came to have of the importance that his life held for history, for posterity, in his attitude toward his papers. Writing from Cambridge outside Boston on August 20, 1775, he told his cousin Lund Washington, who managed affairs at Mount Vernon for the general during his eight-year absence in the war: "I can hardly think that Lord Dunmore can act so low, & unmanly a part, as to think of siezing Mrs Washington by way of revenge upon me"; but I "desire you will if there is any sort of reason to suspect a thing of this kind provide a Kitchen for her in Alexandria, or some other place of safety elsewhere for her and my Papers." The papers that Washington was speaking of—those that he left at Mount Vernon when he went off to war—included detailed records of his extensive farming, trading, and land interests and activities, and also the voluminous letter books that he had kept in the 1750s while he was the wartime commander of the Virginia Regiment. Although the papers in the end, like the house at Mount Vernon, escaped the British torch, the general and the estate manager agitated the matter of their safety for the next year or so, and at one point Mrs. Washington even gathered them together and crammed them into a trunk for removal.[4]

To value the safety of one's papers second only to the safety of one's wife at a juncture such as this perhaps was no more than any prudent man of affairs would have done; yet the range and sheer volume of Washington's pre-Revolutionary War papers bespeak something more than the successful Virginia planter. They are the archives of someone who derived great satisfaction from organizing, setting down, and preserving the detailed record of his own existence. Washington's diary entries recording who came and went each day at Mount Vernon and what the weather was; his careful annual records of when, where, and how individual crops were planted, cultivated, harvested, and disposed of; his elaborate account books recording the financial dealings involving his own and the dower property as well as that of his wife's two children; the orders to and the invoices from British merchants, usually running to hundreds of items, which he either wrote out or copied himself, and then often recopied in his account books; list after list, of slaves, of books; the great sheaves of extracts taken from treatises on agriculture; the separate accounts for his grist mill, fishery, and weaving operation; and finally the voluminous letter books that he kept as commander of the Virginia forces during the French and Indian War, all testify in the first instance to an appetite for paperwork unrivaled by any Virginian of his generation, perhaps including even Thomas Jefferson. As one today follows Washington's trail through the surviving portion of what originally was a far more extensive record of his pre-Revolutionary activities, he is left with the impression of a man driven to master every aspect of his life and to make the most of what life offered.

After the Revolution, Washington returned to these early papers and sought to prepare some of them for future perusal by others; but even as he fretted about the safety of his private papers in Virginia, he was being caught up in the management of the rapidly multiplying papers of the commander in chief. In July 1776, in anticipation of Lord Howe's attack on New York, Washington sent the papers relating to his recent Boston campaign from New York to the Congress in Philadelphia for safekeeping. He soon discovered that he and his staff often had need of these documents and asked that they be returned. Thereafter until 1781 his practice was to have his guards transport the whole body of his papers wherever the demands of war took him.[5]

In the spring of 1781 Washington showed that his concern for his military papers extended far beyond their immediate usefulness. He wrote the president of Congress on April 4, 1781, from his headquarters at New Windsor outside Newburgh, New York, expressing dissatisfaction that so many of his "valuable documents which may be of equal public utility and private satisfaction remain in loose Sheets; and in the rough manner in which they were first drawn." In order "to preserve from injury & loss such valuable papers," it was his wish to have "a set of writers" hired "for the sole purpose of recording them." The work, to "be performed in some quiet retreat" near headquarters, should "be done under the Inspection of a Man of character in whom entire confidence can be placed."[6]

Congress promptly gave its approval, and on May 25, 1781, Washington appointed a New York lawyer, Capt. Richard Varick, to supervise the undertaking. He presented Varick with detailed and precise instructions for sorting into six classes, ordering, registering, and filing all of his official letters, orders, and instructions as well as letters written to him. Varick was to hire "Clerks who write a fair hand, and correctly," to copy, under his supervision, Washington's letters, orders, and instructions and the proceedings of his councils of war, but not the letters written to him. If there could be any doubt about what Washington intended in this undertaking, which occupied Varick and two or three clerks full time for over two years, it is removed by Washington's admonitions: " . . . that there may be a similarity and Beauty in the whole execution, all the writing is to be upon black lines equidistant. All the Books to have the same Margin, and to be indexed in so Clear and intelligent a manner, that there may be no difficulty in the references." Varick was to return to Washington the original documents, properly docketed and arranged, and although belonging to him, both the originals and the transcripts he would look upon, Washington asserted in 1782, "as species of Public property, sacred in my hands."[7]

Before Washington left Newburgh for the march south that culminated in the siege at Yorktown and the surrender of Lord Cornwallis on October 19, 1781, Varick transported the papers from Newburgh upriver to Poughkeepsie, where on July 7 he found "Quarters at Doctor Peter Tappen's an honest Patriot" and began "numbering and digesting into Classes the Copies of Letters & Orders in 1775 & 1776." It took the rest of the summer for him "to indorse, arrange & digest them in proper order," but by September he had three clerks hard at work transcribing the sorted documents at Tappen's house.[8] During his brief stopover at Mount Vernon after the Yorktown campaign, Washington found time on November 15 to write Varick approving the procedures he was following and agreeing that "8 Hours constant successive Writing per Day is as much as almost any Person is able to bear."[9]

In the months that followed, Washington and Varick remained in close touch, and Varick wrote often about the progress he was making.[10] In August 1783, two years after the work began, Varick and his three clerks brought the transcripts up to date, and Varick delivered to Washington twenty-eight completed volumes: six volumes of his letters to Congress, fourteen of letters and orders to his officers, four of letters to civil officials, one of letters to foreigners, two volumes of councils of war, and, finally, one volume of his private correspondence, which Varick and Washington had decided should be transcribed. Varick retained a volume partially filled with transcripts of Washington's letters to the enemy and also the partially filled final volumes of the other six classes of letters.[11] The general and his aides continued to send Varick packets of letters to be sorted and copied,[12] until in December 1783, Varick "bid a happy Adieu to public Services and return[ed] to the pleasant, tho fatiguing, Amusement of a City Lawyer."[13] Washington immediately left New York for Philadelphia, Annapolis, and Mount Vernon. Upon departing from New York, Washington sent home all of his remaining "public and other papers . . . and the Books [in] which they had been recorded," for safety's sake by land instead of by water. They arrived at Mount Vernon in a "Trunk, and two boxes or cases" before the end of the year.[14]

With his treasured war papers, properly sorted and elegantly copied, now "safe to hand" at Mount Vernon, Washington resumed the management of his plantation and found after nearly nine years of absence his private papers in distressing disarray. Despite his best efforts, and the efforts of a series of clerks, Washington never quite succeeded in getting all of his papers in the systematic order that he and Varick achieved with the war papers. The most intriguing and perhaps the most convincing bit of evidence of Washington's belief that the record of his life, his hard-won fame, would be of lasting value to the new nation arises from his efforts in the 1780s to do something about his early papers.

In the French and Indian War, from late 1754 to the end of 1758, during most of which time he was colonel of the Virginia Regiment, Washington entered in a series of letter books copies of the letters, orders, and reports that he wrote. At some point after his return to Mount Vernon, probably in 1786, he went through these very extensive letter books. Finding them marred by awkward constructions, faulty grammar, and misspellings, the hero of the Revolution proceeded to correct what the young Washington had written more than a quarter of a century before. Later, almost certainly after his presidency, Washington went through the same writings of his youth and again made deletions, insertions, and substitutions. That done, he had a clerk copy the corrected letter books.[15]

Although all but two of what must have been twenty or more original letter books in Washington's hand have since disappeared, the two surviving ones allow us to learn how Washington sought to prepare his French and Indian War papers for the sort of treatment that his Revolutionary War papers had received at the hands of Varick. A study of the words Washington added, took away, or substituted in the two original letter books (and a comparison of the letters in the other letter books with a few receivers' copies of letters that have survived) makes clear that the mature man wished only for his younger self to write with greater clarity and correctness. Whatever Washington's intentions, however, his changes in wording occasionally resulted in changes in meaning. More often the new wording produced at worst a shift in emphasis or a change in tone.

Although Washington's tinkering creates problems for the editors of his letter books and for the historians using them, it also provides a valuable indication of his sense of himself in history. An important element in Washington's leadership both as a military commander and as President was his dignified, even forbidding, demeanor, his aloofness, the distance he consciously set and maintained between himself and nearly all the rest of the world. The record of his leadership in his carefully preserved papers was, as he saw it, a part of his legacy to his countrymen. Signs of youthful ignorance and crudity in his early papers might lessen the value of that legacy by allowing future generations to see the father of their country up too close, thereby inviting the sort of familiarity that Washington was at pains to avoid in his lifetime. And so the old man discreetly and circumspectly polished the young man's prose. The impulse perhaps was not much different from that of Jared Sparks, an early editor of Washington's papers, who made no apology for correcting Washington's grammar and other inaccuracies when he felt that the statesman erred from haste or carelessness.

Washington's altered sense of self as the hero of the Revolution is reflected in another aspect of his management of his papers. Before the Revolution he made copies of letters that he wrote and kept letters that he received only if they concerned his business or military affairs. In 1784, soon after his return to Mount Vernon from the army, he hired a private secretary and began to retain copies even of his personal letters and to preserve all letters written to him. As a consequence, far more of his personal correspondence from the post-Revolutionary years has survived, though the reticence of the great man tends to make these letters less revealing than the unguarded texts of rare survivals from earlier years.

When the time came for Washington to give up the presidency in 1797 and return home, he had his clerks set aside the papers that the new president would need and packed the rest for their removal to Mount Vernon. During the next, and last, thirty months of his life, Washington gave a great deal of thought to his voluminous "Military, Civil and private papers," including his presidential papers, and talked of putting up a building at Mount Vernon for their accommodation and security. His papers were on his mind even on the day he died. In his account of Washington's death on December 14, 1799, his secretary Tobias Lear wrote: "I returned to his bed side, and took his hand. He said to me, 'I find I am going, my breath can not last long. I believed from the first that the disorder would prove fatal. Do you arrange and record all of my late military letters and papers. Arrange my accounts and settle my books, as you know more about them than any one else, and let Mr. Rawlings finish recording my other letters which he has begun.'"[16] He died six hours later.

What happened to the papers that Washington preserved for posterity, from the time of his death until 1904 when most of them were deposited in the Library of Congress where they now are, is told in masterful fashion by Dorothy Eaton in the *Index to the George Washington Papers* (Washington, D.C., 1964). For students of history and admirers of Washington, successive editions of Washington's writings appeared, beginning with Jared Sparks's in the 1830s and extending through that of John C. Fitzpatrick in the 1930s. In the late 1960s, at the urging of a group of historians, the University of Virginia decided to sponsor a modern edition of Washington's papers on the scale of the editions under way of the papers of Thomas Jefferson, Alexander Hamilton, John Adams, James Madison, and Benjamin Franklin. After the Mount Vernon Ladies' Association agreed to join the university in sponsoring the project and both the National Endowment for the Humanities and the National Historical Publications Commission gave the undertaking their blessing and promised their support, editorial offices were opened in Charlottesville in 1969 under the direction of Donald Jackson, editor, and Dorothy Twohig, associate editor. Initial efforts were directed largely to the search for letters to and from Washington and to acquiring and cataloging photocopies of manuscripts. A worldwide search, during which staff members spent months working in hundreds of manuscript collections in such places as the Massachusetts and Pennsylvania historical societies in addition to the National Archives and the Library of Congress, uncovered over 100,000 documents from three hundred repositories in the United States and another seventy abroad. Although the process was essentially complete before the first two volumes of Washington's *Diaries* were published late in 1976, a steady trickle of copies of Washington documents, five or six a month, including an occasional hitherto unknown autograph letter of Washington's, still come in from owners of manuscripts, particularly from dealers and collectors.

The editing with extensive annotations of the six-volume edition of *The*

Diaries of George Washington (Charlottesville, Va., 1976–79) and of *The Journal of the Proceedings of the President, 1793–1797* (1981) helped prepare the editors of *The Papers of George Washington* for the daunting task of dealing with Washington's massive correspondence. As it happens, Washington's life, and hence his papers, falls into several distinct segments. These different segments also happened to fit neatly the particular interests and competence of the several historians who were to edit the letters and other papers. It seemed clear that the people awaiting publication of the papers would be as well, or better, served if the editors got on with the publishing of the papers of General Washington and President Washington at the same time they were editing and publishing the papers of Colonel Washington and Squire Washington, and so the decision was made to publish the *Papers* in several chronological series simultaneously, with a single editor having primary responsibility for the volumes in each series.

[Ed. note: Since this essay was written, the editors have completed the publication of the *Colonial Series* in ten volumes, the *Confederation Series* (1784–88) in six, and the *Retirement Series* (1797–99) in four. Ten volumes of the *Revolutionary War Series* have appeared, with thirty or so to go, and nine of the *Presidential Series*, with eleven left to be done. Dorothy Twohig has now edited a one-volume abridgment of the *Diaries* (1999). In addition, all of Washington's surviving papers have been transcribed and stored preparatory to issuing an electronic edition.]

The sheer mass of Washington's papers as commander in chief—more than one half of the 100,000 or so documents cataloged in the editorial offices of the Papers are dated between 1775 and 1783—makes the editing of the Revolutionary War Series particularly complex; but of the four chronological series, it is the Presidential Series that presents the most intriguing problems. No editor has yet dealt with the full corpus of the presidential papers of a man who held office before the twentieth century, before the typewriter, carbon paper, and the telephone began to transform record keeping. The executive branch of government generated tens of thousands of documents between 1789 and 1797, and even with the strictest definition of what constitutes a Washington document, it will take some doing to print or otherwise take note of every one of these—i.e., to honor the commitment to produce a comprehensive edition of the man's papers—without unduly straining the resources of the National Endowment for the Humanities and the University of Virginia, to say nothing of the patience of fellow historians. For instance, letters written to Washington in 1788 and 1789 from men and women seeking offices for themselves or others fill most of the papers in the first two volumes of the Presidential Series.

Yet, not to print letters of application would be to ignore what was one of Washington's main concerns as he went about the task of erecting a new government. Taken together, the letters show in the year that the new government of the United States was formed how an extraordinarily wide range of people, high and low, men and women, young and old, viewed themselves, their recent Revolution, their new federal Republic, and how they saw Washington himself. There is nothing else anywhere quite like this outpouring of personal aspirations at the moment of the nation's founding. The key letter relating to each application, usually the applicant's letter, is printed in the *Papers*, with related letters, such as letters of recommendation or acknowledgment, appearing in whole or in part, in endnotes. Even with such space-saving devices, it will be difficult to get into each volume of six to seven hundred pages more than three or four months of the Revolutionary War or presidential papers.

When the editor of a person's papers talks of his project, he first speaks of the person, then of the person's papers, and ends talking about himself. He loses his audience, even when with fellow editors, when he gets his usual plaint that scholars out there do not attach proper value to the work he is doing. It is the documentary editor's way of asking in moments of doubt for assurance that what he does is worth the doing. As for the editors of George Washington's papers, they may take what comfort they can in the knowledge that the father of their country would think their undertaking worthwhile.

Notes

1. David Humphreys to GW, Jan. 20, 1787, *PGW: Conf. Ser.* 4:528–29.

2. GW to Humphreys, Dec. 26, 1786, to Edmund Randolph, April 9, 1787, ibid., 4:480, 5:135–36.

3. GW to Henry Lee, Sept. 22, 1788, ibid., 6:530–31.

4. GW to Lund Washington, Aug. 20, 1775, Lund Washington to GW, Oct. 29, 1775, GW to Lund Washington Dec. 10–17, 1776, *PGW: Rev. Ser.* 1:335, 2:257, 7:291.

5. See particularly GW to John Hancock, Aug. 13, 18, Dec. 24, 1776, ibid., 6:4–5, 62, 7:431; GW to Caleb Gibbs, May 3, 1777, WPLC. See also Dorothy Eaton, *Index to the George Washington Papers* (Washington, D.C., 1964), introduction.

6. GW to the President of Congress, April 4, 1781, WPLC.

7. GW to Richard Varick, May 25, 1781, to William Gordon, Oct. 23, 1782, ibid.

8. Varick to GW, July 19, 1781, ibid.

9. GW to Varick, Nov. 15, 1781, ibid.

10. Varick, for instance, wrote GW five times in Feb. 1782, ibid.

11. Varick to GW, Aug. 15, 22, 1783, ibid.

12. See, for example, GW to Varick, Oct. 2, 1783, ibid.

13. Varick to GW, Nov. 18, 1783, ibid.

14. GW to Samuel Hogdon, Dec. 13, 1783, ibid.; GW to Varick, Jan. 1, 1784, *PGW: Conf. Ser.* 1:2–4.

15. For a full description of these letter books and for the text with corrections of the letter books that GW kept during the Braddock campaign of 1755, see *PGW: Col. Ser* 1:236–364. For the rest of all of GW's French and Indian War letter books, see ibid., vols. 1–6.

16. W. K. Bixby, *Letters and Recollections of George Washington . . .* (New York, 1906), 133.

12. George Washington

The Aloof American

Edmund S. Morgan

Washington's aloofness came naturally, although we know too little about the personal characteristics of his parents to account for it in genetic terms. His reserve was certainly noticeable by the years following his military service in the French and Indian War. Still, apart from public gatherings, he was often described as amiable in informal and intimate settings. He loved to dance, charmed women, and enjoyed good conversation over long, leisurely dinners with members of his military staff and with family members. His aloofness was not the disadvantage in American public life that it would be after the country adopted a democratic ethos and mass politics. None of the early presidents demonstrated public social skills or eloquence of speech, nor, for that matter, did Andrew Jackson, who was transformed into a democrat and a man of the people by his political managers. Somewhere along the way Washington came to realize that his aloofness, combined with his imposing physique and graceful body language, added an aura to the man who stood out as the undisputed leader of the American Revolution as early as 1775. He treasured his reputation, not because he sought to wear a crown, but because he linked it to his own sense of self-worth and honor.

To some extent, all leaders work at self-construction. In America, according to Daniel Walker Howe's Making the American Self *(1997), the opportunity to accomplish this end has been greater than in any other country, and Howe does not limit his contention to political types. Washington made good use of what he had, and his attributes were supremely compatible with the needs of the country. Even Jefferson, as Robert McDon-*

ald has recently demonstrated, engaged in self-construction, but, to some degree, in ways he did not admit. He was intensely interested in his image and his legacy. Yet at times the master of Monticello inveighed against the dead hand of the past and asserted that the earth belongs to the living. But whereas Washington considered his voluminous personal papers as a probable guarantee that history would treat him fairly, Jefferson eagerly sought out people to set the historical record straight as he interpreted it, in addition to taking other measures—including writing a partial autobiography; compiling his "Anas," a collection of correspondence and notes dealing with the 1790s; and urging his countrymen to make celebration of the Fourth of July the highest ceremony of American civil religion.[1]

Note

1. Robert M. S. McDonald, "Thomas Jefferson and Historical Self-Construction: The Earth Belongs to the Living?" *Historian* 62 (1999): 290–310, and "Thomas Jefferson's Changing Reputation as Author of the Declaration of Independence: The First Fifty Years," *Journal of the Early Republic* 19 (1999): 169–96.

Edmund S. Morgan is Sterling Professor of History Emeritus at Yale University. His numerous books include The Meaning of Independence: John Adams, George Washington, Thomas Jefferson *and* The Genius of George Washington. *His essay first appeared in the* Virginia Quarterly Review *52 (1976): 410–36 and is reprinted by permission of the publisher.*

THE KING OF ENGLAND, GEORGE III, was fond of farming. His favorite diversion was to ride about his lands, chatting with the tenants about the crops. "Farmer George," he called himself. His arch-opponent, George Washington, had the same fondness for farming. He too enjoyed riding about his lands and talking about the crops. Indeed there was nothing else he enjoyed quite so much. But there the likeness ceased. And among the many other matters that differentiated George Washington from George III none was more striking than his greater dignity and reserve. George Washington would never have taken the liberty of calling himself "Farmer

George," nor would he have allowed anyone else to do so. Even his close friends took care to keep their distance; and those who forgot to were apt to be brought up sharp.

A familiar anecdote, though perhaps apocryphal, well illustrates Washington's customary posture toward himself and toward others. During the meeting of the Constitutional Convention in Philadelphia in 1787 a group of Washington's friends were remarking on his extraordinarily reserved and remote manner, even among his most intimate acquaintances. Gouverneur Morris, who was always full of boldness and wit, had the nerve to disagree. He could be as familiar with Washington, he said, as with any of his other friends. Alexander Hamilton called his bluff by offering to provide a supper and wine for a dozen of them if Morris would, at the next reception Washington gave, simply walk up to him, gently slap him on the shoulder, and say, "My dear General, how happy I am to see you look so well." On the appointed evening a substantial number were already present when Morris arrived, walked up to Washington, bowed, shook hands, and then placed his left hand on Washington's shoulder, and said, "My dear General, I am very happy to see you look so well." The response was immediate and icy. Washington reached up and removed the hand, stepped back, and fixed his eye in silence on Morris, until Morris retreated abashed into the crowd. The company looked on in embarrassment, and no one ever tried it again.

It seems a most un-American reaction, not the sort of thing that Americans like to see in the men they honor, certainly not the sort of thing one would look for in the leader of a popular revolution today. Yet Americans then and since have honored George Washington far beyond any other man in their history. Moreover he earned the honor, and his dignity and reserve, the aloofness that still separates him from us, helped him to earn it.

How is part of the larger story of American independence, the story of how the American Revolution transformed some of the least lovable traits of a seemingly ordinary man into national assets. For besides his aloofness, Washington had other characteristics which at this distance appear less than admirable, but which served him and the nation well in the struggle for independence.

Perhaps the most conspicuous of these traits, conspicuous at least in his surviving correspondence, was an unabashed concern for his own economic interest. Although Washington was fair in his dealings and did not ask favor of any man, he kept a constant, wary, and often cold eye on making a profit, ever suspicious (and not always without reason) that other men were trying to take advantage of him. Like most Virginia planters, he complained that London merchants were giving him too little for his to-bacco or charging him too much for the goods he bought from them. When he rented to tenants, he demanded to be paid punctually and dismissed men's inability to meet their obligations as irresponsibility or knavery. If a man was so foolish as to try cheating him, he was capable of a fury that comes through vividly in his letters, as when he wrote to one associate that "all my concern is that I ever engag'd myself in behalf of so ungrateful and dirty a fellow as you are."

In operating his plantation at Mount Vernon he inveighed endlessly against waste of time, waste of supplies, waste of money. "A penny saved is a penny got," he would say, or "Many mickles make a muckle," by which he apparently meant that many small savings would add up to a large one. Even in dealings with his mother he was watchful, for he thought she had extravagant tastes. He was ready to supply her real wants, he said, but found her "*imaginary* wants . . . indefinite and oftentimes insatiable."

Even after he left Mount Vernon in order to win a war and found a nation, his intense absorption with his estate persisted, somehow curiously out of place now, and out of proportion to the historic events that he was grappling with. In the darkest hours of the war and later during some of the tensest national crises he took time to write to the managers of his plantation about making it show a profit. In early December 1776, for example, after fleeing across the Delaware with the remnants of his army, he sent home instructions to make do without buying linen for the slaves "as the price is too heavy to be borne with." And while he was president, his weekly directives to his managers far exceeded in length the documents he prepared for his subordinates in government.

No detail was too small for his attention. In December 1792, while his cabinet was rent by the feud between Jefferson and Hamilton, he sent orders that Anthony's sore toe, "should be examined and if it requires it something should be done to it, otherwise, as usual, it will serve him as a pretence to be in the house half the Winter." Three months later, when Hamilton was under attack in the House of Representatives for alleged corruption in the Treasury Department, Washington was worried that Caroline "who was never celebrated for her honesty," would steal some of the linen she had been entrusted with cutting. And shortly thereafter when war broke out in Europe and the cabinet was debating what attitude the United States should take toward the belligerents, the president professed himself to be "extremely anxious," because he wanted some honey locust seed to be planted before it was too late, and he wanted his sheep to be washed before they were sheared. "Otherwise," he feared, "I shall have a larger part of the Wool stolen if washed after it is sheared."

As the quotations suggest, Washington was continually alert against theft, embezzlement, and shirking by his slaves. Slaves would not work, he warned his managers and overseers again and again, unless they were continually watched. And they would take every opportunity to steal. They would feign sickness to avoid work. They would stay up all night enjoying themselves and be too tired the next day to get anything done. They would use every pretext to take advantage of him, like Peter, who was charged with riding about the plantation to look after the stock, but, Washington suspected, was usually "in pursuit of other objects; either of traffic or amusement, more advancive of his own pleasures than my benefit."

Washington's opinion of his managers and overseers was hardly better. He hired a succession of them who never seemed able to satisfy him. In 1793, after a bad year, he got off a series of blistering letters to the overseers of the five farms into which Mount Vernon was divided. Hyland Crow, for example, was guilty of "insufferable neglect" in failing to get fields plowed before frost. "And look ye, Mr. Crow," wrote the President, "I have too good reasons to believe that your running about, and entertaining company at home . . . is the cause of this, now, irremediable evil in the progress of my business." And Thomas Green, in charge of the plantation's carpenters, got a similar tongue lashing. "I know full well," said Washington, "that to speak to you is of no more avail, than to speak to a bird that is flying over one's head; first, because you are lost to all sense of shame, and to every feeling that ought to govern an honest man, who sets any store by his character; and secondly, because you have no more command of the people over whom you are placed, than I have over the beasts of the forists: for if they chuse to work they may; if they do not you have not influence enough to make them . . ."

And so it went. No one ever worked hard enough at Mount Vernon; and when the owner was there, he felt obliged to ride daily around the place (or so he told himself) in order to keep people at their jobs and to point out to his manager what was not being done right. When a manager took offense at the constant criticism, Washington assured him, "that I shall never relinquish the right of judging, in my own concerns . . . If I cannot remark upon my own business, passing every day under my eyes, without hurting your feelings, I must discontinue my rides, or become a cypher on my own Estate."

A cipher Washington would not be and could not be. He would run his own affairs in his own interest. And he was very good at it. But if that was all he had done, we should never have heard of him, except perhaps as one of many prosperous Virginia planters. Fortunately it was not merely interest that moved him. Dearer by far to him was honor. Honor required a man to be assiduous and responsible in looking after his interests. But honor also required a man to look beyond his own profit, though where he looked and how far might be a question that different men would answer differently.

At the simplest, most superficial level Washington's love of honor showed itself in a concern with outward appearances. His attachment to Mount Vernon, for example, did not stop at the desire to make a profit from it. He wanted the place and its surroundings to look right, to honor the owner by the way they looked; and this meant giving up the slovenly, though often profitable, agricultural practices of his neighbors. He stopped growing tobacco and turned to the rotation of cereal crops that were approved by the English agricultural reformers of the time. He tried, mostly in vain, to substitute handsome English hedgerows for the crude rail fences of Virginia. And he insisted that all weeds and brush be grubbed out of his plowed fields, not simply for the sake of productivity, but because the fields looked better that way. He would rather, he said, have one acre properly cleansed than five prepared in the usual way.

Similarly, as commander-in-chief, he wanted his soldiers to look well. Their uniforms must be kept in order and "well put on." Otherwise, he said, there would be "little difference in *appearance* between a soldier in rags and a soldier in uniform." Appearance mattered especially to him when French troops were coming: his army must not be dishonored by looking shabby or careless. Even the huts for winter quarters must be built of an identical size: "any hut not exactly conformable to the plan, or the least out of line, shall be pulled down and built again agreeable to the model and in it's proper place." And when Washington became president, he showed the same concern for appearances in furnishing his house and decorating his coach in a plain but elegant style that he thought was appropriate for the head of a republican government.

But a man who craved honor could not gain it simply by putting up a good appearance. This was only a shade removed from vanity, and Washington from the beginning betrayed none of the vanity of a John Adams. Indeed his concern with appearances included a horror of appearing vain. He would not assist would-be biographers for fear, he confessed to a friend, of having "vanity or ostentation imputed to me." He would not even allow Arthur Young, the great English agricultural reformer with whom he corresponded, to publish extracts from the letters, for fear of seeming ostentatious or of giving occasion for some "officious tongue to use my name with indelicacy."

But if Washington was not vain, his very fear of appearing so argues that he did care deeply about what people thought of him. Although honor was in part a private matter, a matter of maintaining one's self-respect by doing right regardless of what the world demanded, it was also a matter of gaining the respect of others. Washington wanted respect, and he sought it first where men have often sought it, in arms.

The story of his youth is familiar, how his older brother Lawrence returned from the siege of Cartagena to fill young George with dreams of military glory. We see him at the age of 21 leading an expedition to the Ohio country and the next year another one, in which he fired the opening shots in the final struggle between France and Britain for the American continent. From the outset he made it plain that he was in search of honor: a letter penned at his camp in the Ohio country informed the governor of Virginia in words that Washington would later have eschewed as ostentatious, "the motives that lead me here were pure and noble. I had no view of acquisition, but that of Honour, by serving faithfully my King and Country." Military honor seemed to Washington to be worth any sacrifice. "Who is there," he asked, "that does not rather Envy, than regret a Death that gives birth to Honour and Glorious memory?"

But it was not necessary to die in order to win military honor. Armies were organized to express honor and respect every hour of the day, through the ascending scale of rank, from the lowliest private soldier up to the commander-in-chief. Officers often worried more about their rank than they did about the enemy. On his expedition against the French in 1754 Washington, along with other officers of the Virginia militia, was mortally offended by a captain in the British army who appeared on the scene and claimed to outrank all provincials, even those of a higher nominal grade. Washington later resigned his commission rather than submit to this kind of dishonor. Thereafter he sought in vain for a royal commission in the regular British army in order to avoid such embarrassment. Failing to obtain one, he served again with the provincial troops when the Virginia frontier needed protection and provincial command was urged upon him, because he thought "it wou'd reflect eternal dishonour upon me to refuse it."

Washington continued to regard rank as a matter of high importance. Throughout the Revolutionary War he had to press upon Congress the need for the utmost care and regularity in promotions in order to avoid offending officers who felt that they had not been given the grade they deserved. And the last years of his life were complicated by a dispute with John Adams over the order of rank in the general staff of the army that Congress created to prepare for war with France. But Washington recognized that an officer had to earn the respect that his rank entitled him to. And one of his ways of earning it was by cultivating the aloofness which became so marked a characteristic of his later years.

He may have begun with a large measure of native reserve, but he nourished it deliberately, for he recognized that reserve was an asset when you were in command of others. Mount Vernon, like other large plantations, was a school where the owner learned that giving orders and having them carried out were two different things. Slaves were in theory completely subject to the will of their master or overseer; but they were men, and like other men they gave obedience to those who could command their respect. And respect, in Washington's view, could not be won by familiarity. Familiarity bred contempt, whether in slaves or soldiers. Washington described the posture that he himself strove for in a letter of advice to a newly fledged Colonel in the Continental Army. "Be easy and condescending in your deportment to your officers, but not too familiar, lest you subject yourself to a want of that respect, which is necessary to support a proper command." With regard to enlisted men it was necessary to keep a still greater distance. Officers were supposed to be gentlemen, and they were expected to enhance the respect due them as officers by the respect due them as gentlemen. To make an officer of a man who was not a gentleman, a man who was not considered socially superior by his men, would mean, Washington said, that they would "regard him no more than a broomstick, being mixed together as one common herd." Fraternizing with private soldiers was "unofficer and ungentlemanlike behaviour," cause for court martial in Washington's army. The commander-in-chief, then, must be all the more a figure apart, a figure to be respected rather than loved, a figure like the George Washington on whom so much honor was to be heaped and who, though without ostentation, dearly cherished the accolades.

Interest and honor, in Washington's view, were the springs that moved all men, including himself. And although the two might come in conflict and pull men in different directions, they need not do so. Often they were bound up together in curious ways. When Washington declared that he was seeking only honor in the Ohio country, he demonstrated that this was his motive by offering to serve without pay. But in making the offer he was trying to shame the Virginia assembly into giving provincial officers *more* pay. British officers got 22 shillings a day; Virginia was paying only 12 shillings 6 pence, and Virginia officers were accordingly resentful. But their resentment was not directed so much toward the pecuniary disadvantage as it was toward the implication that they were not as worthy as their British counterparts. It seemed so dishonorable not to be paid on the same scale that Washington would have preferred no pay at all. Interest and honor were intertwined.

Interest and honor were likely to be linked in all public service. In seeking honor a man sought the respect of others, of his family, of his social class, of his friends, his town, neighborhood, province, country. And people, however grouped, generally accorded respect to someone who served their interests. A man seldom looked for honor in promoting the interests of a group to which he did not belong. Consequently in serving the interests of others he might well be serving his own, especially if he took a large enough, long-range view.

How large a view Washington took before 1774 is not easy to assess. It certainly extended to the boundaries of Virginia, for he had served both in the colony's military and in the House of Burgesses. But his quest for a royal military commission looks like a yearning for rank, not for a larger sphere of action. It seems unlikely that Washington, any more than John Adams, would have expanded his horizons beyond his own province, had the colonies' quarrel with England not reached the boiling point. During the tumultuous decade before weapons replaced words Washington imbibed the ideas of republican liberty that animated the spokesmen for American independence. He cannot properly be counted as one of those spokesmen. But he was convinced, long before the fighting began, that the English government was lost in corruption and was determined "by every piece of Art and despotism to fix the shackles of slavery upon us." When Virginians sent him to the Continental Congress to join other Americans in resisting that threat, his horizons, like those of John Adams, expanded in the vision of a national republic. For the rest of his life, instead of serving only a county or province, he would serve a whole new nation. Honor and interest would remain the springs that moved him. But the honor and interest of George Washington somehow became the honor and interest of America.

To announce to the world the independence of Americans required daring, perhaps more so for Washington than for any of the other founding fathers, and perhaps more than he or they could have realized at the time. In accepting command of the yet non-existent Continental Army in June 1775, Washington staked his honor on defeating in battle the world's greatest military and naval power. And he staked it on behalf of a nation that was also as yet non-existent. For a year he commanded a rebel army, high in spirit and low on ammunition. By the time the great Declaration turned the rebellion into a war for independence, the nation was materializing, and it would have been reasonable to expect that those who had embraced independence would rush to defend it with their lives and fortunes. But few Americans were yet as ready as Washington to face the meaning of independence. Washington found that he was in command of an army continually in the process of dissolution and that he was under the direction of a Congress that grew increasingly short-sighted and timid, unwilling to take any steps that the fickle public might momentarily disapprove.

What was worse, the very cause in which he was embarked forbade him to take effective measures to remedy the situation. The republican liberty that Americans espoused required that the military be subject to the civil power, and Washington accepted the condition, even when the civil power became incompetent, irresponsible, and corrupt, even when he was obliged to share the blame for the errors of his Congressional masters. He aimed at honor in the eyes of the people, but as a republican he could not attain his goal by appealing to the people over the heads of their elected representatives.

The most he could do, while he tried to keep his army in being, was to point out to his masters, with unwearying patience, what experience had taught him but not them, namely that while men can be moved by honor, they could not be moved by it for long unless it marched hand-in-hand with interest. Washington had so fully identified his own interest and honor with the interest and honor of the new nation that he served without pay. But he knew that an entire army of men could not be sustained by honor alone. Enthusiasm for republican government would not alter human nature. Nor would it support a man's wife and children. If Congress could not make it in the interest of men to join the army and stay in the army, whether as enlisted men or as officers, the army could not last. Men had to be paid and paid enough to make it worth their while to face the hardships of military life while their neighbors stayed home. Washington acknowledged that men would fly readily to arms to protect their rights—for a short time, as they turned out to drive the British from Concord and Lexington. "But after the first emotions are over," Washington explained, "to expect, among such People, as compose the bulk of an Army, that they are influenced by any other principles than those of Interest, is to look for what never did, and I fear never will happen." And he went on to give the results of his own appeals to men to remain in the army for the honor of it. "A soldier reasoned with upon the goodness of the cause he is engaged in, and the inestimable rights he is contending for, hears you with patience, and acknowledges the truth of your observations, but adds that it is of no more Importance to him than others. The Officer makes you the same reply, with this further remark, that his pay will not support him, and he cannot ruin himself and Family to serve his Country, when every Member of the community is equally Interested and benefitted by his labours."

Washington was never able to persuade Congress to pay his officers what he thought they should get, nor was he able to persuade them to enlist men for long enough terms to give him the disciplined striking force that he needed to meet the British on equal terms. The result, as he continually lamented, was "that we have protracted the War, expended Millions, and tens of Millions of pounds which might have been saved, and have a new Army to raise and discipline once or twice a year and with which we can undertake nothing because we have nothing to build upon, as the men are slipping from us every day by means of their expiring enlistments." For a man in search of honor it was difficult to bear. The public blamed him for not taking action against the enemy, and he was unable even to explain to them why he did not. To have done so would have been to explain to the enemy how weak he was and thus invite an attack he was not equipped to repel.

It hurt his sense of honor, too, to have to rely so heavily on the French. At the beginning of the war Washington had not expected much help from France. He thought that they would supply him with arms and ammunition in return for the trade they would gain, and in order to annoy the British. But he had not counted on military assistance and would have been happier to win without it. In the end French troops and the French navy were essential to his victory for the simple reason that the states would not field a large enough force themselves, even though he was persuaded that they could have done so.

The victory, nevertheless, was his. For eight years he presided over an army that would have dissolved without him. He put up with militia who came and went like the wind. He put up with officers, commissioned by Congress, who scarcely knew one end of a gun from the other. He put up with a horde of French volunteer geniuses who all expected to be generals. He led men who had no food, no shoes, no coats, and sometimes no weapons. He silenced one mutiny after another. He prevented his unpaid officers from seeking to overturn the delinquent government. And he did it all with the aloof dignity which earned the awesome respect of those he commanded, and earned him in victory the honor of the nation that had come into existence almost in spite of itself.

Washington valued his laurels. When he retired to private life at Mount Vernon, it was with a full consciousness that any further ventures in public life might only diminish the honor that was now his. Far better, after so many years' service, to keep out of the political hurly burly, and this he longed to do. There remained, however, a threat that could not merely diminish but perhaps destroy both the honor he had won for himself and the independence he had won for Americans. That could be the consequence if the republic which he had fought to bring into being should itself dissolve.

The threat stemmed from the weakness of the central government. Washington had worried about it all through the war. By 1778 it had become evident to him that the states were sending lightweight men to Congress while the heavyweights stayed at home. The result was that "party disputes and personal quarrels are the great business of the day whilst the momentous concerns of an empire. . . . are but secondary considerations . . . ," that "business of a trifling nature and personal concernment withdraws their attention from matters of great national moment." He could not complain to the public, but he could to his friends in Virginia. "Where are our Men of abilities?" he asked George Mason. "Why do they not come forth to save their Country? let this voice my dear Sir call upon you, Jefferson and others." "Where?" he demanded of Benjamin Harrison, "is Mason, Wythe, Jefferson, Nicholas, Pendleton, Nelson, and another I could name [meaning Harrison himself]?" They had all, it seemed, deserted Congress for Virginia.

Nor did the situation improve as the war dragged to a close, supported by French arms and French credit. While the state governments grew stronger, Congress seemed to hobble on crutches. All business, so far as Washington could see, was merely "*attempted,* for it is not done, by a timid kind of recommendation from Congress to the States." By the time peace came he was convinced that a new constitution creating a more effective national government was necessary to replace the Articles of Confederation. But he was still a republican and knew that this would not be possible until the people of the United States felt, as he did, "that the honor, power and true Interest of this Country must be measured by a Continental scale; and that every departure therefrom weakens the Union, and may ultimately break the band, which holds us together." To work for a more effective national government was, he believed, the duty of "every Man who wishes well to his Country, and will meet with my aid as far as it can be rendered in the private walks of life."

To go beyond the private walks of life was more than his intention, and even there he was wary of becoming associated with any enterprise that might endanger his standing in the public mind. He was uneasy about his connection with the Society of the Cincinnati, the organization formed by the retired officers of his army. To his surprise it had drawn heavy public criticism as the entering wedge of aristocracy. Washington was so baffled by the criticism that he asked his friend Jefferson to explain it to him, which Jefferson did with his usual grace and tact. The principal trouble was that membership was to be hereditary; Washington therefore insisted that this aspect of the Society be abandoned. When some branches of the society declined to give it up, Washington determined not to serve as its president or attend its meetings, even though he thought the public jealousy wholly unwarranted.

Washington believed that as a private citizen pursuing his own interests he could still be working for the good of the nation. He engaged without a qualm in a scheme that would benefit him financially, while it bolstered American independence in a way that he thought was crucial. Before the Revolution he had begun investing heavily in lands in the Ohio country, where as a young man he had made his military debut. While war lasted, the country lay empty of white inhabitants save for a few hardy souls who dared brave the Indian raids organized by the English. With the coming of peace began a great folk exodus from the established regions of the East (mainly from Virginia) over the mountains into the empty West. Washington expected the stream to swell steadily with immigrants, who would leave the monarchical tyrannies of the Old World for the republican freedom of the New. "The bosom of America is open," he declared, to "the oppressed and persecuted of all Nations and Religions. Let the poor, the needy and oppressed of the Earth, and those who want Land, resort to the fertile plains of our western country, . . . "

It was an axiom of the 18th century that the strength of a country lay in its people, and Washington like other Americans wanted the country to grow as rapidly as possible. His only reservation about immigrants from Europe was that they not settle in a group and thus "retain the Language, habits and principles (good or bad) which they bring with them." It was important that they become Americans. It was even more important that all who trekked over the mountains, whether immigrants or natives, remain Americans either by inclination or by force and not slip under the dominion of England or Spain. Both countries had retained footholds in the West, and the rivers flowed relentlessly into the Mississippi toward Spanish territory. The easiest, cheapest mode of exporting whatever the people of the West produced would thus be to ship it downriver to New Orleans. Fortunately, as Washington saw it, the Spanish forbade such shipments, and the Continental Congress was in no position to secure the privilege for Americans, though settlers had no sooner arrived in the western country than they began to demand it.

Washington was persuaded that the West would gravitate to Spain and Britain unless the people there were bound to the East by the only ties that could bind men over the long run, ties of interest. The way to hold them in the nation was by building canals that would give settlers on the Ohio River a shorter water route to the East than the long float down the Mississippi. Washington accordingly devoted his energies to promoting two companies that would build canals from the Ohio and the Great Kanawha to the heads of navigation on the Potomac and the James. "The consequences to the Union," he wrote to his friend James Warren, "in my judgment are immense . . . for unless we can connect the new States which are rising to our view in those regions, with those on the Atlantic by *interest,* (the only binding cement, and not otherwise to be effected but by opening such communications as will make it easier and cheaper for them to bring the product of their labour to our markets, instead of going to the Spaniards southerly, or the British northerly), they will be quite a distinct people; and ultimately may be very troublesome neighbors to us."

It did not bother Washington that in pressing for these canals he was furthering his own speculative interests as well as those of the nation. But he was embarrassed when the Virginia legislature, in chartering the companies to carry out his project, awarded him 150 shares in them. How would this be viewed by the world, he asked himself. Would it not "deprive me of the principal thing which is laudable in my conduct?" Honor and interest could apparently run together if the only benefit he received from the project was an increase in the value of his western lands, but honor would depart if he profited directly from the enterprise he had advocated. On the other hand, if he declined to accept the gift, would it not appear to be an act of ostentatious righteousness? He escaped the dilemma by accepting the shares but donating them to the support of a school in Virginia and to the foundation of a national university, another project designed to foster national feeling. The future leaders of the nation assembled there as students from all parts of the country would learn to shake off their local prejudices.

The canals were not completed in Washington's lifetime and could not fulfill the political function he envisaged for them. Moreover, the union was threatened more by the impotence of Congress than by the disaffection of western settlers. By the terms of the peace treaty, the British outposts in the Northwest should have been given over to the United States, but the British continued to hold them. They were also doing their best to hasten the expected collapse of the republic by refusing to allow American ships in the ports they controlled in the West Indies and elsewhere in the world. Congress, with no authority to regulate American trade, was unable to retaliate.

The debility of Congress seems to have bothered Washington as much for its damage to the nation's reputation abroad as for its depressing effects at home. To be unable to retaliate against the economic warfare of the country he had defeated in battle must render the nation "contemptable in the eyes of Europe." Because he had identified his own honor so completely with that of the nation, the contempt of Europe touched him personally and deeply; and he felt the shame redoubled when the people of western Massachusetts broke out in rebellion and neither the state government nor the national government seemed able to cope with them. "For God's sake," he wrote to David Humphreys, "tell me what is the cause of all these commotions; do they proceed from licentiousness, British-influence disseminated by the tories, or real grievances which admit of redress? If the latter, why were they delayed till the public mind had become so much agitated? If the former why are not the powers of Government tried at once?" Europeans had said right along that a republican government was incapable of the energy needed to support itself in an area as large as the United States. Now the Americans seemed bent on exemplifying the criticism. "I am mortified beyond expression," said Washington, "that in the moment of our acknowledged independence we should by our conduct verify the predictions of our transatlantic foe, and render ourselves ridiculous and contemptible in the eyes of all Europe."

As the situation worsened, Washington argued among his friends for an extension of Congressional power, but at the same time he despaired of its doing much good, for "the members [of Congress] seem to be so much afraid of exerting those [powers] which they already have, that no opportunity is slipped of surrendering them, or referring the exercise of them, to the States individually." By 1786 he was convinced, rightly or wrongly, that the country was fast verging toward anarchy and confusion, to a total dissolution of the union. He thought that the convention called to meet at Philadelphia to recommend changes in the national government offered the only hope of rescue, but it seemed so forlorn a hope that he was wary of attending it. When elected as a delegate, he delayed his acceptance to the last minute.

Washington was ready to do everything possible, he said, "to avert the humiliating and contemptible figure we are about to make in the annals of mankind." He was alarmed to hear that otherwise respectable people were talking of a need for monarchical government, and he feared that his refusal to attend the convention might be interpreted "as dereliction to republicanism." But on the other hand if the effort to save the republican union failed, the persons who made the effort "would return home chagrined at their ill success and disappointment." "This would be a disagreeable circumstance for any one of them to be in," he said, "but more particularly so for a person in my situation." His situation was unique. It was he, after all, more than any other man, who had won independence for the nation. If the nation proved unworthy of it and incapable of sustaining it, the fault would not be his. He would still retain something of the honor he had gained in the struggle, even though it would be sadly diminished. But if he associated himself with a losing effort to save what he had won, he would reduce still further the significance of his achievement.

In the end, of course, he went and inevitably was elected to preside over the convention. The document it produced, whatever its defects, seemed to him the best that could be obtained and its acceptance the only alternative to anarchy. He would not plead in public for its adoption, but to his friends he made plain his total support of it and his opposition to proposals for amending it before it was put in operation. His friends in turn made plain that if it were adopted he would be called upon to serve as the first president.

Again in terms of honor and interest Washington weighed the risks of accepting office. His inclination was to stay at Mount Vernon, to make the place more profitable and keep it looking the way he wanted it to. To preside over the new government "would be to forego repose and domestic enjoyment, for trouble, perhaps for public obloquy." There would be no honor in presiding over a fiasco, and he suspected that there was a sinister combination afoot among the Antifederalists to defeat the effective operation of the new government if they should be unsuccessful in preventing its adoption. But if he should be convinced, he told his friend Henry Lee, that "the good of my Country requires my reputation to be put in risque, regard for my own fame will not come in competition with an object of so much magnitude." The good of the country did require Washington to take the risk.

The good of the country, perhaps its very survival, required above all that its citizens should respect its government, that they should not regard it with the contempt that the state legislatures had shown for the Continental Congress. And no one else but Washington could have given the presidency and the new government the stature they attained by his mere presence. His own honor was already so great that some of it could flow from him to the office he occupied.

Not least of the assets he brought to the task was the commanding dignity that he had won by his deliberately cultivated aloofness, the posture that demanded respect and honor from those below him, magnified now by men's memories of his previous triumphs. There was no need for fancy titles. John Adams and the new Senate worried about how to address him, and to Washington's annoyance Adams made himself ridiculous by arguing for the exalted forms of address employed for the kings of European countries. Washington carried so much dignity in his manner that he required no title to convey it. Though he would not have consented to "Farmer George," he did not need "Your Highness." He nevertheless took his usual pains to avoid familiarity. In Washington's view, the president of the Continental Congress during the 1780's, by opening his doors to all comers, had diminished what little authority the Articles of Confederation allowed him and thus brought the office into contempt. Washington would be less available to every Tom, Dick, and Harry who wished to gawk at him.

He would also keep his distance from the other branches of government. The absence of a strong executive branch had been one of the great weaknesses of the old government that the Constitution tried to remedy. But it was up to the new president to strengthen the new government by maintaining in full vigor all the powers that the Constitution assigned to his office. It was up to him to establish the separation of executive and legislative branches that the Constitution stipulated. That Washington succeeded is a matter of record.

While magnifying the role of the president in government was important to Washington, it seems to have come easily, one might say naturally, to him, and he actually concerned himself more with the international standing of the nation. Improving the strength and reputation of the United States in relation to other nations became his main focus. In this area his special view of human motives proved to be a special asset. His own concern with private interest and his conviction that this was the principal spring of human action had grown with time. And he saw, in the nations of the world, collections of men who had combined in their own interests and pledged their honor, as he had pledged his, to serve those interests. It was in vain, then, to appeal to the honor of any country against the interests of that country and of its people. Honor for a Frenchman lay in serving the interests of the French, as for an American it lay in serving the interests of Americans. Although Washington was convinced, like many men of his time, that the interests of different countries need not conflict, he was certain that no country would or ought to act against its own perceived interests. To expect any country to do so was folly; and it was criminal folly for any man charged with his country's interests to trust another country with them, as for example Congress had done in instructing its envoys to be directed by the French court in the peace negotiations with England.

Washington had first demonstrated the acuity of his understanding of the role of national interest in foreign relations during the war, when Congress developed an enthusiasm for an expedition against Canada to be conducted by French troops. Since Canada was populated mainly by Frenchmen, it was thought that a French invasion would have a much better chance of success than the disastrous expedition that the colonists themselves had mounted in the early months of the war. In the treaty of alliance with the United States France had formally renounced any claim of its own on Canadian territory. If conquered, the area would belong to the United States. The prospect of French troops in Canada had nevertheless alarmed Washington. If the French wished to undertake the move, he was in no position to prevent them. Beggars could not be choosers. But he could plead.

He officially presented to Congress and to the French all the plausible tactical disadvantages he could think of against a Canadian expedition. Then in a confidential private letter to Henry Laurens, the President of the Continental Congress, he explained why the proposal disturbed him. It would mean, he said, "the introduction of a large body of French troops into Canada, and putting them in possession of the capital of that Province, attached to them by all the ties of blood, habits, manners, religion and former connexions of government. I fear this would be too great a temptation to be resisted by any power actuated by the common maxims of national policy." He went on to list the economic and political benefits that France would gain by holding the province in violation of the treaty. It would not be difficult to find a plausible pretext; Canada need only be claimed as a security for American payment of the large debt owed to France. "Resentment, reproaches, and submission" would be the only recourse for the United States. And Washington went on to read a gentle lecture to the gullible members of Congress: "Men are very apt to run into extremes," he said, "hatred to England may carry some into an excess of Confidence in France; especially when motives of gratitude are thrown into the scale. Men of this description would be unwilling to suppose France capable of acting so ungenerous a part. I am heartily disposed to entertain the most favourable sentiments of our new ally and to cherish them in others to a reasonable degree; but it is a maxim founded on the universal experience of mankind, that no nation is to be trusted farther than it is bound by its interest; and no prudent statesman or politician will venture to depart from it."

Whether or not the French merited Washington's wariness had not been put to the test in 1779, for they had not seen fit to undertake the expedition to Canada, though they toyed with the idea. Distrust of foreign attachments nevertheless took firm root beside Washington's other political instincts, and during his years in command of the army and in retirement at Mount Vernon he had advocated a stronger national government, not merely to prevent internal dissolution but to keep the country from falling under the influence of one of the more energetic monarchies of the Old World. Early in 1788, when war clouds were gathering over Europe and the Constitution had not yet been ratified, he had written to Jefferson of his fear that the several states, uninhibited by any effective central direction, might be drawn into the European quarrels.

As president, Washington was at last able to exercise control over foreign relations, and in doing so he never swerved from the maxim of national interest that he had sought to impress upon Henry Laurens. That maxim, as he interpreted it, dictated that, apart from commercial transactions, the United States should have as little to do as possible with any other nation. The true interest of the United States consisted in staying clear of foreign alignments and supplying all sides with the products which its fertile lands could produce in abundance. If the United States could maintain a policy of strict neutrality, the endless wars of the European monarchs would serve both to advance the price of American products and to swell the stream of immigrants needed to fill the empty American West. Accordingly as the threatened European war became reality, it was Washington's consistent policy to build the power of the United States by asking no favors of foreign countries and giving none. The aloofness which he associated with command was the proper posture to give power and respectability to a nation as well as an individual.

Although Washington anticipated commercial benefits from this policy of neutrality, he did not think it wise in negotiating treaties to take undue advantage of the bargaining position offered to the United States by the distresses of other countries. In his view, since he believed nations acted always according to their interest, a treaty was useful only so long as its provisions coincided with the interests of both countries. In 1791 he warned Gouverneur Morris, before he appointed him United States minister to France, that it would be useless to obtain favorable treaties from countries in distress, "For unless treaties are mutually beneficial to the Parties, it is in vain to hope for a continuance of them beyond the moment when the one which conceives itself to be overreached is in a situation to break off the connexion." The treaty with England that ended the Revolutionary War was a case in point. Although Washington complained when the British broke it by carrying off slaves and by refusing to turn over the Northwest posts, he had not really expected them to act differently. The Americans had obtained on paper an agreement that went beyond what their military power entitled them to. It was therefore to be expected that the agreement would be broken.

Washington's foreign policy has sometimes been judged by the two treaties he signed, one regarded as a diplomatic triumph, the other as a defeat. But Washington himself did not set much store by either of them. In Jay's Treaty with England the United States seemed to get much less than it might have, and Washington did not think the treaty a good one. But he thought it better than the uncertain conditions of trade that would have resulted from a refusal to ratify it. If it gave Americans less than they wanted, that was because they did not yet have the bargaining power to demand more—or so at least it seemed to Washington. In Pinckney's Treaty with Spain, the United States got permission for settlers in the West to ship their goods through Spanish territory via the Mississippi. Although Washington in the 1780's had thought contact between the Westerners and the Spanish undesirable, by the 1790's he was ready to insist on the American right to navigate the Mississippi. But he did so only because it had become apparent that a failure to demand the right would alienate the Westerners from the national government more rapidly than the connection with Spanish New Orleans would. He had never doubted that the Westerners would ultimately get the right, because they were growing in numbers so rapidly that it would not be within the power of the light Spanish forces at New Orleans to deny them for long. Pinckney's Treaty gave them only what they would have taken anyhow.

Thus treaties in Washington's view were of little worth. If the interests of two nations happened to coincide, a treaty was scarcely necessary to bind them together. If their interests conflicted, no treaty would be sufficient to hold them. At best a treaty could only regularize and expedite friendly relations between two countries. At worst it might weaken a country by misleading unwary statesmen to act for the benefit of an ally without due regard to their own country's interest.

The important thing, Washington believed, was for Americans to discern their own interest as a nation and to pursue it without trying to take advantage of other countries and without allowing other countries to take advantage of the United States. This was the message of his Farewell Address, both in the version drafted by James Madison in 1792 and in the much different final version drafted by Alexander Hamilton in 1796. He put it more succinctly himself in a letter to William Heath in 1797:

> No policy, in my opinion, can be more clearly demonstrated, than that we should do justice to *all* but have no political connexions with *any* of the European Powers, beyond those which result from and serve to regulate our Commerce with them. Our own experience (if it has not already had this effect) will soon convince us that *disinterested* favours, or friendship from any Nation whatever, is too novel to be calculated on; and there will always be found a wide difference between the words and actions of any of them.

In staking his own honor on the pursuit of national interest, Washington did not come off unscathed. He had committed himself so closely to the nation and its government that every attack on government policies seemed to be an attack on *him*. And by the time he left office the attacks were coming thick and fast, including some that were openly directed at him, charging that he had deserted the republican faith and was squinting at monarchy. Although he professed to be unmoved by these diatribes, his friend Jefferson testified that "he feels these things more than any person I ever yet met with." And because Jefferson himself was a critic of national policies, Washington could not dissociate Jefferson from the assaults.

Washington's last years were saddened by this seeming repudiation of him, but his republican trust in the ordinary man remained unshaken. Less than a year before his death in 1799 he was still affirming that "the great mass of our Citizens require only to understand matters rightly, to form right decisions." And so far as his own honor was concerned his faith was justified. The mass of citizens did not deny him in the end the full measure of honor that was due him. Nor did Jefferson, even though Jefferson thought it was the president rather than the people who needed to understand matters rightly. Fourteen years after Washington's death Jefferson recalled how the president had often declared to him "that he considered our new Constitution as an experiment on the practicability of republican government, and with what dose of liberty man could be trusted for his own good; that he was determined the experiment should have a fair trial, and would lose the last drop of his blood in support of it."

Although Jefferson feared that Washington's emphatic assertion may have hidden a waning confidence in the experiment, there is no evidence that this was the case. To the end Washington cherished his honor, and to the end his honor demanded the preservation of the American republic, free of every foreign connection. That was the meaning of independence for Washington. He was even ready, perhaps a little too ready, to don his old uniform and command a new army in the war with France that seemed so imminent in 1798. When he died the next year, he could not have been sure that his republic would in fact sustain its independence. And had he lived another year he would have found little to cheer him in the election that elevated Jefferson to the presidency. But he need not have feared. The republic did survive and long preserved the aloofness from foreign quarrels that he had prescribed for it. His honor survived with it, and posterity has preserved his image in all the aloofness that he prescribed for himself. Although the mass of citizens have learned to look upon most of their other historical heroes with an affectionate familiarity, they have not presumed to do so with Washington. The good judgment that he was sure they possessed has prevented a posthumous repetition of the folly perpetrated by Gouverneur Morris. Americans honor the father of their country from a respectful distance. And that is surely the way Washington would have wanted it.

13. The Greatness of George Washington

GORDON S. WOOD

Gordon S. Wood makes a major point, expressed in essays by W. W. Abbot and Edmund S. Morgan as well, albeit differently, that Washington, a proud man, zealously guarded his reputation. In the age of the Enlightenment, reputation and character could hardly be separated. Indeed, we have never had a generation of leaders who seemed so preoccupied with their standing in history. This concern appears strange because it appears that their talents and accomplishments in statecraft would have assured them that such apprehensions were needless. Of course, we have the advantage of hindsight. Their mind-set did not reflect a lack of accomplishment but rather derived from their uncertainty whether the nation would survive and achieve stature at home and abroad. And the reputations of those in public life often tended to rise and then fall, often the victim of their corruption and vanity. As famous men, some of them even deified in their own day, our Revolutionary chieftains realized that they lived under a microscope—that everything they did and said mattered. Would they inadvertently do things to sully their accomplishments? It was a heavy burden to bear. Thus, as Wood shows, Washington worried over the propriety of accepting the Virginia General Assembly's gift of canal company shares. He displayed ambivalence about accepting the presidency of the Society of the Cincinnati because critics said its hereditary features conflicted with republican values. He agonized over whether to attend the Constitutional Convention because of what failure would do to his own reputation, to say nothing of what his name's being associated with ill success would do to future endeavors to form a more consolidated union.

Thus, Washington hesitated, seemingly thinking no, before finally agreeing to accept the presidency in 1789. With his reputation secure at that juncture, he wondered why, in the twilight of life, he should venture out on uncharted seas. In conversation with his secretary David Humphreys (a source that only recently has come to light), Washington remarked: "It is said that every man has his portion of ambition. I may have mine as well as the rest; but if I know my own heart, my ambition would not lead me into public life [again]." He had always wished "to merit the good opinion of all good men." As president he might lose all that he had gained.¹ Such episodes confirm Wood's judgment that Washington lived in a world we do not know.

Note

1. Rosemarie Zagarri, ed., *David Humphreys' "Life of General Washington" with George Washington's "Remarks"* (Athens, Ga., and London, 1991), 47.

Gordon S. Wood is Alva O. Way University Professor and Professor of History at Brown University. He is the author of The Creation of the American Republic, 1776–1787, *and* The Radicalism of the American Revolution, *both winners of major historical prizes. His essay originally appeared in the* Virginia Quarterly Review 68 *(1992): 189–207 and is reprinted by permission of the publisher.*

GEORGE WASHINGTON may still be first in war and first in peace, but he no longer seems to be first in the hearts of his countrymen. Or at least in the hearts of American historians. A recent poll of 900 American historians shows that Washington has dropped to third place in presidential greatness behind Lincoln and FDR. Which only goes to show how little American historians know about American history.

Polls of historians about presidential greatness are probably silly things, but, if they are to be taken seriously, then Washington fully deserved the first place he has traditionally held. He certainly deserved the accolades his contemporaries gave him. And as long as this republic endures he ought to be first in the hearts of his countrymen. Washington was truly a great man and the greatest president we have ever had.

But he was a great man who is not easy to understand. He became very quickly, as has often been pointed out, more a monument than a man, statuesque and impenetrable. Even his contemporaries realized that he was not an ordinary accessible human being. He was deified in his own lifetime. "O Washington," declared Ezra Stiles, president of Yale, in 1783. "How I do love thy name! How have I often adored and blessed thy God, for creating and forming thee, the great ornament of human kind! . . . Thy fame is of sweeter perfume than Arabian spices. Listening angels shall catch the odor, waft it to heaven and perfume the universe!"

One scholar has said that Washington has been "the object of the most intense display of hero worship this nation has ever seen." Which helps explain the continuing efforts to humanize him—even at the beginning of our history. Parson Mason Weems, his most famous biographer, was less of a churchman than he was a hustling entrepreneur. He was ready when Washington died in 1799: "I've something to whisper in your lug," Weems wrote to his publisher Matthew Carey a month after the great man's death. "Washington you know, is gone! Millions are gaping to read something about him. I am very nearly primed and cocked for 'em." Weems had his book out within the year.

The most famous anecdotes about Washington's early life come from Weems. He wanted to capture the inner private man—to show the early events that shaped Washington's character, even if he had to make them up. Weems presumed that the source of Washington's reputation for truthfulness lay in his youth. He tells a story that he said he had heard from Washington's nurse. It was, he says, "too valuable to be lost, too true to be doubted." This was, of course, the story of the cherry tree about whose chopping down Washington could not tell a lie.

Despite the continued popularity of Parson Weems' attempt to humanize him, Washington remained distant and unapproachable, almost unreal and unhuman. There have been periodic efforts to bring him down to earth, to expose his foibles, to debunk his fame, but he remained, and remains, massively monumental. By our time in the late 20th century he seems so far removed from us as to be virtually incomprehensible. He seems to come from another time and another place—from another world.

And that's the whole point about him: he does come from another world. And his countrymen realized it even before he died in 1799. He is the only truly classical hero we have ever had. He acquired at once a worldwide reputation as a great patriot-hero.

And he knew it. He was well aware of his reputation and his fame earned as the commander-in-chief of the American revolutionary forces. That awareness of his heroic stature and his character as a republican leader was crucial to Washington. It affected nearly everything he did for the rest of his life.

Washington was a thoroughly 18th-century figure. So much so, that he quickly became an anachronism. He belonged to the pre-democratic and pre-egalitarian world of the 18th century, to a world very different from the world that would follow. No wonder then that he seems to us so remote and so distant. He really is. He belonged to a world we have lost and we were losing even as Washington lived.

In many respects Washington was a very unlikely hero. To be sure, he had all the physical attributes of a classical hero. He was very tall by contemporary standards, and was heavily built and a superb athlete. Physically he had what both men and women admired. He was both a splendid horseman at a time when that skill really counted and an extraordinarily graceful dancer. And naturally he loved both riding and dancing. He always moved with dignity and looked the leader.

Yet those who knew him well and talked with him were often disappointed. He never seemed to have very much to say. He was most certainly *not* what we would today call an "intellectual." We cannot imagine him, say, expressing his views on Plato in the way Jefferson and John Adams did in their old age. Adams was especially contemptuous of Washington's intellectual abilities. It was certain, said Adams, that Washington was not a scholar. "That he was too illiterate, unlearned, unread for his station and reputation is equally past dispute."

Adam's judgment is surely too harsh. Great men in the 18th century did not have to be scholars or intellectuals. But there is no doubt that Washington was not a learned man, especially in comparison with the other Founding Fathers. He was very ill at ease in abstract discussions. Even Jefferson, who was usually generous in his estimates of his friends, said that Washington's "colloquial talents were not above mediocrity." He had "neither copiousness of ideas nor fluency of words."

Washington was not an intellectual, but he was a man of affairs. He knew how to run his plantation and make it pay. He certainly ran Mount Vernon better than Jefferson ran Monticello. Washington's heart was always at Mount Vernon. He thought about it all the time. Even when he was president he devoted a great amount of his energy worrying about the fence posts of his plantation, and his letters dealing with the details of running Mount Vernon were longer than those dealing with the running of the federal government.

But being a man of affairs and running his plantation or even the federal government efficiently were not what made him a world-renowned hero. What was it that lay behind his extraordinary reputation, his greatness?

His military exploits were of course crucial. But Washington was not really a traditional military hero. He did not resemble Alexander, Caesar, Cromwell, or Marlborough; his military achievements were nothing compared to those Napoleon would soon have. Washington had no smashing, stunning victories. He was not a military genius, and his tactical and strategic maneuvers were not the sort that awed men. Military glory was *not* the source of his reputation. Something else was involved.

Washington's genius, his greatness, lay in his character. He was, as Chateaubriand said, a "hero of an unprecedented kind." There had never been a great man quite like Washington before. Washington became a great man and was acclaimed as a classical hero because of the way he conducted himself during times of temptation. It was his moral character that set him off from other men.

Washington fit the 18th-century image of a great man, of a man of virtue. This virtue was not given to him by nature. He had to work for it, to cultivate it, and everyone sensed that. Washington was a self-made hero, and this impressed an 18th-century enlightened world that put great stock in men controlling both their passions and their destinies. Washington seemed to possess a self-cultivated nobility.

He was in fact a child of the 18th-century Enlightenment. He was very much a man of his age, and he took its moral standards more seriously than most of his contemporaries. Washington's Enlightenment, however, was not quite that of Jefferson or Franklin. Although he was conventionally enlightened about religion, "being no bigot myself to any mode of worship," he had no passionate dislike of the clergy and organized Christianity, as Jefferson did. And although he admired learning, he was not a man of science like Franklin. Like many other 18th-century Englishmen, he did *not* believe, as he put it, that "becoming a mere scholar is a desirable education for a gentleman."

Washington's Enlightenment was a much more down-to-earth affair, concerned with behavior and with living in the everyday-world of people. His Enlightenment involved what eventually came to be called cultivation and civilization. He lived his life by the book—not the book of military rules but the book of gentility. He was as keenly aware as any of his fellow Americans of the 18th-century conventions that defined what a proper gentleman was.

Such conventions were expressed in much of the writing of the Enlightenment. The thousands of etiquette books, didactic stories, *Spectator* papers, Hogarth prints, gentlemanly magazines, classical histories—all were designed to teach Englishmen manners, civility, politeness, and virtue. Out of all this writing and art emerged an ideal of what it was to be both enlightened and civilized, and a virtuous leader. Our perpetuation of a liberal arts education in our colleges and universities is a present-day reminder of the origins of this ideal; for the English conception of a liberally educated gentleman had its modern beginnings in the 18th century.

An enlightened, civilized man was disinterested and impartial, not swayed by self-interest and self-profit. He was cosmopolitan; he stood above all local and parochial considerations and was willing to sacrifice his personal desires for the greater good of his community or his country. He was a man of reason who resisted the passions most likely to afflict great men, that is, ambition and avarice. Such a liberal, enlightened gentleman avoided enthusiasms and fanaticisms of all sorts, especially those of religion. Tolerance and liberality were his watchwords. Politeness and compassion toward his fellow man were his manners. Behaving in this way was what constituted being civilized.

Washington was thoroughly caught up in this enlightened promotion of gentility and civility, this rational rolling back of parochialism, fanaticism, and barbarism. He may have gone to church regularly, but he was not an emotionally religious person. In all of his writings there is no mention of Christ, and God is generally referred to as "the great disposer of human events." Washington loved Addison's play *Cato* and saw it over and over and incorporated its lines into his correspondence. The play, very much an Enlightenment tract, helped to teach him what it meant to be liberal and virtuous, what it meant to be a stoical classical hero. He had the play put on for his troops during the terrible winter at Valley Forge in 1778.

One of the key documents of Washington's life is his "Rules of Civility and Decent Behaviour in Company and Conversation," a collection of 110 maxims that Washington wrote down sometime before his 16th birthday. The maxims were originally drawn from a 17th-century etiquette book and were copied by the young autodidact. They dealt with everything from how to treat one's betters ("In speaking to men of Quality do not lean nor Look them full in the Face") to how to present one's countenance ("Do not Puff up the Cheeks, Do not Loll out the tongue, rub the Hands, or beard, thrust out the lips, or bite them or keep the Lips too open or too Close").

All the Founding Fathers were aware of these enlightened conventions, and all in varying degrees tried to live up to them. But no one was more serious in following them than Washington. It is this purposefulness that gave his behavior such a copybook character. He was obsessed with having things in fashion and was fastidious about his appearance to the world. It was as if he were always on stage, acting a part. He was very desirous not to offend, and he exquisitely shaped his remarks to fit the person to whom he was writing—so much so that some historians have accused him of deceit. "So anxious was he to appear neat and correct in his letters," recalled Benjamin Rush, that he was known to "copy over a letter of 2 or 3 sheets of paper because there were a few erasures on it." He wanted desperately to know what were the proper rules of behavior for a liberal gentleman, and when he discovered those rules he stuck by them with an earnestness that awed his contemporaries. His remarkable formality and stiffness in company came from his very self-conscious cultivation of what he considered proper, genteel, classical behavior.

Washington and Franklin, both children of the Enlightenment, had very different personalities, but among the Founding Fathers they shared one important thing. Neither of them went to college; neither had a formal liberal arts education. This deficiency deeply affected both of them, but Washington let it show. Washington always remained profoundly respectful of formal education. Colleges like William and Mary were always an "Object of Veneration" to him. His lack of a formal liberal arts education gave him a modesty he never lost. He repeatedly expressed his "consciousness of a defective education," and he remained quiet in the presence of sharp and sparkling minds. He was forever embarrassed that he had never learned any foreign languages. In the 1780's he refused invitations to visit France because he felt it would be humiliating for someone of his standing to have to converse through an interpreter. He said that it was his lack of a formal education that kept him from setting down on paper his recollections of the Revolution. It was widely rumored that his aides composed his best letters as commander-in-chief. If so, it is not surprising that he was diffident in company. Some even called it "shyness," but whatever the source, this reticence was certainly not the usual characteristic of a great man. "His modesty is astonishing, particularly to a Frenchman," noted Brissot de Warville. "He speaks of the American War as if he had *not* been its leader." This modesty only added to his gravity and severity. "Most people say and do too much," one friend recalled. "Washington . . . never fell into this common error."

Yet it was in the political world that Washington made his most theatrical gesture, his most moral mark, and there the results were monumental. The greatest act of his life, the one that made him famous, was his resignation as commander-in-chief of the American forces. This act, together with his 1783 circular letter to the states in which he promised to retire from public life, was his "legacy" to his countrymen. No American leader has ever left a more important legacy.

Following the signing of the peace treaty and British recognition of American independence, Washington stunned the world when he surrendered his sword to the Congress on Dec. 23, 1783 and retired to his farm at Mount Vernon. This was a highly symbolic act, a very self-conscious and unconditional withdrawal from the world of polities. Here was the commander in chief of the victorious army putting down his sword and promising not to take "any share in public business hereafter." Washington even resigned from his local vestry in Virginia in order to make his separation from the political world complete.

His retirement from power had a profound effect everywhere in the Western world. It was extraordinary, it was unprecedented in modern times—a victorious general surrendering his arms and returning to his farm. Cromwell, William of Orange, Marlborough—all had sought political rewards commensurate with their military achievements. Though it was widely thought that Washington could have become king or dictator, he wanted nothing of the kind. He was sincere in his desire for all the soldiers "to return to our Private Stations in the bosom of a free, peaceful and happy Country," and everyone recognized his sincerity. It filled them with awe. Washington's retirement, said the painter John Trumbull writing from London in 1784, "excites the astonishment and admiration of this part of the world. 'Tis a Conduct so novel, so unconceivable to People, who, far from giving up powers they possess, are willing to convulse the empire to acquire more." King George III supposedly predicted that if Washington retired from public life and returned to his farm, "he will be the greatest man in the world."

Washington was not naïve. He was well aware of the effect his resignation would have. He was trying to live up to the age's image of a classical disinterested patriot who devotes his life to his country, and he knew at once that he had acquired instant fame as a modern Cincinnatus. His reputation in the 1780's as a great classical hero was international, and it was virtually unrivaled. Franklin was his only competitor, but Franklin's greatness still lay in his being a scientist, not a man of public affairs. Washington was a living embodiment of all that classical republican virtue the age was eagerly striving to recover.

Despite his outward modesty, Washington realized he was an extraordinary man, and he was not ashamed of it. He lived in an era where distinctions of rank and talent were not only accepted but celebrated. He took for granted the differences between himself and more ordinary men. And when he could not take those differences for granted he cultivated them. He used his natural reticence to reinforce the image of a stern and forbidding classical hero. His aloofness was notorious, and he worked at it. When the painter Gilbert Stuart had uncharacteristic difficulty in putting Washington at ease during a sitting for a portrait, Stuart in exasperation finally pleaded, "Now sir, you must let me forget that you are General Washington and that I am Stuart, the painter." Washington's reply chilled the air: "Mr. Stuart need never feel the need of forgetting who he is or who General Washington is." No wonder the portraits look stiff.

Washington had earned his reputation, his "character," as a moral hero, and he did not want to dissipate it. He spent the rest of his life guarding and protecting his reputation, and worrying about it. He believed Franklin made a mistake going back into public life in Pennsylvania in the 1780's. Such involvement in politics, he thought, could only endanger Franklin's already achieved international standing. In modern eyes Washington's concern for his reputation is embarrassing; it seems obsessive and egotistical. But his contemporaries understood. All gentlemen tried scrupulously to guard their reputations, which is what they meant by their honor. Honor was the esteem in which they were held, and they prized it. To have honor across space and time was to have fame, and fame, "the ruling passion of the noblest minds," was what the Founding Fathers were after, Washington above all. And he got it, sooner and in greater degree than any other of his contemporaries. And naturally, having achieved what all his fellow Revolutionaries still anxiously sought, he was reluctant to risk it.

Many of his actions after 1783 can be understood only in terms of this deep concern for his reputation as a virtuous leader. He was constantly on guard and very sensitive to any criticism. Jefferson said no one was more sensitive. He judged all his actions by what people might think of them. This sometimes makes him seem silly to modern minds, but not to those of the 18th century. In that very suspicious age where people were acutely "jealous" of what great men were up to, Washington thought it important that people understand his motives. The reality was not enough; he had to *appear* virtuous. He was obsessed that he not seem base, mean, avaricious, or unduly ambitious. No one, said Jefferson, worked harder than Washington in keeping "motives of interest or consanguinity, of friendship or hatred" from influencing him. He had a lifelong preoccupation with his reputation for "disinterestedness" and how best to use that reputation for the good of his country. This preoccupation explains the seemingly odd fastidiousness and the caution of his behavior in the 1780's.

One of the most revealing incidents occurred in the winter of 1784–85. Washington was led into temptation, and it was agony. The Virginia General Assembly presented him with 150 shares in the James River and Potomac canal companies in recognition of his services to the state and the cause of canal-building. What should he do? He did not feel he could accept the shares. Acceptance might be "considered in the same light as a pension" and might compromise his reputation for virtue. Yet he believed passionately in what the canal companies were doing and had long dreamed of making a fortune from such canals. Moreover, he did not want to show "disrespect" to the Assembly or to appear "ostentatiously disinterested" by refusing this gift.

Few decisions in Washington's career caused more distress than this one. He wrote to everyone he knew—to Jefferson, to Governor Patrick Henry, to William Grayson, to Benjamin Harrison, to George William Fairfax, to Nathanael Greene, even to Lafayette—seeking "the best information and advice" on the disposition of the shares. "How would this matter be viewed by the eyes of the world?" he asked. Would not his reputation for virtue be harmed? Would not accepting the shares "deprive me of the principal thing which is laudable in my conduct?"

The situation is humorous today, but it was not to Washington. He suffered real anguish. Jefferson eventually found the key to Washington's anxieties and told him that declining to accept the shares would only add to his reputation for disinterestedness. So Washington gave them away to the college that eventually became Washington and Lee.

Washington suffered even more anguish over the decision to attend the Philadelphia Convention in 1787. Many believed that his presence was absolutely necessary for the effectiveness of the Convention, but the situation was tricky. He wrote to friends imploring them to tell him "confidentially what the public expectation is on this head, that is, whether I will or ought to be there?" How would his presence be seen, how would his motives be viewed? If he attended, would he be thought to have violated his pledge to withdraw from public life? But, if he did not attend, would his staying away be thought to be a "dereliction to Republicanism"? Should he squander his reputation on something that might not work?

What if the Convention should fail? The delegates would have to return home, he said, "chagrined at their ill success and disappointment. This would be a disagreeable circumstance for any one of them to be in; but more particularly so, for a person in my situation." Even James Madison had second thoughts about the possibility of misusing such a precious asset as Washington's reputation. What finally convinced Washington to attend the Convention was the fear that people might think he wanted the federal government to fail so that he could manage a military takeover. So in the end he decided, as Madison put it, "to forsake the honorable retreat to which he had retired, and risk the reputation he had so deservedly acquired." No action could be more virtuous. "Secure as he was in his fame," wrote Henry Knox with some awe, "he has again committed it to the mercy of events. Nothing but the critical situation of his country would have induced him to so hazardous a conduct."

When the Convention met, Washington was at once elected its president. His presence and his leadership undoubtedly gave the Convention and the proposed Constitution a prestige that they otherwise could not have had. His backing of the Constitution was essential to its eventual ratification. "Be assured," James Monroe told Jefferson, "his influence carried this government." Washington, once committed to the Constitution, worked hard for its acceptance. He wrote letters to friends and let his enthusiasm for the new federal government be known. Once he had identified himself publicly with the new Constitution he became very anxious to have it accepted. Its ratification was a kind of ratification of himself.

After the Constitution was established, Washington still thought he could retire to the domestic tranquillity of Mount Vernon. But everyone else expected that he would become president of the new national government. He was already identified with the country. People said he was denied children in his private life so he could be the father of his country. He had to be the president. Indeed, the Convention had made the new chief executive so strong, so kinglike, precisely because the delegates expected Washington to be the first president.

Once again this widespread expectation aroused all his old anxieties about his reputation for disinterestedness and the proper role for a former military leader. Had he not promised the country that he would permanently retire from public life? How could he then now assume the presidency without being "chargeable with levity and inconsistency; if not with rashness and ambition?" His protests were sincere. He had so much to lose, yet he did not want to appear "too solicitous for my reputation."

Washington's apparent egotism and his excessive coyness, his extreme reluctance to get involved in public affairs and endanger his reputation, have not usually been well received by historians. Douglas Southall Freeman, his great biographer, thought that Washington in the late 1780's was "too zealously attentive to his prestige, his reputation and his popularity—too much the self-conscious national hero and too little the daring patriot." Historians might not understand his behavior, but his contemporaries certainly did. They rarely doubted that Washington was trying *always* to act in a disinterested and patriotic way. His anxious queries about how this or that would look to the world, his hesitations about serving or not serving, his expressions of scruples and qualms—all were part of his strenuous effort to live up to the classical idea of a virtuous leader.

He seemed to epitomize public virtue and the proper character of a republican ruler. Even if John Adams was not all that impressed with George Washington, Adams' wife Abigail was certainly taken with him. She admired his restraint and trusted him. "If he was not really one of the best-intentioned men in the world," she wrote, "he might be a very dangerous one." As Garry Wills has so nicely put it, Washington gained his power by his readiness to give it up.

As president he continued to try to play the role he thought circumstances demanded. He knew that the new government was fragile and needed dignity. People found that dignity in his person. Madison believed that Washington was the only part of the new government that captured the minds of the people. He fleshed out the executive, established its independence, and gave the new government the pomp and ceremony many thought it needed.

Sometimes it had more pomp than even he enjoyed. His formal levees, complete with silver buckles and powdered hair, were painful affairs for everyone. These receptions, held at first on Tuesday and Friday afternoons and later on only Tuesdays, were an opportunity for prominent men to meet the president. The invited guests, all men, entered the president's residence at three o'clock, where they found the president standing before the fireplace. Fifteen minutes were allowed for the guests to assemble in a circle. As each guest entered the room he walked to the President, bowed, and without speaking backed to his place in the circle. The only voice heard was that of a presidential aide softly announcing the names. Promptly on the quarter hour the doors were shut; the President then walked around the circle, addressed each man by name, and made some brief remark to him. He bowed but never shook hands. Washington thought that hand-shaking was much too familiar for the president to engage in; consequently he kept one hand occupied holding a fake hat and the other resting on his dress sword. When the president had rounded the circle, he returned to the fireplace and stood until, at a signal from an aide, each guest one by one went to him, bowed without saying anything, and left the room. However excruciatingly formal these levees were, Washington thought they would continue. He thus designed the bowed shape of the Blue Room to accommodate them.

Although many critics thought that the levees smacked of the court life of kings of Europe, Washington was not a crypto-monarchist. He was a devoted republican, at heart just a country gentleman. Martha used to break up tea parties at 9:30 P.M. by saying that it was past the President's bedtime.

As president he tried to refuse accepting any salary just as he had as commander-in-chief. Still, he wanted to make the presidency "respectable," and he spared few expenses in doing so; he spent 7 percent of his $25,000 salary on liquor and wine for entertaining. He was especially interested in the size and character of the White House and of the capital city that was named after him. The scale and grandeur of Washington, D. C., owe much to his vision and his backing of Pierre L'Enfant as architect. If Secretary of State Thomas Jefferson had had his way, L'Enfant would never have kept his job as long as he did, and the capital would have been smaller and less magnificent—perhaps something on the order of a college campus, like Jefferson's University of Virginia.

Washington was keenly aware that everything he did would set precedents for the future. "We are a young nation," he said, "and have a character to establish. It behoves us therefore to set out right, for first impressions will be lasting." It was an awesome responsibility. More than any of his contemporaries, he thought constantly of future generations, of "millions unborn," as he called them.

He created an independent role for the president and made the chief executive the dominant figure in the government.

He established crucial precedents, especially in limiting the Senate's role in advising the president in the making of treaties and the appointing of officials. In August 1789 he went to the Senate to get its advice and consent to a treaty he was negotiating with the Creek Indians. Vice President John Adams who presided read each section of the treaty and then asked the senators, How do you advise and consent? After a long silence, the senators, being senators, began debating each section, with Washington impatiently glaring down at them. Finally one senator moved that the treaty and all the accompanying documents that the president had brought with him be submitted to a committee for study. Washington started up in what one senator called "a violent fret." In exasperation he cried, "This defeats every purpose of my coming here." He calmed down, but when he finally left the Senate chamber, he was overheard to say he would "be damned if he ever went there again." He never did. The advice part of the Senate's role in treaty making was dropped.

The presidency is the powerful office it is in large part because of Washington's initial behavior. He understood power and how to use it. But as in the case of his career as commander-in-chief, his most important act as president was his giving up of the office.

The significance of his retirement from the presidency is easy for us to overlook, but his contemporaries knew what it meant. Most people assumed that Washington might be president as long as he lived, that he would be a kind of elective monarch—something not out of the question in the 18th century. Some people even expressed relief that he had no heirs. Thus his persistent efforts to retire from the presidency enhanced his moral authority and helped fix the republican character of the Constitution.

He very much wanted to retire in 1792, but his advisors and friends talked him into staying on for a second term. Madison admitted that when he had first urged Washington to accept the presidency he had told him that he could protect himself from accusations of overweening ambition by "a voluntary return to public life as soon as the state of the Government would permit." But the state of the government, said Madison, was not yet secure. So Washington reluctantly stayed on.

But in 1796 he was so determined to retire that no one could dissuade him, and his voluntary leaving of the office set a precedent that was not broken until FDR secured a third term in 1940. So strong was the sentiment for a two-term limit, however, that the tradition was written into the Constitution in the 22nd amendment in 1951. Washington's action in 1796 was of great significance. That the chief executive of a state should willingly relinquish his office was an object lesson in republicanism at a time when the republican experiment throughout the Atlantic world was very much in doubt.

Washington's final years in retirement were not happy ones. The American political world was changing, becoming more partisan, and Washington struggled to comprehend these changes. During President Adams' administration he watched with dismay what he believed was the growing interference of the French government in American politics. For him the Jeffersonian Republican party had become "the French Party." It was, he said, "the curse of this country," threatening the stability and independence of the United States. He saw plots and enemies everywhere and became as much of a high-toned Federalist as Hamilton.

His fear was real; his sense of crisis was deep. He and other Federalists thought that the French might invade the country and together with "the French Party" overthrow the government. "Having Struggled for Eight or nine Years against the invasion of our rights by one power, and to establish an Independence of it," he wrote in 1798, "I could not remain an unconcerned spectator of the attempt of another Power to accomplish the same object, though in a different way." He thus listened attentively to all the urgent Federalist calls that he come out of retirement and head the army that the Congress had created to meet the French invasion.

Again he expressed reluctance, and asked whether becoming commander-in-chief would not be considered "a restless Act—evidence of my discontent in retirement." Yet in 1798 he was far more eager to step back into the breach and do his duty than he ever had been before. It was a measure of his despair with this "Age of Wonders"!

Before he could actually commit himself, however, President John Adams acted and, without his permission, appointed him commander of all the military forces of the United States. He accepted, but scarcely comprehended how it had all come about. The next thing he knew he was on his way to Philadelphia to organize the army. Events were outrunning his ability to control them or even to comprehend them, and he more and more saw himself caught up in "the designs of Providence." His command was a disaster. He wrangled over the appointments of the second in command, intrigued against Adams, and interfered with his cabinet. When neither the French invasion nor the American army materialized, Washington crept back to Mount Vernon thoroughly disillusioned with the new ways of American politics.

In July 1799 Governor Jonathan Trumbull of Connecticut with the backing of many Federalists urged Washington once again to stand for the presidency in 1800. Only Washington, Trumbull said, could unite the Federalists and save the country from "a French President." Finally Washington had had enough. In his reply he no longer bothered with references to his reputation for disinterestedness and his desire to play the role of Cincinnatus. Instead he talked about the new political conditions that made his candidacy irrelevant. In this new democratic era of party politics, he said, "personal influence," distinctions of character, no longer mattered. If the members of the Jeffersonian Republican party "set up a broomstick" as candidate and called it "a true son of Liberty" or "a Democrat" or "any other epithet that will suit their purpose," it still would "command their votes in toto!" But, even worse, he said, the same was true of the Federalists. Party spirit now ruled all, and people voted only for their party candidate. Even if he were the Federalist candidate, Washington was "thoroughly convinced I should not draw a *single* vote from the anti-Federal side." Therefore his standing for election made no sense; he would "stand upon no stronger ground than any other Federal character well supported."

Washington wrote all this in anger and despair, but, though he exaggerated, he was essentially right. The political world was changing, becoming democratic, and parties, not great men, would soon become the objects of contention. To be sure, the American people continued to long for great heroes as leaders, and from Jackson through Eisenhower they have periodically elected Washington-*manqués* to the presidency.

But democracy made such great heroes no longer essential to the workings of American government. And Washington, more than any other single individual, was the one who made that democracy possible. As Jefferson said "the moderation and virtue of a single character . . . probably prevented this revolution from being closed, as most others have been, by a subversion of that liberty it was intended to establish."

Washington was an extraordinary heroic man who made rule by more ordinary mortals possible. He virtually created the presidency, and gave it a dignity that through the years it has never lost. But, more important, he established the standard by which all subsequent presidents have been ultimately measured—not by the size of their electoral victories, not by their legislative programs, and not by the number of their vetoes, but by their moral character. Although we live in another world than his, his great legacy is still with us.

Afterword

Washington and the American People

ALTHOUGH WE HAVE numerous essays and articles, as well as exhibition catalogs, on George Washington, there is no comprehensive study of Americans' perception of Washington through two hundred years of history, nothing comparable to Merrill Peterson's volumes on *The Jeffersonian Image in the American Mind* (1960) and *Lincoln in American Memory* (1994). William Alfred Bryan's *George Washington in American Literature* (1952) is dated and unimaginative. The one substantial rendering is limited by a restricted time frame and a confinement to Washington's place in popular culture: Karal Ann Marling's *George Washington Slept Here: Colonial Revivals and American Culture, 1876–1986* (1988). Despite the humorous title, Marling produced a serious work, simultaneously funny and depressing because of the host of ways a reserved, serious-minded man suffered trivialization from Rutherford B. Hayes to Ronald Reagan.[1]

Before Marling's 1876 beginning date, antebellum Americans, as is well known, used Washington for their own purposes, but whatever his alleged virtues or qualities that enamored or inspired them, to say nothing of making him more than human, his countrymen had earlier linked him to the Revolution and nation building. That concern resonated in the speeches of the most prolific, peripatetic Washington orator of the period, Edward Everett of Massachusetts, who hoped the Washington memory might help stave off the impending sectional conflict. In one four-year span, he gave the same two-hour oration 129 times. Everett's endeavors were more successful in helping to raise funds for the rescue and purchase of Mount Vernon, then rapidly deteriorating, in 1858. The estate became the property of a new organization, founded by Ann Pamela Cunningham, a South Carolinian, the Mount Vernon Ladies' Association, which still owns Washington's home and continues its work of preservation and restoration. In the meantime, Washington acolytes gave up their attempts to remove his remains to the national capital, and the Washington Monument project languished until later in the century. All the while, Washington memorabilia appeared everywhere and in various forms as well, from towels and china to tapestries and lithographs.

According to Marling, the passing of time and the political maturing of the nation heralded no growth of more sophisticated, objective ideas about Washington. The sheer outpouring of what she sometimes simply calls junk staggers the mind: bottles, vases, buckles, hats, hatchets, hatchet cookie cutters, medallions, chairs, and on and on, plus two U.S. postal stamps of Washington in prayer.

A second post–Civil War development saw Washington as a sometime captive and even spokesman of the ideological left, the ideological right, businessmen, engineers, sexual profligates, social climbers, consumer advocates, and politicians, especially Republican presidents Coolidge, Hoover, and Reagan.

What are we to make of Washington's public persona today, roughly the time of the bicentennial of Washington's death and a dozen years after Marling's *George Washington Slept Here*? The record of Washington centennials and bicentennials suggests we might well not expect any great lasting accomplishments in terms of Washington's image or the way he is acknowledged. Time will tell. In any case, we have escaped some of the more bizarre happenings of 1932, the two-hundredth anniversary of Washington's birth. Congressman Sol Bloom, the zealous mastermind of what became a patriotic extravaganza, enlisted celebrities right and left. The colorful aviator Jimmy Doolittle, accompanied by a middle-aged great-great-great grandniece of the first president, flew over every part of the nation where Washington had actually traveled, covering 2,600 miles between dawn and dusk on July 25, 1932.[2]

The 1999 bicentennial events have on the whole been quite positive, although it would be naive to claim that the commercial factor has not occasionally reared its head and that it will not continue to do so. The traveling exhibit "Treasures from Mount Vernon: George Washington Revealed" has appropriately drawn high praise from most reviewers. Its objects include the famous Washington dentures, books, letters, clothing, the original key to the Bastille, and an exquisite replica of the mansion and its furnishings built to scale, with sides that open electronically so that one can view the interior of every room. "Treasures" began at the New-York Historical Society before making lengthy stops as far away as California.

The Henry E. Huntington Library and Art Gallery, the Virginia Historical Society, and the Museum of Our National Heritage in Lexington, Massachusetts, staged their own judicious exhibits, and all published excellent scholarly catalogs containing extensive narratives and copious illustrations.[3] A total of at least twenty-four Washington exhibits, conferences, and seminars took place around the country. The National Symphony Orchestra, under the direction of Leonard Slatkin, performed the premiere of "Behold This Man: George Washington" at the Kennedy Center in Washington, D.C. The Mount Vernon Ladies' Association continues to build on its impressive collections for research on Washington and holds lectures and symposia. It cosponsored with the Organization of American Historians a poll of scholars to determine the ten best books on Washington.[4] The Mount Vernon organization, which has stressed Washington's domestic life and plantation management, is raising funds for a museum that will provide an opportunity to include significant coverage of Washington's public life. It concluded its commemoration in 1999 on December 18, staging a full-scale reenactment of Washington's funeral, carried live on C-Span.[5] Moreover, as I observed in the Introduction to this volume, the state of Washington scholarship is vastly improved over what it was during and after the Washington Bicentennial in 1932. The Society of the Cincinnati is contributing to the publication of still more quality works on the Washington era by endowing a number of George Washington Distinguished Professorships.

Even so, there is a threat today to the serious examination of Washington that did not exist when the 1932 bicentennial took place. The problem, a twofold one, is not confined to the first chief executive but seems to impact all the illustrious leaders of the Revolution. First is the matter of race. The Revolutionary generation did not solve or directly confront what appears to us as the principal unfinished legacy of the Revolution. Critics have trained their fire on Jefferson because he spoke so inconsistently about slavery and human equality and because of the renewed furor over the question of whether he kept his bondswoman Sally Hemings as his concubine and fathered children by her. Recent DNA findings connecting the Jeffersons and Hemingses have added fuel to the flames. Yet, as Dorothy Twohig writes in this volume, Washington drew some criticism as a slaveholder in his lifetime, and he is lumped with other southern planters by historians who give low marks to his generation on matters of race. In 1998 New Orleans renamed the George Washington Elementary School because it carried the name of a slave master. A C-Span program on Washington' presidency elicited a call-in opinion that African Americans who visit Mount

Vernon and its slave quarters would be guilty of condoning the owner's racism. It seems probable that a preoccupation with the Founders and racial oppression will not go away any time soon—not as long as prejudice and discrimination remain unresolved issues in American life.

The other dimension of the problem, itself containing racial overtones, is the contention that the study of great white men is now out of fashion. Such a concentration is said to exaggerate the influence of single individuals in the making of history and should take a backseat to fields of history that are new or that have been slighted in the past. This thinking in academic circles shows the rising influence of social history broadly defined, embracing the study of working classes, family, gender, race, and ethnicity. The age-old staples of graduate study, especially political, intellectual, constitutional, and military approaches, have often been shunted to the rear of the discipline as specialists in the older methodologies are replaced on retirement by Ph.D.'s schooled in "new" histories.

There is every reason to think that the old historical avenues will come back. It is the nature of historiography that what goes around comes around. Professors on the cutting edge will rest easier once their specialties are more comfortably in the mainstream. The old staples will revive, additionally, because they have never lost out completely, for politics and statecraft continue at the vital center of public life.

If Marling implicitly faults the American people for their obsession with Washington artifacts and trivia, there is a case to be made for arguing that, in some respects, the public may be wiser than historians whose views of Washington are deeply colored by race and new academic fields of historical interest. The public retains its interest in Washington and the other Framers. In 1997, the year an important book on Jefferson and Sally Hemings appeared and the year of a Ken Burns Jefferson documentary that dealt frankly with slavery, 560,000 people visited Monticello, an increase of 40,000 over the previous year. Mount Vernon in 1998 attracted 1,000,000, its peak year except for 1976, the bicentennial of American independence. These numbers are especially impressive when different kinds of entertainment such as Disney World and Busch Gardens now compete vigorously for the tourist dollar. The Mount Vernon Internet site attracted nearly four million hits that year, leading to the creation of a second site devoted exclusively to the George Washington Bicentennial.[6]

Mainstream studies of the Founders and modern American leaders such as the Roosevelts and Kennedys continue to win prestigious prizes and be adopted by the book clubs. Whatever the elitism and racism of men such as Washington and Jefferson by our twenty-first-century values, their flaws fail to diminish their long record of successful public service, over four decades or so. Americans, for all their amusement with things described by Marling, realize that leaders do make a difference, and not just two centuries ago. Look at Churchill, Roosevelt, Martin Luther King Jr., Mandela, and Gorbachev. As for Washington, he made a difference. He still does. His Revolution looks even better now in view of the failure of Marxist revolutions in the 1990s.[7]

Notes

1. The following provide brief but useful accounts of changing American views of GW: Bernard Mayo, *Myths and Men* (Athens, Ga., 1960), 37–60; Daniel J. Boorstin, *The Americans: The National Experience* (New York, 1965), 337–56; Catherine L. Albanese, *Sons of the Fathers: The Civil Religion of the American Revolution* (Philadelphia, 1976), 141–81; Lawrence J. Friedman, *Inventors of the Promise Land* (New York, 1975), 44–78. Still other accounts, in a general way, deal with GW imagery in the Revolution and the early Republic: Melvin Yazawa, *From Colonies to Commonwealth: Familial Ideology and the Beginnings of the American Republic* (Baltimore, 1985); Len Travers, *Celebrating the Fourth: Independence Day and the Rites of Nationalism in the Early Republic* (Amherst, Mass., 1997); David Waldstreicher, *In the Midst of Perpetual Fetes: The Making of American Nationalism, 1776–1820* (Chapel Hill, N.C., 1997); Simon P. Newman, *Parades and the Politics of the Streets: Festive Culture in the Early Republic* (Philadelphia, 1997).

2. Some of the more outrageous activities of the 1932 bicentennial are detailed in Marling, *Washington Slept Here*, chap. 11.

3. John Rhodehamel, *The Great Experiment: George Washington and the American Republic* (San Marino, Calif., and New Haven, 1998); William M. S. Rasmussen and Robert S. Tilton, *George Washington: The Man behind the Myths* (Charlottesville, Va., 1999); Barbara J. Mitnick, ed., *George Washington: American Symbol* (New York, 1999). For another admirable catalog, based on the National Portrait Gallery's celebration of the 250th anniversary of GW's birth, consult Wendy C. Wick, *George Washington, an American Icon: The Eighteenth-Century Graphic Portraits* (Washington, D.C., 1982). On that occasion the Museum of American History presented its own fine GW display and catalog: Margaret Brown Klapthor and Howard Alexander Morrison, *George Washington: A Figure upon the Stage* (Washington, D.C., 1982).

4. No. 1: James Thomas Flexner, *George Washington: The Indispensable Man*, one-vol. ed. of a longer work (Boston, 1974); no. 2: Marcus Cunliffe, *George Washington: Man and Monument* (1958; Mount Vernon, Va., 1998); no. 3: Edmund S. Morgan, *The Genius of George Washington* (Washington, D.C., 1980); no. 4: Dou-

glas Southall Freeman, *Washington,* one-vol. ed. of a longer work (New York, 1968); no. 5: Don Higginbotham, *George Washington and the American Military Tradition* (Athens, Ga., 1985); no. 6: Forrest McDonald, *The Presidency of George Washington* (Lawrence, Kans., 1974); no. 7: W. W. Abbot et al., eds., *The Papers of George Washington* (Charlottesville, Va., 1983—); no. 8: John R. Alden, *George Washington: A Biography* (Baton Rouge, La., 1984); no. 9: Edmund S. Morgan, *The Meaning of Independence: John Adams, George Washington, Thomas Jefferson* (Charlottesville, Va., 1976); no. 10: Donald Jackson and Dorothy Twohig, eds., *The Diaries of George Washington,* 6 vols. (Charlottesville, Va., 1976–79).

5. *Mount Vernon, Yesterday, Today, Tomorrow* 16 (Winter 1999): 1–3.

6. Mount Vernon Ladies' Association of the Union, *Annual Report* (1998): 5. Additional figures are suggestive of GW's continued appeal. During the tenure of the "Treasures from Mount Vernon" at the New-York Historical Society, attendance there increased almost 400 percent over the same time frame from the previous year. The first weekend of the exhibit's stay at the Henry E. Huntington Library and Art Gallery, near Los Angeles, overcrowded conditions caused the temporary closing of the entry gates; overall visitation exceeded 150,000.

7. One reason for the difficulties encountered by Marxist revolutions has been their emphasis on empowering "the people," making unity a goal of greater importance than individual liberties. The same was true of the French Revolution, which curtailed dissent, a social upheaval that sent at least 17,000 French men and women to the guillotine. During the Russian Revolution, Lenin erected a statue of Robespierre, the French radical leader, in Moscow. Made of faulty stone, it eventually crumbled, as did the Soviet empire a decade or so before the twentieth century ended (Susan Dunn, *Sister Revolutions: French Lightning, American Light* [New York, 1999]).

Index